The Handbook of
Human Resource Management

The Handbook of Human Resource Management

Edited by Brian Towers

BLACKWELL
Business

Copyright © Basil Blackwell Ltd., 1992

First published 1992
Reprinted 1993, 1994

Blackwell Publishers
108 Cowley Road
Oxford OX4 1JF, UK

238 Main Street
Cambridge, Massachusetts 02142, USA

British Library Cataloguing in Publication Data
A CIP catalogue record for this book is available from the British Library.

Library of Congress Cataloging in Publication Data
The Handbook of human resource management / edited by Brian Towers.
     p.   cm. — (Human resource management in action)
     Includes bibliographical references and index.
     ISBN 0-631-18673-5
     1. Personnel management — Handbooks, manuals, etc.   I. Towers,
Brian.   II. Series.
HF5549.H2964   1992
658.3—dc20   92-25491
                                                                        CIP

Typeset in 11 on 13 pt Plantin
by Best-set Typesetter Ltd., Hong Kong
Printed in Great Britain by T. J. Press (Padstow) Ltd., Padstow, Cornwall.

This book is printed on acid-free paper

Contents

Figures

Tables

Contributors

Gordon Anderson is Senior Lecturer in the Department of Human Resource Management and MBA Programme Director at the University of Strathclyde, Glasgow. His research interests centre on the design and implementation of performance appraisal systems, personnel selection and management development. He is writing the book on performance appraisal systems for this series.

Greg J. Bamber is Professor and Director of the Key Centre in Strategic Management, Faculty of Business, Queensland University of Technology, Brisbane, Australia. His publications include *Militant Managers?* (Gower, 1986), and, jointly with Russell D. Lansbury, *New Technology; international perspectives on human resources and industrial relations* (Unwin Hyman, 1989).

P. B. Beaumont is Professor in the Department of Social and Economic Research, University of Glasgow. He has published widely, including a chapter in *The Handbook of Industrial Relations Practice*. His most recent book is *Public Sector Industrial Relations* (Routledge, 1991).

Paul Blyton is Senior Lecturer in Industrial Relations at Cardiff Business School, University of Wales College of Cardiff. His books include (co-edited with J. Morris) *A Flexible Future? Prospects for Employment and Organization* (de Gruyter, 1991); and (co-edited with P. Turnbull), *Human Resource Management conflicts and contradictions* (Sage, 1992). Paul has written the book on flexibility for this series.

Jeff Bridgford is on study leave from Heriot-Watt University, Edinburgh to work as co-ordinator of the European Trade Union College in Brussels. He wrote *The Politics of French Trade Unionism*

(Leicester University Press, 1991). He is co-authoring the book on the European dimension of HRM for this series.

Paul Dobson is Lecturer in Organizational Behaviour at the City University Business School, and a member of the Centre for Personnel Research and Enterprise Development since 1978. He has carried out research in many public- and private-sector organizations, and published in the HRM field.

Roger Farrance is Chief Executive of the Electricity Association and of its two operating companies, Electricity Association Services Ltd and Electricity Association Technology Ltd. He is currently President of the Institute of Personnel Management (IPM).

John Gennard is the Institute of Personnel Management Professor of Human Resource Management and Dean of the Strathclyde Business School. His many publications include the co-authored *The Closed Shop in British Industry* (Macmillan, 1984) and more recently *The History of the NGA* (Unwin Hyman, 1990).

David Guest is Professor of Occupational Psychology at Birkbeck College, University of London. He has written and researched extensively on developments in HRM and personnel management and is also working on related issues of culture change and organizational commitment.

Terry Hercus is Professor in the Faculty of Management, University of Manitoba, Winnipeg, Canada. He has taught and written widely on HRM related research over a number years.

L. C. Hunter is Professor of Applied Economics in the Department of Social and Economic Research, University of Glasgow. His publications include (with J. MacInnes) *Employers' Labour Use Strategies* (Employment Department Research Paper, 1991).

Jeff Hyman is Senior Lecturer in Industrial Relations in the Department of HRM at Strathclyde University. The most recent of his publications is *Training for Work* (Routledge, 1992).

James Kelly is Senior Lecturer in the Department of Human Resource Management, University of Strathclyde. He has written several articles on personnel management related research.

Cliff Lockyer is Senior Lecturer in Industrial Relations at the University of Strathclyde. He worked as an industrial relations officer in the car industry before returning to academic life. His research has included studies of employee attitudes in local government.

Alan McKinlay is Colquhoun Lecturer in Business History in the Centre for Business History, Glasgow University. His current interests are flexibility and the link between strategy, structure and process. He is co-authoring the book on HRM strategy for this series.

Hedley Malloch is Lecturer in Personnel Management and Strategic Management at Teesside Polytechnic Business School. His current research interests are the relationship between competitive strategy and manpower strategy.

Paul Miller is Lecturer in Business Policy and Director of the MBA Programme at the University of Newcastle upon Tyne. He has written on the integration of HRM with business policy and also on economic development in small firms.

Nick Oliver is Lecturer in Organizational Behaviour at the Cardiff Business School, University of Wales College of Cardiff. With Barry Wilkinson he wrote *The Japanization of British Industry* (Basil Blackwell, 1988).

Harvie Ramsay is Senior Lecturer in the Department of Human Resource Management, University of Strathclyde. His research has included employee involvement with work on participation and involvement in the UK; profit-sharing and employee share ownership; attitudes to participation among managers. Publications include the co-authored *People's Capitalism: a critical analysis of profit sharing and employee share ownership* (Routledge, 1989).

Ramsumair Singh is Lecturer in Industrial Relations at the University of Lancaster. He is a chartered electrical engineer, and economist, with training and work experience with the General Electric Company and Texaco Trinidad. He has published on third-party intervention and industrial disputes, and is an ACAS arbitrator.

Ken Starkey is Reader in Organizational Analysis the School of Management and Finance, University of Nottingham. He is currently researching the link between strategy and HRM in a variety of organizational settings. He is co-authoring the book on HRM strategy for this series.

Mairi Steele is Lecturer in the Department of Human Resource Management at the University of Strathclyde. Her research interests include recruitment and retention of women in the labour market, public policy attitudes towards internal trade union affairs and employment law. She has published in these areas.

John Stirling is Principal Lecturer in Industrial Relations and Trade Union Studies at Newcastle upon Tyne Polytechnic. He has research interests in worker co-operatives and trade union education and has published widely in both fields. He is co-authoring the book on the European dimension of HRM for this series.

George Strauss is Professor of Business Administration in the School of Business Administration of the University of California at Berkeley, USA. He has written widely in the HRM field. His latest work is 'Workers' participation in Management' in J. Hartley and G. Stephenson (eds), *Empolyment relations: the psychology of influence and control at work* (Oxford, Blackwell, 1992).

Brian Towers is Professor of Industrial Relations in the Department of Human Resource Management, Strathclyde Business School, University of Strathclyde. He is founder and editor of the *Industrial Relations Journal* and editor of *The Handbook of Industrial Relations Practice* (Kogan Page, 1987).

Barry Wilkinson is Professor of Human Resource Management at Cardiff Business School, University of Wales College, Cardiff. With Nick Oliver he wrote *The Japanization of British Industry*, the second edition of which is forthcoming. He is currently researching into the social impact of Japanese direct investment in the UK and elsewhere.

Allan Williams is Professor of Organizational and Occupational Psychology at the City University Business School. He is also Pro-Vice-Chancellor of the University, and Director of its Centre for Personnel Research and Enterprise Development. He has published widely in the HRM and organization development literature.

Foreword

ROGER FARRANCE

Throughout history there have been periods when new ideas and change have swept through nations like prairie fires. Not infrequently revolution and violence have been the ugly accompaniments of the sometimes forceful introduction of the new and the resistance of the old. The Reformation, 1848, the World Wars and the establishment of Communist Republics are all examples.

The 1980s have been another such period, culminating in the collapse of Communism and the hesitant introduction of democratic government in the former Iron Curtain Countries. Western Europe and America with their stable governments, mature institutions and complex, integrated economies have not suffered political upheaval, but they have been substantially affected by the changes in concepts of the structure of society, political, industrial and economic, and the place of individuals within it.

It is not possible in the space of a short foreword to analyse the causes of the movement for change, or where they began. There are many elements, including advances in technology, communications and transport. Globalization of issues, population growth, concern for the environment and increasing knowledge of what is happening beyond local boundaries have all played a part. The sheer dimensions of these developments, be they the growth of multinational organizations, the remoteness of government, or just the size of national and world problems, seem on the one hand to have created a sense of helplessness, and on the other a determination by people to participate in and to control the events that affect them as individuals.

These trends have found expression in industry, and to some extent in government, in the rejection of corporatism and the definition and projection of individual rights and freedoms. At the same time, many of the inhibitions of earlier days have been discarded so that the demand for the respect of the rights of the individual and for each to have a say in what happens to them, becomes more articulate and difficult to ignore.

In industry, commerce, and the public sector there has been substantial decentralization and devolution of decision-making. Accountability has been pushed down to the lowest possible levels while hierarchies have been reduced and organizations have become flatter. Where this has happened managers' responsibilities have been extended far beyond simply getting the goods out of the door. The motivation of employees, team building, quality and the resolution of work-place problems are all part of his or her accountability. Personnel departments may provide support and advice, but are no longer there to take the people problems off the manager's shoulders.

Collectivism does not fit happily into this new framework. The collective organization needs an institution or corporate body to confront. In the United Kingdom trade unionism was at its strongest where people were employed in large numbers, often in one place, and where their pay and conditions were determined remotely from the individual. The shipyards, coal industry, and motor vehicle manufacture, for example, encouraged collectivism as did the public services and utilities. Employee participation was for the most part non-existent and where it was attempted it was largely through the involvement of union representatives in joint committees.

While on the European Continent collective systems of Works Councils, employee representatives on two-tier boards and industry-level, or even nationwide collective bargaining continues, in Britain we have been moving towards decentralization and more direct relations between management and employees. This has been accelerated by the various reforms of the law affecting trade unions and collective bargaining, although it could be argued that these reforms were reflecting the changes taking place rather than initiating them.

Many enterprises in the new technology industries simply do not recognize trade unions. In others, single union agreements and other arrangements provide a role for unions, but within the context of the new individualist concepts and not the old collectivist ones. Western Continental Europe is not exempt from the tide of events. EC Directives may prescribe minimum employment conditions, and Works Councils or other joint partnership arrangements may be embedded in the system by legal requirements, but the same need exists to meet the changed perceptions of employees of how their employer should behave towards them.

Human resource management must be the route by which companies and employing organizations can come to terms with the new situation. It provides the means by which the fullest potential of employees can be developed and used for the benefit of both themselves and their employers. Good HRM practice will ensure that every employee knows that they matter as an individual and a human being while the employer will have the confidence that the work force will perform to the levels needed and beyond for success in today's competitive world. Brian Towers and the distinguished contributors to this handbook are to be congratulated on providing an essential, authoritative and most timely volume that will be welcomed by all practitioners in the field of HRM.

Roger Farrance, CBE
President
Institute of Personnel Management

Introduction
HRM: an overview

BRIAN TOWERS

The practice of human resource management originated in the United States some forty years ago. By the 1960s and 1970s HRM was being successfully developed in companies such as IBM and Hewlett Packard, which had no experience of trade unions. These companies and others provided examples for imitators so that by '. . . the end of the 1970s the new non-union model had been clarified sufficiently to support its more systematic use by firms in most sectors of the economy.' (Kochan et al. 1986, p. 53).

Non-unionism, at least in the US, remains a significant characteristic of HRM companies. This was, of course, even in the 1960s readily available to US companies with HRM aspirations. It was particularly the case for those with locations in the many states which discouraged union organization, i.e. the 'right-to-work' states; and even in the industrial heartlands of US unionism the non-union option was increasingly available as membership density continued to decline from its peak in the 1950s (Troy 1986). Non-unionism was a necessary condition for the success of the early US pace-setters which required their employees to be involved in and committed to their companies and to accept willingly the flexible utilization of their labour. These goals and values and the emphasis upon the individual employee, could not coexist with the collectivist, and then characteristically confrontational, approach of trade unions.

But if non-unionism was a necessary condition for the development of HRM it was certainly not sufficient. HRM strategies in US companies were not simply motivated by a desire to avoid trade unions (Kochan et al. pp. 249–50). They offered their employees, and still largely do, positive benefits in return for their commitment and involvement. The pay was better than they could get elsewhere; non-pay benefits were broadly equalized; training and career progression were built into employee expectations; and most important of all employment security, if not related to a particular job, was far more than a slogan. These were tangible, and historically rare, gains for employees. In the case of IBM its commercial success went hand-in-hand with its human resource policies and its no-redundancy commitment was a reality until the 1980s. Its human resource blueprint was exported with equal success, not least to the UK. In 1977 IBM even had sufficient confidence in its philosophy to test, successfully, its view that its employees had no need for trade union organization in its plants (Beaumont 1987, pp. 120–1).

But what exactly is this 'blueprint' and how extensive is it? These questions are difficult to answer. In defining HRM we are always thrown back on the all-too-familiar examples of IBM and Hewlett-Packard. Guest (1987), drawing upon US research, defines it as comprising '. . . a set of policies designed to maximize organizational integration, employee commitment, flexibility and quality of work'. (p. 503) This 'model' presents both a satisfying internal consistency and something which is recognizable at IBM and Hewlett-Packard. These companies seek to integrate the policies and interests of the organization with those of their employees through sophisticated communication programmes and tangible evidence of commitment – good pay, single status, career progression and job security. Once the organization has this commitment it can use it to increase the quality of its employees through recruitment, training and development and raise its productivity and efficiency levels via a willingly flexible and adaptable workforce (Guest 1987).

IBM and Hewlett-Packard have been successful not just com-mercially but have also, as Guest points out, shown a capacity to change and adapt as well as enjoying low turnover, low absenteeism, few grievances and a good record on problem-solving. But how unique are they? Japanese companies operating in the UK, for example (such as Toshiba, Nissan, Toyota and Honda), are also commercially successful and largely come within Guest's HRM model, yet remain committed to trade union recognition, albeit the tightly circumscribed single union variant. If, therefore, HRM is 'an idea whose time has come' (*Financial Times* 1991) how far should the 'idea' be restricted to the four-cylinder, high-performance model identified by Guest but with a limited existence on the ground? Furthermore, what should we make of the '. . . plethora of ini-tiatives, programmes and innovations of all kinds . . .' and the '. . . increasing recognition that something significant may be happening in the management of the employment relationship.' (Storey 1989, p. 4)? More precisely, should analysts now be ready to talk of a modified, diluted or hybrid HRM approach more easily assimilated into structures, cultures and traditions which are different from those of the USA?

On the first question, intensifying competition from the Japanese in United States domestic markets has rendered the Guest model even more limited. As Kochan et al. put it as early as 1986: 'Many of the totally unorganized firms that started up and grew rapidly in the 1960s and 1970s are now facing the challenge of adapting their human resource management practices to maturing, more price-competitive markets. Like their unionized counterparts, these firms will experience increased pressure to lower labor costs, streamline staffing levels, adopt labor-saving technologies, and redeploy workers and assets. Human-resource management professionals will be asked to adjust policies away from those that were designed to serve a business strategy that valued low turnover and high commitment to ones that better serve emerging strategies that depend on low labour costs. As these pressures increase, so does the potential for the emergence of conflict between employee expectations of employment continuity and career progression and management's efforts to contain costs. Moreover, these pressures are likely to affect employees at all levels of the firm, from hourly employees to middle managers and executives.' (p. 246)

These prescient comments became a reality for IBM in 1991 when it suffered the first (and massive) loss in its corporate history, forcing it to abandon its no-redundancy policy – a policy which had in any case been clouded in ambiguity in the latter years of the 1980s. And it may yet be that within the USA Japanese companies are in the process of becoming the new flagbearers of the fully-fledged HRM model, given the ease of operating in contexts without a trade union presence.

In the UK, and mainly reflecting the weakening but still relatively strong trade union movement, the position is more confused. Survey evidence (Sisson 1989, pp. 28–40) tells us that:

- New appointments and changes of title are indicating a shift away from 'personnel' towards 'human resources'. Examples include British Airways, Tube Investments, GKN and Whitbread.
- There is a shift in the responsibility for 'people' issues from personnel to line management.
- Organizations have been reconsidering their collective relationship with

employees through trade unions in favour of a direct, individual relationship and even where trade unions continue to be important there has been a growth in consultation at the expense of joint regulation. Single union agreements have not been extensive but are significant and influential.

- More organizations are putting emphasis on the individual in the application of selection, testing, appraisal and performance-related pay.
- Participation and employee involvement have been extended, primarily through 'team briefing' and 'quality circles'.
- The distribution between manual and non-manual employees is being blurred through the introduction of single-status programmes.

It is also clear that these developments are continuing. British Airways, for example, is now seeking to move towards a single union agreement as Japanese companies conclude such deals on their greenfield sites, most recently with Toyota at Derby. Ford may also still harbour ambitions in this respect despite its failure in 1989 to build a new, single union plant at Dundee. Derecognition is also causing some consternation in trade union circles. The TUC is pressing for a statutory policy under a future Labour government and an important straw-in-the-wind is BP's intention to derecognize its still numerically strong trade unions other than for representational purposes (*Financial Times* 1992). Trade union weakness is also making it easier for organizations to develop participation and employee involvement programmes and introduce more sophisticated selection, testing and appraisal techniques. Performance-related pay may have lost some of its shine but it is increasingly easier to implement as collective bargaining continues to be devolved to the level of the business unit or cost centre (Towers 1992).

Whilst these changes should not be exaggerated since their actual incidence is still limited to a small proportion of all organizations – Storey's observation that 'something significant may be happening' seems to be soundly based. But should this 'something significant' be considered as a growth in HRM or an amorphous, diluted response to its influence?

The question is clearly rhetorical: IBM, Hewlett-Packard and their imitators cannot be considered as bridgeheads but perhaps rather as outposts. These organizations have undoubtedly been influential, but British contexts and traditions remain unfavourable to replication not least because of the still strong remaining commitment to collective bargaining despite the weakening of trade unions in the 1980s and 1990s. Nor, given a free hand, would British companies necessarily opt for HRM. As Guest (1987, pp. 517–18) reminds us, a viable alternative is the 'professional' personnel management of many successful companies which organizationally may not suit the strategic planning nature of HRM. What really matters to the practitioner is what works. A package of traditional policies and practices allied to some of the more innovative reforms associated with HRM may be more viable than a grand design. HRM in Britain may therefore be seen as an influential movement which has been adapted to British circumstances. It is an 'approach' to consider rather than a 'model' to imitate.

Outside the UK similar constraints inhibit the spread of an HRM culture on the US model. In Europe most of the individual members of the European Community as well as the EC's supranational institutions are culturally and ideologically the least fertile soil for the HRM plant to flourish. The concept of a 'social partnership' between public and private-sector employers and trade unions is deeply rooted in the EC offering limited scope for the growth of HRM policies acting directly upon individual employees rather than collectively through their trade unions. Beyond Europe, assessment is clearly more difficult but a recent survey has found that diverse cultural contexts in countries such as Japan, Korea and Singapore are not all favourable to HRM policies and, that taking an international comparative perspective, HRM is '. . . more a theoretical construct than an applied reality. What companies generally practise is personnel management rather than HRM.' (Pieper 1990, p. 180)

The overall picture is therefore, a mixed one. HRM is unlikely to be just another modish and transitory idea – indeed, it is part of a longer tradition going back to the early human relations theorists of the 1930s. However, nor is it necessarily ushering in a revolution in organizational approaches to the management of employees. There are too many philosophical, institutional, cultural and political constraints preventing that outcome. Yet it is having an influence upon organizational thinking and behaviour which goes beyond HRM organizations themselves. In that sense it will probably have a more widespread and lasting effect than its present extent would suggest. This judgement that HRM is not just one of the passing fads which litter business history is the rationale for this book.

The nature, extent, influence and implications of HRM are comprehensively discussed in Part One, drawing on the experience of the UK, USA (and Japanese companies in both of these countries) as well as Europe and Australia. The two concluding chapters of Part

One also remind us that HRM can arouse strong fears and suspicions among trade unions and that it is important to subject it, as any other development, to close critical scrutiny.

These wider issues are important and give perspective to the more practically based contributions which follow and which earn this volume its description as a 'handbook'. The authors in Part Two offer detailed description, analysis and critique, drawing upon research and experience of the practice and limitations of the human resource manager's approach to the employment relationship. Part Three rounds off the book with a selection of case studies from a range of organizations which have handled change using HRM approaches.

References

Beaumont, P.B., *The Decline of Trade Union Organisation*, Croom Helm, 1987.

Financial Times, 28 January 1991.

Financial Times, 17 January 1992.

Guest, D.E., 'Human resource management and industrial relations', *Journal of Management Studies*, vol. 24 no. 5 September 1987, pp. 503–21.

Kochan, Thomas, A., Katz, Harry, C. and McKersie, Robert, B. *The Transformation of American Industrial Relations*, Basic Books, 1986.

Pieper, R. (ed.), *Human Resource Management: an International Comparison*, de Gruyter, 1990.

Sisson, K. (ed.), *Personnel Management in Britain*, Basil Blackwell, 1989.

Storey, J. (ed.), *New Perspectives on Human Resource Management* Routledge, 1989.

Towers, B., *Choosing Bargaining Levels: UK Experience and Implications*, Institute of Personnel Management, 1992.

Troy, L., 'The rise and fall of American trade unions: the Labor movement from FDR to RR' in S.M. Lipset (ed.) *Unions in Transition: Entering the Second Century*, Institute for Contemporary Studies, 1986, pp. 75–112.

Part I
Contexts

1

Human Resource Management in the United Kingdom

DAVID GUEST

Introduction

The development of human resource management (HRM) in the UK is a story of considerable talk, much promise and extensive activity which all too often has failed to deliver much in the way of improved performance. Its emergence in the 1980s as a seemingly new topic coincided with a wide variety of changes in the economic and industrial environment, giving rise in some quarters to the impression that HRM had some causal influence. But in one of the most thorough reviews of developments in the field of personnel management in the first half of the 1980s, Legge (1988), supported in relation to more recent developments by Storey and Sisson (1989), concluded that the dominant pattern was not so much one of change but of 'business as usual'. How can we reconcile this conclusion with the impression of considerable change and progress in HRM? By reviewing some central features of recent developments and current practice, this chapter attempts to provide some answers. At the same time it points to some of the lessons to be drawn by those eager to make some real progress.

Two points must be emphasized in attempting to understand current UK practice. The first is the danger of imposing a false sense of uniformity. There is in fact an enormous amount of diversity of policy and practice parading under the label of HRM and this is reflected in the differing conclusions of those who attempt to arrive at judgements about the nature of HRM by distilling what they see in practice. The second is the danger of 'talking up' and exaggerating the amount of change that has occurred and especially of confusing activity with outcomes. In this respect we need to be clear about the kind of changes we are concerned with. These can range from superficial changes in department titles through innovations in policy and practice to the outcomes of such policy and practice. It is important to disentangle HRM policy levers, such as selection, training and job redesign, from HRM policy goals, such as flexibility and commitment, and in turn to distinguish these from organizational outcomes with which they might be associated such as labour turnover and productivity (Guest 1987). And considerable caution must be exercised in asserting cause and effect. Here HRM is used in its widest sense to cover any type of innovative personnel management or industrial relations policy and practice. It therefore overlaps with what others (e.g. Kelly 1990) have discussed under the rubric of 'the new industrial relations'.

This chapter will use the two issues outlined above as the point of departure. The first section therefore tries to map the diversity in HRM. The second examines some of the evidence about the extent and impact of developments in HRM in the UK; and a third section assesses the implications for the practice of HRM in the UK.

Forms of Human Resource Management in the United Kingdom

All analyses of HRM which adopt a strategic perspective argue for the need to fit HRM to the business strategy. Since these business strategies differ, it is logical that HRM policy and practice should also differ. On the other hand, there are sometimes opportunities to choose a particular HRM strategy. This can occur when HRM considerations help to shape the business strategy. For example, a firm may choose to compete on the basis of quality of service, including quality of staff, rather than on the basis of competitive costs and does so after taking account of the quality of its existing human resources. One of the contexts in which choice is most apparent is in setting up new plants or 'greenfield sites'. These are of particular interest because they more closely reflect the policies managers would like to pursue if freed from the constraints found in most established plants. They represent one strand of HRM in the UK to be discussed below.

Whether as a result of considered strategic choice or of loose analysis or as a reflection of the particular concerns and interests of writers and practitioners, HRM has been used in a variety of ways to focus on a range of issues. Predictably, those who are interested in the future of trade unionism from a radical perspective focus on different issues from others more interested in ways of raising productivity and exploring the role of HRM in the strategic decisions of the firm. There is a strong case for imposing a tight conceptual framework on the definition and therefore on the empirical analysis of HRM (Guest 1987). However, this section recognizes and tries to capture some of the diversity of the definitions, the debates, the research and the practice of HRM in the UK.

Human resource management as anti-trade unionism

Human resource management has been conceptualized as essentially unitarist and individualistic (e.g. Guest 1987) and therefore anti-union. So one pattern we might expect to find is the use of a planned anti-union strategy possibly combined with a set of HRM policies designed to enhance individual employee commitment to the employing organization. One example might be a preference for individual contracts of employment. This approach contains many features of what has been characterized as a 'hard' (Storey 1987) version of HRM and by others as a form of 'macho management' (Mackay 1986). Those discerning greater subtlety in management's approach have described HRM as 'a wolf in sheep's clothing' (Keenoy 1990).

Despite the extensive publicity given to a few well-known cases such as International News at Wapping, there have been only a small number of examples of union derecognition. Indeed the evidence of the Labour Research Department (1988), which has been monitoring derecognition attempts, suggests that even allowing for some under-reporting there were less than 100 successful cases during the 1980s.

There are also a number of instances where a single union has replaced multi-unionism (Guest 1989). However, these too are few and far between. In the great majority of cases, personnel and industrial relations managers, even if they bear the new title of human resource (HR) manager, have been content to continue with the existing industrial relations system of collective bargaining. The implication is that either HRM is rarely overtly anti-union or, if it is, it is ineffective. Perhaps the wolf has no teeth.

Human resource management as non-trade unionism

An alternative to positive anti-unionism is to recognize that HRM, with its unitarist perspective, should consist of a set of positive policies that remove any felt need for trade unions among employees. Unions simply become irrelevant. Again the key to this is the HRM policy goal of seeking high commitment to the employing organization. The importance of this perspective was reinforced by Foulkes (1980) in the USA who associated some of the most advanced HRM practices and most successful companies with non-unionism. This rarely started out as a deliberate policy on trade unionism but had subsequently developed into a positive set of policies to avoid any felt need for trade unions.

Many managers appear to be attracted by the prospect of no unions but do not have sufficient power to remove them. Instead there has been some attempt to bypass or marginalize unions in the hope that they will 'wither on the vine'. This has led to the 'empty shell' hypothesis (Legge 1988) that the traditional collective bargaining machinery appears to be intact but in practice has diminished considerably in significance. Evidence does not permit any firm conclusions on this although we do know that there has been substantial growth in systems of communication and consultation which bypass traditional union channels (Edwards 1987; Batstone and Gourlay 1986).

Human resource management in greenfield sites

Many of the most innovative HRM practices in the UK during the 1980s were associated with new plants, often set up in Scotland or Wales and usually by foreign companies (Bassett 1986). Much publicity has been given to the practices of Japanese firms. It appears that they adopt a hybrid which is neither entirely Japanese management as practised in Japan nor typically British (White and Trevor 1983; Wickens 1987). For example, they have not always been swift to embrace conventional Japanese quality circles (Oliver and Wilkinson 1990). One criterion for their success is a minimum level of statistical competence among those workers involved in the circles and this is much harder to achieve among British workers with their typically low level of basic education.

Features of the Japanese approach to HRM include very careful attention to recruitment, selection and socialization, built around realistic job previews; extensive, continuing and largely on-the-job training; detailed and considerable communication and feedback, particularly of job-related information; constant attention to total quality management; an emphasis on group identification and

group or team working; and low tolerance of substandard performance, including poor attendance. Usually there will be some form
of plant council and in many cases this will include trade union
representation. However, almost all Japanese firms have sought
special arrangements with one union, often the EETPU, and this has
sometimes included special arrangements such as no-strike clauses
and pendulum arbitration (Oliver and Wilkinson 1990).

American firms setting up plants in the UK have adopted a similar set of HRM policies but with some important differences in
emphasis. Due in part to their greater concern for individualism
and a sometimes more explicit anti-trade unionism, they have given
greater weight to individual–organization linkages and, following the
pattern described by Foulkes, have adopted very extensive mechanisms for tying individuals into the company through communications and generous pay, while avoiding any form of representative
system. Normally, therefore, there will be no trade union representation nor even any non-union representation. However, there may
well be well-developed systems through which individuals can air
grievances. Beaumont (1985, 1990), reviewing the introduction of
new electronics plants in Scotland during part of the 1980s, found
that none of the American plants recognized trade unions and that
many had deliberately taken care to avoid any felt need for unions by
careful planning of their HRM. Toner (1985) found that in Ireland
this approach was working successfully, with employees in new non-
union plants displaying higher satisfaction than their counterparts in
established union plants in the same sector.

The contrast between Japanese and American greenfield sites
can be summarized in terms of the contrast between some of the
well-known, much studied and now well-established plants. The
American plants are best captured by the practices of IBM and
Hewlett Packard, the Japanese ones by Nissan and Toshiba. It is
interesting that in considering the firms that have gained a reputation
for their innovative HRM practices, it is usually the foreign owned
and more particularly the American and Japanese companies that
spring most readily to mind. European multinationals operating in
the UK have provided less dramatic examples of HRM. They have
been more conscious of the traditions of social partnership in which
trade unions have a recognized role. The practices of multinationals
represent one important development and serve as useful examples of
what might be achieved. Although the practices of American and
Japanese firms have tended to attract the headlines in the past, it

may well be that in the future it is the European companies that will provide the more useful models. At the same time it must be recognized that foreign-owned greenfield sites are only a small part of the overall pattern. What then have British companies in the UK been doing?

The discovery of strategic human resource management

One of the apparently novel developments in the UK during the 1980s has been the discovery of the need for an HR strategy. This can take a number of forms. Firstly, it can represent an attempt to integrate HR policies with business strategy. Secondly, it can mean ensuring that the various HRM policies cohere and complement rather than contradict each other. Thirdly, it can reflect a conscious decision to use HRM strengths as a basis for competitive advantage. There are other weaker variants, such as the development of a mission statement in which some primacy is given to the importance of human resources.

There is good evidence to support the recognition of the importance of strategy. Brewster and Smith (1990) in their survey of a cross-section of organizations found that a little over 70 per cent claimed to have a formal HRM strategy and half the heads of the function contributed to the development of corporate strategy. Detailed information to back this up and illustrate the substantive implications were less forthcoming and Marginson et al. (1988) have reinforced the case of the sceptics in their research which found that many of those claiming an HR strategy were unable to describe the content of that strategy. This type of evidence appears to reinforce the impression that companies are often paying lip-service to the idea of HR strategy rather than taking it seriously.

One manifestation of this lip-service may be the growth of the company mission statement. Many companies have now developed some sort of formal statement of their mission and it invariably refers to the importance of human resources. The process of developing a statement may be extremely useful for those involved in that it forces them to think through their priorities. However, what happens to it afterwards is more important and it would appear that the most popular option is to publicize it for a while and then file it away. This scepticism is reinforced in the American research by Schein (1986) who found little evidence that mission statements provided a strong lever for culture change.

The most comprehensive research on strategy and HRM in the UK has been undertaken by the team directed by Pettigrew at Warwick. They report the experience of a limited number of cases where significant change took place. The emphasis of their research (Hendry and Pettigrew 1990; Hendry et al. 1989) has been on the factors shaping the HR strategy. One of the conclusions from this and Pettigrew's other work is that sustaining the kinds of change needed, which typically range across business strategy, structure, culture and HRM is extremely tricky and few British companies have risen successfully to the challenge. Instead they have 'played' with strategy and culture.

The culture route to human resource management

Linked to strategy, many companies in the UK have sought to change their culture. The goals of such culture change have varied and it is possible to discern companies which wish to move to a 'production culture', a 'quality culture', a 'service culture', a 'people first culture' and a 'risk-taking, entrepreneurial culture'. Whatever the direction of change, it has become widely accepted that this vague concept of culture is a key to competitive success and that a central part of any culture change requires change in a number of HR levers and therefore in HR policy.

Schein's American analysis distinguishes between primary and secondary levers of culture change. His primary, and more effective, levers focus on the leader's behaviour, including what is the object of attention and the response to key events, and the criteria for selection, promotion and the allocation of rewards. A survey of UK experience shows that while these are used, the most popular primary lever for change is off-the-job training (Williams et al. 1989). There is every chance that this approach will have limited impact since the energy typically goes into organizing and implementing the training courses and not into what happens after the training. Indeed it may be an evasion of the more important structural changes that are required.

Pettigrew's work has highlighted the importance of managing change on several fronts, over a long period of time and with a degree of strategic coherence. Typical attempts at culture change in the UK have been safe and administratively convenient. As a result they will often have had at best only a limited impact and HR specialists will be seen as unable to deliver significant organizational change.

Despite this pessimistic summary, the picture is not entirely gloomy. Grinyer et al. (1988) have shown how a number of British companies have achieved a significant positive transformation. Sadly, most had to be pushed to change by strong external pressures. Thereafter, a change of leadership was often a key factor in implementing and sustaining improved performance, reinforcing Schein's analysis. The role of HRM issues is summarized by the authors (p. 150):

> Sharpbends are heavily dependent on people. A change at the top is one of the main triggers for a sharpbend. Successful bends are aided by careful choice of the right people to undertake the main tasks and made much easier by motivating and involving the whole workforce.

Companies such as British Airways and Rank Xerox, in their different ways, have achieved significant changes in culture, with HR considerations playing a central role. Often with less fuss, some of the well-established companies such as ICI, BP and Shell have been introducing significant changes in their HR strategy coincidentally with, and often as a stimulus to, shifts in culture.

The quality route to human resource management

For many organizations, quality has become a fashionable and essential goal to pursue. One of its attractions is that it can be considered at a number of levels from an overall concept of total quality management to specific and concrete initiatives such as quality circles and Pareto analyses. Quality improvement is inextricably linked to HRM in a number of ways. Firstly, the normal vehicle for communicating the importance of quality is training. Secondly, the ability to improve the quality of processes and outputs depends in part on the quality and commitment of the workforce. This leads to an emphasis on careful selection and training as well as to the wider issues of organizational culture and climate discussed above. Thirdly, the quality of the management of the workforce is likely to be a key feature in establishing the credibility of top management commitment to any quality initiative. Finally, quality implies a process of involvement and flexibility more consonant with an organic high-trust organization, pointing to a number of issues of structure and management style.

The ability to pursue quality improvement with varying degrees of commitment and enthusiasm, despite the claims by leading advocates that what is required is total quality management, makes it particularly attractive to the typically pragmatic British manager. There is therefore evidence of widespread initiatives to improve quality. As noted earlier, the impact of specific activities such as quality circles has often been disappointing (Hill 1991; Oliver and Wilkinson 1990) and has reinforced the importance of setting such activities within a wider strategic framework. The need for total quality management, closely linked to and integrated with HRM, is increasingly recognized.

More of the same, but more determined

While a number of companies have attempted significant change in their HR strategy, the majority have been more modest and pragmatic or perhaps opportunistic. They have seized opportunities as they arose and adopted or at least tried out a number of new HR techniques from time to time. Most have introduced changes slowly and cautiously, particularly where they affected industrial relations. An exception seems to have occurred during the depth of the recession in the early 1980s. This provided a severe jolt to many companies and, coupled with the new political spirit in the country at the time, led to a number of initiatives designed to ensure a more determined management of the workforce.

Marsden and Thompson (1990) have charted the growth of flexibility agreements, some of which reflected a significant shift in the content of collective bargaining. Indeed flexibility suddenly became a goal of many organizations as they sought to break down traditional demarcations which were perceived by managers as barriers to productivity increases. One of the more damaging consequences was that the price for change was high. Wage increases averaged 8–9 per cent throughout the 1980s. In the manufacturing sector this was largely compensated for by increases in productivity (Metcalf 1989). But in the expanding service sector and much of the public sector, similar productivity gains were hard to achieve.

For a while a more determined management of industrial relations was aided by anxieties on the part of trade unions about the future of their members and indeed their own trade union organizations. In the public sector this was manifested in a number of major disputes.

A second widespread trend, again reflecting a new spirit of

industrial relations, was a more or less tentative exploration of the scope for employee involvement. This took a variety of forms, but the most prevalent was the introduction of new or improved forms of communication (Millward and Stevens 1986). Briefing groups returned to fashion, managing directors produced videos and public relations departments presented glossy employee reports designed to inform employees of company progress and exhort them to greater efforts. Enthusiasm for such initiatives was often short-lived and there is little convincing evidence that they produced any significant benefits, more particularly when introduced in isolation.

The third trend within the field of HRM has been to change the structure of payment systems and the pattern of rewards. Many companies have tried to simplify structures and reduce the number of grades as one step towards greater flexibility. There has also been a greater emphasis on performance-related pay. A particular manifestation of this, encouraged by government legislation, has been the growth of employee share ownership programmes and profit-sharing schemes. However, the motivation theory underpinning most schemes is naïve and there is little evidence that on their own such schemes have had much effect (Dewe et al. 1988). In contrast to employee share ownership and profit-sharing, attempts to develop local schemes, linking individual, group or plant performance to pay have a better chance of success. Such schemes have been widely introduced throughout both the public and private sector (Kinnie and Lowe 1990).

If the trends outlined above are primarily concerned with devising mechanisms to improve performance, others have been more interested in getting workers to the standard where they have the potential to perform effectively. There has been a growing sophistication in the use of selection techniques. Comparisons of changes during the 1980s show a growth in the use of selection tests and assessment centres (Shackleton and Newell 1991). There has also been a major debate about training which in some cases has led to improvements in quality and quantity (Training Agency 1989), but the picture is very patchy and some observers believe that despite more activity, particularly in management development, significant improvements in practice are confined to a minority of often well-publicized cases (Keep 1989).

Overview of forms of human resource management initiative

All the evidence suggests a growing awareness among HR professionals about the potential benefits of changes of some of the initiatives outlined above. At the same time we also know that HR specialists have often been slow to innovate (Guest 1991). The problem appears to lie less in any lack of awareness than in an inability to take positive action and follow initiatives through to the point where improvements in performance can be delivered. One reason for this has been the sheer amount and pace of change of all sorts affecting organizations. As a result, HR managers have often failed to find the time to ensure that initiatives are integrated into a broader policy framework or to follow them through. The result has often been a series of piecemeal initiatives, lacking overall coherence or strategic thrust.

Nowhere is the lack of integration more apparent than in public-sector organizations or those which have moved to private owner-ship. Short-term changes have been piled one on top of the other, usually without a sufficiently coherent strategy and usually without allowing time fully to implement each initiative. This is a recipe for employee scepticism and uncertainty. And it helps to explain why HRM has failed as yet to achieve its potential impact in the health service, in education and local government, in the coal and railway industries and even in organizations like British Telecom.

The various models of HRM outlined above are very much private-sector models. During the 1980s, the public sector was encouraged to ape the private sector in various ways and HRM has undoubtedly been one of the areas in which this has appeared attractive and feasible. Indeed, each major reorganization has been seen as both a threat to, and an opportunity for the development of, a more strategic and more effective HRM (see, e.g. Kessler 1990, with respect to local government and Spry et al. 1991 on the NHS). To date the structure of public-sector organizations and the uncertainties of state control have severely limited the scope for any sustained HRM strategy. Instead, like many private-sector organizations, most action has focused on the use of particular techniques. For example, in local government there has been an increased use of psychological testing in selection (LGTB 1989) and a growth in performance-related pay (LACSAB 1990). In the NHS, training provisions and management development have increased as the importance of the process of management becomes more widely appreciated.

Overall, then, the pattern in the UK is one of mixed and diverse development. Sometimes this is for good reasons, such as the demands of different markets or industrial sectors. Sometimes it is a reflection of loose thinking about HRM coupled with a degree of window-dressing. In still other cases, diversity is a product of poor implementation and the lack of a sustained strategy. We should not be surprised by this diversity but it also produces a sense of disappointment in the limited and uneven progress of HRM in the UK.

The Impact of Human Resource Management in the United Kingdom

The main justification for pursuing innovative HR policies is their positive impact on organizational performance. The previous section painted a picture of diversity in the processes – the policies and practices – being pursued under the label of HRM. It revealed a lot of often piecemeal activity but found little good evidence of a coherent strategic approach to HRM. This leads to the plausible hypothesis that HRM innovations have had little impact on organizational performance. Testing this hypothesis or its opposite has, however, proved to be extremely difficult.

First we must specify the kind of organizational outcomes it is plausible to expect. Researchers have often been more interested in intermediate outcomes such as the existence of a clearly formulated and integrated HR strategy, the degree of decentralization of policy, increases in employee commitment to the organization or a better trained workforce. These are important topics for research. However, while they are legitimate HR goals, they are only a step on the way to organizational outcomes and have little legitimacy within organizations when viewed in isolation from these outcomes (Guest 1987).

There appear to be four classes of organizational outcome that might reasonably be linked to HRM. The first is changes in HR and industrial relations-related outcomes such as disputes, including strikes, labour turnover and absenteeism. A second group of variables are concerned with organizational processes and include innovation and achievement of change. A third is productivity and the fourth is the range of conventional financial criteria for business performance. Apart from organizationally relevant outcomes, others that might legitimately be considered include improvements in employee well-being and in community satisfaction. Here, however, we shall restrict ourselves to organizational outcomes.

Attempts to research the links between HRM and these outcomes have not got far, partly because of the inherent research problems. Surveys can provide some sort of correlational data but they cannot demonstrate causal links. Even careful studies have run into difficulties because of the absence of adequate performance data (see e.g. Edwards 1987). One way of trying to overcome this is through case studies. However, it has proved difficult to generalize from the limited case material available and the organizations studied are often selected precisely because they are atypical in some important respect.

What we ideally need is a combination of longitudinal surveys and case material. It should be industry specific and it should be wide-ranging enough to take into account a range of contextual and industry-specific factors. In the absence of such research, we can only infer from the limited evidence that is available. We therefore turn to a brief review of this.

Industrial relations outcomes

The kinds of changes in industrial relations that have attracted most attention in recent years have included the level of trade union density, the power of trade unions and the maintenance of collective bargaining. From an organizational perspective the more important outcomes are associated with performance. Productivity, discussed below, is one such outcome; others, which can have a direct impact on the financial performance of the firm, include disputes and strike activity, labour turnover and absenteeism. It is possible to obtain aggregated national data on each of these, although labour turnover in particular will have little meaning at this level.

Strike activity during the 1980s, and particularly the late 1980s, fell compared to the 1970s. It is tempting to attribute this to changes in policy and practice, including legislation, at both governmental and company level, but it appears that strike activity in the 1980s is similar to the 1960s and other decades and it is the 1970s not the 1980s that are out of step (Milner and Metcalf 1991). There is evidence from case studies that companies practising HRM policies are likely to have lower levels of absence and labour turnover but this has not been systematically studied in the UK. Furthermore the research on organizational commitment, which theoretically provides the clearest causal link to lower absence and turnover, shows that its impact is invariably slight (Guest 1992). In summary, there is no good evidence showing that HRM policies in the UK are associated with positive industrial relations outcomes. However this is due to an absence of relevant research rather than to any negative evidence.

Innovation, change and human resource management

There is no direct evidence of the link between HRM and innovation. In the USA, a number of commentators have suggested that only those organizations that practise HRM have a capacity for the kind of innovation required to survive in a rapidly changing world and even large organizations can change their structures to facilitate innovation (Kanter 1989). In the UK, Deloitte, Haskins and Sells (1987) have surveyed perceptions of the link between company innovation and HRM policy and practice, in a partial replication of an American study by Kanter (1984).

Interviews were conducted with 198 senior managers from 105 of *The Times* 1000 companies. One question asked for nominations of the most innovative companies. Top of the list came Amstrad, IBM and Marks and Spencer. Ironically, fourth equal were ICI and Clive Sinclair's companies. A separate survey among the 105 senior personnel managers in the same organizations asked for nominations of the most innovative companies on HR issues. Top of the list, and well ahead of the rest, came Marks and Spencer and IBM. They were followed by ICI, Shell, Mars, Rank Xerox and Hewlett-Packard. A crude calculation of the financial performance of the HRM innovators compared with other firms in the same sector, matched on size and structure, revealed that they appear to be more successful.

Allowing for all the methodological weaknesses, this study could be interpreted to show a relationship between perceived HRM innovativeness and financial performance. It is less clear that there is an association between HRM and reputation for general innovativeness. However, the main sample of senior managers emphasized the importance of HR factors in facilitating innovation. In all this, there are problems of identifying causality and it appears that reputation derived from publicity for innovativeness influenced managers' responses. If we couple these kinds of data with the results of the study by Grinyer et al. (1988) which highlighted the importance of human resources in achieving sustained change and improvement, it points to the need to get HR issues right. It is less clear that the process whereby this is achieved always fits HRM principles. For example, in the 'Sharpbenders' an external threat justified a power-coercive strategy of change (Chin and Benne 1976), at least initially. This contrasts with the implicit requirement within the philosophy of HRM for a normative re-educative strategy of change focusing on values and culture.

Human resource management and productivity

Productivity in manufacturing industry in the UK rose impressively during most of the 1980s. There are several possible explanations for this, some of which might be traced back to HRM. Metcalf (1989) has reviewed the evidence and concluded that industrial relations factors and better utilization of labour contributed to the productivity increases. He identified the importance of a 'fear factor' in the early 1980s which facilitated a more determined management. This in turn led to an intensification of labour and the introduction of a range of flexibility agreements. The specific industrial relations processes operating to influence productivity, and their long-term significance, have been disputed (Nolan and Marginson 1990).

Any possible intensification of work is rarely directly associated with HRM, although it does fit with claims of a more aggressive, more determined management. HRM and this more determined management may come together in the form of flexibility agreements. A flexible workforce is often seen as one of the important HRM goals. Marsden and Thompson (1990) have attempted to estimate the impact on productivity of flexibility agreements. They conclude that these agreements account for a significant percentage of the increase in productivity in the manufacturing sector.

The claims for productivity gains arising from flexibility agreements provide perhaps the clearest indication yet of positive gains from policies often associated with HRM. Yet the Marsden and Thompson findings are very speculative, due largely to the poor quality of the data available. They must also be set against the evidence from the service sector. It is here that HRM has generally been perceived as more applicable but it appears that productivity gains in this sector, in so far as it is possible to estimate them, have lagged well behind manufacturing, suggesting that other factors have been considerably more important. Finally we should not ignore the possibility that policies masquerading under the label of HRM and sometimes purporting to take account of workers' concerns are primarily aimed at HR utilization through more efficient organization of work. This requires more intensive working but not through the path of greater commitment to the organization or to the work (Nolan and Marginson 1990).

Human resource management and company performance

Peters and Waterman (1982), in *In Search of Excellence*, claimed to have found a link between American company performance and the kind of concentration on the 'human' side of enterprise that is consonant with HRM. The British attempt to cover the same ground, Goldsmith and Clutterbuck's (1984) *The Winning Streak*, revealed similar, loosely demonstrated links. Edwards (1987), however, found no clear link between HRM-type policies and practices at plant level and company performance. Those practising more innovative HRM policies did not report better company performance. There are several possible explanations for this. One is that the measures and the use of different levels of organization in the analysis are inappropriate; another is that the HRM practices are not properly implemented and integrated into a coherent strategy; a third is that there really is no link; and a fourth is that it takes a very long time for the benefits to filter through into company measures.

The study cited earlier by Grinyer et al. (1988) is one of the few UK studies that has started from company performance and worked back. They compared companies where the performance had suddenly been positively transformed with others in the same sector and a similar previous performance trend where this had not happened. The key factor seemed to be a change in leadership, but it was what the leader did that was most important and one of the things the latter paid attention to were HR factors. This is indirect evidence of the importance of HRM for company performance, but like the 'excellence' studies it is tied into leadership and culture, reinforcing the view that these are essential elements in any HR strategy.

An overview

The review of outcomes of HRM has not been very helpful. This is less because of negative evidence than the absence of good quality evidence. While we can claim that the jury is out and issue the conventional plea for more research, this ignores the scale of the problem of change. It has been argued that the values of top UK industrialists are unsympathetic to HRM (Thurley 1981). They will therefore only take significant initiatives in HRM if they are convinced that there is a link between HRM and performance of the company or utility. As this review has shown, such evidence does not exist in a form that will convince the sceptics.

Before we leave this issue, it is worth noting that there is evidence on the impact of specific techniques which could form part of an HRM strategy. These include quality circles, job redesign and various forms of financial participation. Here again the evidence is not encouraging (see e.g. Dunn et al. 1991; Guest 1991; Hill 1991). The impact of these initiatives on performance is generally limited and short-lived. The problem with many of them is that they are introduced in a piecemeal fashion. The exception, and probably the best model of what can be achieved, is found in many of the foreign-owned greenfield sites. At these plants a more integrated set of policies has often been introduced. The problem in convincing the sceptics is that it can be hard to find direct comparators. However, where such evidence is available, as for example in the case of Toshiba's Plymouth plant, then it is very impressive (Trevor 1988). The more astute American observers (see e.g. Lawler 1986) have argued strongly for just such a widely based approach. Indeed there are parallels between the concept of total quality management (see Hill 1991) and Lawler's notion of 'total involvement management'. This can be extended to the similar concept of 'total human resource management' reflecting the advocacy by some HRM analysts of an integrated HRM strategy.

Implementing Human Resource Management

One implication of the preceding analysis is that there is insufficient good quality research establishing causal links between HRM and performance outcomes. Another is that the process of introducing HRM into organizations is poorly understood and often poorly managed. However, there is some good case study material about HRM strategy formulation and a limited number of cases of companies that have managed successful organizational change where HRM had a central part to play (Hendry et al. 1989). Based on this type of research evidence and the wider literature on the management of organizational change, it is possible to identify factors that should be taken into account by those seeking to implement innovative HRM successfully in the UK.

This final section therefore moves from analysis and review to a more prescriptive perspective and draws out the lessons from the available cases for effective implementation of HRM. In so doing we will omit any discussion of the link to business strategy. Clearly, however, establishment of that link is an essential first step.

Clarify the meaning of human resource management

This may seem an odd topic to start with, but the confusion over the concept creates the risk of misdirection of efforts. There are a range of possible definitions; the key issue in the present context is to be aware of the range of possibilities and ideally of the evidence about the impact they have had. The range of approaches extends from the redefinition of the personnel function through an extension of employee involvement to a full and coherent HR strategy based on a distinctive set of values. Those hoping to copy the models provided by firms like IBM and Toshiba need to be aware of the scale of the strategic implications, of the resources required and of the disappointments that will inevitably follow from a low-key or piecemeal attempt at change. Too many British companies appear to have pursued HRM innovations without a clear strategic view or an awareness of the complexities, resulting in limited progress and scepticism about HRM.

Develop realistic strategic human resource goals

Once the range of possibilities has been considered, the next step is to analyse the factors inhibiting and facilitating change. It will be helpful to use an analytic framework such as that presented by Hendry and Pettigrew (1990) to consider the relevant contextual and processual influences and especially the range of possible barriers to the introduction of HRM changes. The range of constraints will include technology, the attitudes and skill levels of the workforce, trade union strength, the financial resources for investment in human resources and, above all, the assumptions and beliefs of those in power in the organization.

Successful implementation of any new HR policies and more especially the more radical forms of HRM require strong and sustained commitment from the top. Many chief executives pay no more than lip-service to HRM, immediately reducing its potential impact. In practice this means that any changes will need to be long term, step by step and evolutionary. From this analysis it may become apparent that a radical change of values to embrace a high-commitment HRM strategy is not a viable option, at least not in the short or medium term.

Improve/ensure delivery systems

Once realistic HRM goals have been set, they need to be sold to the whole workforce and especially to those managers who have to work at day-to-day implementation. One way of selling the goals is to stick with them, avoiding the widespread tendency towards favouring the 'flavour of the month'. A second is to create a number of specific implementation systems. Typically British firms have looked to off-the-job training and development. The problems of transfer and reinforcement have often reduced its impact. Alterations to reward systems and structures and working arrangements have a better chance of ensuring a longer-term change.

A further factor in the implementation of change is the part played by the chief executive and the HR specialists. Both should practise what Peters and Waterman (1982) labelled 'simultaneous loose–tight properties'. They must display consistent and strong commitment to the HRM goals and strategy, but empower others to implement it. For HR specialists this can be particularly difficult since it appears that they must give power away by encouraging others to take over part of their role. All the evidence suggests this ultimately makes them more highly valued partly because they learn to become facilitators and change agents rather then controllers and administrators. For chief executives, the key is the need constantly to reinforce the importance of human resources through their actions. It is in this context that reward systems can be particularly powerful.

Integrate the application of 'hard' and 'soft' techniques

Many British companies have tried to introduce HRM by changing attitudes in the hope that this will lead to changes in behaviour. Typically, as noted above, this involves the use of mechanisms of employee involvement designed to increase commitment to the organization. The evidence indicates that this is not enough (Guest 1992). It may be an essential but not sufficient condition for effective HR utilization. A more integrated and coherent approach also needs to include changes that focus more directly on behaviour. These include the changes in structure, job design, reward systems and problem-solving mechanisms already noted. Total quality management seems to be a particularly promising way of integrating many of these changes in a manner which reinforces the HRM strategy. A common feature of all these approaches is that they need to be implemented at the local level where they focus on behaviour designed to improve performance. For this to succeed, middle- and junior-level managers must be committed to the approach. In the UK, this commitment has not always been forthcoming (Bradley and Hill 1987).

Sustaining change and improvement in human resource management

Much of the wider literature on organizational success emphasizes the need to accept constant change (e.g. Peters 1988). So too do advocates of total quality management, with its never-ending quest for improvement. One way of facilitating this is to create what is increasingly described as a learning organization. Again, we know from the available research that most British organizations are a long way away from this and have a very lukewarm approach to training and learning in general.

Based on the evidence of some of the well-known and more successful implementors of HRM, it appears that organizations need first to maintain a flexibility of structure so that they can rapidly respond to changing requirements and opportunities, for example in the labour market. Secondly, it is necessary to learn through information and especially feedback. This will involve a range of feedback loops including local job-related feedback but extending to a range of communication systems such as careful use of staff attitude surveys. It also implies feedback through systematic evaluation of policies and progress. Again we know that most personnel departments have been notoriously slow to obtain feedback for evaluation and adjustment of most types of policy (Guest et al. 1991).

A third factor, linked to the quality movement, is the search for constant means of improving HR performance. This is another kind of information and learning, reflected in close contact with those at the forefront of new developments in the HR field, including academics. Sifting of new developments should lead to selection of those approaches and techniques which can provide renewal and redirection within the framework of the long-term strategy and value system.

Conclusion

Many of the prescriptions outlined in the previous section fit in with general programmes for effecting and sustaining change in organizations. They are adjusted to take account of the specific features of HRM and the evidence of the progress to date in the UK. As the previous sections have outlined, that progress is in many respects disappointing. Foreign companies have generally made the running while British companies, with a few exceptions, have paid lip-service to HRM and at best introduced piecemeal improvements. Many may think they are doing rather better than this; possibly they are, but relevant performance improvements seem to have arisen mainly through more determined management of employment relations than through any coherent belief in HR utilization.

The evidence about any change related to HRM is very restricted by the tendency to ignore the need for evaluation and systematic feedback as a basis for continued improvement. Elsewhere (Guest 1991) it has been argued that personnel/HR specialists are poor at HR innovation and that senior line managers rarely innovate in HRM because of their limited commitment to it. It is essential to break into this vicious circle if the more sophisticated versions of HRM are to be implemented in the UK. The UK practices of some foreign companies provide a model of what can be achieved. Admittedly much of the evidence comes from relatively new plants or from a few establishments in a limited number of industrial sectors, and it would be unrealistic to expect the same results in many older establishments. But there is much more that can be done and needs to be done to improve management of human resources in the UK.

References

Bassett, P. 1986: *Strike Free*. London: Macmillan.
Batstone, E. and Gourlay, S. 1986: *Unions, Unemployment and Innovation*. Oxford: Blackwell.
Beaumont, P.B. 1985: *High Technology Firms and Industries: a consideration of some industrial relations features*. Department of Management Studies Working Paper no. 3. Glasgow: University of Glasgow.

Beaumont, P.B. 1990: *Change in Industrial Relations*. London: Routledge.

Bradley, K. and Hill, S. 1987: Quality circles and managerial interests. *Industrial Relations*, 26, 68–82.

Brewster, C. and Smith, C. 1990: Corporate strategy: a no go area for personnel? *Personnel Management*, July, 36–40.

Chin, R. and Benne, K. 1976: General strategies for effecting change in human systems. In W. Bennis, K. Benne, R. Chin and K. Corey (eds), *The Planning of Change*, 3rd edn, New York: Holt, Rinehart & Winston, 22–45.

Deloitte, Haskins and Sells 1987: *Innovation: the management challenge for the UK*. London: Deloitte, Haskins and Sells.

Dewe, P. Dunn, S. and Richardson, R. 1988: Employee share ownership schemes: why workers are attracted to them. *British Journal of Industrial Relations*, 26(1), 1–20.

Dunn, S., Richardson, R. and Dewe, P. 1991: Employee share ownership schemes: their influence on employee attitudes. *Human Resource Management Journal* 1(3), Spring, 1–17.

Edwards, P.K. 1987: *Managing the Factory*. Oxford: Blackwell.

Foulkes, F. 1980: *Personnel Policies in Large Non-Union Companies*. Englewood Cliffs, NJ: Prentice-Hall.

Goldsmith, W. and Clutterbuck, D. 1984: *The Winning Streak*. London: Weidenfeld & Nicolson.

Grinyer, P., Mayes, D. and McKiernan, P. 1988: *Sharpbenders*. Oxford: Blackwell.

Guest, D. 1987: Human resource management and industrial relations. *Journal of Management Studies* 24, 503–21.

Guest, D. 1989: Human resource management: its implications for industrial relations and trade unions. In J. Storey (ed.), *New Perspectives on Human Resource Management*, London: Routledge, 41–55.

Guest, D. 1991: Personnel management: the end of orthodoxy? *British Journal of Industrial Relations*, 29(2), 149–75.

Guest, D. 1992: Employee commitment and control. In J. Hartley and G. Stephenson (eds), *The Psychology of Employment Relations*, Oxford: Blackwell, 111–35.

Guest, D., Peccei, R. and Rosenthal P. 1992: The role of training and development in explaining career success. In K. Bradley (ed.), *People and Performance*, Aldershot: Gower (in press).

Hendry, C. and Pettigrew, A. 1990: Human resource management: an agenda for the 1990s. *International Journal of Human Resource Management*, 1(1), 17–43.

Hendry, C., Pettigrew, A. and Sparrow, P. 1989: Linking strategic change, competitive performance and human resource management: results of a UK empirical study. In R. Mansfield (ed.), *Frontiers of Management*, London: Routledge.

Hill, S. 1991: Why quality circles failed but total quality management might succeed. *British Journal of Industrial Relations*, 29(4), 541–68.

Kanter, R. 1984: *The Change Masters*. London: Allen & Unwin.

Kanter, R. 1989: *When Giants Learn to Dance*. London: Simon & Schuster.

Keenoy, T. 1990: HRM: a case of the wolf in sheep's clothing? *Personnel Review*, 19(2), 3–9.

Keep, E. 1989: A training scandal? In K. Sisson (ed.), *Personnel Management in Britain*, Oxford: Blackwell, 177–202.

Kelly, J. 1990: British trade unionism 1979–1989: change, continuity and contradictions. *Work, Employment and Society*, Additional Special Issue, May.

Kessler, I. 1990: Personnel management in local government: the new agenda. *Personnel Management*, November, 40–4.

Kinnie, N. and Lowe, D. 1990: Performance-related pay on the shopfloor. *Personnel Management*, November, 45–9.

Labour Research Department 1988: *Labour Research*, no. 77, April.

Local Authorities Conditions of Service Advisory Board (LACSAB) 1990: *Performance Related Pay in Practice: a survey of local government*. London: LACSAB.

Lawler, E.E. 1986: *High Involvement Management*. San Francisco: Jossey Bass.

Legge, K. 1988: Personnel management in recession and recovery. *Personnel Review*, 17, 2–70.

LGTB (Local Government Training Board) 1989: *Use of Testing Survey Results*. Luton: LGTB.

Mackay, L. 1986: The macho manager: it's no myth. *Personnel Management*, 18(1), 25–7.

Marginson, P., Edwards, P.K., Martin, R., Purcell, J. and Sisson, K. 1988: *Beyond the Workplace: managing industrial relations in the multi-establishment enterprise*. Oxford: Blackwell.

Marsden, D. and Thompson, M. 1990: Flexibility agreements and their significance in the increase in productivity in British manufacturing since 1980. *Work, Employment and Society*, 4(1), 83–104.

Metcalf, D. 1989: Water notes dry up: the impact of the Donovan proposals and Thatcherism at work on labour productivity in British manufacturing industry. *British Journal of Industrial Relations*, 27, 1–28.

Millward, N. and Stevens, M. 1986: *British Workplace Industrial Relations, 1980–1984*. Aldershot: Gower.

Milner, S. and Metcalf, D. 1991: *A Century of UK Strike Activity: an alternative perspective*. Centre for Economic Performance, Working Paper no. 75. London: LSE.

Nolan, P. and Marginson, P. 1990: Skating on thin ice? David Metcalf on trade unions and productivity. *British Journal of Industrial Relations*, 28(2), 227–47.

Oliver, N. and Wilkinson, B. 1990: *The Japanization of Britain*. Oxford: Blackwell.

Peters, T. 1988: *Thriving on Chaos*. London: Macmillan.

Peters, T.H. and Waterman, R. 1982: *In Search of Excellence*. New York: Harper & Row.

Schein E. 1986: *Organizational Culture and Leadership*. San Francisco: Jossey Bass.

Shackleton, V. and Newell, S. 1991: Management selection: a comparative survey of methods used in top British and French companies. *Journal of Occupational Psychology*, 64(7), 23–36.

Spry, C. Caines, E. and Selkirk, A. 1991: Big bang hits the health service. *Personnel Management*, January, 23–5.

Storey, J. 1987: *Development in the Management of Human Resources: an Interim Report*. Warwick Papers in Industrial Relations, no. 17. Coventry: IRRU.

Storey, J. and Sisson, K. 1989: Limits to transformation: human resource management in the British context. *Industrial Relations Journal*, 21(1), 60–5.

Thurley, K. 1981: Personnel management in the UK – a case for urgent treatment? *Personnel Management*, August, 24–8.

Toner, B. 1985: The unionization and productivity debate: an employee opinion survey in Ireland. *British Journal of Industrial Relations*, 23(2), July, 179–202.

Training Agency 1989: *Training in Britain: a study of funding, activity and attitudes*. London: HMSO.

Trevor, M. 1988: *Toshiba's New British Company*. London: Policy Studies Institute.

White, M. and Trevor, M. 1983: *Under Japanese Management*. London: Heinemann.

Wickens, P. 1987: *The Road to Nissan*. London: Macmillan.

Williams, A., Dobson, P. and Walters, M. 1989: *Changing Culture*. London: Institute of Personnel Management.

2

Human Resource Management in the USA

GEORGE STRAUSS

This is a brief sketch of some of the main issues facing human resource management (HRM) in the USA during the 1990s. It focuses on policy problems rather than techniques, though the latter are of great importance to practitioners. Two themes run through the discussion: a major theme relating to increasing public regulation of the human resource (HR) function and a weaker theme of increasing interest in participative management and high-commitment systems.

The Human Resources Function

Personnel administration, for many years a stepchild in management, was rechristened human resource management during the late 1970s and early 1980s and is enjoying a renaissance in both academia and the real world.

Personnel, as a function, can be traced back before 1900 (Jacoby 1985). It grew in status during the 1930s and 1940s largely because of the wartime labour shortage, the union threat and the later need (in many companies) to adjust to being unionized. Then as union–management relations 'matured' and became routinized, other, seemingly more pressing functions, such as production, marketing, finance and law, began to receive the bulk of top management's attention.

In the early 1970s things began to change again. New laws, dealing with safety, equal employment opportunities and the like, forced radical changes in selection, evaluation and promotional procedures, among others. These developments in turn raised HR specialists' status and budget. In the late 1970s, as the economic climate turned sour, many top managements began to view HR policies as critical for reducing costs, increasing organizational flexibility and even ensuring survival. Industrial relations, personnel and organization development policies became increasingly closely co-ordinated.

In some cases this meant using hard-ball tactics to keep unions out of non-union worksites and to extract deep economic concessions at locations where unions already existed. In other instances, it involved developing co-operative new relationships in which the union serves as equal partner. Regardless of strategy, managements' purpose was to increase shop-floor efficiency and to soften the effects of rigid work rules, often developed for an earlier technology. In general, however (particularly where the companies employ few blue-collar workers), policy towards unions was subsidiary to broader interests, especially efficiency, flexibility and management development. Indeed – a point to be stressed – HRM in most companies was and is primarily concerned with managers and white-collar employees, not blue-collar workers.

Many of the new initiatives came from top management itself as line managers began 'asserting greater control over industrial relations policy issues because industrial relations and human resources professionals were slow to change' (Kochan et al. 1986:494). In some companies, these new policies meant wholesale replacement of old-time industrial relations experts who had 'become increasingly isolated, conservative, and less influential' by 'a new set of human resource management specialists who were more conversant with different types of planning, behavioral science-based innovations in work organization and personnel systems' (Kochan and Piore 1985:5). Thus, when General Motors' Vice President of Labour Relations retired, he was replaced by the former director of the company's quality of working life programme, not by someone whose career had been in industrial relations (Kochan and Cappelli 1984). Similar changes occurred at Ford and Chrysler.

As top management demonstrated greater interest in HR policies, the status and perhaps the clout of the newly named HR departments seemed to grow, especially according to such indices as title of top officer, staff size, budget, salary level (Strauss 1987) and number of masters of business administration (MBAs) hired. The HR department, for example, became more frequently involved in long-run strategic planning. As a consequence, according to a *Wall Street Journal* article (27 April 1983, p. 1), former personnel workers received 'at least 30% higher pay . . . if the company uses the trendy "human resources" title'.

Along with this came some other developments. First, there have been some important technical breakthroughs in selection, evaluation and performance appraisal. These rather dull areas suddenly became rather hot. Second, there was much greater willingness to experiment. Often new policies were tried out in several departments or plants before being introduced uniformly.

These developments have occurred in the context of increasing government regulation.

The Role of Law

At one time a sharp contrast could be drawn between the HR practices in the USA and those in continental Europe: continental practices were tightly regulated by law while those in the USA were comparatively unfettered. This began to change during Roosevelt's New Deal when laws were passed which protected unionization and established some fairly minimum wages. The New Deal also introduced tax-supported unemployment and old-age (superannuation) benefits. But, aside from union–management collective bargaining agreements, management's HR practices remained relatively unregulated.

Beginning in the 1960s, however, a series of major laws were enacted which dealt with such topics as occupational safety, employer-funded superannuation funds, discrimination and equal employment. These laws have had some major impacts, as will be discussed later in this chapter.

In 1980 President Reagan was elected on a platform calling for deregulation. His administration was marked by a considerable slackening in the rigour with which the executive branch enforced the laws, a policy followed to a lesser extent by George Bush, his successor. Nevertheless, none of the old legislation was repealed or significantly weakened. Indeed a series of new laws were enacted, some strengthening previous laws (regarding, for example, discrimination against women, minorities, the aged and disabled) and others branching out into completely new directions, for example severely restricting employers' use of polygraphs (lie detectors). No single recent law has had a major impact, but their cumulative effect has been substantial. Furthermore, Congress is considering a long list of HR-related bills, many of which will eventually be passed, though some are likely to be vetoed by the President.

The legal push comes not just from the federal Congress. As permitted in the federal system, state legislatures have been passing laws on similar topics. Further, the USA is a litigious society, and state courts have been actively expanding employee rights, creating a new body of common law, especially with regards to employers' ability to discharge employees 'at will'. The net effect is much broader governmental intervention into HR practices, from hiring to discharge. Some call this the Europeanization of American HRM.

These relatively new legal developments have considerably affected HR decision-making processes. These processes have become more formal, more time-consuming and more bound by paperwork. All this has helped upgrade the HR function and to link it more closely with the corporate legal department.

Labour Relations

Unions have become substantially weaker, in a process not much different from that occurring in the UK. From a 1955 peak of approximately 33 per cent of the labour force, union density has declined to 16 per cent in 1992. The decline in the private sector has been even greater, from over 35 per cent in 1955 to about 12 per cent today (and the percentage continues to drop). Meanwhile the public sector has assumed an increasingly important union role. Public-sector unionism was minimal in 1955; today, close to 37 per cent of governmental employees belong to unions and this figure is holding constant.

Why the private-sector decline? One reason is that traditionally unionized industries, especially manufacturing, mining, transportation, utilities and construction, have grown much less rapidly than the non-union industries, such as trade and services. Factories have moved to the non-union southern states. Additionally, non-union employers have adopted tougher, more sophisticated and more effective techniques to keep their organizations 'union free'. Often they compete with unions through the adoption of high-commitment policies providing participation, job security, individual job rights and due process. Further, in government-run elections designed to determine whether workers want union representation, employers campaign vigorously, taking advantage of every technicality the law allows. Often their tactics skirt or even violate the law, since the penalties for doing so are minimal.

An increasing (though still small) number of already unionized firms have rid themselves of unions altogether. A common technique is to provoke a strike and then to replace the striking workers with new employees. More commonly management has sought to negotiate 'concessions', new contracts which provide fewer benefits than those which are expiring. Often they do this through 'whipsawing', that is through threatening to close the plant in question and moving its work to another plant, either in the USA or overseas. Bargaining as a whole has become much more decentralized. As union strength has declined, so have the number of strikes.

On the other hand, a considerable number of union–management relations might be characterized as being relatively co-operative. Unions and managements in steel, motor car and a few other industries have sought to work together. Though the adversarial aspects of their relationship will never be eliminated, numerous joint efforts have been undertaken to resolve common problems such as productivity, substance abuse and the like.

Though unions are still significant in some industries, their role in HRM generally is much reduced. Forty years ago it was the union movement which took the initiative in proposing new HR ideas – and management reacted. Unions were largely responsible, for example, for the spread of private pension and health plans and for the widespread acceptance of the principles of seniority and discipline based on just cause. Today management has the upper hand. In some cases management has exercised its power in ways that I view as antisocial and short-sighted. In other cases, its influence has been quite positive.

While many recent HRM initiatives have come from management, others have been derived from the women's agenda (if not from the women's movement itself): comparable worth, flexitime, child care, elder care, and the freedom to move in and out of the labour force. Some of these new ideas have been widely adopted already. Others are likely to be adopted during the 1990s.

High-commitment Policies

There is much discussion of 'high-commitment' policies, though perhaps more talk than practice. By high-commitment policies I mean policies designed to develop broadly trained employees who identify with their organization and who are prepared and trusted to exercise high orders of discretion. Along with this comes a commitment from the firm to provide job security and the opportunity to develop a satisfying career (not just a job). Aside from trust, key components of this strategy are participation, lifetime employment, career flexibility and new forms of compensation. Together they constitute a 'high-commitment culture'.

High-commitment policies require heavy investment in human capital, and in some ways are like the stereotype of Japanese management. But they are not like Japanese management in that they give employees a considerable amount of free choice and individual rights.

Some of the leaders in this development, IBM and Hewlett-Packard (HP), for example, are non-union. However, General Motors' new Saturn Division, NUMMI (the GM–Toyota joint venture) and Xerox show that equally innovative plans can be adopted in genuine collaboration with unions. After all, there is nothing basically inconsistent between the high-commitment HR and collective bargaining. In fact the chances of such firms as IBM and HP backsliding from their present good intentions would be much reduced were they unionized. Unions might keep them honest.

Though high-commitment organizations may constitute the wave of the future, this wave has hit some big rocks. The US economy is shifting from manufacturing to service. Firms once protected from competition are now subject to its full rigours. Many previously stable industrial giants (e.g. AT&T) have been forced to 'restructure' and 'downsize', sometimes as a result of take-overs, leveraged buy-outs and the like. Quite often organizations emerge from such restructing with a high debt level and a desperate need for cash flow. As a result they liquidate their human assets at a rapid rate. Not only are skilled managers, professionals and workers thrown on the scrap heap, but expensively nurtured 'corporate cultures' are quickly shattered. (If companies are treated like commodities, to be bought and sold on an auction market, people are likely to be treated similarly.) At the moment, disinvestment in human resources seems to predominate over high commitment. Over the long term this trend may switch.

Participation

Expanded employee involvement is at the heart of the high-commitment strategy, and there is much experimentation with various forms of participation. Participation, it is hoped, will increase employee satisfaction and commitment as well as organizational effectiveness. If successful, all parties gain.

Participation is hardly new. Informal participation, as a style of consultative management, has been preached for a long time, but the last few years have seen a considerable increase in *formal* participative schemes. These schemes can be grouped under three heads: (1) job redesign, for example, job enrichment, (2) quality circles and autonomous work groups, and (3) joint union–management or employee–management committees (see Ramsay in chapter 11). All three forms of participation seem to have proliferated more widely in the USA than in the UK (compare Millward and Stevens 1986 with Cooke 1990).

Job enrichment, quality circles and autonomous work groups appear to be more common in non-union plants. In some companies they have been introduced to keep unions out. Joint commitees exist primarily in the unionized sector.

According to the limited research to date, most US participation schemes succeed in bettering something. They increase satisfaction, productivity or quality or they improve turnover, safety or union–management relations. A problem in the USA as in the UK (MacInnes 1985), is that many of these schemes are short-lived. They succumb to a variety of ills: opposition by unions, workers, supervisors or top management or merely half-hearted support; problems with regards to equitable compensation; or distrust, too high expectations or burn-out (Strauss 1992).

There are critics who argue that participation is merely a fad, which will pass. In some instances this is certainly the case. Participation does not come naturally; generally it represents an unstable social system. Autocracy is simpler. Fortunately, however, managements and unions are now learning the organizational skills required to make participation work. Over time participative work techniques may become more satisfying for workers and more efficient for management. Like drug use, participation is an acquired habit, but a habit which is difficult to shake. In time its success rate should improve.

Work Schedules and Careers

Many workers are more interested in *when* they work than in participating *at* work. This is shown by the considerable interest in new approaches to work scheduling, such as the compressed work week, flexitime and job sharing, as well as the expansion of an older arrangement: part-time work. And 'telecommuting', the opportunity to work at home via computers, has become more popular.

What these plans have in common is that they are designed to permit employees to enjoy their life off the job, as opposed to on it. For some workers, these new schedules represent a changing lifestyle which downgrades work as a source of satisfaction. But for many women and some men it is important chiefly as an opportunity to combine work with family life. Indeed, work schedules have become a major issue for some women's groups.

The demand for change is expressed most frequently by university graduates and MBA-trained women who are competing with men for managerial careers. For some women the 'mummy track', which slows the promotion timetable enough to allow for family obligations, meets the need. For others it does not. Lately neo-feminists have become interested not just in equality on the job, but in equality plus the chance to bring up a family without undue harm to career.

Beyond flexitime, there are open, flexible career systems. These include the freedom to move back and forth from full to part-time to zero-time work (for example, in response to family demands) – and to do so without jeopardizing one's status as a permanent employee. It may mean calculating seniority cumulatively rather than consecutively, thus permitting one to take long leaves of absence without forfeiting previously earned seniority. It also involves the right to a phased retirement (a right especially important since mandatory retirement has become illegal). The demand for career flexibility is also associated with greater concern with burn-out and the opportunity to shift work if one gets stale.

In 'open career systems' individuals are given considerable freedom to manage their own careers. In such settings one finds features like realistic job previews, (RJP, a procedure in which job applicants are frankly told a job's disadvantages), a chance to bid on jobs and training opportunities, and the freedom to accept or decline transfers. To assist employees in making wise career choices requires assessment centres to evaluate skills, as well as more opportunities for counselling.

Although many of these demands came from the women's movement, they are of interest to men, too, and particularly to professionals and managers. Flexible careers systems are certainly
consistent with the philosophy of participation and high commitment. On the other hand, flexibility may be hard for organizations to
provide. Individual and organizational needs often mesh quite badly.
The Utopia in which everyone does his or her own thing may be far
off. As yet, open career systems are more talked about than
practised.

Core versus Peripheral Employees

One of the objectives of high-commitment companies is to provide
something akin to Japanese-style lifetime employment. In this, their
objectives are much like those of unions, which typically insist that
their members receive a constant stream of income from the day they
are hired to the day they die: they get it in the form of wages,
vacations, sick leaves, jury pay, unemployment benefits, pensions
and the like. High-commitment companies provide similar benefits
for their core employees. In both cases, most of the economic
uncertainties of life are transferred from the employee to the
employer.

Maintaining lifetime employment, in the face of the vagaries of the
market, is difficult for many businesses. An increasingly common
solution among American high-commitment companies is to do this
in the Japanese way. They absorb peak workloads through overtime,
subcontracting, 'agency temporaries', part-time and on-call work
and the like. In slack times they protect their core employees by
reversing this process, i.e. eliminating overtime and dismissing
peripheral workers, such as temporaries and subcontractors.

Consistent with this policy the number of part-time and on-call
employees has grown considerably. Subcontracting also has increased.
The kind of work subcontracted ranges from janitorial and equipment maintenance to top-management decision-making (in the latter
case the subcontractors are called management consultants).

Quite a lot of people like the independence of being subcontractors.
Some employees (especially working mothers) dislike being tied
down to full-time permanent jobs and prefer flexibility. But few of
these people enjoy much security. On the whole they are low paid,
have few fringe benefits, and most are women. A high percentage

of part-time workers, possibly a majority, would prefer full-time regular employment. At least, they might like the choice whether to be full time or part time to be theirs, not the employer's.

Thus, the growing distinction between core and other employees accentuates what economists call the 'segmented labour market' and creates serious social dilemmas. The substantial job security enjoyed by core employees merely accentuates the insecurity suffered by the rest. A severely disadvantaged secondary labour force is the ugly backside of high-commitment policy.

Downsizing and Outplacement

When business is seriously depressed, there may be too little work even for core employees. Then management must choose between making layoffs as soon as the need seems apparent and so maintaining a 'tight shop', or of delaying the decision until absolutely necessary and meanwhile finding some sort of activity for surplus workers. High-commitment firms tend to follow the policy of delay. They search for temporary assignments for unneeded workers and perhaps provide them special training or subsidize their transfer to other plants. If business gets still worse they accelerate attrition through fairly lavish voluntary early retirement schemes. Indeed early retirement has become a favourite strategy for downsizing companies which, in effect, bribe workers to quit.

Even these steps are often not enough. Many Silicon Valley companies, with well-publicized high-commitment policies, have begun to make layoffs. As a *Wall Street Journal* headline put it, 'Torrent of job cuts shows human toll as recession goes on. Firms values shift as lean and mean win, big happy family loses' (12 December 1991). Indeed the 1980s in the USA have seen the largest number of layoffs since the Depression. They have occurred even in such presumably stable industries as banking, telephones, retail groceries and chemicals. According to one estimate, almost one-quarter of the jobs in major (Fortune 500) companies permanently disappeared during this period (*Daily Labor Report*, 6 April 1990). Managerial positions, which once were viewed as sacrosanct, have become just as much at risk as blue-collar jobs. In many instances middle managers have been harder hit than blue-collar workers.

What distinguishes current 'outplacement' from the earlier 'sack' is the delicacy with which it is made. A whole new art of firing people has been developed. Aside from the considerable expenses which are incurred to induce older employees to accept early retirement, some companies finance training for new occupations, subsidize job-finding trips, continue employee pay and benefits, and give them time off to look for a nice job. Thus IBM in order to persuade its employees to resign has offered severance allowances of up to two years' pay plus $25,000. Outplacement counsellors, a new breed of morticians, listen to outplaced workers' emotional traumas, assist in writing job applications, coach interview skills and generally help in the job search.

These HR policies are not uniformly followed, of course, not even in hi-tech industry. A large percentage of employers offer little or no protection against layoffs. During the 1980s job security became a major union objective, often given higher priority than wage increases. When long-time unionized employees in the car and steel industries are made redundant, they now enjoy guaranteed income streams equalling or close to equalling their pre-redundancy pay. In some cases these streams continue until the worker is ready for retirement. To support this programme General Motors has committed $4.3 bn over the current contract period. Employees in other industries are rarely so fortunate. Often they receive only limited government-financed unemployment insurance (the dole) at a rate no more than half the employee's pre-redundancy pay, paid for no more than 26 weeks.

There are relatively few legal restrictions on employers' right to make layoffs. In 1988 Congress passed a law (over President Reagan's veto) requiring 60 days notice before making 'mass layoffs' or closing down a plant. Experience to date suggests that complying with the law is less of a burden than management had feared; on the other hand, it has done less than its proponents had hoped to reduce unemployment or to ease the transition to new employment.

Discrimination and Equal Employment

Equal employment – not collective bargaining – has been the most significant HR issue in the USA since the mid-1960s. Beginning in 1960 a series of state and federal laws have banned discrimination on the basis of ethnic origin, religion, gender, age and physical disability. These laws and their interpretation are complex and technical and have provided employment for a large number of lawyers and testing experts.

Such laws have real teeth. They are enforced in a number of ways, through action by the federal Equal Employment Opportunities Commission or its state counterparts, through special regulations applying to government contractors, and through class-action suits filed on behalf of categories of job applicants or employees alleged to have suffered from discrimination. Settling these suits has cost companies substantial sums of money. As this is written, AT&T has agreed to a $66 m settlement to compensate employees discriminated against because of pregnancy. Earlier it had agreed to pay $75 m to settle two other cases.

Equal employment regulations cover many aspects of work: hiring, promotions, redundancies, compensation and even training opportunities. As the US Supreme Court put it, the law 'proscribes not only overt discrimination but also practices that are fair in form, but discriminatory in operation. The touchstone is business necessity. If an employment practice operates to exclude [minorities] and cannot be shown to be related to job performance, the practice is prohibited.' This means that if a selection practice (such as a recruitment procedure, test, interview protocol or a weight requirement) screens out proportionally more individuals from any one ethnic or gender category, then the procedure's 'business necessity' must be validated. For example, job applicants' test scores must be statistically correlated with relevant aspects of work performance. In practice, too, the legal process often requires 'goals' and 'timetables' and even flexible 'quotas' ('affirmative action'), especially where the employer can be shown to have discriminated in the past.

These requirements have forced a radical change in the procedures used to select, evaluate and promote employees at all levels. Performance appraisal procedures have been overhauled to reflect actual behaviour rather than attitudes or traits. Promotional ladders have been redesigned to ensure that women are not held down by 'glass ceilings'. Great efforts have been made to recruit minorities, including offering university scholarships to promising candidates. 'Work sample' tests have been introduced which test the specific skills required for the job in question. Applicants for the job of customer service representative, for example, may be evaluated in terms of how they respond to simulated customer telephoned complaints.

As a consequence of these efforts there has been significant increase in the employment of women and ethnic minorities in occupations that were once entirely white and male. Nevertheless wide disparities in employment and earnings remain. Women may have gained more ground than blacks. A large black underclass is only marginally in the labour force. Still, real progress has occurred.

By now the legally mandated adjustments in company policy have largely been made. Organizations have learned how to live under equal employment rules and yet preserve a degree of flexibility. For this reason, big business showed little interest in following the Reagan administration's call to dismantle the regulatory machinery.

Recently a series of Supreme Court decisions has disturbed this equilibrium by interpreting the laws more narrowly. In response, women and minority groups have sought legislation which would both overturn these decisions and extend the reach of the law. Significantly, when big business representatives agreed to a tentative compromise with women and minority groups, their efforts were vetoed by the Bush administration which sought to make political capital of the issues of 'quotas' and 'reverse discrimination'. Eventually pressure, chiefly from women's groups, forced the administration to agree to a new strengthening legal protection.

In fact, equal employment for women and minorities is much less an issue than it was in the 1970s. The main undecided questions today relate to promotions and to the aged, handicapped, homosexuals (in some jurisdictions), and opportunities for women to combine maternity and careers.

'Comparable worth' is an issue which received more attention in the mid-1980s than it does now. Current law requires that men and women be paid equally when they perform the same or closely similar jobs. But women's groups have argued that jobs which are performed primarily by women should be paid wages equal to those of male jobs of 'comparable worth', even if the jobs are not closely similar. They object, for example, to the common practice of paying truck drivers and electricians more than nurses, even though nurses require considerably more training and bear much more responsibility. In effect, comparable worth advocates seek a major reorganization of wage-setting in American industry. Meeting their demands would require a massive job evaluation scheme in which the requirements of every job would be compared to every other.

Understandably this proposal met considerable resistance. Arguing that an unfair wage structure constitutes a form of discrimination, women's groups made some progress in a few lower courts, but higher courts hesitated to become involved in the difficult process of wage determination. In some states, female government employees won major adjustments, either through legislation or collective bargaining. At the moment, however, comparable worth is making little headway.

Mandatory retirement is now prohibited in most occupations. Likewise, discrimination on the grounds of age (over 40) is illegal. Together these provisions make it difficult for employers to replace older, presumably less energetic employees, with younger, possibly more enthusiastic ones. Elaborate documentation of poor performance is required before older employees may be demoted or replaced.

For a variety of reasons many of the key age discrimination cases here have involved top executives. Evaluations of executive performance are inevitably subjective and subject to dispute. Displaced executives can better afford to hire lawyers than can low-paid production workers. Additionally, juries may grant punitive as well as remedial damages in age discrimination cases, thus making these cases attractive to lawyers. There have been some dramatic awards (some reduced on appeal). In some of these cases employees have produced 'smoking guns' confirming the employer's purpose, with for example, a memo stating an intent to 'rejuvenate the organization and bring in fresh, young blood'.

In recent years, companies have learned to avoid obviously discriminatory statements. Instead they document performance, provide periodic performance appraisals and give employees opportunities to improve their performance before firing them. As a result the number of cases won by plaintiffs has declined.

An estimated 43 million Americans suffer from some form of mental or physical disability, and a high percentage of disabled individuals are unemployed. In 1990 the Americans with Disabilities Act strengthened previous legislation designed to protect this disadvantaged minority. The new law prohibits employers from discriminating in hiring disabled persons, provided that with 'reasonable accommodation' they can perform the essential functions of the job in question.

The meaning of 'reasonable accommodation' is bound to lead to extensive litigation. For example, variations in the way the job is done may be required. Special equipment may have to be provided. Ramps may need to be built for those in wheelchairs. But accommodation is required only so long as it does not cause an 'undue hardship' to the employer. In determining 'undue hardship' (another fuzzy term) the cost of the accommodation must be balanced against the employer's size.

Experience under the older regulations suggests that large employers can make necessary accommodations relatively easily, provided they show flexibility and imagination. Perhaps the most noticeable change will be an increase in the number of ramps and toilets suitable for those in wheelchairs. But small employers, in particular, will object to the seeming pettiness of some regulations.

Individual Job Rights

Recent years have shown a growing concern for individual job rights. By contrast with participation and flexible career systems, both of which give individuals freedom to make choices within the organization, the rights to be discussed here protect the individual from the organization and its members. In effect they say the organization can go so far – and no further. Some of these rights have been obtained primarily through legislation, others through court decisions or union contracts.

Many raise controversial questions. For example: what rights does a professor have to see confidential evaluations of his/her work by his/her peers? What rights does anyone have to prevent dissemination of material in his/her file to others?

Who can have access to reports prepared by company doctors and psychiatrists? Under what circumstances can a supervisor search an employee's desk or clothes locker?

What freedom of dress and hairstyle does one have on the job? Under what circumstances can one's employer inquire about one's sexual or political behaviour off the job?

What rights does one have to smoke on the job? What rights does one have not to be bothered by other people's smoking?

May clerical workers place pictures of their family on their work desks? Is it sexual harassment for employees to post 'girlie' pictures in locations where women can see them? (A recent court has ruled it is.)

For the most part these are new, recently articulated issues. For instance, they were not on traditional union agendas, and indeed they stem largely from changes in overall social values. Perhaps the greatest controversy relates to drug testing. Can/should the employer test everyone? Only those in critical jobs, such as aircraft pilots, who might do serious harm were they influenced by drugs? Or only those who demonstrate overt signs of being currently drugged? What deductions can the employer draw from a single positive test (since false positives are common)? Suppose the test is accurate, what is the employer's obligation: to inform the police? To discharge the employee quietly? Or to send him to an expensive, employer-paid cure?

A 1988 law requiring federal contractors to maintain drug-free workplaces has contributed to the growing use of drug tests. Controversy has been greatest with regards to random testing, with civil libertarians arguing the employees should not be penalized for off-the-job drug use as long as it does not demonstrably affect their on-the-job performance.

Unions have been ambivalent on the drug-testing issue, fearing being seen as supporting drug use. For the most part they have insisted on procedural safeguards and that drug users receive treatment rather than discipline.

Analogous issues are involved with genetic testing, polygraphs, AIDS and alcoholism. Do polygraphs or testing for AIDS or for genetic defects violate individual privacy? Are AIDS, alcoholism and drug addiction occupational handicaps to which the employer must make a reasonable accommodation? Where does one draw the line?

With union endorsement, bills have been introduced into Congress and state legislatures which would restrict electronic monitoring in the office and the use of undercover agents to check on sales clerks. For example, they would prohibit assessing job performance by counting the number of key strikes an employee makes on computer keyboards, or through listening into telephone conversations with customers. Unions argue that these practices place workers under excess stress.

Most uses of polygraphs (lie detectors) are now illegal. Challenges are being mounted against paper-and-pencil 'honesty' and personality tests on the grounds that these are often invalid and that the latter frequently probe sexual preferences and political and religious values.

Standards are unclear here, and they are rapidly changing. Until recently, for instance, the right to smoke on the job was generally recognized, and non-smokers had to accommodate themselves as best they could. Now the reverse is the case. The Occupational Safety and Health Administration has been asked to declare tobacco smoke a workplace hazard. Employees have won compensation awards from employers for injuries to health caused by being forced to work in smoke-filled rooms. Many companies now heavily restrict smoking, with most of these policies being introduced over the last few years.

Some localities now require employers to offer a smoke-free work-place for all employees who request one. A few employers go further: they forbid employees smoking (or even drinking) off the job on the grounds that this increases health costs. Counter-attacking, smokers and tobacco companies have lobbied for laws establishing 'smokers' bills of rights' which prohibit discrimination against smokers.

Emotions over such issues run high. All of them invite the legislature or the courts to set general standards, although neither management nor civil libertarians may be happy with the results. Clearly management has less freedom in these areas that it had a few years ago. Further its freedom is likely to decline even more.

Due Process

Formal due process procedures to protect job rights are becoming increasingly common. There is growing use of ombudsmen, formal grievance and appeals procedures, and even binding arbitration in non-union (particularly high-commitment) companies.

Along with this employees are having easier access to the courts. There are three developments here. First, judicial decisions are rapidly eroding the traditional common law view that employment is 'at will' and can be terminated for any reason – or none. Second, unless a company is careful in how it fires an employee, it may be subject to defamation or libel suits. Third, when an employer dis-charges a woman, a member of an ethnic minority or an older worker, it may be subject to a discrimination suit. While courts are unlikely to defer entirely to the company's internal adjudication process, the existence of such a process may constitute a defence against charges of procedural, if not substantive, unfairness.

Thus US workers are gradually gaining the protections given to British workers under the industrial tribunal scheme, the main dif-ferences being that the grounds according to which American workers can appeal are somewhat different from what they are in the UK and the damages awarded a successful complainant can be con-siderably more liberal.

Compensation

There is a growing dissatisfaction with traditional compensation practices, which for US blue-collar workers, are typically based on job classifications and seniority, adjusted by cost-of-living changes. It is argued that this system is inflexible (especially in bad times), rewards longevity rather than performance, and discourages team-work and job-switching.

As a consequence there is considerable experimentation with alter-native compensation schemes, most of which place a considerable part of the employee's earnings 'at risk'. Among others the most common new approaches are the following:

- the abandonment of individual piece-work for 'gainsharing' (incentive) programmes based on departmental, plant or organization-wide performance;
- profit-sharing and employee stock ownership plans (ESOPs);
- basing individual managers' pay on the contribution which they (or the unit under their direction) make to overall organizational performance;
- greater use of one-off awards and bonuses which provide recognition for meeting specific goals but which do not enter into base pay (lump sum bonuses have taken the place of wage increases in many recent labour–management contracts);
- finally, for blue-collar workers, pay for knowledge, that is pay based on the number of skills one has learned rather than the particular job classification one is in.

Each of these approaches has its problems and limitations. Some, such as ESOPs, have been introduced primarily for their tax reasons. Others represent symbolic quid pro quos given in return for blue-collar pay cuts. Attempts to extend top-management bonus systems to lower levels of management have frequently caused much dis-satisfaction and charges of unfairness. There has been much criticism of the excessive compensation paid to top managers of unprofitable companies. In numerous instances rank-and-file workers have been asked to do without pay increases while top management has given itself seemingly outrageous bonuses.

Taken as a whole, these new approaches to compensation seek to reward teamwork and performance and to provide the employer with a more flexible wage bill, one which is responsive to fluctuations in the business cycle. Profit-sharing, ESOP, various bonus and incen-tive systems, all shift some of the risk of employment back from the company to the worker, and for this reason often meet union and worker resistance. Still, by emphasizing the fact that company and worker somehow share a common fate, they remain consistent with the high-commitment philosophy. On the up side, they reward participative efforts.

Fringe Benefits

The costs of fringe benefits – forms of compensation other than pay and bonuses – are increasing faster in the USA than are wages. Understandably they lead to considerable controversy. Although vacations are shorter in the USA and holidays less frequent than in many European countries, the total cost of fringes is greater because pension (superannuation) and health costs are privately financed to a greater degree than in Europe.

The USA has nothing like the British National Health Scheme. Tax-supported 'social security' pays part of the medical costs for the very poor and those 65 and over. The bulk of the population, however, relies on employer-financed health insurance which many small employers do not offer. The adequacy of this protection varies widely and some 37 million Americans are not covered by any scheme, public or private. These are usually low-income people to begin with. Once taken ill, they can quickly exhaust their meagre savings, leaving them dependent on charity.

Another problem: health costs have increased dramatically. Today they consume 12 per cent of GDP in the USA, compared with 6 per cent in the UK and 9 per cent in France. Some of the causes for high costs are common throughout the world: an ageing population and an increasingly expensive medical technology (a liver transplant can cost over $100,000). But one source of expense is uniquely American, the increasing cost of malpractice suits filed against hospitals and doctors whenever an apparent mistake is made. Not only is malpractice insurance terribly expensive (typically tens of thousands of dollars per doctor per year), but to prevent suits, doctors engage in 'defensive medicine'; for instance, they order an excess number of expensive tests. Adding further to the costs, neither doctors nor patients have much incentive to keep costs down. Expenses are too easily passed on to either the employers or insurance funds.

Becoming alarmed at these skyrocketing costs, unions and management have experimented with a variety of cost-containment measures. For example, 'second opinions' may be required before non-urgent operations are undertaken, medical bills may be more closely monitored, or patients may be fully reimbursed only if they use the services of approved physicians and hospitals who have agreed in advance to limit their charges. These measures have been only modestly successful in controlling expenses. Though the cost of direct medical service is reduced, that of administration is increased.

As the population ages, pension costs will also increase. The problem is lessened for the moment because pension funds are heavily invested in stocks, and in recent years stock prices have increased faster than pension costs, thus providing a financial buffer. This windfall is unlikely to continue for long. Other problems: some employers have under-contributed to their funds, others have 'recaptured' allegedly excessive contributions, and still others have inappropriately invested them or have used these funds in struggles for corporate control.

Over time, both pensions and health care benefits will consume an increasing portion of both GNP and total compensation. As resources get tighter, tensions may increase. Already we see some conflict between childless people and those with large families, and between younger people who want income now and older people who want improved pensions.

Additional problems derive from the fact that our current fringe benefit systems were developed to meet the needs of a traditional family with a working husband and a non-working wife. Problems arise when both spouses work and the family acquires children. Immediately, there is a demand that the employer provide child care (one of the most difficult HR issues today).

Beyond this, sick leave which initially covered only a woman's period of confinement (if that) has been frequently extended to include the first few weeks in which the new baby is home. But children are frequently ill and many employers now allow employees to use sick-leave time to take care of their ailing offspring. And if it can be used for sick children, how about for dependent, elderly parents? Or a sick spouse, or 'significant other'? As time goes by the distinction between vacations and sick leave may decline. Eventually it may be eliminated.

All this points towards the greater use of 'cafeteria plans' in which employees are given a choice as to the fringes they use. The range of possible benefits will increase but a reasonably firm cap will be placed on their total cost. The employers will pass the buck to the employee to make the difficult choice among the many benefits available.

But this will do little to resolve another issue: the widening differences between core employees and the remainder of the population in terms of the benefits, especially retirement and health benefits, enjoyed by the two groups. The only reasonable solution is for fewer benefits to be provided privately and more by the state, either directly or through legally established minimum standards.

Conclusion

To the extent a single theme runs through recent developments, it is that of increasing public regulation of the HR function. There was a time in the USA when employers were almost entirely unregulated, either by unions or by the government. Employees were looked upon as commodities. The employer had no obligation towards them except to pay their regular wages. The financial burden of life's risks – illness, unemployment, old age, death – were borne exclusively by the employee. The employee's only right was to quit, a right more than counterbalanced by the employer's right to discharge the employee at will.

Unions arose to redress this balance. Unions gave workers a series of rights, defended by the grievance procedure. Strong unions also won a comprehensive stream of benefits for their members. These shifted the risks of life to the employer. Though unions have now been greatly weakened, the reforms they introduced have been widely adopted, particularly by large, 'progressive' non-union companies. Indeed these reforms play a major part in the HR policies of high-commitment organizations.

But voluntary adherence is not enough. Relieved of the union threats, many companies became as arbitrary as of old. Further, unions had given relatively low priority to the grievances of women, minorities and the handicapped. In the face of growing public pressures to deal with these issues, Congress and the courts have gradually begun fashioning new rights and regulations. For some companies, these do little more than formalize what they already feel to be good HR policies. For others, adjustment is proving difficult, but rarely impossible.

This general trend towards greater formalization and regulation is occurring simultaneously with a somewhat weaker trend towards participative management and high-commitment policies. Both trends strengthen the HR function.

Acknowledgements

My thanks for support go to the Institute of Industrial Relations, University of California, Berkeley and to Eric Auchard for editorial assistance.

References

Cooke, W. 1990: *Labor–Management Cooperation. New Partnerships or Going in Circles?* Kalamazoo, MI: Upjohn.

Jacoby, S. 1985: *Employing Bureaucracy: managers, unions, and the transformation of work*. New York: Columbia University Press.

Kochan, T.A. and Cappelli, P. 1984: The transformation of the industrial relations and personnel function. In P. Osterman (ed.), *Internal Labor Markets*, Cambridge: MIT Press, 133–61.

Kochan, T.A., McKersie, R. and Chalykoff, J. 1986: The effects of corporate strategy and workplace innovations on union representation. *Industrial and Labor Relations Review*, 39, 487–502.

Kochan, T.A. and Piore, M. 1985: US industrial relations in transition. In T. Kochan (ed.), *Challenges and Choices Facing American Labor*, Cambridge: MIT Press, 1–12.

MacInnes, J. 1985: Conjuring up consultation – the role and extent of joint consultation in post-war private manufacturing industry. *British Journal of Industrial Relations*, 23, 93–114.

Millward, N. and Stevens, M. 1986: *British Workplace Industrial Relations, 1980–84*. Aldershot: Gower.

Strauss, G. 1987: The future of human resources management. In J.B. Daniel Mitchell (ed.), *The Future of Industrial Relations*, Los Angeles: Institute of Industrial Relations, University of California, 91–118.

Strauss, G. 1992: Workers' participation in management. In J. Hartley and G. Stephenson (eds), *Employment Relations: the psychology of influence and control at work*, Oxford: Blackwell Publishers, 291–313.

3

Human Resource Management in Japanese Manufacturing Companies in the UK and USA

BARRY WILKINSON AND NICK OLIVER

Introduction

In the 1980s the major Japanese manufacturing corporations have played a leading role as a model for new patterns of manufacturing management and work organization in the West. This role has been increasingly assumed by inwardly investing Japanese companies in North America and the UK, many of whom now confront indigenous manufacturers on their home ground. This is not to say that the Japanese have simply transferred all the practices for which they are renowned from home ground on to foreign shores. However, they have selectively applied some of their key management tools, introduced suitably modified others, and demonstrated that, thus far, they appear to work. Many non-Japanese companies in the USA and UK deny that their recent experiments with manufacturing methods and employee relations practices such as harmonization, flexible work roles and single union deals owe anything to the Japanese model, a position which some commentators have ascribed to Western fears of 'cultural violation' (Kelman 1990).

The new package of manufacturing and human resource management (HRM) techniques is found under a variety of labels, including 'Japanization' (Oliver and Wilkinson 1988); 'flexible specialization' (Piore and Sabel 1984); 'world class manufacturing' (Schonberger 1986) and 'lean manufacturing' (Womack et al. 1990). No one would argue that Japanese practice does not heavily influence, if not dominate, these approaches. Therefore the activities of Japanese manufacturing companies in the West are of considerable practical and theoretical significance. In setting up on greenfield sites and using state-of-the-art management methods these companies are indicative of the direction in which many indigenous companies would like to go.

This chapter describes the management practices used by Japanese manufacturing companies in the UK and USA, focusing in particular on their HRM activities. It does not follow a specific definition of HRM, but uses the term to cover a package of practices concerning employee relations and work organization. These practices are contrasted with those found in Japan itself, and with traditional British and American policy and practice.

Human Resource Management in Japan

In the search by Western pundits for the 'secret' of Japan's economic success during the 1970s and 1980s, several bestsellers emerged which focused on HRM in Japan (Ouchi 1981; Pascale and Athos 1982). These accounts centred on the provision of lifetime employment, company welfarism, seniority-based wages and promotion and enterprise unionism. It is alleged that these confer a high level of legitimacy on management actions and generate a commitment and loyalty to the company not typically found in the West. Such company paternalism in Japan was underpinned by the ideology of loyalty to one lord as derived from Japanese Confucianism and the feudal legacy (Morishima 1982; Nakane 1973; Dore 1973), though such practices emerged as responses to specific labour market problems prevailing earlier this century (Littler 1982; Sethi et al. 1984). Enterprise unions, on the other hand, developed as late as the 1950s following the suppression of independent trade unions (Cusumano 1986; Littler 1982).

During the 1980s the strong yen, trade friction with the USA and Europe, competition from other East Asian producers, increased labour costs and an ageing population have placed a variety of pressures on Japanese manufacturers. One effect has been that lifetime employment obligations have not always been met. Some companies, especially in the declining coal, steel and shipbuilding industries, have been forced to shed labour, while others are attempting to eliminate, or at least dilute, seniority-dominated pay and promotion systems in favour of performance-related ones (Japan Institute of Labour 1984; Sakasegawa 1988).

Given the expectation of lifetime employment (at least for an elite of core workers – women and peripheral workers are largely excluded from the system) it is not surprising that recruitment and selection by the major Japanese corporations is a careful process. The major corporations recruit direct from the educational institutions with the best reputations and look for potential rather than specific skills. Careful screening, sometimes with the assistance of private investigators, is used to eliminate radicals or 'unbalanced personalities' and to ensure the recruitment of candidates likely to endorse company values and philosophy (Pucik 1985; Robbins 1983). Job training is typically provided by the company, this being preceded by induction programmes more akin to those provided by religious orders or military schools which familiarizes the recruit with the philosophy and ways of the company (Azumi 1969; Ishida 1977; Naylor 1984). Training and socialization continue throughout the employee's career, typically on the job and involving frequent rotation. This, together with the playing down of visible hierarchical status symbols, encourages an acceptance of flexible work roles. Managerial job rotation encourages managers to have a company-wide orientation and makes them generalists rather than specialists (Clegg 1986).

In manufacturing industry work is typically organized around work teams which have a high degree of internal flexibility, the foreman or team leader having significant production planning, quality and other responsibilities. White-collar workers also often find themselves working in teams and open-plan offices are commonplace. Consultation and communication in the form of team briefings and problem-solving activities such as quality circles are extensive.

These HRM practices need to be seen in relation to the manufacturing methods of total quality control and just-in-time production which evolved in Japan from the early 1950s onwards. Just-in-time requires that a production system is run with minimal stocks. This means that material passes through the system very quickly, but this carries a price; the system is inherently fragile and vulnerable to disruption (from any source). Total quality control is an umbrella term covering a range of practices: an emphasis on error prevention; responsibility for quality at the point of production and continuous improvement. Like just-in-time, the effect of total quality is to heighten the strategic position of labour in the production process.

In the major Japanese corporations, HRM practices and manufacturing practices appear to have found a happy 'fit'.

Japanese Manufacturers Move Overseas

Overseas investment by Japanese companies grew markedly in the 1970s, then surged in the 1980s under strong political and economic pressure from the West. The surge was particularly strong in Europe and the USA as the Japanese sought locations within the major markets for their products (Morris 1988). According to the Japanese Ministry of Finance between 1984 and 1988 North America received some 46 per cent of Japanese overseas manufacturing investment, the corresponding figure for Europe being 18 per cent. Within Europe, the UK has been the favoured location, and in the period 1984–8 absorbed 6.4 per cent of Japanese overseas investment. Between 1987 and 1990 the number of Japanese manufacturing plants – the major employers of labour – more than doubled to over 130 (Anglo-Japanese Economic Institute 1990). According to Dillow (1989) the UK is the favoured location because of a warm political welcome (France and other EC countries have occasionally expressed hostility), low wages and relatively weak trade unions. In the USA, by 1988 there were over 300 Japanese manufacturing plants in the car assembly and component sectors alone, and hundreds more in a range of other sectors. It has been estimated that by the turn of the century Japanese companies will employ well over 100,000 in the UK (Dillow 1989), and somewhere between 850,000 and 1 million in the USA (Rehder 1990). Hence by the 1990s employment in Japanese companies has become a phenomenon worthy of study in its own right, though the greater significance of Japanese investment may be the lead Japanese companies have offered in providing a model of HRM for indigenous companies to follow. Indeed, Ford UK went so far as to call its productivity campaign of the early 1980s the 'After Japan' campaign, because of its avowed intention to be 'best of the rest – after Japan' (BBC 1986).

Human Resource Management in Japanese Companies in the UK and USA

The first point to note is what the Japanese have not brought with them to Western shores. Omissions are the extensive paternalistic welfare provisions and seniority-based pay and promotion systems which, as noted above, have recently become problematic in Japan itself. Similarly, promises of lifetime employment have not been in evidence, though the objective of long-term employment has frequently been expressed (Brown and Reich 1989; Gleave and Oliver 1990; Yu and Wilkinson 1989). What they have brought is an approach to organization based on teamwork and devolved responsibility, careful selection procedures, extensive and intensive consultation and communications, appraisal-based pay, and employee relations systems designed to safeguard managerial prerogatives and minimize the likelihood of industrial action.

Selection, induction and training

Recruitment into Japanese companies in the UK and the USA is characterized by careful selection procedures which emphasize attitude and potential rather than experience and acquired skills. The type of recruitment practice varies according to the operations of the companies concerned. In the UK, about 40 per cent of the jobs created up to 1989 were in the consumer electronics field (JETRO 1989), largely in light, relatively low-skill assembly work. These companies have largely gone for young, female labour, often avowedly because such workers possess the speed and nimbleness necessary for electrical assembly work. Thus, recruitment practices tend to combine the effects of both nationality (e.g. rigorous selection) and technology (e.g. nature of the work).

Many companies have tended to recruit people straight from school or college with no previous work experience. As many of the inward investors set up on greenfield sites in areas of high unemployment, they have largely been able to recruit those with no experience of the industry in question (Oliver and Wilkinson 1988). At Komatsu (manufacturers of earth-moving vehicles) in the north-east of England candidates undergo skills, numeracy and dexterity tests, and throughout the whole selection procedure there is emphasis on teamwork ability and co-operative attitudes. Those with team leader potential undergo psychological tests exploring abilities for teamwork, flexibility and responsibility (Gleave and Oliver 1990). At Toyota's new Kentucky plant in the USA the first 1700 recruits were selected from 100,000 applications after over 20 hours of tests spread over several months. Adaptability and the ability to learn and to work in teams were primary criteria (Economist Intelligence Unit

1989). On-the-job training is typically preceded with induction: at Komatsu new recruits undergo a 10-week induction period during which there are five formal and five informal sessions, including Japan familiarization classes, a common feature across many companies. It is usual for those recruited to supervisory grades or above to be sent on trips to parent plants in Japan itself.

Job training is typically provided internally, though at least in the early stages of operations there has been a tendency to buy in managerial talent (Pang 1987). British and American managers in Japanese transplants, however, do not always enjoy the degree of autonomy they might prefer. Pucik (1989) alleges tight control of US subsidiaries by their Japanese parents. In the UK Lowe and Oliver (1990) report a case in which there existed a 'shadow system', whereby British managers were shadowed by Japanese counterparts, who regularly reported back to Japan. Fucini and Fucini (1990) report a similar arrangement at Mazda's Flat Rock plant in the USA. In the UK example, the shadow system was a temporary arrangement until the Japanese parent built up confidence in the UK subsidiary. In some UK companies non-Japanese staff are unlikely to be promoted to senior director levels (Gleave and Oliver 1990), a pattern also found in the USA (Fucini and Fucini 1990).

Teamwork
As described in the section on HRM in Japan, the team concept is an important component of the Japanese manufacturing package, and involves vesting a high degree of 'ownership' of the process in the hands of relatively self-contained teams. Processes of selection and induction typically emphasize abilities to work in teams, and to accept responsibility and flexible work roles. These working practices are directly imported from Japan, and are part and parcel of Japanese total quality philosophy. Team organization typically places the supervisor in a much more demanding role than has traditionally been the case in either the USA or UK.

At Nissan in the north-east of England supervisors select their own staff and take responsibility for on-the-job training, communication, some maintenance, and for capitalizing on workers' ingenuity in improving quality and production processes (Kirosingh 1989). The numbers of specialists such as maintenance and inspection staffs are minimized, and those remaining may be brought under the jurisdiction of the team leader. Public displays of individual and group performance and a meticulous attention to detail are characteristic of the approach, as is the maintenance of strict discipline and bell-to-bell working (Brown and Reich 1989; Rehder 1990; Slaughter 1987; Takamiya 1981; Wickens 1987). Some trade unionists in both the USA (Brown and Reich 1989; Holmes 1989) and UK (Oliver and Wilkinson 1988) have themselves accepted the need for such discipline. A senior official from the UK electrician's union who had negotiated a number of agreements with Japanese firms commented to the authors:

> The Japanese believe in bell-to-bell working. They cannot understand the mentality of the British people where they have to go to the toilet at times other than their natural break because they have conditioned themselves to do that. They can't understand why they are not prepared to co-operate with the company and give back to the company the two and a half minute washing time before the end of the bell because the Japanese say 'Well it's our company and that two and a half minutes, if added up throughout the week is 70 television sets.' Whichever way you look at it they are absolutely right.

Fucini and Fucini (1990) describe how the team system at Mazda's Flat Rock plant created a 'self-regulating attendance system' which relied on peer pressure to discourage tardiness and absenteeism. The Big Three US vehicle producers keep a reserve pool of labour to fill in for absentees. Thus it is the absentee alone (and indirectly the company) who pay for the transgression (Fucini and Fucini 1990: 136–7):

> To his fellow workers [the absentee] is the other driver, pulled off to the side of the road for speeding. His problems are not theirs. This is not the case at Mazda. The speeding driver is not ticketed at the side of the road, but in the middle, forcing all traffic to come to a halt. The transgression of one team member creates problems for all team members. When one team member is absent, his team mates will have to work that much harder to pick up the slack.

Similar arguments apply to production errors or problems with work rate – a worker's team mates suffer the consequences if someone is slow or error prone by having to perform more rectification work, or having to work overtime to meet production quotas.

While both the advocates and critics of Japanese-style teamwork agree that expectations on workers regarding quality, productivity and attendance are higher under the team system, there is debate as to whether the result is best characterized as 'work humanization' or 'work intensification'.

Consultation and communication

Frequent feedback of quality, productivity, etc. information to work teams and Japanese managers' common practice of spending time on the shop-floor (White and Trevor 1983) mean day-to-day management–worker communication is frequent and direct. Typically these are backed up by formal consultation and communication groups such as team briefings, *Kaizen* (continuous improvement) groups, quality circles and company advisory boards. Team briefings are typically used for the transmission of detailed information to work teams regarding performance and quality levels, and are often an opportunity to set targets for the shift, the week or the month. Company advisory boards are similar to works councils and provide a forum for managers and workers' representatives (who need not be trade unionists) to discuss a wide range of issues, such as company performance, markets and a range of company policies. *Kaizen* groups and quality circles are examples of formal sessions where employees are encouraged to generate and pursue ideas for the improvement of productivity and quality in their work areas.

Authors such as Wickens (1987) and Trevor (1988) stress the positive points of the two-way sharing of information and the involvement of workers in Japanese transplant operations. Crowther and Garrahan (1988) on the other hand, have pointed to the problems trade unions can face when communication from management to workforce bypasses the shop steward. Rehder (1990), describing Japanese transplants in the USA, argues that the *Kaizen* process can mean the ingenuity of informal work groups is brought under management control, and put to the purpose of intensifying work.

Single status and harmonization

Japanese transplants in the USA and UK have facilitated the team concept and flexible work practices by using relatively few job classifications, and through reducing the extent of status distinctions – especially between blue- and white-collar workers – so common in the West. Company uniforms, common car parks and canteen and toilet facilities, and clocking on for all (or none), sometimes followed by group exercises and/or team briefings at the start of the shift, are commonly found (Pang and Oliver 1988; Gleave and Oliver 1990). The danger of demarcation disputes is also reduced by there being only a handful of job classifications. The extent of change from traditional Western practices is well illustrated by Toyota's joint venture with GM at the NUMMI plant in California. Prior to Toyota's involvement there were over 80 blue-collar job classes and over 200 overall. This was reduced to one job class for production workers and four altogether (Brown and Reich 1989). At Nissan in the north-east of England, a greenfield site, there are only two blue-collar job titles – 'manufacturing staff' and 'manufacturing technician' (Wickens 1987). Elsewhere in the UK and USA many companies have attempted to reduce the number of job classes and harmonize terms and conditions in order to gain more flexibility, though in some cases this has proved difficult, and the attempted violation of job demarcations was probably the central issue behind the Ford UK strike in 1988 – Ford's first national strike for over a decade (Wilkinson and Oliver 1990).

Reward systems are also designed to encourage flexible working practices. Instead of linking pay to an elaborate and complex system of job classes and job evaluation, remuneration systems in Japanese transplants pay workers to be flexible. At Toshiba in Plymouth, for instance, there are 18 recognized production skills, and increments are paid for each one mastered. A formal assessment of each employee is carried out annually.

Pay and appraisal

It is in the area of reward systems that we find the most marked divergence from practices believed to be common in Japan. As noted above, company provision of housing, health and educational facilities is typically left behind. Further, seniority carries relatively little weight in consideration of decisions on pay and promotion. Japanese companies have not, however, gone for large-scale job evaluation exercises typical in many American and British companies at least up until the 1980s.

In the UK, in the labour markets in which many Japanese manu-facturing companies operate – relatively low-skill light assembly work – the companies themselves report that they pay average or above-average wages (Pang and Oliver 1988; Yu and Wilkinson 1989). Wage levels are generally determined by the company in relation to industry and regional labour markets; many companies in both the USA and UK have avoided unionization and hence wage bargaining, and even some of those companies in the UK which recognize single unions claim collective bargaining has no influence on wages. Rather, wages are often established via the recommendation of the company advisory board or company council – a company institution in which union officials play only a minor role.

A striking aspect of pay systems – at least in Japanese companies in the UK – is the widespread use of formal performance appraisal schemes. While being more common in the USA, appraisal in the UK has typically been restricted to managerial and white-collar staffs, and the results have tended to be kept separate, at least officially, from reward reviews and considerations of promotion (Wickens 1987). Such a separation is supported by prescriptions in British personnel management textbooks (Torrington and Hall 1987). In contrast, a recent survey showed all Japanese respondents employing over 200 used performance appraisals, nearly all applied

Table 3.1 Appraisal criteria in Japanese companies in the UK

Criteria	No. of companies using criteria
Teamworking ability, co-operation	11
Self-organization, problem-solving skills	10
Leadership, persuasiveness	9
Attendance, punctuality	8
Quantity of work, efficiency, productivity	8
Communication skills	7
Job knowledge	7
Accuracy, attention to detail	7
Attitude, motivation, loyalty	7
Creativity, initiative	6
Flexibility, adaptability	5
Quality of work	5
Ability to work under pressure	4
Enthusiasm, willingness to work	4
Safety, housekeeping	4
Reasoning, analytical skills	4
Persistence, determination	3
Work skills	3

Source: Yu and Wilkinson (1989)

the scheme to all staff including blue-collars, and the great majority indicated an influence of appraisal results on job grades, wage level, promotion and task allocation (Yu and Wilkinson 1989). This has been compared by Nissan's personnel director with traditional British practice, where 'frequently the only use to which [appraisals] are put is as a reference document for the next review' (Wickens 1987:123).

Of 13 sets of Japanese companies' appraisal documentation recently collected by the authors, 11 included forced choice question-naires inviting the appraiser (typically the immediate superior or team leader) to grade the appraisee against a range of criteria. These criteria are indicated in table 3.1.

The criteria, a mix of task performance indicators and personal qualities, are striking for the frequent use of subjectively assessed factors such as teamwork, communications, co-operation and attitude. This orientation fits the Japanese emphasis on flexibility and teamwork in the operation of their organizations, serving constantly to reinforce the message initially given in selection and induction. Whether judging people on their co-operation serves to resolve the apparent contradiction between individualized appraisal and reward on the one hand and co-operation and teamwork on the other is a question we unfortunately have to leave open.

Employee relations

In the UK, apart from a few joint ventures or where the Japanese company has taken over a going concern, the norm has been the avoidance of trade unions in new towns and semi-rural locations, and the recognition of a single union in established industrial areas. Many non-Japanese companies setting up on greenfield sites have also had success with the single union option in the 1980s.

The advantages to companies of single union recognition are primarily: the facilitation of flexible working in the absence of union demarcation lines; the reduced likelihood of industrial disputes 'spilling over' from plant to plant; and the simplification of bargaining and consultation structures and procedures. In itself single union recognition is hardly new to the UK, as the trade union defenders of such deals have pointed out. However, when we look closely at the additional features of the single union deals signed at Toshiba and other companies in the 1980s, a marked departure is indicated. This is because the deals typically incorporate most or all of the following:

company advisory boards; binding arbitration; specific clauses on flexible working; and a strongly unitarist language and sentiments.

Company advisory boards come under a variety of names such as staff council, company council and advisory committee. Like many traditional joint consultative committees, members are not necessarily trade union officers, or even trade union members, but the boards' responsibilities typically extend to areas normally the preserve of collective bargaining, including pay and terms and conditions. In addition, such boards are important mechanisms for the transmission of company information. At Toshiba UK, manufacturers of colour televisions, union representatives are requested to sign a form stating that:

> It is recognized that the Company Advisory Board is the best and first means of resolving all collective issues between the company and its employees, and the representative fully supports and encourages the role of the Company Advisory Board in the conduct of relationships between the company and its employees.

The shift of responsibilities from shop stewards to worker representatives on advisory boards poses a threat to the traditional role of the shop steward. Describing Nissan UK's agreement with the engineering union, the AEU, Crowther and Garrahan (1988:57) argue that 'it allows virtually no independent role for shop stewards, and whilst it appears that the company does not intend to actively obstruct union activities, the mechanisms for representation are highly supportive of non-union participation'.

This is one explanation suggested by Crowther and Garrahan for the low union membership at Nissan. At other Japanese companies in the UK, however, strong support of union membership from managements helps membership levels to be similar to those for the rest of British manufacturing industry (Oliver and Wilkinson 1988).

Some single union agreements incorporate a binding arbitration clause, and all those deals seen by the authors include procedures which greatly reduce the likelihood of an official dispute. 'Signing away the right to strike' has been vehemently criticized, though collective agreements are not legally binding in the UK. What is important is that dispute procedures in such deals may contribute, at least symbolically, to the industrial relations stability which is so important to the vulnerable Japanese system of production (Wilkinson and Oliver 1989).

Specific flexibility clauses are typical in these agreements. These generally assert in unambiguous terms the managerial prerogative over labour deployment, reinforcing the potential for flexible working that comes with single union recognition. The agreement between Hitachi and the electricians' union in the UK, for instance, reads:

> All company members will agree the complete flexibility of jobs and duties within and between the various company functions and departments. The main flexibility principle will be that when necessary to fit the needs of the business, all company members may be required to perform whatever jobs and duties are within their capability.

The language of 'harmony', 'mutual benificence' and 'commitment to company success' features prominently in many of the agreements between Japanese companies and unions, on both sides of the Atlantic. This indicates a redefinition of the role of the trade union as 'partner' rather than 'adversary'.

Attitudes of trade unionists to the new style of employee relations (which, it must be stressed are not the exclusive preserve of Japanese companies) have been mixed. In the UK some trade unionists have been critical of the employment practices of Japanese companies, and against those unions who have been party to agreements with these companies. In the USA some trade unionists have also been vocal in their denouncement of the Japanese approach to industrial relations. Following one dispute in 1989 between workers and the Japanese construction company Ohbayashi, labour leaders announced an anti-Japanese investment rally on 7 December, Pearl Harbor Day (Kane 1989). (The dispute was settled before the rally took place when Ohbayashi agreed the US union federation AFL–CIO could play the role in labour assignments it wanted.)

In the UK, in the context of declining trade union membership, inter-union competition has been the response of the trade union movement to the new industrial relations strategies of newly investing companies, and some trade unions, notably the Electrical, Electronic, Telecommunication and Plumbing Union (EETPU), the Amalgamated Engineering Union (AEU) and the Managerial, Administrative, Technical and Supervisory Association (MATSA), have taken a proactive approach in offering model agreements on the above lines to potential investors. In the well-rehearsed debate, the advocates of the new unionism claim 'realism' and 'mutual benefit', the critics complain of a 'beauty contest' syndrome resulting in 'sweetheart deals'. What is clear is that the unions party to such deals are explicitly accepting a collaborative rather than adversarial role, a role which implies a new kind of trade unionism with similarities to Japanese company unionism.

In the USA, the majority of Japanese manufacturers have avoided the recognition of trade unions altogether, with employee relations being conducted through the various consultative and communication mechanisms described earlier. However, in those situations where unionization has occurred, similar issues have surfaced. The GM–Toyota joint venture, NUMMI in California, is instructive in this respect, and it is worth explaining the implications for industrial relations in the US car industry.

In the context of fierce competition from the Japanese, it was as early as the late 1970s that the desire on the part of car sector employers in the USA to shift from 'pattern bargaining' was being strongly expressed. Pattern bargaining was a well-established system of bargaining in the Canadian as well as the US car industry which more or less ensured standard industry-wide wages, conditions and working practices. The desire was to move towards company- or even plant-level bargaining. In the early 1980s, with several Japanese assemblers moving into non-union plants on greenfield sites in the Midwest, the pressure grew even greater. According to Holmes (1989:21–2): 'by 1985 the top UAW leadership . . . were implicitly endorsing the team concept as a strategy to make the US auto industry competitive. . . . It involves a shift towards enterprise unionism where the union views itself as a partner in management.' Since the mid-1980s the team concept and local bargaining have become widely established in the USA, and are making inroads into the Canadian car industry as well.

The Toyota–UAW local agreement at NUMMI was probably the single most important deal, and since then NUMMI has provided a model of management–union relations as well as work practices in GM and other plants across the USA. Toyota Motor Corporation President, Soichiro Toyoda, was directly involved in 'efforts to communicate to the UAW our wish to introduce Japanese methods to the greatest possible degree . . . in my opinion the most critical area is labour–management relations' (cited in *Productivity Digest*, Singapore, 3/11 January 1985).

In the UK Toyota was a relatively late investor, and at the time of writing (early 1991) had not commenced production. Direct comparison with the US experience is therefore problematical. However, Toyota's chosen site is in Derbyshire, outside the traditional car-producing areas of the UK, and it is known that the company will be signing a single union agreement. Honda, in contrast, are attempting to pursue a non-union route at their plant at Swindon in the UK. Local producers are alarmed at the cost advantages they fear the Japanese will have, and are attempting to move towards the Japanese model themselves. Being on established sites, the indigenous producers are finding this a slow and difficult process.

Summary and Conclusions

Comparison between the UK and US experiences with Japanese companies reveals some differences but many similarities. What is less than clear is the extent to which these companies are reflecting current 'international' perceptions of best management practice versus their Japanese origin. Certainly the fact that they are setting up on greenfield sites gives them a scope for experimentation not open to companies on established sites. Moreover, it is clearly mistaken to regard inwardly investing 'Japanese companies' as a homogeneous mass; although there are some similarities in HRM style between these companies, there are also important differences which are mediated by a whole variety of locational and technological factors. The nation of origin is only one of many factors which impacts on management practice.

When the inwardly investing companies are considered relative to those operating in Japan itself, there are clear differences. Left behind in Japan are the extensive welfare provision, lifetime employment and seniority wages and promotion. The Japanese manufacturers have brought total quality and just-in-time manufacturing systems and the team concept which goes with them.

On both sides of the Atlantic Japanese HRM policies entail careful attention to selection, training, consultation and communication, single status facilities, harmonized terms and conditions, the minimization of job classes, and individual appraisals emphasizing co-operation, teamwork and flexibility. Such practices underwrite an efficient manufacturing system dependent on teamwork, strict discipline, flexibility and attention to detail. And despite scepticism about British or American workers' ability or inclination to work 'the Japanese way', they have generally achieved the sorts of productivity and quality levels found in Japanese companies in Japan.

The context in the 1980s, however, for both the USA and UK, has been one of high unemployment, weakening trade union strength, and generally a political climate hostile to labour movements and organized industrial action. This context, together with the fact that many (in the USA) or most (in the UK) Japanese companies are setting up on greenfield sites without the baggage of established organizational cultures and traditions, probably helps account for the apparent ease with which Japanese companies have established new practices. In both countries, too, most Japanese manufacturers have been welcomed by local trade union leaders, businessmen and civic dignitaries for the new life they promise to put into communities suffering from the decline of their traditional industries.

As we enter the 1990s, there is still a clear 'honeymoon' effect surrounding many of these investments. The extent to which the HRM practices we have discussed in this section will be sustained in the longer term, and the extent to which they will be modified in the light of local conditions remain an open question.

References

Anglo-Japanese Economic Institute 1990: *Japanese Addresses in the UK*. London: AJEI.

Azumi, K. 1969: *Higher Education and Business Recruitment in Japan*. New York: Columbia University Press.

BBC 1986: Process capability and control. *Quality Techniques*, PT 619. Milton Keynes: OU/BBC Productions (film).

Brown, C. and Reich, M. 1989: When does union–management cooperation work? A look at NUMMI and GM-Van Nuy's. *California Management Review*, 31(4), 26–44.

Clegg, C. 1986: Trip to Japan: a synergistic approach to managing human resources. *Personnel Management*, August, 35–9.

Crowther, S. and Garrahan, P. 1988: Invitation to Sunderland: corporate power and the local economy. *Industrial Relations Journal*, 19(1), 51–9.

Cusumano, M. 1986: *The Japanese Automobile Industry: technology and management at Nissan and Toyota*. Cambridge, Mass.: Harvard University Press.

Dillow, C. 1989: *A Return to Trade Surplus? The Impact of Japanese Investment in the UK*. London: Nomura Research Institute.

Dore, R. 1973: *Origins of the Japanese Employment System*. London: Allen & Unwin.

Economist Intelligence Unit 1989: *Japanese Motor Business*, no. 19, March.

Fucini, J.J. and Fucini, S. 1990: *Working for the Japanese*. New York: Free Press.

Gleave, S. and Oliver, N. 1990: Human resources management in Japanese manufacturing companies in the UK: five case studies. *Journal of General Management*, 16(1), 54–68.

Holmes, J. 1989: From uniformity to diversity: changing patterns of wages and work practices in the North American automobile industry. Paper presented to the Annual Employment Research Unit Conference, Cardiff Business School, UWCC, 19–20 September.

Ishida, H. 1977: *Exportability of the Japanese Employment System*. Tokyo: Japan Institute of Labour.

Japan Institute of Labour 1984: *Wages and Hours of Work*. Japanese Industrial Relations Series, no. 3.

JETRO 1989: Issue no. 1.

Kane, M. 1989: *Regional Underpinnings of the US-Japan Partnership Commonwealth of Kentucky: a case study*. University of Kentucky.

Kelman, S. 1990: The Japanization of America. *Public Interest*, 98, 70–83.

Kirosingh, M. 1989: Changed work practices. *Employment Gazette*, 97(8), 422–9.

Littler, C. 1982: *The Development of the Labour Process in Capitalist Societies*. London: Heinemann.

Lowe, J. and Oliver, N. 1990: New look employee relations: the view from the inside. Paper presented to the Employment Research Unit Conference on Employment Relations in the Enterprise Culture, Cardiff Business School, UWCC, 18–19 September.

Morishima, M. 1982: *Why has Japan 'Succeeded'? Western Technology and the Japanese Ethos*. Cambridge: Cambridge University Press.

Morris, J. 1988: The who, why and where of Japanese manufacturing investment in the UK. *Industrial Relations Journal*, 19(1), 31–40.

Nakane, C. 1973: *Japanese Society*. Harmondsworth: Penguin.

Naylor, L. 1984: Bringing home the lessons. *Personnel Management*, 16(3), 34–7.

Oliver, N. and Wilkinson, B. 1988: *The Japanization of British Industry*. Oxford: Blackwell.

Ouchi, W. 1981: *Theory Z: how American business can meet the Japanese challenge*. Boston: Addison-Wesley.

Pang, K.K. 1987: Japanese management practices in overseas subsidiaries: a case approach. MBA dissertation, Cardiff Business School, UWCC.

Pang, K.K. and Oliver, N. 1988: Personnel strategy in eleven Japanese manufacturing companies in the UK. *Personnel Review*, 17(3), 16–21.

Pascale, R. and Athos, A. 1982: *The Art of Japanese Management*. Harmondsworth: Penguin.

Piore, M. and Sabel, C. 1984: *The Second Industrial Divide*. New York: Basic Books.

Pucik, V. 1985: Managing Japan's white collar workers. *Euro-Asia Business Review*, 4(3), 16–21.

Pucik, V. 1989: *Management Culture in Japanese-owned US Corporations*.

Tokyo: Egon Zehnder International.

Rehder, R. 1990: 'Japanese transplants: after the honeymoon. *Business Horizons*, January–February, 87–98.

Robbins, S. 1983: Theory Z from a power-control perspective. *California Management Review*, 25(2), 67–75.

Sakasegawa, K. 1988: Technological innovation and wage systems: the Japanese experience. In International Labour Office (ed.), *Technological Change, Work Organization and Pay: lessons from Asia*, Labour–Management Relations Series no. 68, Geneva: ILO, 171–84.

Schonberger, R. 1986: *World Class Manufacturing*. New York: Free Press.

Sethi, S., Namiki, N. and Swanson, C. 1984: *The False Promise of the Japanese Miracle*. London: Pitman.

Slaughter, J. 1987: The team concept in the US auto industry. Paper presented to the Conference on the Japanization of British Industry, Cardiff Business School, UWCC, 17–18 September.

Takamiya, M. 1981: Japanese multinationals in Europe: international operations and their public policy implications. *Columbia Journal of World Business*, Summer, 5–17.

Torrington, D. and Hall, L. 1987: *Personnel Management*. London: Prentice-Hall.

Trevor, M. 1988: *Toshiba's New British Company*. London: Policy Studies Institute.

White, M. and Trevor, M. 1983: *Under Japanese Management*. London: Heinemann.

Wickens, P. 1987: *The Road to Nissan*. London: Macmillan.

Wilkinson, B. and Oliver, N. 1989: Power, control and the Kanban. *Journal of Management Studies*, 26(1), 47–58.

Wilkinson, B. and Oliver, N. 1990: Obstacles to Japanization: the case of Ford UK. *Employee Relations*, 12(1), 17–22.

Womack, J.P., Jones, D.T. and Roos, D. 1990: *The Machine that Changed the World: the triumph of lean production*. New York: Rawson Macmillan.

Yu, C. and Wilkinson, B. 1989: *Pay and Appraisal in Japanese Companies in Britain*. Japanese Management Research Unit Working Paper no. 8. Cardiff.

4

The European Dimension: Employee Relations in Europe

JEFF BRIDGFORD AND JOHN STIRLING

Introduction

There can be little doubt that since the late 1970s the existing employee relations systems in Europe have been the subject of significant and pervasive challenges. Structural shifts in labour markets, movements of capital into different sectors and the alterations of patterns of ownership have taken place alongside the introduction of organizational strategies which are moving from industrial relations to human resource management (HRM). All this within changing patterns of trade union power and membership and shifting government policies on employment and industrial relations. The creation of the Single Market within the European Community (EC) and the development of the Social Charter and its related directives add to an ever-expanding catalogue of change.

However, the apparent wholesale shifts in direction must be counterbalanced by the evidence of continuity and the different pace of change between industries and countries. In the UK, for example, we are faced with a choice between those who suggest that employee relations in general and trade unions in particular will never be the same again and those who emphasize stability and the resilience of existing structures (Bassett 1986; MacInnes 1987; Kelly 1990).

Judgements about the relative merits of the arguments and the level and significance of change are enhanced by placing the developments in a broader context. Comparison on a European basis becomes not simply an end in itself, albeit an interesting one, but also a mechanism for developing understanding, and an agent of policy-making. However, this is not to suggest that what is successful in one country can simply be transposed to another with every prospect of equal success. Codetermination in Germany or the Scandinavian system of centralized bargaining are integral parts of broader social structures and industrial relations frameworks which cannot simply be bolted on to existing systems elsewhere.

We should be equally wary of suggesting that characteristics of employee relations policies are predetermined to be culturally specific. Large organizations will adopt and adapt policies from other countries, although the process is not necessarily a straightforward one as Ford's 'After Japan' policy illustrates (Starkey and McKinlay 1989). They may also seek to impose particular employee relations models. Some transnationals have sought to establish a degree of uniformity in their practice. Non-unionism in companies such as IBM has been the most evident and controversial export, but collective bargaining strategies, payment systems and work organization policies may also be decided centrally and exported to branch plants.

The EC itself has also sought to establish a 'levelling' of employee relations practices by pursuing common standards through the Community Charter of the Fundamental Social Rights of Workers and its associated Action Programmes. In the field of equal opportunities policies in particular, the Court of Justice has been successful in imposing EC-wide decisions on individual countries. These developments have caused some commentators to suggest that 'in a fully blown form, the social dimension could result in the creation of a European industrial relations framework standing above, but at the same time interacting with, the national systems already in place' (Teague 1989:9).

However, it is far too early to talk about a European industrial relations system. The creation of a common legal framework in such areas as dismissal or retirement presents formidable obstacles. These may seem small beer when compared, for example, to the co-ordination required for trade unions to co-operate in European-wide collective bargaining even if organizations were prepared to accept it. The whole picture then becomes even more complex when we take into account European countries outside the EC and the developments in the former command economies. In such circumstances, a coherent European industrial relations system is a long way off.

In the remaining sections of this chapter we explore the elements of the industrial relations process which contribute to both uniformity and diversity, and provide the context within which human resource (HR) policies are developed. We conclude with some comments on the impact of Europe for British employee relations.

Labour Market Contexts

Employment patterns both shape and reflect organizational HR policies. Public-sector employers and large corporations have a significant impact on local labour markets while, at the other end of the spectrum, small and medium-sized enterprises remain responsible for employing the majority of workers.

It has become commonplace to suggest that radical changes have been taking place in European labour markets since the 1980s and that these have had a major impact on the development of employee relations processes. The main features of this are the persistently high levels of unemployment related to the restructuring of manufacturing industry and the continued decline of the primary sector. This was paralleled in the past by the growth of employment in the public and service sectors. In OECD countries, the former grew from 14.2 per cent of the labour force in 1970 to nearly 18 per cent by 1979 (ILO 1984:49). In the service sector, all the EC states experienced growth between 1970 and 1980. The increases ranged from 5.2 per cent in Greece to over 10 per cent in countries as diverse as Denmark, Spain and Luxemburg (Eurostat 1989). More recently, public-sector employment growth has reached a plateau and even declined but the service sector remains the most significant growth area. It is now suggested that these overall changes in employment patterns are irreversible (European Commission 1989:8).

The shifts in sectoral employment have been related to more controversial changes in modes of employment which have been linked to the growth of female participation in the labour force. It has been suggested that there are now a range of 'new forms of work' (European Foundation 1988:19). In reality, employment on part-time and temporary contracts is long established. What is suggested as different is 'their irresistible, unprecedented spread in all member states', their increasing legal recognition and their promotion by government policy (European Foundation 1988:19).

This 'irresistible' spread is much debated (Hakim 1990; Phillimore 1989; Pollert 1988) but remains central to the development of HRM. It is the core workforce that has become the focus of policy development in such areas as recruitment, training, appraisal and retention through organizationally specific rewards systems.

However, a crude core and peripheral European model can conceal more than it reveals. Firstly, references to 'new forms of work' begs the question of who is doing the work. The early analysis of dual labour markets focused on the significant role of urban black and migrant workers in peripheral jobs (Rosenberg 1989). The changes in Eastern Europe suggest that some migration may occur again but it is unlikely to be on the scale that we have seen in the past. The emphasis in the analysis has now shifted to the overwhelming importance of women, particularly in part-time employment. In the past much of this has been in agriculture, and in countries such as Italy, Ireland and Greece where the decline in that sector has been less dramatic and more recent, the proportion of women's labour accounted for by part-time work actually fell between 1975 and 1985 (European Commission 1989).

Women also dominate temporary employment in non-manufacturing industry although the importance of this sector is the subject of considerable debate. 'Figures for the member states suggest that while temporary employment has increased in all countries except Italy, it remains relatively small' (Brewster and Teague 1989:249).

Secondly, there is the question of whether the suggested growth of atypical work patterns is one of choice either for employers or workers. The flexible firm model would certainly suggest that employers are making conscious decisions in their employment policies. Where this is so, it is likely to coincide with an overall restructuring of HR policies. However, it is clear that the 'flexible firms' are still on the edge of economies which remain dominated by traditional employment patterns. The evidence as to whether employees 'choose' atypical jobs must also be tempered by the question of what alternatives are available. However, it is clear that a significant proportion of Europe's part-time workers would prefer full-time jobs if they were available (European Commission 1989:75).

Finally, there is the question of how transient the changing patterns of employment are. By the year 2025 there will probably be 2 per cent fewer people in Europe. By the time the Single European Market becomes effective the number of net entrants to the labour market could fall close to zero. In such circumstances employment policies become either to replace people with capital through new technology or to introduce HR policies that train and retain staff. This could lead to tendencies to expand rather than contract core workforces and for the adoption of atypical forms of work to be based on genuine personal choice. All of this has profound effects for employee relations policies and, in particular, the role of trade unions in a restructured European labour market.

Trade Unions and Europe

The trade unions of Western Europe present a diverse pattern in terms of their membership, modes of organization and political ideologies. This has significant implications for the development of collective bargaining and the implementation of HR policies within organizations.

There are long-standing differences in trade union membership density levels between European nations. In general terms, the Scandinavian countries have traditionally had high levels. Countries such as the UK, the former West Germany, Belgium, Ireland and Italy have been in the middle range with densities of between 40 and 60 per cent. At the bottom of the range have come France, Portugal and Spain with membership varying between 15 and 30 per cent.

The restructuring of European industry has led to an overall decline in union membership since the high point of the 1970s. However, there is significant variation within the Community in the rate and direction of change although variability in the statistics make accurate international comparisons difficult (Walsh 1985). Nevertheless, as Visser (1988:127) records, 'in all but the three Scandinavian countries union membership declined during the first half of the 1980s. A real reversal occurred in France, Italy, the Netherlands and the United Kingdom.' Since then, membership has stabilized and some countries, including losers like Italy and the Netherlands, have regained members. For example, after a three-year decline, the Deutscher Gewerkschaftsbund (DGB) had a membership increase to bring the 1988 level to 7.8 million which is close to the 8 million peak of 1981. The reunification of Germany means that this figure can only continue to grow and make the German trade union movement the biggest in the EC.

Poole (1986:67) has suggested that 'divergences in trade union density amongst nations may be best explained by public policies which support collective bargaining and which, while partly a reflection of labour strategies, are also affected by managerial and state policies on trade union recognition'. While this approach appears to reduce trade unions themselves to being the passive recipients of members it has the merit of focusing attention on the sources of trade union power at both the political and workplace level.

A further factor affecting union membership and density is the level of organization. In a number of European countries, the 1970s were characterized by trade union strength in the workplace coupled with considerable influence over social democratic governments. A 'corporatist' industrial relations model emerged which saw the high point of union power (Taylor 1989). Corporatism itself was relatively short-lived although it has left a legacy of labour law and might be said to have passed its traditions to the EC. The fragile alliance of unions and political parties was undermined by continued economic problems and a deregulatory political backlash. Furthermore, few other European nations have a unified trade union movement along British lines. Alongside the social democratic or labourist federations the most commonly found have been communist-linked centres and Catholic organizations.

It might be argued that 'corporatism' has shifted to the European level for those trade union movements within the EC. The European Trade Union Confederation (ETUC) was founded in 1973 to bring together confederations across Europe and it has tried to transcend ideological and confessional divisions. This situation is now very fluid with the changes in Eastern Europe and the disruption of communist-influenced international centres. The ETUC itself has an important 'corporate' role in the development of EC policy and has been influential in such areas as the Social Charter. Alongside this development at confederation level, individual unions are developing closer links. The process is particularly interesting in Germany where unions from the former 'East' and 'West' are forming joint federations or signing co-operation agreements (*Labour Research* May 1990). On 1989 figures, the united German trade unions will have 17 million members and dominate the European movement. In the UK, John Edmonds, general secretary of the GMB, has suggested that his union 'would be linked to at least six European trade unions through cross-frontier amalgamations and agreements in the next few years' (*The Guardian*, 31.8.90).

The European trade unions face considerable challenges in the next decade and joint action across national frontiers will assume increasing importance. The legal framework established by the Community itself will have a significant effect but it will continue to focus on individual rights. The development of collective bargaining will remain at the centre of trade union activity.

Collective Bargaining

There is no simple model of European collective bargaining and wide variations in the structure of negotiating arrangements exist between countries. Collective agreements may be concluded at all levels from national to local. The UK has probably the widest variety in its bargaining arrangements whereas the former West Germany had a well-established and highly formalized system. Bargaining structures have come under increasing challenge as the economic and employment structure has altered and the political importance of corporatism has declined. Employers' organizations in particular have sought to decentralize bargaining. The most notable example was the abandonment of the commitment to centralized negotiations in Sweden during the 1980s. Other examples have occurred in France, Belgium and Italy. In addition, HRM strategies based on individualized contracts reduce the necessity for collective agreements.

However, these developments must be interpreted with great caution as traditional bargaining arrangements show great resilience and seemingly fundamental changes can be rapidly reversed. In France, for example, the growth of company bargaining in the 1980s had declined by the end of the decade. From 1988 onwards there has been a shift to sector-level negotiations and the establishment of 'orientation' agreements at national level (IRS Employment Trends 1990).

If decentralized bargaining patterns do become characteristic of EC states, then we might anticipate the development of European-wide 'framework' agreements as a counterbalance. The trade unions in particular will seek to achieve their objectives through their political influence on the European institutions, and there is some evidence to suggest that this is precisely what is happening.

Employee Relations and Community Policy 1958–1990

Although the EC was established as primarily an economic entity, the 'social dimension' has grown in importance in recent years. There have been three distinct phases of developments in terms of employee relations which correspond roughly to the following periods: 1958–72, 1973–84, and 1985–91. The key events were the setting up of the EC, the first enlargement, the impact of Thatcherism at the European level and the nomination of Jacques Delors as

President of the European Commission with the ensuing push towards the Single European Market.

1958–1972

The first phase of EC development concentrated on the creation of a customs union and common market, and issues relating directly to employee relations were generally neglected. There were, nevertheless, two significant exceptions. A common market presupposes the freedom of movement of labour, but in practical terms employees are less likely to move from one country to another in search of work if they lose their entitlement to social security benefits. As harmonization of the different social welfare systems was out of the question for technical, financial and political reasons, it was decided to move gradually towards the co-ordination of the different systems in line with article 51 of the Treaty of Rome, thus ensuring that migrant workers could aggregate their entitlement to benefits. The other issue was that of equal pay, whose significance we discuss in more detail below. However, it should be noted here that the establishment of the principle of equal pay had more to do with economic than social policy. As Quintin (1988:71) notes, France 'already had legislation establishing the principle of equal pay and it considered that it would be at a competitive disadvantage unless all member states adopted the same principle'.

1973–1984

The second period coincided with a more interventionist phase during which the provisions of EC law were used to improve and harmonize living and working conditions. The summit conferences held in the Hague and Paris (1969 and 1972) paved the way for the completion, further development and enlargement of the EC. In the wake of this the Council of Ministers agreed to a number of directives on workers' rights in relation to redundancies and equal opportunities. In addition, in the mid-1970s, the Council of Ministers agreed to an action programme for safety, hygiene and health and, as a result of this, a number of other directives were introduced.

The Council of Ministers was, however, unable to agree on a number of other issues particularly those relating to employee participation and information. The most famous was the so-called Fifth Directive on the structure of public limited companies which was initially proposed in 1972 and which, in certain circumstances, aimed to guarantee employee participation (OJ C131/72). Later on, there was the so-called Vredeling Directive. This would have required public limited companies with more than 100 employees (in the first version) to give the workforce information on matters such as the company's economic and financial situation, its employment outlook, production and investment plans, rationalization activities and the introduction of new working methods (OJ C240/83). Opposition to both sets of proposals was widespread both within and outwith the institutions of the EC, and so no decisions were reached. Unanimity was required within the Council of Ministers for a proposal to be adopted and this process only worked when consensus prevailed. In the UK the 1979 elections returned a government which was committed to liberalizing the economy and reducing the power of trade unions and which was not prepared to see this crusade nullified by restrictive industrial relations policies at the EC level. Consequently any further proposals such as the directives granting part-time and temporary employees the same rights as full-time workers (OJ 62/82 and OJ C128/82) and on parental leave for family reasons (OJ C333/83) were systematically blocked by a British veto in the Council of Ministers. This intransigent British opposition to EC social affairs effectively brought the second stage of Community development to an end.

1985–1991

Stage three coincided with the appointment of Jacques Delors, a former French Socialist Minister of Economic and Financial Affairs, as President of the European Commission in 1985. It is a period characterized by contradictory trends. On the one hand the Community has formally abandoned any pretension of being the 'overseer' of European employee relations. The adviser to Jacques Delors on social affairs has claimed that the Commission was moving from a strictly 'normative' approach which 'aims at applying a single harmonising framework to the Community as a whole' to a 'de-centralised' approach which 'rejects as counterproductive any kind of social legislation at the Community level' (Venturini 1989:62). On the other hand, the pressures of the Single Market and the Social Dimension are forcing further attempts at regulation. Overall, the Commission's approach has been based on four elements: the Single European Act, the Single European Market, the social dimension and the social dialogue, all of which have significant consequences for employee relations in Europe.

In an attempt to speed up decision-making in the Council of Ministers the Single European Act introduced qualified majority voting for certain measures 'which have as their object the establishment and functioning of the internal market' (Art. 100 a i) and which encourage improvements 'especially in the working environment, as regards the health and safety of workers' (Art. 118 a). However, unanimity is still required for provisions 'relating to the rights and interests of employed persons' (Art. 100 a ii). The situation is confused, and legal definitions of the 'working environment' are ultimately required from the Court of Justice.

Linked to the Single European Act were further proposals for the Single European Market. The Commission published a White Paper entitled *Completing the Internal Market* which was approved by the Council of Ministers in June 1985. It contained a total of approximately 300 proposals designed to remove physical barriers to trade between countries within the EC and to establish the Single European Market by the end of 1992. The consequences for industrial relations in Europe are still not completely clear, not least because some of the more contentious proposals are yet to be agreed. Nevertheless, evidence would suggest that competition will intensify and, in an attempt to respond, employers will aim to reduce labour costs either by putting a brake on wage increases and shedding labour in countries with high labour costs or, where appropriate, by engaging in 'social dumping', i.e. moving investment to countries with low labour costs. It is precisely because of these fears that the social dimension has assumed greater significance.

The Social Dimension

The Commission of the EC has attempted to add a social dimension to the Single European Market. It has proposed a directive on European company statutes which would require mandatory employee participation in the decision-making of transnational companies. Participation would be achieved by one of three means of representation: on the board of directors (the German model); on a separate enterprise committee (the French/Italian model); after a process of negotiation subject to minimum requirements (the Scandinavian model). The Vredeling Directive was revived in the form of a new proposal 'for informing and consulting the employees of undertakings with complex structures'. It stipulated that in EC companies with more than 1000 employees their representatives would be given information on the company's structure; its economic and financial situation; the probable development of the business, production and sales; the employment situation and probable trends in investment. In addition employers would have to consult employee representatives on decisions 'liable to have serious consequences for the interests of the employees of its subsidiaries in the Community'. These measures have been bitterly opposed by the British government in the Council of Ministers, and no decision has been forthcoming.

The European Commission has also published a Community Charter of the Fundamental Social Rights of Workers. It was to act as a partial counterweight to the Single European Market and was described in an introductory remark by Jacques Delors as 'a keystone of the social dimension in the construction of Europe'. It calls for minimum standards in major areas of labour law and was agreed by eleven heads of state and government at a European Council meeting held in Strasbourg in December 1989 (the UK was alone in voting against). It addresses such issues as working conditions; freedom of movement of labour; minimum pay; social welfare schemes; freedom to join a trade union, to engage in collective bargaining and to participate in strike action; vocational training; equal opportunities; information, consultation and participation; health and safety; child labour; pensioners; and the disabled. Although the Charter is not legally binding on member states, it is supported by a legislative action programme with 47 proposals; 17 of these are draft directives, 10 of which are in the field of health and safety. Some of the more sensitive issues such as wages are only the subject of opinions and are not, therefore, binding on member states. Indeed, it would seem that the Charter has been considerably reduced in scope through redrafting and the limitations of the Action Programmes. Furthermore, the principle of 'subsidiarity' which delegates decisions to the lowest possible Community level has meant that, for example, the positive right to strike, which may have posed difficulties for a British government, has been left to member states' own arrangements.

The final aspect of this fourfold approach, the social dialogue, is indeed less 'normative'. The Single European Act stated that 'the Commission shall endeavour to develop the dialogue between management and labour at European level which could, if the two sides consider it desirable, lead to relations based on agreements' (Art. 118 b). The Commission arranged a series of meetings which became known as the Val Duchesse discussions. They took place between the representatives of the employers in the private sector (UNICE) and the trade unions (ETUC) at the European level. The first set of discussions centred on the issue of macro-economic policy and the second on new technology. UNICE insisted that the discussions were not negotiations, and, according to the TUC, the results were 'disappointing' (1988:18). However, the fact that these discussions had taken place at all was somewhat surprising and heralded a slight improvement in relations between UNICE and the ETUC. After a hiatus, discussions started up again and CEEP, the public-sector employers' organization, signed a draft framework agreement with the ETUC.

A further development has been a pioneering form of social dialogue set up independently by the European Metalworkers' Federation (EMF) and a small number of transnational companies. Thompson Grand Public and the EMF signed a two-year agreement in 1986 and an indefinite one in 1988 establishing two distinct bodies – a liaison committee and a European branch committee. The former, composed of union representatives from France, the Federal Republic of Germany, Italy, Spain and now the UK, meets once every six months at the company's expense, and the representatives are to be informed of the economic, industrial and commercial activities of the company as well as of major structural and industrial changes prior to their implementation, and also of plans for technical change. The latter, composed of 26 employee representatives elected on a proportional basis, meets annually at the company's expense, and has the same information rights. Although not typical, this agreement forms a landmark in European industrial relations and has acted as a model for about a dozen other agreements. It is the first time that a company has recognized an international union secretariat as an official representative of its workforce. It also creates the first example of a fledgling European 'works council' and incorporates the spirit of the proposed Vredeling Directive. British companies were slow to emulate Thompson Grand Public's attempts to set up a European works council. However, one union Manufacturing, Science and Finance (MSF), claims that it 'has been able to set up company councils with 12 multinational employers, among them Nestlé, Continental Can, Pechiney and BSN. Pressure is also being applied on Ford, Unilever and Philips for similar deals' (*The Guardian* 31.8.90).

The United Kingdom in Europe

What impact have these European developments had on employee relations in the UK? There are three potential levels at which change can take place: organizational strategy, employment law and public policy.

It is clear that transnational investment policies are influenced by the development of the Single European Market particularly as non-EC companies seek to establish a Community base. It is no coincidence that Rowntree was taken over by the Swiss firm Nestlé and that the last major independent British computer firm ICL was taken over by a Japanese competitor, Fujitsu. However, evidence suggests that many UK firms have yet to develop coherent strategies for Europe. This is particularly so in the HRM field. One survey concluded that the companies covered had 'no immediate concern about having to adjust pay and conditions to make them comparable with those in Europe. Even in unionized firms, there was little or no concern about most of the issues of the Social Charter' (Wood and Peccei 1990:84). The competing pressures of uniformity and autonomy which have bedevilled the Commission's action pro- grammes are repeated at company level. European strategies will have to cope with national diversity and, as Thurley (1990:57) argues, 'this implies that decision making and organisational definitions within the European firm can never be clear-cut or unambiguous'. Human resource management policy developments in Europe range from the minimalist response to new legislation through to proactive initiatives. While most organizations will develop pragmatically it is interesting to note the action of at least one new company. Keiper Recaro, a West German car seat manufacturer setting up in the UK, has agreed to incorporate the European Social Charter into its own employment contract (*The Guardian* 22.5.90).

The second area that we identified as important was that of em- ployment law. Much of what has been passed at the EC level has had limited effect on British employee relations. There are nevertheless a few exceptions of which the most important has been in the field of equal opportunities. There is evidence to suggest that the British Labour government in the 1970s was keen to pre-empt the decisions

taken by the EC by introducing its own laws on employment protection and equal pay. Legislation parallel to European directives in
the areas of collective redundancies and employee rights on company
mergers were introduced and, under a Conservative government, the
1980 Directive on the financial protection of employees in the event
of their employer's insolvency, was implemented. However, the best
example of EC labour law impinging on British employee relations is
in the field of equal opportunities and more specifically equal pay.
The Equal Pay Act (1970) brought the notion of equal pay into
English law, but the 1975 Equal Pay Directive made legal, claims for
equal pay for work of equal value. This feature was missing from
British law at that time. A successful European Court of Justice case
changed this situation and opened the way of amendments to British
law. As a direct result of the Community decision, over 150 equal
value claims had been brought by mid-1990 with a 15 per cent
success rate at the industrial tribunal. It is also likely that a significant proportion of the one-third of claims that were withdrawn
were successfully settled (*Bargaining Report* June 1990).

Further changes in UK law followed the Community's Equal
Treatment Directive and the Sex Discrimination Act of 1986 brought
private households and companies with less than five employees
within the scope of the law. More significant were the changes made
by European Court decisions with regard to pensionable ages. In one
case, Miss Marshal won a claim against the Southampton and South
West Hampshire Health Authority that allowed her to remain at
work until the same retiring age as a man. In a second, it was a man
who was to claim victory when he established that he was entitled to
receive a company pension at the same age as a woman (*Barber* v.
Guardian Royal Exchange).

European developments have had interesting consequences for the
debate on public policy in the UK. The Conservative government's
approach to the Single European Market has been very straightforward: 'to gain the maximum benefit individual measures should
be designed and implemented within a clear framework which allows
markets as much freedom as possible and avoids unnecessary
bureaucratic intervention' (*Economic Progress Report* October 1988).
The Social Charter clearly falls within the ambit of 'bureaucratic
intervention' and, as well as refusing to sign, the Conservative
government have resisted the subsequent draft directives.

The Labour Party's approach to Europe has been in marked
contrast. As *The Guardian* (15.8.90) has suggested, it 'has endorsed

the Social Charter as part of its march to European style social democracy'. Indeed, Europe has provided a useful taking-off point for many of its employment policy proposals and has provided the solution to at least one potentially controversial issue. The Labour Party has abandoned its commitment to the closed shop and used the Social Charter's rights of union membership and non-membership as the basis for its decision. It has incorporated the principles of the draft directives giving part-time employees the same legal rights as full timers into its policy statements (Labour Party 1989). In addition it has now accepted a policy establishing a national minimum wage on the basis that it will bring the UK into line with the rest of the EC even though the Social Charter itself has been considerably weakened on this point. On equal opportunities it has used European standards as the basis for proposed measures on child care and parental leave. There is no doubt that Europe is playing an increasing role in shaping British party political approaches to industrial relations policy-making.

Summary and Conclusions

It is now quite simply impossible for employers, managers and trade unions to ignore the influence of European employee relations processes on their own HRM policies. Labour market changes are taking place at a European level; British labour law is influenced by European decisions; the major political parties have clear stances on European policies and there are tentative steps towards co-ordinating trade union action and even collective bargaining. It may be that a declining trade union movement will resurrect itself through a European strategy.

Trade unions have been under pressure throughout the Community from changes in the labour market; the decline of corporatism and the development of employee relations policies which, if not openly hostile, simply have no place for them. It is important to place these changes in context. Formal collective bargaining arrangements, employee participation systems such as works councils as well as legal rights still give trade unions a major role in European industrial relations frameworks. They are also responding to the changes that confront them and may find that they provide opportunities as well as threats. In general, prospects of labour shortages are likely to shift bargaining power back towards those unions that have maintained an organizational hold. Similarly, tightly integrated international production systems offer potentially greater bargaining power through the increased disruptiveness of industrial action. This would, however, require considerable improvement in trade union co-operation at a European level. On a less conflictual basis there is no reason why HRM policies cannot be adapted to union-organized environments and, in practice, that is precisely what will happen.

The EC itself is also providing its own pressures for change within the field of employee relations. After years of relative inactivity, the Commission moved into a phase where it attempted to deal with employee relations issues by resorting to a normative approach which favoured the introduction of EC-wide directives. The results were mixed. The Commission then appeared to change tack, moving towards a more decentralized approach. While it is true that it has been anxious to encourage 'social dialogue' between representatives of employers and employees at the European level, the emphasis remains firmly within a normative approach. Moreover, now that 'recalcitrant' member states can, in certain circumstances, be isolated within the Council of the EC (as a result of the move towards qualified majority voting), there is evidence to suggest that this normative approach will prevail. Employee relations in the UK will be increasingly affected by the decisions taken outside its borders. The Single European Market will exert pressures on many aspects of employee relations, not least, wages and jobs. More specifically, it would seem that the Commission will attempt to introduce more social measures that the British government will find increasingly hard to veto. There can be no doubt that the European dimension is increasingly influencing the state of employee relations in the various countries of Western Europe.

References

Bassett, P. 1986: *Strike Free*. London: Macmillan.

Brewster, C. and Teague, P. 1989: *European Community Social Policy*. Institute of Personnel Management.

European Commission 1989: *Employment in Europe*. European Community.

European Foundation for the Improvement of Living and Working Conditions 1988: *New Forms of Work*. European Community.

Eurostat 1989: *Employment and Unemployment*. European Community.

Hakim, C. 1990: Core and periphery in employers' workforce strategies: evidence from the 1987 ELUS survey. *Work Employment and Society*, 4(2), 157–88.

International Labour Office 1984: *World Labour Report*, Vol. 1. ILO.

IRS Employment Trends 1990: *Developments in European Collective Bargaining*, no. 460.

Kelly, J. 1990: British trade unionism 1979–1989: change, continuity and contradictions. *Work Employment and Society*, special issue, May.

Labour Party 1989: *The Social Charter: how Britain benefits*, Labour Party.

MacInnes, J. 1987: *Thatcherism at Work*. Open University Press.

Phillimore, A.J. 1989: Flexible specialisation. Work organisation and skills: approaching the 'second industrial divide'. *New Technology, Work and Employment*, 4(2), 79–91.

Pollert, A. 1988: The flexible firm: fixation or fact? *Work Employment and Society*, 2(3), 281–316.

Poole, M. 1986: *Industrial Relations: origins and patterns of national diversity*. Routledge.

Quintin, O. 1988: The policies of the European Communities with special reference to the labour market. In M. Buckley and M. Anderson (eds), *Women, Equality and Europe*, Macmillan, 71–7.

Rosenberg, S. 1989: From segmentation to flexibility. *Labour and Society*, 14(4), 363–407.

Starkey, K. and McKinlay, A. 1989: Beyond Fordism? Strategic choice in labour relations in Ford UK. *Industrial Relations Journal*, 20(2), 93–100.

Taylor, A.J. 1989: *Trade Unions and Politics*. Macmillan.

Teague, P. 1989: *The European Community: the Social Dimension*. Kogan Page.

Thurley, K. 1990: Towards a European approach to personnel management. *Personnel Management*, September, 54–7.

TUC 1988: *Maximising the Benefits, Minimising the Costs*. TUC.

Venturini, P. 1989: *The Social Dimension of the Internal Market*. European Community.

Visser, J. 1988: Trade unionism in Western Europe: present situation and prospects. *Labour and Society*, 13(2), 120–77.

Walsh, K. 1985: *Trade Union Membership*. European Community.

Wood, S. and Peccei, R. 1990: Preparing for 1992? Business-led versus strategic human resource management. *Human Resource Management Journal*, 1(1), 63–89.

5

Industrial Relations and Organizational Change: is Human Resource Management Strategic in Australia?

GREG J. BAMBER

Is strategic human resource management (HRM) being practised in Australian workplaces? What are the links between HRM strategies, organizational change and business strategies? In confronting such questions, it is helpful to distinguish between three levels of decision-making about industrial relations (IR) and HRM issues: first, a macro (national) level, second, a micro (workplace) level, and third, an intermediate level, the enterprise (cf. Kochan et al. 1987). This contribution reviews some macro patterns of IR and human resource (HR) policies in Australia. It then turns to a micro perspective, which focuses on the workplace level. Against this background, it discusses an enterprise-level analysis of business strategies and organizational change. It starts, however, with an introduction to the Australian context.

The Australian Context

Political power is more devolved in Australia than in such unitary countries as the UK, France and Japan. Like Germany and the USA, Australia is a federation of states, each having considerable independence. The independence extends to IR because the federal government's formal powers in this arena are constrained by Australia's Constitution. Nevertheless, most IR arrangements are more centralized in Australia than in the UK.[1] In recent years, the Australian Council of Trade Unions (ACTU) has been much more influential in the Australian polity and economy than the Trades Union Congress (TUC) has been in the UK.

By the 1980s the ACTU had a cadre of leaders who were, in general, younger and who had more formal education than those of the TUC. Since 1983 the federal government and a majority of the state governments have been in the hands of the Australian Labor Party (ALP). Its former prime minister, Mr Bob Hawke, had been the ACTU full-time president until 1980.

The close connection between the ACTU and the ALP allowed them to attempt to introduce a more consensual approach to national policy-making by forging the ALP–ACTU Accord on prices and incomes, the economy and wider social issues. Its advent marked a change of direction from the confrontational approaches of earlier governments. The Accord had some similarities with the post-1974 UK Social Contract between the Labour government and the TUC, but the Accord has lasted longer than the Social Contract and appears to have been more successful (Chapman and Gruen 1990).

Perhaps the Social Contract and the Accord are examples of negotiated-corporatist politics rather than of 'pure' corporatism characterized by Hitler's Germany or Mussolini's Italy (cf. Hearn 1987:436). The Accord did not formally embrace the employers, who have been less united and appear to have had less influence with the government than has the ACTU.

By contrast with the British traditions of voluntary collective bargaining, Australian employment relationships are regulated by legally binding arbitrated industrial awards. Many of these are, in effect, voluntary collective agreements, but are subsequently endorsed either by a state arbitration commission or the federal Australian Industrial Relations Commission (AIRC).

In many larger enterprises, there used to be a demarcation line between IR and personnel management. Few Australian enterprises still observe such a demarcation. By the 1990s, they generally treated IR as one aspect of the broader field of HRM. None the less, to a greater extent than in the UK, corporate chief executives still see IR issues as important. This perception may have been reinforced because Labor governments dominated Australian politics for most of the 1980s and IR reform has remained high on most public-policy agendas.

Despite such contrasts, in comparison with most other countries, Australian IR shows more similarities than differences with the UK.

Australia inherited a British legacy of unions with craft foundations and labourist ideologies. In both countries there is considerable *ad hocery* in management and fragmentation among the employers' organizations; there are traditions of adversarialism rather than social partnership. The national political spectrum is broadly similar in both countries, with government alternating between Labour and the Conservatives.[2]

In Australia (as in the UK), there are occasional and much publicized examples of confrontational unionism and employerism, including serious industrial disputes and legal action, much media coverage and threats of dismissals. However, 72 per cent of Australian workplaces (with at least five employees) have never experienced any industrial action (Callus et al. 1991:62).

At present most practitioners are using the term HRM in a broad sense, as a generic label which is beginning to subsume personnel management (and to some extent IR too). This accords with the approach of the *Human Resource Management Journal* (UK) and we adopt such a generic usage. The Australian experience can inform the international debates about HRM. Many of these debates are concerned with the interface between personnel management and IR, and between HRM and organizational change, as well as with notions of strategy (cf. Fombrun et al. 1984; Hendry and Pettigrew 1986), so the present discussion focuses on such issues.

Union Policies[3]

Some influential leaders of the Australian labour movement have recently been focusing particularly on the national or macro level of HR policy, even though they generally do not use the term HR. It is such a focus which links labour, HR and economic policies that Kochan and McKersie (1989) propose as a suitable strategy option for the (American) nation (p. 229). Nevertheless, in recent years there have been few signs of such macro-level HR strategies either in the USA or the UK.

Perhaps because it has been closer to the centre of the political stage than the TUC in recent years, the ACTU has developed more coherent economic strategies, notably the Accord. In brief, under the Accord, the industrial and political wings of the Australian labour movement aimed to ensure that living standards of employees and non-income-earning sectors of the population requiring protection would be maintained and, through time, increased with movements in national productivity. The government would introduce national health insurance and fairer taxation; pay special attention to the 'social wage' by increasing expenditure on social security, public services and education; change the elements of labour law most disliked by the unions; improve policies on occupational safety and health, HR planning, industrial and technological development, multiculturalism, regulation of prices, employee participation and industrial democracy.[4]

In exchange for such government action, apart from its national wage case claims, arbitrated by the AIRC approximately on an annual basis, the ACTU agreed to make no extra claims (except when there were special and extraordinary circumstances). This was a remarkable concession in view of the Australian adversarial traditions.

Concern about revitalizing Australia's economy, in 1986, prompted the ACTU to send a senior delegation on a mission to Europe. The mission's objectives included a consideration of 'the implications of technology, work organizations, education and productivity for international competitiveness' (Australia 1987:xi).

In spite of Australia's strong links with the UK, the mission's influential report, *Australia Reconstructed*, saw the UK as providing an inappropriate model, which Australia should avoid. It observed that the UK's policies 'had been pursued in a socially disruptive and inefficient way, and had resulted in disastrous levels of unemployment and high social and regional inequality'. In addition, the report was critical of Australia's 'passive' approach to labour market policy. It also expressed concern about Australia's corporate planning (e.g. the accent on short-term returns versus longer-term planning and investment) (pp. xii–xiii).

On the other hand, the mission was especially influenced by its observations of tripartite HR policies in Sweden and Austria 'where low inflation, reasonable growth and improved balance of payments have been accompanied by low unemployment, social cohesion and more balanced regional growth' (p. xii). The mission saw these two countries as models to emulate, particularly as, in general, they seemed to reinforce the Accord. The mission's recommended strategies included the development of a national economic and social objective, negotiated and supported on a tripartite basis. This 'should aim to achieve full employment, low inflation and rising living standards which are equitably distributed . . . an innovative, positive and consensual approach to the management of change and to the removal of all impediments to achieving these objectives . . . [and] the generation of productive investment' (p. xii).

It is worth giving two illustrations of the implementation of such union strategies. First, federal and state governments have legislated to promote equal employment opportunity, occupational health and safety and more flexible educational arrangements, for example, to establish a 'unified national system' of tertiary education, which included abolishing the distinction between universities and colleges of advanced education (polytechnics) and promoting credit transfer and articulation arrangements between institutions, embracing those in the technical, as well as the tertiary, sector. Moreover, in 1990, Hawke asserted that Australia should become 'the clever country'.

To this end the government launched its Training Guarantee Scheme which aimed to induce all except the smallest employers to spend at least 1.5 per cent of their payroll on structured training by 1992. Historically, Australia has devoted relatively little funding to skill formation. Neither its general workforce nor most of its managers appear well prepared for employment in comparison with its foreign competitors. Australia shares this distinction with the UK (Storey and Sisson 1990); both countries compare unfavourably with Japan or the other mission countries. But the Australian federal Labor government appears to be intervening in this aspect of the labour market rather more than the UK Conservative government.

The AIRC has been involved in a second front for implementing the union policies. In 1988, it endorsed a fundamental programme of workplace change to restructure Australia's numerous antiquated industrial awards. Such restructuring was long overdue, for some major awards had their origins in the early twentieth century. Many newer awards copied the concepts of the older ones. These had reflected nineteenth-century craft demarcations and fragmented forms of work organization, with outdated management and union structures.

Under this programme to enhance 'structural efficiency', employers and unions were obliged to engage in a form of productivity bargaining. To a greater extent than the general UK experiences of the 1960s and 1970s, however, there were explicit aims in Australia to move away from Taylorist forms of management and work organization. These aims included:

- establishing skill-related career paths which provide an incentive for workers to continue to participate in skill formation;

- eliminating impediments to multi-skilling and broadening the range of tasks which a worker may be required to perform;
- ensuring the working patterns and arrangements enhance flexibility and . . . efficiency;
- developing appropriate consultative procedures. (AIRC 1989; see also CAI 1990.)

Employer Policies

Although the ACTU leadership played a catalytic role in initiating the above policies, much of the burden of implementing them inevitably involves employers. How did the employers (and unions) attempt to implement such policies? Two contrasting ideal types of approach can be identified: a cost minimization approach (CMA) and a productivity enhancement approach (PEA). Enterprises that are most exposed to international competition are most likely to adopt a PEA, as they endeavour to compete with their rivals. Conversely, those that are most sheltered (e.g. by tariffs) are more likely to adopt a CMA. Those that compete in terms of quality and higher added value will tend to adopt a PEA while those that compete in terms of price will tend to adopt a CMA (Curtain and Mathews 1990).

Variants of either approach are likely to be adopted in particular enterprises depending on the knowledge, imagination, effort deployed and mutual trust and the political capacity shown by the key players. The policies mentioned above and the moves towards structural efficiency could precipitate a step away from adversarial IR, especially in cases that approximate to the PEA type. These moves have an integrative potential; besides institutional IR issues they also embrace the management of the labour process (work organization, job classifications and work procedures), and other aspects of HRM (selection, skill formation, career development, performance appraisal and productivity-linked pay systems).

Besides aiming to raise the level of consciousness about skills, careers, productivity and competitiveness in the workforce, the above policies have tended to lift the level of debate in Australia's business community. The Accord appeared to bring relative industrial peace and reductions in real wages, despite being accompanied by increases in managerial salaries (especially for senior executives). After the election of the Hawke government in 1983, its negotiated-corporatist approaches initially received a warm welcome from many opinion leaders and most managers, particularly those in larger enterprises.[5]

In 1983, the chief executives of about 80 of these began meeting regularly as the Business Council of Australia (BCA). They endeavoured to adopt a more proactive rather than a reactive stance on HR and other issues. The BCA established a Study Commission chaired by Professor Fred Hilmer.[6] The Commission was asked 'to identify means of achieving changes to the current industrial relations system that will improve the way people work together at places of employment. The overriding aims of such changes must be to increase the competitiveness and performance of Australian enterprises' (BCA 1989:x).

The Commission developed a series of policies designed to accelerate a shift from an IR to an employee relations (ER) mind-set and to replace national or industry-level negotiated corporatism with a devolved and deregulated (or, as Hilmer puts it, a 'self-regulated') approach at the enterprise level.[7]

This approach includes: promoting enterprise unionism (rather than occupationally based unionism); devolving ER responsibilities from staff specialists to line managers; flattening organization structures; opening up management–employee communications; encouraging training and skills development; installing performance appraisal, incentive pay schemes and improved grievance procedures (Hilmer 1989).

To What Extent Are the Union and Employer Policies Compatible?

Restructuring unions was a keystone of the policies developed by the ACTU and the BCA. Both concluded that the UK legacy of occupationally structured unions was no longer appropriate. In proposing a change towards about 20 large industry unions, the ACTU was inspired by the Scandinavian and Austro-German examples. In proposing enterprise unionism,[8] the BCA was inspired by the Japanese (and American) examples.

Some faltering progress has been made towards both objectives. Within a few years, the current plethora of unions will have been rationalized further. Most union mergers are determined as much by ideological considerations as by industrial logic. Nevertheless, at a micro level, there will be more progress towards a form of enterprise unionism, albeit within these larger union structures.

As in the UK, 'single-union deals' are being agreed at some new establishments. For instance, although the Federation of Industrial, Manufacturing and Engineering Employees is a large conglomerate union, it is, in effect, an enterprise union for the new ICI Australia plant in central Queensland, just as the Amalgamated Engineering Union is, in effect, an enterprise union for Nissan's plant in north-east England (but at ICI Australia there is a high union density, compared with a much lower density at Nissan).

By 1991, there was an attempt to find some common ground between the union and employer positions; there were some talks which could develop a future form of Accord from a bipartite into a tripartite arrangement that would embrace the government, ACTU and at least one employers' organization. Each party aimed to promote some devolution of job regulation or 'managed decentralism' as one of the most influential employers' organizations, the Metal Trades Industry Association (MTIA), put it (Evans 1989, after McDonald and Rimmer 1989), whereby there would continue to be centralized pay regulation, but increasing scope for workplace-level enterprise bargaining.

The 1990–2 version of the Accord specifically proposes a form of enterprise pay bargaining; this would involve minimum rates being set at an industry level, but with employers and unions able to negotiate additional payments depending on enterprise productivity improvements.[9] Arguably this could be an 'Australian model' of regulated flexibility, which can be seen as an alternative to the form of 'unregulated flexibility' developed at enterprise level in the UK and USA (Mathews 1989).

The ACTU generally seeks to promote workers' interests and adopts more of a macro orientation with a pluralist/collective perspective, while the BCA generally seeks to promote employers' interests and adopts more of a micro orientation with a unitary/individualistic perspective (cf. Fox 1966; Purcell 1987; Sutcliffe and Sappey 1990). Despite these different sets of general objectives, perspectives and values, the differing emphases on macro- and micro-level reforms are complementary and there are significant overlaps between the two policies. Both parties are seeking to move away from Australia's traditional reliance on external labour markets, towards a more highly skilled workforce, with better career paths, which would more often be developed in internal labour markets (cf. Curtain 1990). Both are aiming towards several other similar goals: greater productivity and international competitiveness through improved work organization and HRM, particularly at workplace level.[10] Both parties' policies are ahead of their constituents' views, rather than merely reflecting them. At a local level, many managers and stewards are not fully cognizant of such policies, let alone fully convinced about the appropriateness and methods of implementing them. Hence it is important to explore the impact of these policies at workplaces.

Strategic Human Resource Management at Workplaces?

As in the USA and UK, in Australia some writers seek to distinguish HRM from personnel management, on the grounds that HRM implies specifically a move away from seeing employees merely as a cost (to be cut), towards an 'investment orientation' and a more innovative and strategic view of the management of people (Boxall and Dowling 1990:158; Blunt 1990:48). When referring to such a specific implication, we add the prefix strategic HRM.

There is no general agreement on the characteristics of strategic HRM. However, there are some demanding claims about it which emphasize, among other things, its links with business strategies and organizational change (which we discuss later), and its use of such techniques as: the measurement of productivity, performance appraisal, training, performance-related pay, profit-sharing and share ownership schemes, and job redesign, with a management philosophy that espouses teamwork, consultation, communications and information-sharing.

To what extent are these techniques found in practice, as well as in the rhetoric? We can draw some inferences about the pervasiveness of such HRM techniques from the Australian Workplace Industrial Relations Survey (AWIRS).[11] For instance, half of its random sample of workplaces admitted that they did not measure labour productivity in a quantifiable way.[12] However, 'workplaces in mining and communication were more likely to measure labour productivity than other industries'. As many as 61 per cent of workplaces claimed to have performance appraisal schemes for their employees. This percentage was similar in all size categories and sectors, but was the highest (80 per cent) in the finance and property sector (Callus et al. 1991:266).

Why might managers take the trouble to appraise their employees? HRM textbooks indicate that the general purpose of these schemes is to facilitate the choice of appropriate training and to link pay with performance (e.g. Schuler et al. 1992). Only 52 per cent of the private-sector workplaces claimed to provide formal off-the-job training, in comparison with 71 per cent of the public-sector ones. There was a positive correlation between workplace size and training: proportionately more larger workplaces offer such training than smaller workplaces (Callus et al. 1991:303).

Only 32 per cent of workplaces claimed to provide performance-related pay to any of their non-managerial employees. Such a form of pay was more common in the private (44 per cent) than in the public sector (8 per cent). It is more common (42 per cent) in small work-places (5–19 employees) than in larger ones; such pay is provided in only 31 per cent of workplaces with over 500 employees. Two sectors were particularly prone to provide performance-related pay: retailing (61 per cent) and finance and property (52 per cent) (p. 243).

Only 8 per cent of private-sector workplaces had a profit-sharing scheme for non-managerial employees; 13 per cent had a share ownership scheme to which any employee could belong. None the less, these two types of scheme were more widespread in finance and property than in most other sectors (p. 244). Within the previous five years, only 44 per cent of workplaces had implemented any job redesign.

Managers in only a third of workplaces claimed that their employees were consulted about changes affecting them. Also, managers in only a third of workplaces claimed to have a philosophy of teamwork/consultation. A higher proportion (43 per cent) of larger workplaces (over 200 employees) claimed to have such a philosophy than medium-sized (20–99) workplaces (31 per cent). Furthermore, more workplaces in the public sector (47 per cent) than private sector (28 per cent) adopted this philosophy (p. 269).

As an indication of the quality of employee communications, workplace managers were asked: 'On which, if any, of these issues affecting this workplace does management regularly provide information to employees or their representatives?' As shown in table 5.1, on every issue listed, the majority of workplaces did not regularly provide information to employees. However, with the exception of 'marketing strategies', public-sector workplaces were more likely to provide such information than private-sector ones.

The rhetoric about HRM also suggests that personnel decisions are increasingly decentralized from head office to workplaces, and from staff to line managers. Nevertheless, such devolution of power

Table 5.1 Issues about which management regularly provide information to employees or their representatives, by sector

Issue	% of workplaces		
	Public (%)	Private (%)	All (%)
Future staffing plans	65	41	48
Marketing strategies	25	42	36
Investment/corporate plans	57	38	43
Financial position of workplace	54	38	43
None of the above	15	26	23

Population: Australian workplaces with at least 20 employees.
Figures are weighted and are based on responses from 2004 workplace managers.
Source: Callus et al. (1991:136)

is not exclusively associated with modern HRM. Late nineteenth-century foremen had a great deal of power to hire, fire and establish work rules (cf. Gospel 1983:98), to a much greater extent than most contemporary supervisors and line managers, whose autonomy was constrained after the First World War, not least by the growth of personnel and IR departments. (This illustrates that historical reflections can be valuable in putting contemporary debates into a broader context.)

Renewed decentralization to supervisors and line managers is relatively recent. As yet, such managers have much less autonomy than their nineteenth-century predecessors. We can infer from the AWIRS data that supervisors and line managers on average made only 14 per cent of the key personnel decisions. Responsibility for such decisions is shared between a variety of managers within and beyond the workplace (Callus et al. 1991:79–80). Public-sector workplace line managers had a particularly low level of autonomy. Otherwise, there were relatively few differences between the various sectors and sizes of workplaces (p. 257).

A full analysis of the AWIRS data on these issues has not yet been completed. But from a preliminary analysis enthusiastic advocates of HRM could argue that, at most, there is an uneven use of the techniques commonly associated with strategic HRM. Furthermore, there does not yet appear to be a consistent pattern to imply that enterprises in particular sectors or size categories are more likely to adopt strategic HRM. Evidently, there has been less training, consultation, devolution and so on than is sometimes implied by the rhetoric about modern HRM.

On the other hand, it can also be inferred from these data that there has been a great deal of workplace change in recent years; 86 per cent of workplaces had experienced at least one type of significant change in the previous two years (p. 186). Many different approaches to change have been adopted, depending on the degree to which they embrace initiatives such as those discussed earlier. Moreover, there has been much proselytizing about the ACTU and BCA policies. Their proponents each imply that their approach is the way in which to manage change in HR strategies, unions and employing organizations.

The AWIRS data throw a great deal of new light on the contours of employment relationships and change. None the less, when trying to explain the dynamics and processes of change, such extensive survey methods are generally less useful than more intensive methods. Therefore, it is important also to consider organizational change explicitly and to draw on some more intensive case study data.[13]

Business Policies, Organizational Change and Human Resource Management Strategies

An intermediate corporate level, the enterprise, is important not least because most opinion leaders in Australia are advocating that it is increasingly appropriate to adopt an enterprise focus (though there are significant differences between them on how to operationalize such a focus).

Recent forms of enterprise-level change have been analysed by researchers at the Australian Graduate School of Management. They consider two critical questions: first, how radically must an organization change (scale of change) to survive and seize the opportunities that will provide it with a critical competitive advantage? Second, what kind (style) of leadership is needed to manage the transition? (Dunphy and Stace 1990:65). Depending on the answers to these questions, the position of any case can be located on dimensions of scale and style.

Gradual increases in scale and participative styles have been prescribed by many organizational development (OD) practitioners, but not all implementation of change adopts this approach. Dunphy and Stace give the example of Murdoch's transformation strategy at Wapping in the 1980s. First, Murdoch thought that a radical scale of change was necessary. Second, he formed the view that it could not be negotiated; therefore, he adopted a coercive quasi-military style of change leadership to transform his London newspaper production. Although controversial, in his own view Murdoch's plan appeared to be successful in financial terms, at least initially (Dunphy and Stace 1990:66 after Harris 1987).

By contrast, there are many examples of successful outcomes following longer-term and more gradual OD-type interventions. In spite of such successes, many OD specialists can be criticized for prescribing universalist human relations-type remedies. These advocate careful environmental scanning and 'the building of an organizational consensus about the need for and direction of change through widespread workforce participation' (Dunphy and Stace 1990:67). For example, the authors of the 'excellence' genre such as Peters and Waterman (1982) prescribe appealing remedies, but they are rather general and ethnocentrically American.[14]

In the wake of such criticisms, following their research Dunphy and Stace devised a useful contingency model of organizational change. They conclude that, in practice, leaders of enterprises that maintain medium to high levels of corporate performance do not use universalist prescriptions, but do use a situationally based approach to change, which is designed to help the organization to maintain 'fit' with its changing environment. They rightly warn executives to choose an appropriately customized change strategy, rather than to rely on packaged change solutions that may be inappropriate to their organization.

To facilitate such a choice, figure 5.1 illustrates four types of change strategies. This model combines the above dimensions of scale and style. The management of change can thereby be categorized into four contrasting strategies.

Type 1 Participative evolution (incremental adjustment, achieved by collaborative means). During most of the 1980s, around the world, IBM changed mainly by incremental adjustment, though there were some exceptions and, in general, IBM has not welcomed union participation.

Type 2 Charismatic transformation (large-scale discontinuous change, achieved by collaborative means). Australia's largest financial institution, Westpac Bank, employed type 2 methods of managing change in the early 1980s.

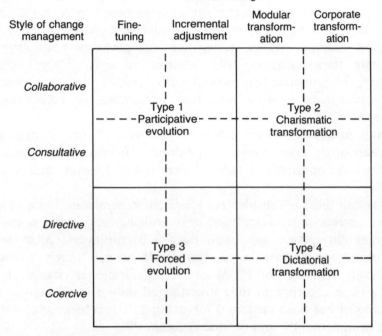

Figure 5.1 Dunphy and Stace's types of change stategies
(*Source*: Dunphy and Stace 1990:82)

Its then managing director led the changes, strongly, from the top, though the process was facilitated by a major OD intervention, designed by a prominent Canadian OD consultant. Kanter (1983) gives other examples mainly from the USA.

Type 3 Forced evolution (incremental adjustment, achieved by coercive means). Several Australian state-owned electricity generation and supply utilities typify type 3 change strategies. However, the major disputes at the South East Queensland Electricity Board in the mid-1980s imply that it was more typical of type 4 (see Bamber and Watson 1992).

Type 4 Dictatorial transformation (large-scale discontinuous change, achieved by coercive means). The Sydney Water Board cut its employees from 15,300 to 12,300 within two years. The organization structure was reduced from (in some cases) 14 levels between the line workers to the chief executive, to a maximum of 7 levels. The Board aimed at a fundamental culture change. After some success with type 4 change, the Board appears to have moved to type 3.[15]

The Sydney Water Board case illustrates that, even within one organization, change strategies may vary over time, or between

different sectors of the workforce or different parts of the organization. However, in a turbulent environment, these researchers
argue that fine tuning was not considered a viable strategy, so
the most common change strategy of high performers was type 4,
corporate transformation, with a directive style (52 per cent).
Further, 'They assume that transformative change must occur quickly
and hence there is little time for consultation or collaboration'
(Dawson:1990).

Many American writers generally prescribe change strategies in
the charismatic transformation quadrant. However, this quadrant
describes the approach of only 12 per cent of Dunphy and Stace's
sample.

Although there is considerable scope for generalizing Dunphy and
Stace's enterprise-level analysis, it is probably applicable primarily
to larger enterprises, say, with over 200 employees. Most other
enterprises see themselves as too small to pay much attention
specifically to issues of HRM or of organizational change. Even
among large enterprises, they investigated only a small sample and
their model has been criticized for using an unproblematical notion
of 'environmental fit' and of 'management'.[16]

Nevertheless, most organizational change consultants would have
much to learn from the model, for too many of them have preferred
general strategies that are irrespective of the context. As Dunphy
and Stace point out, OD consultants tend to prefer type 1, but
increasingly some adopt type 2. Type 3 tends to be preferred by
consulting firms who make change primarily by devising and implementing management techniques and control systems. Lastly, the
big corporate strategy consultants usually prescribe type 4 strategies.
If they wished, each category of change agent could broaden their
repertoire in order to use the strategy most appropriate to the
situation. Dunphy and Stace conclude that 'A critical issue is the
balance of coercive/directive and consultative practices needed to
overcome resistance and to win commitment of all levels' (1990:92).

It is arguable that, as levels of education and skill increase, more
employees will expect a participative approach to change management, so that they may be more receptive to change in organizations
that encourage employee involvement. Hence similar research in
the 1990s may find a higher percentage of high performers adopting
a more consultative style, despite the continuation of a turbulent
economic environment.

On the other hand, with the almost inevitable swing of the

national political pendulum, there may be a change from Labor to a conservative federal government. Such a government is less likely to encourage notions of industrial democracy and employee participation. Thus, change in the external economic and political context could encourage a different choice of management style. At the time of writing, it appears likely that a future conservative government would dismantle much of the current negotiated-corporatist apparatus and aim to deregulate the labour market, which could have many implications, including the end of the Accord and of the training guarantee and structural efficiency schemes, and possibly a return to more confrontational approaches, at least in the short term.

Current Developments and Future Patterns

How is HRM developing? Dunphy and Stace found three trends in all of the medium- to high-performing organizations in their sample: first, a decentralization of the HRM function to business units, away from centralist HRM departments. Second, there was a trend for organizations to move to a more strategic orientation in the way that HRM policy is instigated, considered and linked into the corporate planning process; they found the most senior HRM executives reporting directly to the chief executive, and an increasing importance of HRM issues in formulating business plans. Third, these enterprises had developed comprehensive performance management systems as an integrated form of management-by-objectives approach to goal setting, appraisal, development and reward structures.

In the early 1980s none of these trends would have been widely observed, as most personnel departments were centralized, personnel policies were precedent-based, rather than strategically focused, and performance management was either absent or control-based (i.e. an appraisal rather than an appraisal–training–reward orientation). Such trends may reflect changing environmental circumstances. However, another inference from these trends is that there may be fashions in HRM as in other fields of management (and in the designs of consumer goods).

Apart from the above-mentioned common trends, Dunphy and Stace also found four distinct types of HRM strategies, as illustrated in table 5.2.

First, the 'structural' HRM strategy type 'was characteristic of the

Table 5.2 Dunphy and Stace's contrasting types of HRM strategy

STRUCTURAL HR STRATEGIES[a]	TURNAROUND HR STRATEGIES
HR strategy is strongly focused on the business unit	HR strategy is driven for a short period by the executive leadership, characterized by challenging, restructuring or abolishing HR systems, structures and methodologies
Features:	
• Strong bottom line orientation	
• Emphasis on workforce planning, job redesign and work practice reviews	**Features:**
• Focus on tangible reward structures	• Major structural changes affecting the total organization and career structure
• Internal or external recruitment	• Downsizing, retrenchments
• Functional skills training and formalized multiskilling	• Lateral recruitment of key executives from outside
• Formalized IR/ER procedures	• Executive team building
• Strong business unit culture	• Breaking with the old culture

DEVELOPMENTAL HR STRATEGIES[a]	PATERNALISTIC HR PRACTICES
HR strategy is jointly actioned by the corporate HR unit and business units	HR practice is centrally administered
Features:	**Features:**
• Emphasis on developing the individual, and the team	• Centralist personnel orientation
• Internal recruitment, where possible	• Emphasis on procedures, precedent and uniformity
• Extensive developmental programmes	• Organization and methods studies
• Use of intrinsic rewards	• Inflexible internal appointments policy
• Corporate organizational development given high priority	• Emphasis on operational and supervisory training
• Strong emphasis on corporate culture	• Industrial awards and agreements set the HR framework

[a] Both of the above give high priority to performance management systems
Source: Dunphy and Stace (1990:126)

majority of enterprises' in their sample. The HRM orientation of these enterprises appeared 'to cluster around business unit, work team and job redesign; functional skills training; lateral recruitment as a norm' rather than the exception, and more emphasis on HRM systems driven by line managers rather than by corporate staff. The approach appeared 'more oriented to structural solutions, role definition and technical skill development and less concerned to create the involvement of employees in planning personal, professional or corporate-level organizational change. In all cases, this type of HR strategy was associated with a directive management style at the corporate level'.

Second, the 'developmental' HRM strategy appeared compatible with the arguments in much of the current HRM literature; it was characteristic of a few medium- to high-performing enterprises in the sample. These placed strong emphasis on workforce and organizational change 'in areas like personal development, management development, career management and culture management (internal marketing, culture surveys, employee communication strategies). In each case this type of HR strategy was associated with a consultative style of corporate change leadership.'

The structural and developmental strategies 'were not completely discrete categories: organizations with a dominantly structural' HRM orientation would often include some developmental HR policy in their HRM strategies. 'Similarly, enterprises with a dominantly developmental HRM orientation would often include some structural HR practices' in their HRM strategies. The implication is that even when pursuing a structural strategy, some culture building and management development will be necessary. Similarly a developmental HRM strategy should not avoid the difficulty of workforce and job restructuring.

Third, the 'turnaround' HRM strategy type was characteristic of some of the enterprises 'in the period three years before the study', a time when they were undergoing a period of organizational change. These enterprises had substantially contracted, redefined or abolished their central personnel departments; 'were in the process of radically reviewing' their HRM systems and policies; were implementing voluntary or forced redundancies and 'had opened their recruitment' to the external labour market at key executive and other levels.

The fourth HRM type, 'paternalistic', was associated with the lower-performing enterprises making change by fine tuning. A paternalistic HRM strategy exemplifies the 'traditional mechanistic'

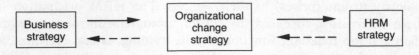

Figure 5.2 Dunphy and Stace's model of relations between business strategy and HRM strategy
(*Source*: Dunphy and Stace 1990:133)

personnel management policies of the 1960s–1970s. It is strongly influenced by Tayloristic scientific management, standard IR practices, and a wish to maintain the status quo. This paternalistic type featured a centralist approach to HRM, an emphasis on procedures, 'heavy reliance' on work study 'as a form of personnel/control, and formalistic employer–employee . . . relationships' (Dunphy and Stace 1990:127–9).

What determines the type of HRM strategy adopted? Dunphy and Stace conclude that, potentially, the type of HRM strategies adopted can be related to the broader business strategy. But, the type of organizational change is the important intervening variable which modifies the relationship. They found that an enterprise's organizational change strategy tends to drive its HRM strategy rather than vice versa, as illustrated in figure 5.2.

The inferences from this analysis reinforce the idea of contingency, that decision-makers should choose the HRM strategy which is most compatible with an enterprise's business circumstances and organizational change strategies. A loose collection of non-customized HRM interventions and gimmicks will not suffice if an enterprise is to develop the internal synergies likely to be necessary for high performance.

The models summarized above help our understanding of the complementary nature of IR issues, organizational change and HRM policies. Corporate and change strategies are generally initiated by senior executives, but HRM policies may be formulated by personnel departments, then implemented by supervisors and line managers. As Dunphy and Stace argue, it is important for us to formulate a more integrated understanding of how various management choices relate to each other. This is particularly in relation to organizational change and HRM strategies, which are introduced into some enterprises in ways that are mutually contradictory.

Dunphy and Stace's enterprise-level models are not yet strongly grounded in theory. Nevertheless, they are helpful conceptual tools to sharpen the debates about types of organizational change, styles of leadership and varieties of HRM policies. Such novel approaches are stimulating a growing appreciation of the potential strategic contribution that can be made by HRM at an enterprise level. More analytical approaches would be welcome. Practitioners as well as academics could help to develop such contributions. Besides providing a basis for theory building, models like these can facilitate improved management practices.

Summary and Conclusions

We discussed macro- and micro-level policies and their implementation (or lack of it) by employers, governments and unions. At a macro (national) level, unions and employers are devising alternatives to the crude, militant approaches which have attracted much media attention and have been divisive in the employment and political arenas. The approaches by ACTU and BCA in the late 1980s and early 1990s are more subtle and each aims to achieve some consensus, albeit on its own terms. The contrasts between confrontational and consensual approaches have some similarities with the distinctions, for example, between distributive and integrative bargaining (Walton and McKersie 1965), low-trust and high-trust relations (Fox 1974), and between automating and informating approaches to managing innovation (Zuboff 1988).

There are signs of strategic thinking about HR issues at the macro level, for instance, by the federal government, ACTU and BCA. There appear to be more signs of such strategic thinking in Australia than in the UK or USA. It remains to be seen, however, to what extent such national-level thinking in Australia is translated into consistent local-level practice.

In comparison with most other Western market economies, Australia has a high degree of foreign ownership of its large enterprises; 52 per cent of private-sector workplaces with 500+ employees are partly or wholly foreign owned (Callus et al. 1991:27). Many of the most important strategic decisions that induce organizational change in such enterprises are taken at corporate headquarters overseas. If based in Australia, it is difficult, even for champions of strategic HRM, to exert much influence on corporate strategies that are formulated overseas.

Nevertheless, certain enthusiasts claim that, in general, employers in Australia are implementing strategic HRM. But we should be sceptical about many of these claims, especially those that seem to regard a particular form of HRM as a universalistic management prescription. At a micro (workplace) level, we can infer from the AWIRS data cited earlier that short-term, inconsistent and *ad hoc* forms of personnel and IR management have by no means yet been displaced by long-term, consistent and strategic HRM. At the first signs of a change in business circumstances, the instinctive reaction in many enterprises still seems to be the declaration of redundancies, especially among their personnel and IR specialists and programmes, not least those in education and training. Such short-term responses are the antithesis of strategic HRM, with its notion of investing in people, over the longer term.

In Australia, as in the UK, many of the claims about strategic HRM are exaggerated and rhetorical, rather than being realistic and generally implemented, apart from in a few leading-edge enterprises (cf. Guest 1987; Legge 1989). Short-term responses, including such cuts, can be observed even in enterprises that in other respects may appear to be at the leading edge.

However, perhaps those 'newer-style' HRM managers who align their approaches with the appropriate business and organizational change strategies may illustrate their greater usefulness to corporate power-holders than the 'older-style' personnel and IR managers, who were usually more detached from the power-holders. Therefore, possibly the HRM-oriented people will be more likely to escape the worst cuts, especially if they can demonstrate the lasting value of their contributions to the enterprise.

Some of these more enlightened HRM specialists who survive, are playing a vital role as catalysts for and implementors of change. They are helping to restructure management, IR and work organization by rethinking and improving their policies and practices. To this end, they are also trying to learn, selectively, from the approaches promoted by some of the policy-makers with a longer-term orientation, from the labour movement, the employers and others. If broadly defined and based on a realistic contingency approach, even if not necessarily strategic, modern HRM practices, then, have considerable potential to provide constructive and much-needed links between the formerly separate territories of business policy, personnel and IR, and also between the three levels of analysis: national, workplace and the enterprise.

Acknowledgements

Dexter Dunphy and Doug Stace commented on an earlier draft and kindly permitted the reproduction of figures 5.1 and 5.2 and table 5.2. The editor and several other colleagues including Chris Baker, Richard Curtain, June Hearn, Dick Sappey, Keith Sisson and George Strauss also made helpful comments on an earlier draft, which were much appreciated. As usual, Jan Nixon provided invaluable research assistance.

Notes

1 For more background on Australian IR and HRM arrangements, see Lansbury and Davis (1987); Palmer (1988); Isaac (1989); Dabscheck (1989); Howard (1990); Deery and Plowman (1991); Schuler et al. (1992); Bamber and Davis (1992).

2 In Australia, when the conservatives form the federal government, it is usually as a coalition between the Liberal and National parties.

3 We discuss union, before employer, strategies because in the 1980s the Australian labour movement leaders seemed more likely to be the initiators of new strategies than most of their employer counterparts.

4 The Accord and related ACTU policies include many more elements about a wide range of important issues, for instance, macro-economic and trade policies (see ALP–ACTU 1983; Davis 1983), but it is not appropriate to explore this whole range here.

5 Many of the recommendations in *Australia Reconstructed* were also accepted by the government, and some by certain employers' organizations, albeit less enthusiastically. But other employer interests strongly criticized *Australia Reconstructed* (e.g. see Nurick 1987).

6 He was a prominent management consultant who became Dean of the Australian Graduate School of Management.

7 While the BCA Study Commission was deliberating at national level, the NSW state government commissioned Niland (1989, 1990) to prepare two green papers on IR reform at the state level. He also proposes, among other things, the adoption of an enterprise focus, which, like the BCA's proposal, has aroused much controversy (e.g. see Dabscheck 1990; Rimmer 1990).

8 The BCA notion of enterprise unionism approximates in US terms to industrial unionism whereby one union has exclusive coverage over all workers at an establishment.

9 In effect following its October national wage case decision the AIRC

(1991) endorsed the 1990–1 version of the Accord (Mark VI), even though the AIRC had rejected the Accord Mark VI in its May 1991 decision.

10 However, some employers are also seeking to segment their workforce into core and peripheral components (Bamber 1990).

11 This survey was completed shortly before implementation of the above-mentioned training guarantee and award restructuring schemes, so, unfortunately, we cannot evaluate the effects of those two initiatives from the AWIRS data. Most of the data cited here are from Callus et al. (1991), but I am currently conducting further analysis of the AWIRS data, together with Paul Boreham, Richard Hall, Bill Harley and Julie McMillan. The AWIRS project was inspired by the UK series of Workplace Industrial Relations Surveys.

12 In spite of these data, it is inferred that many more workplaces did not really measure productivity systematically. When responding to such questions, there is probably a tendency for respondents to try to offer socially desirable answers. To some extent these may reflect the current rhetoric about HRM, which appears to have been widely accepted with remarkable rapidity. Hence, if anything, this and the following paragraphs are likely to overstate the pervasiveness of HRM techniques in practice.

13 Apart from the differing objectives and methods between the extensive survey and intensive case studies on which this next section draws, it is worth noting that the AWIRS 1989–90 survey adopted a broad view of IR and also covered HRM more generally. It was of randomly selected stratified samples of 2353 workplaces with over four employees from throughout the Australian economy, except for agriculture and defence. Most of the present comments draw from the sample of 2004 workplaces with at least 20 employees. The following analysis by Dunphy and Stace was primarily based on 13 prominent employing organizations in 1988–9 and each organization was also researched retrospectively in an earlier period to give a total sample of 26 cases, which were all in service-sector industries that have been, or are being, confronted by deregulation. These organizations have their head offices in one of three Australian states. Their analysis also drew on their consulting experience. Therefore, AWIRS data provide a map of the contemporary terrain, while Dunphy and Stace identify and explain some prototypical trends.

14 However, for an exmaple of the 'excellence' literature tailored to the Australian context, see Limerick et al. (1984); also see Bamber and Lansbury (1989:23ff.).

15 Except where another source is cited, more details of the cases mentioned as exemplifying these four types are given in Dunphy and Stace (1990), which this whole section is based on.

16 See Dunford (1990). As Hendry and Pettigrew (1990:24) point out, perhaps coherence and appropriateness are less rigid terms than fit.

References

AIRC 1989: *National Wage Case Decision.* Melbourne: Australian Industrial Relations Commission (Print H9100).

AIRC 1991: *National Wage Case Decision (October 1991).* Melbourne: Australian Industrial Relations Commission (Print K0300).

ALP–ACTU 1983: *Statement of Accord by the Australian Labor Party and the Australian Council of Trade Unions Regarding Economic Policy.* Melbourne: Australian Labor Party – Australian Council of Trade Unions.

Australia, Commonwealth of 1987: *Australia Reconstructed: ACTU/TDC Mission to Western Europe – A Report by the Mission Members to the Australian Council of Trade Unions and the Trade Development Council.* Canberra: Australian Government Publishing Service.

Bamber, G.J. 1990: Flexible work organisation: inferences from Britain and Australia. *Asia-Pacific Human Resources Management*, 28(3), 28–44.

Bamber, G.J. and Davis, E.M. 1992: Employment relations in Australia. In R.C.D. Nacamulli, M. Rothman and D.R. Briscoe (eds), *Industrial Relations Around the World: labour relations for multinational companies*, Berlin: de Gruyter, forthcoming.

Bamber, G.J. and Lansbury, R.D. (eds) 1989: *New Technology: international perspectives on human resources and industrial relations.* London: Unwin Hyman.

Bamber, G.J. and Watson, K. 1992: *The Prevention and Settlement of Industrial Disputes in Australian 'Essential Services.'* Working paper. Brisbane: Key Centre in Strategic Management, Queensland University of Technology.

BCA 1989: *Enterprise-based Bargaining Units – A Better Way of Working: Report to the Business Council of Australia by the Industrial Relations Study Commission, 1.* Melbourne: Business Council of Australia.

Boxall, P. and Dowling, P.J. 1990: Human resource management: employee relations and the industrial relations tradition in Australia and New Zealand. In G. Griffin (ed.), *Current Research in Industrial Relations: Proceedings of the 5th AIRAANZ Conference*, Sydney: Association of Industrial Relations Academics of Australia and New Zealand, 152–68.

Blunt, P. 1990: Recent developments in human resource management: the good, the bad and the ugly. *International Journal of Human Resource Management*, 1(1), 45–60.

CAI 1990: *Award Restructuring: guidelines for employers.* Melbourne: Confederation of Australian Industry.

Callus, R., Morehead, A., Cully, M. and Buchanan, J. 1991: *Industrial Relations at Work: the Australian Workplace Industrial Relations Survey.* Canberra: Australian Government Publishing Service.

Chapman, B.J. and Gruen, F.H. 1990: *An Analysis of the Australian Consensual Incomes Policy: the Prices and Incomes Accord.* Canberra: Australian National University, Centre for Economic Policy Research, Paper 221.

Curtain, R. 1990: Internal versus external labour markets: choosing an appropriate enterprise skill formation strategy. *Business Council Bulletin*, November, 10–19.

Curtain, R. and Mathews, J. 1990: Two models of award restructuring in Australia. *Labour and Industry*, 3(1), 58–75.

Dabscheck, B. 1989: *Australian Industrial Relations in the 1980s.* Melbourne: Oxford University Press.

Dabscheck, B. 1990: Industrial relations and the irresistible magic wand: the BCA's plan to Americanise Australian industrial relations. In M. Easson and J. Shaw (eds), *Transforming Industrial Relations*, Sydney: Pluto/Lloyd Ross Forum, 117–30.

Davis, E.M. 1983: The 1983 ACTU Congress: consensus rules OK! *Journal of Industrial Relations*, 25(4), 507–16.

Dawson, P. 1990: Review of Dunphy and Stace (1990). *ANZAME News.* 1990.

Deery, S.J. and Plowman, D. 1991: *Australian Industrial Relations*, 3rd edn. Sydney: McGraw-Hill.

Dunford, R. 1990: A reply to Dunphy and Stace. *Organizational Studies*, 11(1), 131–4. (On the following pages, there is a rejoinder by Dunphy and Stace.)

Dunphy, D. and Stace, D. 1990: *Under New Management: Australian organizations in transition.* Sydney: McGraw-Hill.

Evans, A.C. 1989: *Managed Decentralism in Australia's Industrial Relations.* 11th Sir Richard Kirby Lecture, University of Wollongong. Sydney: Metal Trades Industry Association.

Fombrun, C.J., Tichy, N.M. and Devanna, M.A. 1984: *Strategic Human Resource Management.* New York: Wiley.

Fox, A. 1966: *Industrial Sociology and Industrial Relations.* Research Paper 3, Royal Commission on Trade Unions and Employers' Associations. London: HMSO.

Fox, A. 1974: *Beyond Contract: work, power and trust relations.* London: Faber and Faber.

Gospel, H. 1983: The development of management organisation in industrial relations: a historical perspective. In K. Thurley and S. Wood (eds), *Industrial Relations and Management Strategy*, Cambridge: Cambridge University Press, 91–110.

Guest, D.E. 1987: Human resource management and industrial relations.

Journal of Management Studies, 24(5), 503–21.

Harris, R. 1987: Rupert Murdoch: media tycoon, strikebreaker and citizen of the world. *The Listener*, 27 January, 7.

Hearn, J.M. 1987: Corporatism Australian style: the Prices and Incomes Accord. In G.W. Ford, J.M. Hearn and R.D. Lansbury (eds), *Australian Labour Relations: readings*, Melbourne: Macmillan, 424–37.

Hendry, C. and Pettigrew, A.M. 1986: The practice of strategic human resource management. *Personnel Review*, 15(5), 3–8.

Hendry, C. and Pettigrew, A.M. 1990: Human resource management: an agenda for the 1990s. *International Journal of Human Resource Management*, 1(1), 17–44.

Hilmer, F. 1989: *New Games, New Rules: work in competitive enterprises.* Sydney: Angus and Robertson.

Howard, W. 1990: Industrial relations and human resource management: different or differentiated products? In G. Griffin (ed.), *Current Research in Industrial Relations: proceedings of the 5th AIRAANZ Conference*, Sydney: Association of Industrial Relations Academics of Australia and New Zealand, 192–200.

Isaac, J.E. 1989: The arbitration commission: prime mover or facilitator. *Journal of Industrial Relations*, 31(3), 407–27.

Kanter, R.M. 1983: *The Change Masters: innovation and entrepreneurship in the American corporation.* London: Allen & Unwin.

Kochan, T.A., Katz, H.C. and McKersie, R.B. 1987: *The Transformation of American Industrial Relations.* New York: Basic Books.

Kochan, T.A. and McKersie, R.B. 1989: Future directions for American labor and human resources policy. *Relations Industrielles*, 44(1), 224–44.

Lansbury, R.D. and Davis, E.M. 1987: Australia. In G.J. Bamber and R.D. Lansbury (eds), *International and Comparative Industrial Relations*, Sydney: Allen & Unwin, 97–115.

Legge, K. 1989: Human resource management: a critical analysis. In J. Storey (ed.), *New Perspectives on Human Resource Management*, London: Routledge, 19–40.

Limerick, D., Cunnington, B. and Trevor-Roberts, B. 1984: *Frontiers of Excellence.* Brisbane: Australian Institute of Management, Queensland.

McDonald, T. and Rimmer, M. 1989: Award restructuring and wages policy. *Growth*, 37, 111–34.

Mathews, J. 1989: *Towards an 'Australian Model' of Wages-Linked Regulated Structural Adjustment.* Stockholm: Swedish Centre for Working Life.

Niland, J. 1989: *Transforming Industrial Relations in New South Wales*, Vol. 1. Sydney: NSW Department of Industrial Relations and Employment.

Niland, J. 1990: *Transforming Industrial Relations in New South Wales*, Vol. 2. Sydney: NSW Department of Industrial Relations and Employment.

Nurick, J. 1987: *Australia Reconstructed*: a review. *Economic Witness*, 19 August, 1–7.

Palmer, G. (ed.), 1988: *Australian Personnel Management: a reader.* Melbourne: Macmillan.

Peters, T.J. and Waterman, R.H. 1982: *In Search of Excellence: lessons from America's best-run companies.* New York: Harper & Row.

Purcell, J. 1987: Mapping management styles in employee relations. *Journal of Management Studies*, 24, 533–48.

Rimmer, M. 1990: The Niland Green Paper: a critical review. In M. Easson and J. Shaw (eds), *Transforming Industrial Relations*, Sydney: Pluto/Lloyd Ross Forum, 6–17.

Schuler, R.S., Dowling, P.J., Smart, J.P. and Huber, V.L. 1992: *Human Resource Management in Australia*, 2nd edn. Sydney: Harper Collins.

Storey, J. and Sisson, K. 1990: Limits to transformation: human resource management in the British context. *Industrial Relations Journal*, 21, 60–5.

Sutcliffe, P. and Sappey, R. 1990: Human resource management and industrial relations: towards a framework for analysis. In G. Griffin (ed.), *Current Research in Industrial Relations: proceedings of the 5th AIRAANZ Conference*, Sydney: Association of Industrial Relations Academics of Australia and New Zealand, 201–21.

Walton, R. and McKersie, R. 1965: *A Behavioral Theory of Labor Negotiations*. New York: McGraw-Hill.

Zuboff, S. 1988: *In the Age of the Smart Machine: the future of work and power*. New York: Basic Books.

6

Trade Unions and Human Resource Management

P. B. BEAUMONT

Introduction

The existing HRM literature has been very much dominated by organizational practice and academic work in the USA. This literature suggests that the leading individual components or elements of a relatively sophisticated, cohesive and integrated HRM package are:

1 relatively well-developed internal labour market arrangements (in matters of promotion, training and individual career development);
2 flexible work organization systems;
3 contingent compensation practices and/or skills or knowledge-based pay structures;
4 relatively high levels of individual employee and work group participation in task-related decisions;
5 extensive internal communications arrangements.

More generally, the key messages in the US HRM literature are a strategic focus, the need for HRM policies and practices to be consistent with the nature of overall business strategy, the need for individual components of an HRM package mutually to reinforce each other, and be consistent with corporate culture; teamwork, flexibility, individual employee involvement and commitment are the leading watchwords of this approach.

Perhaps not surprisingly, a body of literature with such a message has attracted an above average number of sceptics, not to say critics. For example, in the USA a number of the older, institutionally orientated labour relations academics have argued that HRM is nothing terribly new and that it is anti-union and anti-collective bargaining. Such sentiments are ones which appear to have found a relatively receptive audience among a number of industrial relations academics in the UK.

This chapter seeks to depart from the growing practice of drawing together the various criticisms of HRM made by academic commentators. Instead it proposes to let the unions speak for themselves by looking at a number of the observations and comments they have made about the concept or notion of HRM. Such a task is not, however, a particularly straightforward one, for basically two reasons. Firstly, we find that the unions (in various countries) have been more inclined to discuss individual elements of an HRM package (e.g. quality circles) rather than to discuss the concept, package or approach as a whole. And secondly, we need to be alert to the possibility of some divergence between what unions are saying and what they are actually doing in practice. For example, one may find instances of individual unions condemning, as statements of national level policy, membership involvement in quality circles, but it would be a brave, not to say rather foolish, commentator who would therefore conclude that no members of the unions concerned will actually be involved in quality circles in individual workplaces.

Nevertheless in this chapter we seek to provide a number of different union perspectives on HRM. The individual perspectives we consider are basically those (1) between different countries or national systems, and (2) between different unions in a single system or country; in the case of the USA there will also be some reference to different views within a single union. As well as identifying or highlighting differences along these lines we also attempt to offer some explanation for the occurrence of such differences. For obvious reasons we are particularly interested in the views of unions in the UK, although this review contains considerable discussion of the union position(s) in North America. The latter seems an appropriate starting-point because, as noted earlier, HRM is very much a concept or practice which originated in the USA. Accordingly in what follows we examine, in turn, the union positions in the USA and Canada, differences between individual unions in the USA and differences within a single union in the USA. This is then followed by an examination of the position within the UK.

A Canadian–US Comparison of Union Views

In general, the available evidence (albeit far from perfect in nature) suggests that the extent of workplace innovation along the HRM lines has been more extensive in the USA than in Canada throughout

Table 6.1 Canadian Auto Worker Union guidelines on work reorganization

1 We reject the use of Japanese production methods which rigidly establish work standards and standard operations thereby limiting worker autonomy and discretion on the job.

2 We reject the use of techniques such as *Kaizening* (pressure for continuous 'improvement') where the result is speed-up, work intensification and more stressful jobs.

3 We oppose workplace changes which limit mobility, weaken transfer rights and erode seniority provisions.

4 We reject the introduction of alternative workplace structures and employee-based programmes which purport to represent workers' interests while circumventing the union.

5 We reject efforts to shift compensation from wages to incentives and to individualize the rewards of productivity improvements.

6 We oppose the process of union nomination or joint appointees to new jobs created to perform company functions.

7 We oppose initiatives which undermine worker solidarity – structures which require conformity to company-determined objectives and which divide workers into competing groups internally, nationally and internationally.

8 We oppose the use of peer pressure in company campaigns to discipline and regulate the behaviour of workers.

9 We reject workplace reorganizations which threaten job security by subcontracting or transferring work outside the bargaining unit.

10 We oppose efforts to render workplaces so lean that there is no place for workers with work-related, age-related or other disabilities.

11 We oppose efforts to involve and reward workers in the systematic elimination of jobs or the disciplining of other workers.

Source: CAW (1989:9–10)

the 1970s and 1980s (Verma and Kochan 1990). And one of the major reasons for this difference between the two national systems is that the Canadian unions have been relatively more opposed to innovations along these lines than their US counterparts. For example, 'anti-QWL' (quality of working life) convention resolutions were passed in 1982 and 1983 by the Ontario and the British Columbia Federations of Labour respectively, while the Canadian Auto Workers Union (CAW) and United Steel Workers Union in Canada have officially adopted policies opposing various forms of innovation along HRM lines. Table 6.1 indicates the position of the CAW on the issue of work reorganization.

Although the CAW has been particularly outspoken in its opposition to HRM-type innovations, it appears that its general position is shared by a number of other unions in Canada. For example, an interview-based study of 17 top-level union officials in Canada basically concluded that (Kumar and Ryan 1988:8–9):

> Union leaders are convinced that management attempts towards employee involvement, and demands for greater flexibility in work arrangements are nothing but a 'misguided desire for a union free environment'. They are of the view that management is more interested in speed up, more productivity, than in the worker input. Labor leaders strongly believe in the adversarial system of labor relations citing the fundamentally different roles of union and management at the workplace. Participation in management decision-making initiative, according to them, is largely cost driven, motivated by management's desire to abdicate its responsibility by transferring to the union the role of disciplining workers, setting one worker against the other.

The obvious question posed here is why have the Canadian unions in general been much more opposed to HRM-type developments than unions in the USA? Clearly a major factor in accounting for this difference is the divergent movement in the overall levels of workforce unionization in the two countries. The overall level of union density and collective bargaining coverage has increased in recent decades in Canada, whereas there has been substantial decline apparent in the USA over the same period; currently, the level of union density in Canada is some 34 per cent of the workforce compared to some 16 per cent in the USA. In short, in terms of a standard model of organization development and change (with its three stages of unfreezing, change and refreezing) the Canadian unions, at least to date, have experienced less pressure or incentive to 'unfreeze' their historical commitment to the traditional, adversarial model of collective bargaining.

Inter-Union Variation within the USA

The 1970s and 1980s have witnessed a considerable internal debate within the US trade union movement as how best to respond to management-initiated HRM developments. For example, a study in the mid-1980s suggested that, although the American Federation of Labour–Congress of Industrial Organizations (AFL–CIO) did not have an official policy on QWL or worker participation programmes, there were basically the following different approaches adopted by national unions (Kochan et al. 1984):

1 *general opposition*, with the most well-known example being that of the International Association of Machinists;
2 *decentralized neutrality*, which was perhaps the most common case, whereby it was up to each local branch of the national union to decide if it wanted to be involved;
3 *decentralized policy with national union support*. In this category were unions, such as the United Auto Workers (UAW), where local union experimentation was encouraged from the top, although such efforts were not endorsed by the international president of the unions concerned;
4 *the Communication Workers' case*, where the international president (Glen Watts) publicly supported such efforts as an integral part of the union's longer-term strategy.

One of the authors of this particular study pursued the theme of union diversity in a subsequent paper, and pointed to a basic dichotomy between a 'co-operatist' and 'militant' strategy within the North American labour movement (Katz 1986). These two groups held very different views on a number of matters, including work reorganization and the roles of workers and unions, with these differing views deriving from (1) different assumptions regarding product demand and technological developments and (2) different ideological premisses. Table 6.2 sets out the differing positions of these two groups towards the issue of work reorganization.

Whatever the position of 'principle' taken by individual unions at the national level in the USA towards HRM developments, it is apparent that such developments have proceeded at some considerable pace at the level of the individual workplace throughout the 1980s. Indeed, it now appears

1 that the initial rather narrow, self-contained quality of working life or employee participation innovations has been considerably broadened in nature, through the introduction of associated changes in work organization (i.e. functional flexibility through teamworking);
2 the extent of such developments in the unionized sector is essentially similar to that in the non-union sector;
3 rather more national unions appear to have encouraged or at least not actively resisted such innovations, particularly in industries which are relatively exposed to the threat of foreign competition (Verma and Kochan 1990); in such cases national union officers have sought to ensure

Table 6.2 Co-operatists' and 'militants' position towards work reorganization in the USA

Group	Position	Assumptions	Ideology
Co-operatists	Willing to introduce team forms of work organization, with reduced numbers of individual job classifications and increased responsibilities for production workers (may be accompanied by pay-for-knowledge systems)	Product market uncertainty, the Japanese competitive example, micro-electronics and other flexible production techniques have provided the (desirable) opportunity to move to non-Tayloristic forms of work organization	Workers and unions can gain more meaningful participation rights as economic and technological pressures will 'force' management to move, albeit reluctantly, in this direction
	Such developments will enhance worker and union participation in decision-making at the shop-floor level, although participation at other levels should also occur		
Militants	Oppose teamworking (and associated pay structures) as they are designed to speed up work and by weakening workforce identification with the union may help bring about	The micro-electronics technology as with all technological change in the past, will further deskill the workforce and enhance management's control capability	More meaningful participation arrangement led developments will enhance the growth of the non-union sector

Table 6.2 Cont.

Group	Position	Assumptions	Ideology
	quiescent company or enterprise unions		
	The associated participatory arrangements will divide and manipulate the workforce and thus undermine collective bargaining		

Source: Drawn from Katz (1986)

certain quid pro quos for involvement, such as partnership in the ad-ministration of the arrangements and no management encouragement of non-union developments elsewhere in the company.

However, these HRM innovations (particularly teamworking) in the motor car industry in the USA have produced some notable internal debates and disagreements within the UAW. The nature of this debate is briefly outlined below.

Intra-Union Variation: The UAW in the USA

In the previous section we noted a mid-1980s study which identified the UAW as being one of the leading examples of a union with 'a decentralized policy with national union support' towards QWL and worker participation initiatives. It was in fact the UAW which negotiated the first ever QWL clause to be included in a national-level bargaining agreement (i.e. the UAW–GM agreement in 1973), while throughout the 1970s and 1980s it had the two spokesmen, in the persons of Vice Presidents Irving Bluestone and Donald Ephlin, who were among the most well-known advocates of such programmes within the US union movement. From the early beginnings in relatively narrow QWL and worker participation schemes, shop-floor work teams, reduced job classifications, and a variety of participation programmes have evolved and spread throughout the US car industry in the 1980s. National officers like Ephlin have been in favour of such developments on the grounds that they are essential for competitive survival, enhance the variety and skill content of jobs and are consistent with the union's long-term goal of increasing the level of worker and union participation in organizational decision-making (Ephlin 1988). However, within the UAW itself there has emerged a vocal body of opposition among local officers (as opposed to rank and file members) who have increasingly challenged the national leadership in internal union elections in recent years ('the new directions' movement), arguing that the union membership has suffered from the spread of teamworking (Bramble 1990). The 'intellectual ammunition' for these local officials has largely been provided by the well-publicized writings of Parker and Slaughter (1988) who have argued that teamworking weakens the traditional role and importance of seniority, increases the workload of individuals by adding new responsibilities (such as quality control), results in team leaders acting as *de facto* foremen, and pits individual workers against each other (via the influence of peer pressure within teams), all of which works to management's advantage through an increase in the level and extent of their discretion. Indeed to Parker and Slaughter the team concept is simply 'management by stress'.

The extent and vocalness of the opposition within the UAW to teamworking may well be greater than in other unions if only because such working arrangements have proceeded relatively far in the motor car industry in the USA. However, the existence and nature of such opposition are unlikely to be unique to the UAW, and thus may be a useful pointer, not to say source of concern, to other unions, in the USA and indeed elsewhere as they are forced to respond to management's attempts increasingly to move in the HRM direction.

Taking Stock of the North American Situation

We have deliberately spent some considerable time examining the views and responses of unions in the USA and Canada towards HRM developments. The reason for this approach has been twofold. Firstly, given the essentially US origins of HRM and hence the unions' longer experience with the concept and practice, it seemed likely to be of interest in its own right. And secondly, it seemed likely to yield a number of useful lessons and insights for more fully appreciating and understanding the union position in the UK. Indeed on the basis of our examination and discussion to date, one might expect to find:

1 British unions being closer to the US than to the Canadian unions, if a major determinant of their attitude towards HRM is the recent direction of movement in the level of overall unionization;[1]
2 some inter-union variation in attitudes for reasons of ideology, differences in present operating circumstances and differing assumptions about the nature of ongoing developments;
3 the reasons for accepting, or opposing, HRM developments are likely to be relatively similar in nature.

Hopefully we will have more to say about these matters following our review of the union scene in the UK.

Some TUC-Level Statements

In the introductory section we observed that in general unions have tended to comment more on some of the individual elements or components (e.g. quality circles, teamworking) of an HRM package, rather than on the concept or practice as a whole. However, in the *First Report of the TUC Special Review Body*, the discussion of the contextual pressures on unions observed that 'more generally, union influence is being challenged because of other management trends such as the increasing management emphasis on winning the commitment of the individual employee ("human resources management")' (TUC 1988:6). This view that HRM is in essence the development of a set of policies, practices and arrangements designed essentially to 'individualize' industrial relations, and thus circumvent the unions and weaken individual membership commitment and loyalty to the union, is one that is probably widely accepted throughout the British union movement. However, where individual unions may well disagree is on whether they see all individual components of HRM as equally threatening in this way, and on how to respond appropriately to employer initiatives along these lines.

The TUC has also commented on a number of the leading individual components or elements of HRM. For example, in 1981 the TUC observed that (IDS 1985:9):

> Trade unions have been urging employers for decades to give workers more control over the jobs they do. QCs are a belated recognition of employees' expertise and knowledge and the need to put them to use. At the same time trade unionists may be understandably sceptical about the merits of the latest in a succession of 'vogue' management techniques.

The generally 'suspicious' attitude or tone in this document concerning quality circles was reflected in the issuance of certain safeguards or guidelines which included the following:

1 consultative arrangements may already exist which could deal with production and quality matters;
2 quality circles should not be imposed without reference to existing negotiating procedures;
3 quality circles should not challenge or bypass existing trade union structures;
4 at least some of the savings generated by quality circles should be distributed to the workforce by negotiation.

The TUC have also commented on the notions of numerical and functional flexibility which are widely viewed as a central feature of HRM developments (1985:14–15). For instance, they questioned whether flexibility moves are being driven by a coherent management strategy, and raised some concerns about the potential of some flexibility moves to fragment the workforce, worsen terms and conditions of employment, intensify work pressures, reduce employment oppotunities and attack union organization. At the same time, however, the TUC recognized the inevitability of certain product market and labour market pressures pushing in this direction and suggested that flexibility moves will be acceptable to unions provided that certain safeguards are observed and certain quid pro quos are obtained by the workforce and the unions. Specifically, they suggested that flexibility moves which involve or are accompanied by a strengthening of job security, improved work organization, job enhancement, better training, shorter hours and improved access to information should be viewed in a relatively positive light by unions. Finally, in a recent note to the CBI Wider Share Ownership Taskforce, the TUC indicated that (1) they are in favour of schemes (e.g. employee share ownership plans, ESOPS) which give employees a share in their employer's prosperity, although (2) they are opposed to a substantial proportion of an individual's income being contingent upon the variable performance of a single organization, and (3) question the extent to which such schemes significantly enhance the motivation and commitment of individual employees (1990:4).

In summary, it appears that the TUC (1) views HRM developments in total as having the potential to 'individualize' industrial relations, but (2) recognizes the inevitability of certain environmental pressures on employers encouraging some moves along these lines and (3) feels that individual unions should basically judge their value and worth on a situation-by-situation basis, although (4) certain safeguards and quid pro quos should be ensured and obtained in situations where such moves actually take place.

If we move beyond the TUC to consider the position of certain individual unions towards HRM, do we observe the sort of diversity of viewpoint between unions which has been documented in the USA? This is a matter which we explore in the next section through an examination of certain union views of employee involvement and quality circles which are such a central feature of HRM developments.

Unions and Employee Involvement: A Diversity of Views?

An IDS study observed that 'trade union views on quality circles are not monolithic. While a major TUC statement in 1981 and a recent TGWU pamphlet both are generally suspicious of quality circles, other reactions have been more enthusiastic' (IDS 1985:9). For example, this study noted the following view of the Electrical, Electronic, Telecommunication and Plumbing Union (EETPU) general secretary (p. 9):

> I have no hesitation in advising trade unionists to explore with their management and with their fellow workers how forming such [quality] circles can bring benefit to them as individuals as well as to their organisation. Such involvement would improve personal satisfaction and pride in the job as well as boosting our national performance at the level where a real remedy to our problems lies – in the plant and in the company.

The EETPU is, arguably, the leading example of a union in the UK which appears to have positively embraced HRM developments via its single recognition package approach in which, for instance, a commitment to flexible working practices is involved. Their position contrasts strongly with that of the Association of Scientific, Technical and Managerial Staffs (ASTMS) (as it then was) in 1987 which saw quality circles as having the potential to undermine union organization and collective bargaining arrangements. Specifically, the ASTMS document made the following points (1987:15–16):

1 quality circles only extend worker participation on management's terms;
2 as an alternative channel of workforce–management communication, quality circles can undermine the position of supervisors and challenge existing collective bargaining arrangements;
3 in comparison to collective bargaining, quality circles have a number of disadvantages, namely that members are self-appointed or selected by management, discussion is restricted to the immediate work area, management retains the right to accept, reject or amend proposed solutions and they promote a 'false identification' with management aims;
4 however, as individual employees appear to gain some personal satisfaction from quality circle involvement, their possibilities should not be rejected out of hand. But management's motives for introducing them should be fully examined and the union needs to be in a strong enough position to have the circles operating in a context where there is an expansion of collective bargaining;
5 in situations where quality circles cannot be resisted, there need to be safeguards and quid pro quos, including the provision of extensive company information, regular updates on the savings generated through the circles and union input into the selection of circle volunteers.

The Transport and General Workers' Union (TGWU) is another union which has for some considerable time been relatively sceptical about employee involvement and quality circle developments. For example, in a foreword to a 1989 publication on the subject, the general secretary stated (p. 2):

In approving this report for publication and distribution to our membership, we wish to make it clear that the union does not advocate or promote participation in these new style management techniques. But we do recognise that many of our members are already caught up in them, and need guidance about how to apply basic principles of control to them. There is a particular concern about members in small and medium sized firms who may not have either the organisational strength or the comprehensiveness of existing agreements to enable them to resist the application of these techniques and strategies. Experience indicates to date that certain large, well organised plants have seen them as methods aimed at undermining collective bargaining and eroding trade union influence. This is, in essence, the view the union takes overall. Nevertheless, the approach set out in this report should be of assistance to members involved in them, either in reviewing existing arrangements or in responding to management initiatives.

In fact, in an earlier publication (1985) the TGWU provided the following advice on quality circles:

1 quality circles and employee involvement schemes should not be introduced without union scrutiny and consent;
2 employee representatives on such schemes should be chosen in line with union representative machinery;
3 where schemes already exist they should be brought into line with union structures and be put under union control;
4 in no case should schemes be allowed to undermine union structures or collective bargaining.

The 1989 publication of the TGWU went considerably beyond that of 1985 by distinguishing between essentially narrow, self-contained quality circles and a broader concept of employee involvement, the latter being linked to the notion of larger cultural change. In table 6.3 we set out the guidelines contained in the TGWU publication concerning quality circles and the broader notion of employee involvement.

Summary and Conclusions

The material presented above suggests that the British union position (with all the dangers of over-generalizing being borne in mind) towards HRM falls somewhere between 'decentralized neutrality' and 'decentralized policy with national union support', using the terms utilized in the US study referred to earlier.

Perhaps one can reasonably label the British union approach towards HRM as that of 'decentralized policy with national union guidelines' which means, in essence, that:

1 British unions are concerned about HRM developments as potentially undermining union organization and collective bargaining arrangements;
2 product and labour market circumstances will inevitably lead some employers to favour such initiatives;

Table 6.3 TGWU guidelines on quality circles and employee involvement, 1989

---

1 Quality circles, where they are not part of a bigger package of employee involvement, should be approached on the basis that:
   (a) they should only be introduced subject to the mutuality principle;
   (b) shop stewards should play a full and representative role in them, and their operation should be subject to proper procedure for grievances and disputes;
   (c) they should not discuss individual worker performance;
   (d) claims for monetary reward for participation in them should be approached on a productivity basis, with any payment available to the whole work group involved;
   (e) full disclosure of management costings, both direct and indirect, should be demanded as one of the conditions of participation.
2 Full employee involvement (EI), based on culture change, should only be pursued on the clear basis that:
   (a) all aspects of the EI are subject to negotiation by the union;
   (b) union access is negotiated to the decision-making structure which runs parallel to production management for the purposes of producing permanent change. The 'dual structure' or 'parallel structure' cannot remain a management prerogative;
   (c) while new working practices may, in some cases, improve working conditions, health and safety monitoring agreements should be made especially in relation to 'stress' syndromes. Since many of these new practices are coming into existence to bring productivity to new thresholds through high-risk organization, often referred to as 'management by stress', it is only common sense to safeguard against the human consequences of organizational stress;
   (d) team or group working, however it comes into existence, should be matched by the presence of a shop steward, and workers' control should be pursued as far as possible both within the team or group structure, and in the management control process which sets the strategy and objectives of this form of work organization.

Source: TGWU (1989:10–11)

3 the case for membership involvement (or not) must be made at the individual organizational level on a situation-by-situation basis;
4 hopefully local-level negotiators will be wary about such involvement through the inclusion of appropriate safeguards and the obtaining of certain quid pro quos.

In short, it appears that the union approach towards the leading, individual items or elements of HRM is very similar to the basic approach adopted towards the introduction of new technology, although most assessments of the new technology agreement approach have highlighted the often considerable divergence between the contents of model agreements issued by national union offices and the contents of actual agreements at the individual workplace. One suspects that this type of experience will not be unique to new technology agreements in the UK.

Finally, does this mean that the vast majority of British trade unions have at best simply reacted to management-led initiatives in HRM? Are there no signs of a more strategic, proactive approach from the unions? Probably most 'outsiders' would answer yes and no to these two questions. However, both individual unions and the TUC are clearly at present seeking to make training the centre-piece of a more proactive position in relation to HRM. The EETPU role in training is well known and a number of other unions (e.g. Manufacturing Science and Finance (MSF), the TGWU) have recently produced model joint training agreements. This is obviously a line of development that should be watched with considerable interest in the future.

Acknowledgements

The author is grateful to Larry Cairns, TUC Education Officer for Scotland, for the provision of a good deal of information. Morley Gunderson and Tom Kochan also provided some useful material for Canada and the USA respectively.

Note

1 At the end of the 1980s the overall level of union density in the UK was higher than that in Canada, and, obviously, in the USA. This fact alone may 'complicate' any suggestion that the direction of change in the level of union density largely shapes the nature of the unions' response to HRM.

References

ASTMS 1987: *IRR&R* no. 385.

Bramble, T. 1990: *Industry Restructuring and Union Organisation: a case study of the United Auto Workers of America, 1979–89.* Discussion Paper no. 1/90. School of Economics and Commerce, Latrobe University.

CAW 1989: *CAW Statement on the Reorganization of Work.*

Ephlin, D.F. 1988: Revolution by evolution: the changing relationship between GM and the UAW. *The Academy of Management Executive*, 2(1), February, 63–6.

IDS (Incomes Data Services) 1985: *Study no. 352.* IDS.

Katz, H.C. 1986: The debate over the reorganization of work and industrial relations within the North American labor movements. Mimeographed paper. ILR School, Cornell University.

Kochan, T.A., Katz, H.C. and Mower, N.R. 1984: *Worker Participation and American Unions: threat or opportunity?* The WE Upjohn Institute for Employment Research, Michigan, ch. 6.

Kumar, P. and Ryan, D. 1988: *The Canadian Union Movement in the 1980s: perspectives from union leaders.* Research and Current Issues Series no. 53. Industrial Relations Centre, Queens University, Ontario, 8–9.

Parker, M. and Slaughter, J. 1988: Managing by stress: the dark side of the team concept. *ILR Report*, Fall.

TGWU 1989: *Employee Involvement and Quality Circles?* A TGWU Policy Booklet.

TUC 1985: *IRR&R* no. 357.

TUC 1988: *Meeting the Challenge: first report of the Special Review Body*, 6.

TUC 1990: *IRR&R* no. 465.

Verma, A. and Kochan, T.A. 1990: Two paths to innovations in industrial relations: the case of Canada and the United States. Paper presented at the Spring Meeting of the Industrial Relations Research Association, Buffalo.

7

Human Resource Management: a Sceptical Look

RAMSUMAIR SINGH

Introduction

Within recent years human resource management (HRM) has assumed considerable importance in both the theory and practice of the management of organizations. Many firms have been implementing HRM strategies, and the claim is often made that they are spending more on the development of their human resources than ever before (Schuster 1986; Peters and Waterman 1982; Tichy et al. 1982). In a rapidly changing and competitive environment HRM is seen as a strategic factor in influencing not only the success of companies, but also that of nations (Zhong-Ming 1990). Universities have not been slow to respond to these developments. Some have established Chairs in HRM, and new courses in HRM have been introduced. Journals dealing specifically with HRM have been founded, and there is a growing body of literature within the field. These developments are not confined to any particular country, being found internationally in both developed and developing countries. This is not to say that there is a universal model of HRM applicable to all countries. For, as with industrial relations, it is profoundly influenced by the particular traditions and circumstances of the countries in which it is practised. As Pieper (1990:11) rightly noted: 'the industrialized nations of the Western world have developed characteristic approaches to HRM which do show some similarities, but are different, often contradictory, in many respects. It seems that in practice, a single universal HRM concept does not exist.' What can be said with certainty, however, is that HRM has now become a very fashionable area of study and attention for both the practitioner and the theorist concerned with the management of organizations.

While there are many advocates of HRM, it has not been embraced with open arms by some influential commentators (Legge 1989; Keenoy 1990). There is an increasing scepticism about the practice and theoretical underpinning of HRM. Even the extent of its application is questionable. Guest (1990:377) in his recent study of HRM in the USA noted that:

> the evidence casts some doubt upon any assumptions that HRM is widely applied in the USA. Indeed, as far as we can judge from published evidence, it appears to be limited to a small number of well-known cases. This raises questions about how we can reconcile the enthusiasm and the 'talking up' with the substance.

If this be true of the USA – the home of HRM – then clearly a pertinent question is: why all this fuss about HRM?

It is the purpose of this chapter to examine the emergence and attributes of HRM; to analyse the function played by HRM in organizations with a view to understanding why it has been so readily and, perhaps, uncritically accepted by so many organizations. Finally, it is proposed to make some comments in support of the growing scepticism with regard to HRM.

The Nature and Purpose of Human Resource Management

What is HRM? With so much at stake one would hope for a precise definition. Yet a perusal of the literature soon reveals a considerable diversity of opinion. Description and prescription are not easily separated. Some authors argue that HRM is a modern term for what has been traditionally referred to as personnel administration or personnel management (Byars and Rue 1987). Others use this term in addition to personnel management, and this is reflected in the fact there are now several textbooks on 'personnel and human resource management' (PHRM) (Schuler 1987; Leap and Crino 1989). Yet others see the integration of the traditional personnel function into strategic management as the major difference between personnel management and the concept of HRM, and the term 'strategic human resource management' (SHRM) is gaining a foothold in the literature. Most authors are agreed that the key to competitive advantage of an organization lies in making optimal use of human resources, and in the fostering of co-operation between employer and employees in the pursuit of organizational goals.

According to this analysis, HRM has been defined as consisting of the following elements:

- traditional personnel administration (staffing, rewarding, work design);
- a specific management philosophy that values labour as the major asset of an organization and that regards human beings as being able and willing to grow and develop;
- the integration of the personnel function into strategic management (Pieper 1990:13).

None of these perceptions of HRM is right or wrong in any absolute sense; however all are incomplete. An adequate understanding of the nature and purpose of HRM requires us to probe further into the way in which organizations are managed in society. At the most basic level it requires us to articulate more specifically the changes that are taking place in the society in which we live and to have some vision of the aspirations of that society as reflected in the ordering of the structures and processes of employment relations. The role of particular topics which constitute HRM such as 'strategic integration' and 'strategic management' and the like can be assessed only within such a framework. Concepts such as high quality, high commitment and high flexibility do not possess only one interpretation and each must be analysed within its particular societal traditions and circumstances. The very meaning and importance of such concepts will differ depending upon the special characteristics of the country in which they subsist. Or to put the same point in a different way, every society will have some ideas as to what it considers to be the nature and purpose of HRM, but these will differ depending upon the nature of that society.

All this is not to deny that HRM is a universal phenomenon and that there will be some commonality of application of strategies and techniques in many countries, and particularly those with multinational corporations. Yet a practice which is successful in Japan may be inapplicable in the UK where the traditions and circumstances are different. Likewise some Third World Countries face very specific problems which cannot be compared with those of the advanced industrial countries. This is not to deny that countries can learn from each other's HRM practices. Indeed it is imperative to do

so: 'For all practical purposes, all business is global. Those individual businesses, firms, industries, and whole societies that clearly
understood the new rules of doing business in a world economy will
prosper, those that do not will perish' (Mitroff 1987:ix). The point
being made is that international transferability of HRM systems, no
less than that of industrial relations systems, must be undertaken
with the utmost caution.

Theory in Human Resource Management

While there has been a growth of the practice of HRM, however
loosely defined, there has been very little theoretical development in
the field. As Guest (1987:509) noted: 'There is, as yet, no theory of
human resource management.' Yet many authors have attempted to
develop theory and, in particular applicable theory. Although it is
not the purpose here to review the various theoretical approaches, a
brief review of some of the more important ones is necessary in any
critical evaluation of HRM.

Beer et al. (1985) at Harvard proposed a model which they described as 'a broad causal mapping of the determinants and consequences of HRM policies' (p. 16). Attention has frequently been
drawn to the fact that there are a number of difficulties with the
Harvard framework. A central difficulty – which the authors themselves acknowledge – lies in the postulate that employees and unions
be considered as 'stakeholders' in the organization; they also postulate
individual well-being as an important outcome of their HRM model.
The concept of 'stakeholder', as Guest (1987:510) notes, 'owes more
to idealism than to realism', and would be difficult to apply in many
countries, and in particular in the UK and USA without new legislation relating to the ownership and control of firms.

In sharp contrast, the researchers of the Michigan group (Devanna
et al. 1984) argue that strategic HRM should be seen as the over-
lapping part of both strategic or general management on the one
hand, and personnel management on the other. Such an integration
of the personnel function into strategic management forms the major
difference between traditional personnel management and HRM.
As such, it is claimed, HRM becomes a particular approach to
the management of organizations, distinct from other approaches
(Fombrun et al. 1984).

There have been other influential attempts at theorizing in HRM:

human asset accounting (Likert 1967); human capital theory (Schultz 1972); human resource (HR) indexing (Schuster 1986). The unifying feature of all these approaches is that they treat human labour as the most important asset of an organization rather than viewing it primarily as a cost factor. It is explicitly recognized that no organization can attain its goals without labour of the right quality and quantity. This is particularly true for those organizations concerned with high technology. Thus an organization must invest in the development of its human resources.

A Framework for Analysing Human Resource Management Issues

Most of the literature on HRM takes the goals of the organization as its starting-point and builds models primarily to help managers to make and implement strategic decisions to achieve the firm's objectives. Yet it is evident that any model of HRM needs to go beyond the primary goals of management to consider the strategic interactions of other actors in the HRM system, notably individual workers, trade unions and, most importantly, society at large. Such a model is proposed in the hope that it will assist in the understanding and indentification of national differences in HRM approaches. By its very nature, however, such a model is a heuristic device by means of which data may be analysed; it has no predictive capabilities.

A framework for the analysis of HRM issues is presented in figure 7.1. It is based on the fundamental premiss that HRM processes and outcomes are determined by a continuously evolving dynamic interaction of environmental factors and organizational responses to them. Of particular importance is the role of the external environment, its values, history and institutional structures, as is also the nature of the desired optimal HRM and performance outcomes.

A number of factors which are important in analysing HRM in particular countries are enumerated in the list entitled 'external environment'; this list is by no means exhaustive but does draw attention to some of the critical variables. Since nations have different cultures, they consequently have different legal, political and industrial relations systems. Differences in the external environment profoundly affect HRM practices. Employers and workers have rights and obligations towards each other and this fidelity relationship is now recognized as bilateral. Thus the legal system is a particularly important determinant.

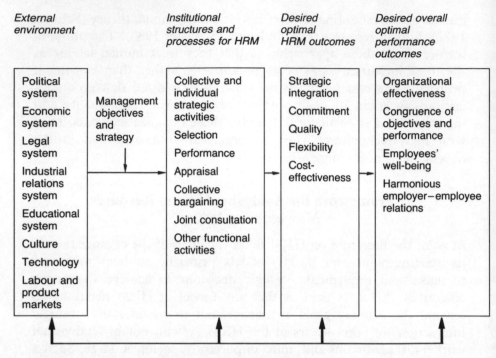

Figure 7.1 A framework for analysing HRM issues

The parameters embodied in the desired optimum organizational goals of strategic integration, high quality, high flexibility and cost-effectiveness, would seem to be universal objectives of organizations; yet there are no universal solutions as to how to achieve them. The institutional structures and processes in pursuit of these objectives are undoubtedly culture bound. The HRM outcomes are, however, a means to an end: they are intended to achieve the overall optimum performance of the organization, not least the well-being of its employees.

The output from each component of the system helps to shape and balance the entire system. Some, market forces, for example, may set in motion a series of responses from all the actors in the system. The interaction of market forces and the responses of employers, trade unions, workers and governmental policy together may determine the setting and the outcome of HRM strategies. Whether or not the organization achieves its objectives, the output of the system is fed back into the external environment and influences the environment itself.

While the framework does not constitute a fully developed new theory of HRM, there are several advantages in considering the relationship of the various elements of the system, and the roles played by environmental pressures and strategic choices. First, the framework recognizes the interrelationships among activities at different levels of the system and helps to explain any prevailing internal contradictions or inconsistencies among the various levels of HRM activities. For example, it helps us to understand how unions and workers have responded to the increased importance of decisions made unilaterally by employers. The framework also facilitates analysis of the effects that increased participation in workplace decisions by individuals and work groups have for the trade union movement and, indeed, for industrial relations. Since HRM policy-making with its concomitant effects on traditional collective bargaining have become increasingly important, researchers can no longer justifiably isolate the strategic levels of HRM into separate and isolated fields of study, any more than practitioners or policy-makers can segregate them into independent domains. The framework encourages analysis of the roles that management, trade unions, workers and the government play in each other's domain activities. In this way, HRM research, theory and policy or perspective analysis are brought together.

The test of whether the analysis provides a more insightful and useful understanding of the dynamics of HRM systems lies in the ability to explain why HRM evolved as it did and to identify the alternative choices the parties face as they shape the future of the system.

A combination of factors has led to the development of HRM in the 1980s. A major factor was the increasing international competition faced by firms not only in the UK but also in other countries, notably the USA. The old models for the management of labour seemed not to be working effectively in a rapidly changing environment. The quest for new models became an urgent task for organizations. The climate of the period was fertile for the development of HRM. The impact of new technology, notably in manufacturing and office computerization, facilitated flexible working arrangements and new reward systems. Another significant development in the UK facilitating management initiatives in HRM was the diminishing power of trade unions coupled with a strong trend towards individual achievement encouraged by governmental policy. Trade unions have been losing their traditional membership reservoir, as the coal, steel and manufacturing industries decline, and thus their influence. Simultaneous and parallel with this development is the decline in the number of blue-collar workers as the services sector has been growing (Guest 1989). As a consequence the representation of such diverse groups has become difficult. Indeed so strong was this trend that the question was posed as to whether the working class can still be seen as a socially homogeneous group with shared interests and common values, life-styles and political views (Pieper 1990). While new technology was available to all organizations globally the only variable parameter to give competitive advantage to organizations appeared to be labour. Within this context HRM appeared to offer something new which both management and workers could embrace. For most organizations the question posed was: how best to use our human resources?

Thus the acquisition of new technology is not the only important factor in determining economic success: a decisive determinant is whether people are educated and trained to a standard to use the new technology effectively. Technology, technological knowledge and finance for investment transcend national boundaries; by contrast the workforce of a nation to a large extent remains within the nation to be educated and trained, and for employment. Whether a plant is built in the UK or in Japan, even if the same technology is used, the effectiveness of the plants would be profoundly affected by the quality of the labour force.

The economic and political circumstances of the UK are major determinants of the speed of introduction of HRM strategies in the 1980s by so many firms. The Conservative government was elected in 1979, and claimed that there was a need to create 'a climate in which enterprise can flourish, above all by removing obstacles to the market, especially the labour market' (HMSO 1985). In pursuit of this objective they introduced a number of statutes relating to employment relations. Ewing has suggested that intervention in the labour market has taken two distinct forms: the first has been to 'deconstruct' the edifice of collective labour law which had been introduced by the Labour government in the 1970s, thereby 'providing a surer and better-balanced framework of law for responsible and constructive industrial relations'; the second was to 'deregulate' the employment protection laws and to undermine the role played by Wages Councils which laid down minimum terms of employment for workers in some industries (Ewing 1990:2).

An important strand of government policy, conducive to the

introduction of HRM strategies, has been to weaken the collective power of trade unions in the areas where they continue to operate. This has been achieved by reducing the coercive power which trade unions have over workers, by means of legislation conferring rights for those not wishing to join trade unions. Secondly, the law has also been used to weaken the coercive power which trade unions have over their members. The statutory immunities relating to secondary picketing, secondary boycotts and other forms of sympathetic action have been removed. All industrial action must now be supported by a secret ballot, unions being liable in damages if they fail to comply. The upshot of the labour laws introduced in the 1980s is to weaken the trade unions further, and thus make them more amenable to the HRM initiatives of employers.

The quest for new forms of management initiatives was further accelerated by the recession in the UK in the early 1980s. There were large job losses in a number of industries. Firms had to operate in an increasingly competitive environment both nationally and internationally. During this period there were many public corporations privatized, and as these firms moved into the private sector they implemented new policies for the management of labour. Cost-effectiveness and efficiency became the strategic objectives of organizations during this period. Traditional industrial relations, characterized by an adversarial relationship between management and unions, were of declining importance as they were associated with conflict and the decline of industry. Against this background there emerged what is loosely called 'the new industrial relations' – a term used to describe industrial relations in the UK in the 1980s, one feature of which is closely associated with HRM.

Another factor, often overlooked when HRM is evaluated, is demographic change (Storey and Sisson 1990). In recent years there has been an increasing proportion of women in the workforce, many of them part-time workers. Young people also constitute a significant and growing proportion of those in employment. It is therefore of interest to note that in many firms in the electronics industry and in services, notably Toshiba, and Marks and Spencer, where it is claimed that HRM is practised, there is a high proportion of women workers. Historically, women workers have been more difficult to organize into trade unions than men and more compliant to management initiatives.

Undoubtedly a most powerful influence in the introduction of HRM initiatives in the UK was the fact that in the 1980s a number of Japanese companies established plants in greenfield sites which provided the opportunity for the introduction of new initiatives in the management of labour. Included in these initiatives, for example, is new machinery for the prevention and settlement of industrial disputes, notably pendulum arbitration (Singh 1986). There are a number of distinguishing characteristics of these companies which provide fertile ground for the introduction of innovative HRM practices: a highly professional management; a carefully selected and trained labour force, and intrinsically rewarding work and security of employment. These companies actively pursue a careful and deliberate policy of marginalizing the influence of trade unions or of avoiding the need for them altogether. Management-led initiatives to achieve this result are commonplace in these organizations: quality circles, single status, staff consultative committees and the like. The outcome is that in these Japanese companies there is either no role for trade unions or at best one where unions are allowed to operate but on management's terms (Guest 1989).

These very successful Japanese companies have been trying to present a new vision of the employment relationship in contemporary society: a vision of unity, co-operation, purpose and inspiration and managerial wisdom unfettered within a compliant single-union or non-union environment. Not surprisingly, several writers have noted that there is a link between the competitive threat posed by Japanese companies and the interest in their HRM policies (Guest 1989). For the guiding principles of the new HRM strategies British firms have turned to Japan. The Japanese are viewed as leaders in modernization strategies and managers in the UK are enthusiastically borrowing methods of control of the employment relationship from Japan, with little regard for the Japanese society in which these practices have their origin. The Japanese approach to HRM appears to be characterized by a high commitment to quality, productivity, competitiveness, and a philosophy of organizing the work environment to achieve these objectives. Convincingly, and with profitable results to sustain their approach, these companies expound the virtues of their HRM techniques (Wickens 1987).

Conflict between the interests of employers and workers is seen as an aberration in these new-design organizations, and so is the idea that workers shall organize into independent trade unions. The critical issues of the joint regulation of the employment relationship are glossed over as too outmoded. HRM is based on a simple and seductive idea: harmony between the interests of employers and workers. Indeed, the paramount interests are: the efficient pro-duction of high-quality goods at a competitive cost. Once this is understood any conflict between management and workers becomes superficial, a matter for HRM, not conflict of interest.

It is now almost a necessity for firms in the UK wanting to appear modern and progressive to embark upon some form of HRM stra-tegy. The primary concerns with productivity, quality and cost-effectiveness have posed serious questions about the ordering of the employment relationship. As already noted, the traditional industrial relations have been blamed for the country's current industrial problems. A closer and more positive relationship between man-agement and workers is widely advocated. Thus HRM would fill this gap, but it has likewise put tremendous pressure on its practitioners to justify it.

The Legal System

Whereas economic, cultural and technological factors form a general framework for HRM, a country's legal system has to be seen as an all-important specific constraint since it determines the nature of the relationship between employers and employees. In many countries the legal environment for HRM is unique and closely tied to the country's history and structure. But most countries are also bound by international laws and conventions as, for example, those of the International Labour Organization (ILO). And, of course, this is true for the UK.

It is therefore significant to note that some of the practices of HRM would appear to be contrary to the spirit and purpose of both national and international law. The term 'human resource' is itself, in many respects, synonymous with 'human commodity' perceived as a cost of production. In 1944, in the Declaration of Philadelphia, the ILO adopted a declaration which defined the aims and the purposes of the organization and this was incorporated in the ILO Con-stitution. The declaration reaffirmed, in particular, that 'labour is not a commodity'; that 'freedom of expression and of association are essential to sustained progress' (Valticos 1985:75).

One consequence of HRM policies has been a decline in the importance of industrial relations, and therefore in the role of trade unions and their representatives in the workplace. Collective bargaining either has no role or only a marginal role in the organizations which claim to practise HRM. This is clearly against the stated aims of British national law. For example, the general duty of the Advisory, Conciliation and Arbitration Service as laid down in the Employment Protection Act 1975 requires the promotion of the improvement of industrial relations and in particular encouragement of the extension of collective bargaining and the development and reform of collective bargaining machinery (HMSO 1975). The law establishes the framework for industrial relations but HRM strategies seem designed to impede its progress.

The contributions made in recent years by European Community (EC) law to the development of industrial relations in the UK have been enormous, in particular, in the fields of sex discrimination and equal pay. The UK government has been forced by actions in the European Court to bring UK sex discrimination and equal pay law into line with the requirements of Community law. While it is not intended to review all such reforms here, some of them are particularly important for HRM, and require comment.

One concept is worthy of particular attention as we enter a stage in European integration at which Community lawmaking will become ever more significant, particularly in the broadly defined 'social law' field. This is the emerging concept of 'indirect effect' whereby Community law is given effect through the intermediary of national law. In consequence, the fullest effect can be given to the principle that while, under the EC Treaty, a directive leaves to national authorities the choice of form and methods for its implementation in national law, it is none the less binding upon member states as to the result achieved (Hartley 1988). The impact of this principle is potentially enormous for HRM, as it would be felt right across the field of social laws, where it is proposed by the Commission that the Community should legislate in the coming years to put in place a network of guarantees of minimum standards in employment, as well as in other fields such as company law and environmental law.

The Community Charter of Fundamental Social Rights of Workers provides a framework of principle for the future development of a European 'social dimension'. The Charter sets out some 12 categories of 'fundamental social rights' both at Community level and at national level. The 'social rights' set out in the Charter form an essential part of the process of completing the 'internal market' which is due to be established by the end of 1992 (CEC 1990).

The Charter proposes a number of rights for workers: equal pay for men and women; paid holidays; the right of association and collective bargaining; improvements in the working environment as regards health and safety of workers; information, consultation and participation by workers; and freedom of movement between member states. The Charter envisages implementation at both national and Community levels. Member states are required to guarantee the fundamental social rights in the Charter and to implement the 'social measures', 'indispensable to the smooth operation of the internal market as part of a strategy of economic and social cohesion' (CEC Directorate-General, 1990:2; Hepple 1990:643).

The implementation of the Charter poses difficult problems. Article 28 invites the Commission to submit initiatives 'which fall within its powers' with a view to the adoption of legal instruments for effective implementation, as and when the internal market is completed, 'of those rights which come within the community's area of competence'. The Commission responded promptly to this invitation by publishing in November 1989 an Action Programme (AP). The proposals set out in the AP are to be put forward and work programmes for the years 1990–2 (CEC 1989). In addition, both the Charter and the AP foresee, as an important means of implementation, the development of the 'social dialogue' in the spirit of the Treaty.

A highly relevant question that has arisen is whether key parts of the AP can be introduced by majority voting of the member states as allowed by the Single European Act, or whether unanimity is required. As yet, there appears to be no settled answer to this question. In the event the Commission has adopted the technique of separating parts of the proposals for implementation so as to avoid the requirement of unanimity. However, there are some rights, such as freedom of association and collective bargaining, for which the Commission is unlikely to find a route towards a qualified majority. Partly for this reason, the Commission has refrained from proposing initiatives in respect of these rights.

Clearly, the Charter and the AP represent a massive advance in employment protection, providing 'a floor of rights' on which working and living standards can be secured by new laws and new forms of relations between employers and employees across the Community.

There can be little doubt that industrial relations, and with it HRM, are moving centrally into the field of human rights, and that human rights at the workplace are likely to assume greater importance than hitherto. The ILO Conventions, the provisions of the

European Convention of Human Rights (ECHR) and EC laws are combining to extend the statutory rights of workers, and to regulate and influence HRM profoundly.

Evaluation

The rise of HRM in the 1980s seems to have taken most organizations and commentators by surprise. Yet resources, including human resources, have always been managed, although the forms of management had to be adapted to changing economic, technological and social conditions. HRM has emerged as a pace-setter by emphasizing high employee commitment and flexibility in the utilization of labour. The great majority of firms can be expected to continue to face intense foreign and international competition, and more dramatic changes in the way labour is managed may become a permanent feature of organizational life. The changing market and technological conditions will interact with equally important changes in the characteristics of the labour force and in the aspirations of workers.

Since the 1960s there has, moreover, been a great expansion in education at all levels in the UK. Thus the techniques of management control used in the past may not be appropriate to the changing environment. HRM strategies aimed at a better educated and trained labour force require more sophisticated methods of management. HRM manages 'power' and 'control'; in the present climate most workers accept management's edicts from a lack of choice. HRM requires a 'unitary' frame of reference; in this setting the possibility of a conflict of interests is seldom recognized. Conflict does not originate inside the structures in organizations practising HRM; when it does appear – as it nearly always does – solutions are focused on the problems of individuals. It is the individual that has to be dealt with, not the organization.

Expansion of the areas of consensus between management and labour, and the reduction of the areas of conflict, form a primary management task. To this end, HRM is a strategic management tool. The effective implementation of HRM policies calls for the training of line managers in HRM strategies as they will find themselves at the leading edge of HRM implementation. At the same time, very few workers or trade union leaders are so trained. Management appears to have the competitive advantage in this regard.

Attention has been drawn to the recent developments in employment law, particularly those emanating from the EC. The impact which these laws are likely to have would inhibit the development of HRM strategies as applied in the UK today. In Germany and France, for example, workers have rights which are guaranteed by law; in the UK workers have, for the most part, only immunities. In Germany, at the company and plant levels the system of legally guaranteed codetermination is a major determinant of the way in which trade unions become involved in the management of enterprises. As the Single Market approaches, legal rights for British workers and their unions may be created, thus limiting the scope of HRM as practised today. In this context contemporary HRM may be just a passing fad.

If HRM is to be a respectable area of academic study it must develop theory and, so far, its exponents have demonstrably failed to do so. Its underpinning has been drawn from the attics and basements of other disciplines and, indeed, it could be characterized by 'what is true is not new and what is new is not true'.

Legge has argued that the new enterprise culture of the UK is 'one that demands management's rights to manipulate, and ability to generate and develop resources'. For her, HRM is, in many cases, a 'new label' as personnel management evokes images of do-gooding specialists (Legge 1989:40). Keenoy (1990) in a perceptive article posed the question 'HRM: a case of the wolf in sheep's clothing?' The list of sceptics is growing and not without justification.

Acknowledgement

The author is grateful to Professor Ewing for making available a copy of his unpublished paper.

References

Beer, M., Spector, B., Lawerence, P., Mills, D.Q. and Watton, R. 1985: *Human Resource Management: a general manager's perspective.* Glencoe, Ill.: Free Press.

Byars, L.L. and Rue, L.W. 1987: *Human Resource Management.* Homewood, Ill.: Irwin.

CEC (Commission of the European Communities) 1989: *Communication from the Commission concerning its Action Programme Relating to the Im-*

plementation of the Community Charter of Basic Social Rights for Workers. Com. (89), 568 Final. Brussels, 29 November.

CEC 1990: *The Community Charter of Fundamental Social Rights for Workers.* Brussels.

CEC Directorate-General for Employment, Industrial Relations and Social Affairs 1990: *Social Europe 1/90.* Brussels.

Devanna, M.A., Fombrun, C.J. and Tichy, N.M. 1984: A framework for strategic human resource management. In C.J. Fombrun, N.M. Tichy and M.A. Devanna (eds), *Strategic Human Resource Management*, New York: Wiley, 33–55.

Ewing, K. 1990: Labour law under the 1980's Conservative government. Unpublished paper.

Fombrun, C.J., Tichy, N.M. and Devanna, M.A. (eds) 1984: *Strategic Human Resource Management.* New York: Wiley.

Guest, D.E. 1987: Human resource management and industrial relations. *Journal of Management Studies*, 24(5), September, 503–21.

Guest, D.E. 1989: Human resource management: its implications for industrial relations and trade unions. In J. Storey (ed.), *New Perspectives on Human Resource Management*, London: Routledge, 41–55.

Guest, D.E. 1990: Human resource management and the American dream. *Journal of Management Studies*, 27(4), July, 377–97.

Hartley, T.C. 1988: *The Foundations of European Community Law*, 2nd edn. Oxford: Clarendon Press.

Hepple, B. 1990: The implementations of the Charter of Fundamental Social Rights. *The Modern Law Review*, 53, September, 643–54.

HMSO 1975: *Employment Protection Act 1975.* London.

HMSO 1985: *Employment: the challenge for the nation.* Cmnd 9474. London.

Keenoy, T. 1990: HRM: a case of the wolf in sheep's clothing? *Personnel Review*, 19(2), 3–15.

Leap, T.L. and Crino, M.D. 1989: *Personnel/Human Resource Management.* New York: Collier-Macmillan.

Legge, K. 1989: Human resource management: a critical analysis. In J. Storey (ed.), *New Perspectives on Human Resource Management*, London: Routledge, 19–40.

Likert, R. 1967: *The Human Organisation.* New York: McGraw-Hill.

Mitroff, I.I. 1987: *Business Not as Usual.* San Francisco: Jossey-Bass.

Peters, T.J. and Waterman, R. 1982: *In Search of Excellence.* New York: Harper Row.

Pieper, R. (ed.) 1990: *Human Resource Management: an international comparison.* Berlin: Walter de Gruyter.

Schuler, R.S. 1987: *Personnel and Human Resource Management.* St Paul: West Publishing Co.

Schultz, T.W. 1972: *Investment in Education.* Chicago: University of Chicago Press.

Schuster, F.E. 1986: *The Schuster Report: the proven connection between people and profit.* New York: Wiley.

Singh, R. 1986: Final offer arbitration in theory and practice. *Industrial Relations Journal*, 17(4), Winter, 329–38.

Storey, J. and Sisson, K. 1990: Limits to transformation: human resource management in the British context. *Industrial Relations Journal*, 21(1), Spring, 60–5.

Tichy, N., Fombrun, C. and Devanna, M.A. 1982: Strategic human resource management. *Sloan Management Review*, 23(2), Winter, 47–61.

Wickens, P. 1987: *The Road to Nissan.* London: Macmillan.

Valticos, N. 1985: International labour law. In R. Blanpain (ed.), *Comparative Labour Law and Industrial Relations*, Antwerp: Kluwer, 75–92.

Zhong-Ming, W. 1990: Human resource management in China. In R. Pieper (ed.), *Human Resource Management: an international comparison*, Berlin: Walter de Gruyter, 196–210.

Part II

Practice

8

Integrating Strategy and Human Resource Management

PAUL MILLER

Introduction

This chapter outlines the main techniques associated with the integration of human resource management (HRM) and business strategy and in addition discusses some of the main issues in a wide-ranging way. In the 1990s this task is by no means a straightforward one.

Clearly, we approach the notion of integration from both the 'strategy end' and the 'HRM end' and we embark on this journey in the belief that a meeting between the two will be productive and practically useful.

Unfortunately, the journey we make is made hazardous by the fact that both strategy and HRM are entering an era of some confusion. In the strategy arena, there is debate about the nature of strategy and the way that it is taught in business schools (Mintzberg 1990), and in HRM there is similar debate on the distinctive nature of HRM and whether or not it exists as a concept distinct from personnel management (e.g. Storey 1989; Guest 1990).

Having made these cautionary comments, however, we should note that many of the contributions which seek to integrate HRM and strategy remain valuable and useful. They may not have been wholeheartedly embraced by US or UK industry and they may be more easily described than implemented, but they remain useful guides to the range of issues associated with implementing strategy and HRM. Furthermore, there is a range of strategic issues associated with the management of human resources in organizations which it is vital to address if the UK economy is to grow and prosper.

The chapter therefore, is divided into a number of sections. The first identifies a working definition both of HRM and strategy. The second briefly considers the four functions traditionally associated with HRM. As these functions are considered in detail in chapters 9, 10, 12 and 13, comment is confined to areas where there is a particular linkage to strategy. This section also deals with the important issue of whether initiatives affecting human resources in the organization have a positive effect on firm performance. Finally, we consider the strategic role of the corporate human resource (HR) function.

Defining Strategy/Defining Human Resource Management

Although defining a concept is a complex task and often one which gives rise to controversy, it remains useful in order to sketch out the field on which we play. It is not the intention here to review the many definitions of HRM and strategy, rather it is the intention simply to state those that are most useful in the context of this chapter.

The word 'strategy', as it has come to be applied in business, is a market-oriented concept – it is fundamentally concerned with products and competitive advantage. Furthermore, it is a stratified concept – it is found at different levels in the organization. Thus, we may expect to find a business-level strategy or perhaps a functional-level strategy – linked to and dependent upon the corporate or 'master' strategy. An essential point to note is that the strategy process is a 'cascade'. It starts at the corporate level and has a number of logical and related steps flowing from it. (We should perhaps note that this general conception of the strategy formulation process has recently been called into question (e.g. Mintzberg 1990).) Notwithstanding these broad conclusions, we should, of course, emphasize that there is a range of definitions of the term (Andrews 1971; Hofer and Schendel 1978; Ansoff 1965).

The notion of HRM is, by comparison with strategy a relatively new concept (although its antecedents in business are, of course, older). As a result, there are fewer definitions and rather less consensus on the nature of the concept. For our purposes, there are, however, a number of elements that might be associated with a working definition of HRM. The first is that the notion of HRM, like strategy, should be market oriented. There is no reason why our notion of what constitutes a market might not be very broadly defined, but it should relate to the activities of the business. Thus, we can include 'not for profit' as well as profit-oriented organizations in our understanding of market relatedness.

The second element is that, again like the notion of strategy itself, the notion of HRM is stratified. Thus, the issues associated with the management of those employees at the top of the organization are different from those associated with the management of people at the bottom. Having said this, we should perhaps note that all issues associated with the management of human resources should be derived issues. In other words (Miller 1987:348), 'we are probably dealing with a "functional" or "business" level strategy. HRM cannot be conceptualised as a stand alone corporate issue. Strategically speaking, it must flow from and be dependent upon the organisation's [market oriented] corporate strategy.'

It follows that all initiatives taken by the specialist HR team should be explicable in the context of the organization's strategy. There may, of course, be a plea here that there are some things that all organizations should do for their employees 'as good employers'. When asked for examples of such things, many practitioners are inclined to allude to high-profile companies such as Marks and Spencer and Hewlett-Packard. Such companies do have well-articulated HRM strategies; these strategies do, however, appear to be well matched to the business strategy. We can never be certain of this matching but anecdotal evidence and comments by chief executives would appear to support the assertion.

One of the implications of these characteristics for the integration of strategy with HRM is the fact that we can distinguish strategic HRM. We can obviously distinguish strategic HRM from non-strategic HRM (Miller 1987), but we can also distinguish, conceptually, HRM which is downstream of corporate strategy and HRM which is downstream of business-level strategy. Broadly speaking, we may consider non-strategic HRM to be a function which is:

- separate from the business (i.e. not integrated with it);
- reactive;
- short term;
- of no interest to the board of directors;
- constrained by a legalistic and institutional definition such that it is concerned principally with unionized employees and lower-level employees (Miller 1987).

Figure 8.1 A model for linking HRM to strategy

Figure 8.1 illustrates the possibility of distinguishing the various 'levels' of HRM, consistent with the levels of strategy within the organization.

For the purposes of much of the discussion that follows, we shall be considering principally the integration of HRM with corporate strategic issues. In other words, we shall be focusing on strategic HRM. This is not to say that issues associated with the management of, for example, shop-floor employees are unimportant – on the contrary. It is the argument here, however, that if the broad notion of a 'cascading' process is reasonable, it follows that it is vital to ensure that activity at the higher levels is optimized. If it is not, nothing at the lower levels in the organization will be, however sound and well thought out managerial activity at those levels might be.

The Four Functions of Human Resource Management

There are four 'generic' HRM functions that are performed within all organizations (Fombrun et al. 1984). These are selection, appraisal, reward and development. These same authors also say that these functions are performed by specialist HR managers in organizations. This is not necessarily so. Many organizations are either too small to have a specialist HRM function or unwilling to allocate these functions to a specialist. It remains important nevertheless to recognize that these functions are indeed performed within all organizations more or less systematically.

In relation to two of the four generic functions this point is obvious. Thus, all organizations select employees and all organizations reward employees. In practice, all organizations also appraise and develop their employees. In other words, in the day-to-day interaction of subordinate and superordinate there will be frequent displays of disapproval and approbation for work – *de facto* performance appraisal. Similarly, in all organizations there will be frequent examples of 'don't do the job that way, do it this' type interactions which are developmental activities of a rather crude, but nevertheless useful variety.

The fact that all organizations perform the four generic activities is perhaps an obvious point to make. It remains nevertheless important and one that should be made also in relation to strategy development itself. Thus, there is a range of formal and systematic tools for the development of strategy in organizations that senior executives may or may not use. If the organization does not use these tools and techniques, it does not mean it ceases to 'act'. The organization continues to respond to its product market environment and the skilled researcher may observe these responses and detect a strategy – a 'pattern' in behaviour and activity (Mintzberg 1990).

In summary, all organizations make strategy and all organizations select, appraise, develop and reward their employees. The proposition that doing these things systematically is better than doing them unsystematically is contentious and an empirical question. For the manager the issue is an important one and for the manager of human resources it is particularly pertinent because with the exception of forays into 'manpower planning' in the 1960s, the planned and systematic management of employees is not a common feature of UK practice. It is, in other words, a reasonable question to ask whether or not the effort associated with integrating HRM with strategy is going to impact upon organizational performance. This question is vital and one that has been asked in relation to strategy development over the years – in particular to strategic planning. As the question is asked and answered, there are useful pointers to the impact of strategic HRM on firm performance. These are particularly apposite if we consider the whole issue of employee development.

Employee Development and the Performance of the Firm

The development of managers (together with the reward of managers) constitutes one of the key tasks of a corporate personnel department. Development in this context may be defined as the identification of those skills and knowledge needed by managers in order for the organization to meet its strategic objectives and the management of those processes necessary to produce them. Although some would tinker with this definition, most would support the main thrust. Its implications are profound for the organization.

The first implication is that management development should be directed towards the organization's goals and not (necessarily) the individual's. Secondly, the definition implies articulated strategies. Thirdly, the definition implies a systematic process linking one to the other.

If employee development is crucial to the implementation of organizational strategies then the question of the relationship of development to firm performance is highly relevant. This relationship has been given particular prominence in the UK recently: 'Individuals are now the only source of sustainable competitive advantage. Efforts must be focused on mobilising their commitment and encouraging self development and lifetime learning' (CBI 1989). However, on the general relationship of development to performance there is

> a paucity of hard, detailed evidence of direct causal links . . . insufficient account may have been taken of the many other factors that intervene in the relationship between investment in education and training and the resultant return in the form of increased performance (Keep and Mayhew 1987:219–30).

This argument is very similar to that which is associated with the effectiveness of formal planning systems. Formal HRM systems have one major feature in common with planning systems generally. This is the relative difficulty of conceptualizing them. This may come as something of a surprise to HRM specialists, but it is nevertheless the case that for at least 25 years managers have applied 'planning techniques' in the belief that they do indeed improve profitability. This in spite of the fact that there has never been any real agreement on what 'planning' means with the resulting difficulty of transferring experience from one business to another. Partly responsible for this assumption were early studies that there was indeed a link between profitability and the use of planning (e.g. Thune and House 1970). Since these early studies, research has been ambiguous.

In a recent review of the research (Pearce et al. 1987) (which incidentally found only one conceptual definition of strategic planning in 18 studies of the subject), the authors argue that the reason for the lack of any proven relationship between planning and performance may be because the research has tended to ignore the contextual influence of such factors as competitive conditions. (For 'contextual influences' we may, of course, substitute 'intervening factors' from the earlier quotation (Keep and Mayhew 1987).) We are also reminded that although profitability is a long-term goal of businesses, strategic planning has other intended and unintended consequences which deserve recognition and study (as, of course, does employee development).

The similarities between the issues raised can be taken further. Thus, a key element in the decision to invest in employee development rests in the belief that the investment can be considered in much the same way as any other investment. In other words there will be a positive return on it. Yet research has shown that organizations are frequently ignorant of the full costs associated with development programmes or of the cost implications of not making the investment:

> Many companies were not aware of the volume of their own expenditure on training. Whilst most had a training budget, what was included varied from company to company . . . some covered only the direct costs of the training department, very few counted the costs of wages and salaries during training (MSC/NEDO 1985).

So much so true. Many HRM practitioners will recognize the statement of the problem and it will resonate with the situation in their own organizations. However, the situation described is by no means unique. Again we can say the same thing of strategic planning. In other words, few organizations will know the costs associated with the implementation and ongoing process of strategic planning and none will know the costs of 'not planning'.

The moral here is to avoid the tendency to condemn initiatives in HRM because their effectiveness is not empirically proven. Such heart searching does not prevent initiatives in other fields of business – and in particular strategy. The factors that encourage these initiatives may, at the end of the day, be described as 'gut feeling' or anecdotal – but they are nevertheless tried.

However, in the case of management development, there really is no valid reason to apologize for substantial investment. In his recently published study which seeks to explain why some nations perform better competitively than others, Michael Porter (1990:498) says the following about the UK (see aso chapter 13):

> there is a serious problem confronting the bulk of [British] industry. The British workforce is well behind in education and skills compared with that of many other advanced nations. There is a shortage of managers trained in technology entering manufacturing industries, and a technical background has become uncommon in top management.
>
> Most British companies have done little in-house to offset a weak education system. Investment in training by industry is estimated at far less than one percent of revenues (0.15% in 1980) in Britain, compared to 2 percent in Germany and 3 percent in Japan. The net result is that Britain has lagged badly in upgrading the average quality of human resources. This is in many ways the most fundamental problem for the nation's economy.

In summary, it may not be possible for any one firm to establish the relationship of strategic investment in employee development to firm performance, but the anecdotal evidence and the macro evidence are now overwhelming.

Implementing Development Activities

If we pursue the issues associated with management development, we may consider a further contextual point. We have already noted aspects of the recent debate about the nature of strategy. An important aspect of this debate is the extent to which strategy is articulated within organizations (Mintzberg 1990; Quinn 1980). This problem is not merely one of accessing a strategy, it is a recognition of the possibility either that organizations' strategies are not articulated at all (but no less successful for all that) or that they are developed incrementally and they are not susceptible to articulation at any one point in time.

If this is true, and there is now considerable evidence to support this view of how organizations develop strategy, then it places the HR specialist in something of a dilemma in seeking to construct systematic management development programmes. 'Development for what?' would not be an inappropriate question.

In answer to this question, we may perhaps respond that any

development process will enhance the human capital in the organization and will be an appropriate investment. Certainly, this is a view that would be supported by those considering the UK scene from a macro perspective. From the perspective of the firm, this problem may well be more theoretical than real. The relationship between management development and strategy may operate at a number of levels of complexity and it is possible that there are other conceptualizations of strategy at firm level which may appropriately inform development activities. We simply do not know the answer to this question in detail.

Nevertheless we can make a number of general comments on this relationship which are, inevitably, a little simplistic. If we consider the most common models for management development activity, we find that two predominate. The first we might call the 'hierarchical location' model. In this model, firms tend to organize development activities by hierarchical level – junior, middle and senior management. The alternative model used by many organizations to construct development activities is the 'high-flyer' model – the picking out of a cohort of individuals based upon an assessment of their potential.

The suggestion here is that there is a third model. This model is based on the belief that organizations should be able to stratify development activities by level of strategy in the organization (i.e. those levels indicated in figure 8.1), by age of participant and by strategy content.

As an example, we could imagine a business-level development activity built around a mature business strategy – a 'mature industry managers' course. This would cover such topics as interpersonal/ negotiating skills (to implement cost reduction activities in a cash-generating business); strategies for maintaining market share (there is probably little growth in the market place); preparation for retirement (the manager will be among the oldest of the organization's executive group); and so on.

Furthermore, we would construct a development process which was congruent with the overall strategic thrust of the activity. For example, we could make a good case for suggesting that 'interpersonal skills' are a key feature of any development activity. However, having determined this, we have a range of choices available to us to determine the pedagogy – how it was to be taught. In process terms, we might distinguish between high-pressure, fast-response learning and a more relaxed form of activity. Our choice should be based upon the strategic situation faced by managers. Young manager in a fast-moving, competitive environment – high-pressure development. Older manager, managing a mature business – slower-moving process congruent with the strategic situation he or she faces in the workplace.

This model is, of course, an idealized one. The essential point made is that the activity is designed around a common strategic need of the organization rather than the supposed common needs of a group of individuals joined together solely by their similar location in the organizational hierarchy.

Neither the high-flyer model, or the hierarchical location model referred to earlier adequately addresses the problem of matching the development needs of individuals to the strategic needs of the organization. The mature business managers' course is recognizably simplistic, but it does start from the organizational end of the spectrum.

Selection/Reward/Appraisal – the Integration of Strategy

Having considered employee development in some detail, we shall briefly consider the remaining HRM functions and their linkage to strategy.

Selection

Of the four generic functions of HRM, selection is the one whose integration with strategy is perhaps most conceptually developed. In an early contribution Miller and Norburn (1981) used the product life-cycle model to map out the characteristics of the manager who was most likely successfully to implement the strategies logically to be found at the differing stages of the life cycle. The model is shown in table 8.1.

The concepts identified are not, in themselves, complex. Thus, in a mature business whose overall strategic thrust is directed towards the generation of cash, it is relatively easy to recognize the personality traits necessary. Most employees here are likely to be long-serving so that change is going to be difficult to implement; an executive used to achieving change speedily and with little con-sultation is unlikely to have the diplomatic/interpersonal skills necessary.

Table 8.1 Matching managers to strategy

The objective of the business	*The main business activities*	*The chief executive should be*
Growth	1 Pursuit of increased market share 2 Earnings generation subordinate to building dominant position 3 Focus on Longer Term results 4 Emphasis on technical innovation and market development	A Young, ambitious, aggressive B Strong development and growth potenital C High tolerance for risk taking D Highly competitive by nature
Earnings	1 Pursuit of maximum earnings 2 Balanced focus on short range/long range 3 Emphasis on complex analysis and clearly articulated plans 4 Emphasis on increased productivity, cost improvements, strategic pricing	A Tolerates risk, but does not seek it B Comfortable with variety and flexibility C Careful but not conservative D Trade-off artist; short/long, risk/reward
Cash flow	1 Pursuit of maximum positive cash flow 2 Sell off market share to maximize profitability 3 Intensive pruning of less profitable product/market segments 4 Intensive short-range emphasis/minimize 'futures' activities	A Seasoned and experienced B Places high premium on efficiency C High tolerance for stability no change for sake of it D *Not* a dreamer, turned on by results now

Source: Miller and Norburn (1981).

Conversely, a manager who is required to respond and act quickly – for example in a fast-growing product market situation – should display the opposite characteristics. An overall ability to force through actions, often in the face of opposition, is important. And although not a prerequisite for success, the post-holder in this situation is, as table 8.1 indicates, likely to be young.

In summary, the managerial characteristics that match particular strategic situations are not difficult to identify. In practice, however, the widespread implementation of such schema has not happened. Why not? There are four main reasons. The first is that the product life-cycle 'map' and other representations of strategic situations were recognized as simplistic. The second reason is that selection techniques, although increasingly sophisticated, do not directly match the task identified here. In other words, they do not by and large answer the question 'I want someone with these characteristics, does this candidate have them'? By and large, they provide data on a candidate and they must be moulded to the strategic situation in hand. In other words, selection techniques provide the answer; the problem is to find the right question! In a recent article comparing selection testing techniques, the author(s) concluded: 'Normative tests allow you to compare people . . . ipsative tests [referring to individual scores] give some indication of the relative strengths of various aspects of a person within himself or herself' (Fletcher et al. 1989:51). From a strategic perspective, we would wish (as in many other aspects of this problem) to start at the organizational end of the spectrum and work towards the individual. Not vice versa.

A third problem not addressed by the model is that of the organization's culture and the need to incorporate employees within it. This issue was relatively dormant until recently. Now, the problem of implementing major strategic change has been identified by some as the problem of changing the organization's culture. Put another way, should the selection process seek matches to the organization's current culture or the culture that it aspires to?

And finally, there is the overall complexity of the task of managing a system which matches manager to strategy, particularly when the organization is made up of many strategic situations. This complexity may be attributable to the most basic of issues such as the difficulty of finding a young manager to lead a growth situation. Or, the difficulty of putting this trait alongside the search for a risk-taking personality (however this may be defined and identified).

Table 8.2 Matching reward systems to strategy

The objective of the business	The main business activities	The chief executive's remuneration should be
Growth	1 Pursuit of increased market share 2 Earnings generation subordinate to building dominant position 3 Focus on longer-term results 4 Emphasis on technical innovation and market development	High, incremental, incentive element based on market share (with identified ceiling) No incremental element to basic salary No pension scheme if under 35 Few fringe benefits Payments in lump sums
Earnings	1 Pursuit of maximum earnings 2 Balanced focus on short range/long range 3 Emphasis on complex analysis and clearly articulated plans 4 Emphasis on increased productivity, cost improvements, strategic pricing	High, incentive element based on earnings (without identified ceiling) Stable element in salary – incremental, with fair number of steps Fairly large fringe benefits package (based on cafeteria principle)
Cash flow	1 Pursuit of maximum positive cash flow 2 Sell off market share to maximize profitability 3 Intensive pruning of less profitable product/market segments 4 Intensive short-range emphasis/minimize 'futures' activities	No incentive element (except perhaps based on group profits) High basic salary, few incremental steps

Source: Miller and Norburn (1981).

Reward

Consideration of reward systems, particularly in the UK context, illustrates an interesting paradox. On the one hand, we observe considerable confidence that reward does motivate. This is particularly the case at board level where there has been a proliferation of executive schemes ranging from simple bonuses to share options. On the other hand, we have to make the point that there is precious little evidence that schemes such as these do impact positively on the financial performance of the business. (See Schuller 1989 for a review of some of the evidence on financial participation primarily at below board level.)

In spite of this apparent paradox, it remains the case that there is considerable room for innovation in the implementation of reward systems. Table 8.2 (Miller and Norburn 1981) illustrates some of the possibilities. Again we observe a number of practical barriers in the way of implementing the schema illustrated here. Perhaps the most obvious is the near impossibility of recruiting managers and not offering them any fringe benefits! However, having recognized the barriers, we should not throw out the baby with the bathwater. In other words, we should recognize that difficulty in implementation does not mean the impossibility of implementation. Miles and Snow (1978) illustrate the extent to which innovation is possible by quoting practice in the Canadian Pacific Railways; Galbraith and Nathanson (1978) illustrate comparable innovation in the Boeing Corporation.

Appraisal

The appraisal system 'is the cornerstone of an effective human resource system' (Fombrun et al. 1984:452). Certainly, appraisal of some kind is vital in any system that attempts to link the performance of the organization with the performance of people. However, labelling appraisal as the 'cornerstone' may be something of an exaggeration. Like many techniques in HRM, it is subject to trends in fashion. This chapter will not discuss the various appraisal techniques, nor the barriers to the successful introduction of an appraisal system (see chapter 10).

In summary, in the two key areas of development and reward, there is some room for innovation – testing of ideas. There is, as research is constantly revealing, very little evidence of businesses experimenting with ideas which seek to link strategy with HRM.

Yet, in the realm of strategy, taken in isolation, there is a wealth of experimentation with equally 'undeveloped' notions such as strategic planning. The reasons for this paradox are partially to be found in the ambiguous role of the corporate HR function and it is to a consideration of this topic that we now turn.

The Role of the Corporate Human Resource Function

The role of the corporate function in integrating HRM with strategy is, of course, central. The difficult role faced by personnel departments has been discussed at length by a number of authors (e.g. Legge 1978) and others have offered prescriptions for that role (Purcell 1985). The role is often, in the UK, an ambiguous one. The ambiguity fundamentally arises as a result of its structural location at the centre of the organization, while at the same time often being distanced from strategic decisions taken at that centre. This ambiguity manifests itself most obviously when the HR function gives 'advice' to constituent parts of the organization.

A case study

When the author was a member of the corporate personnel department of a large UK business, he arranged for the completion of a survey of attitudes to the department to be administered in the divisions of the company. Some of the responses, reproduced below, illustrate the 'problem of ambiguity':

> You don't come out and say what you think is really best for us in our situation.
>   When invited to a company, you should be less equivocal and instead give positive [directional] guidance.
>   I don't think it is likely that this Division will be one of your customers.
>   I'm not sure what you are trying to achieve.
>   There is a suspicion of you people generally in the Division.

These comments indicate that some parts of the group value their autonomy and guard it jealously. Others want help. Some want to be told what to do, others would prefer to be advised. Some do not know whether they are being offered advice for the division's benefit or for the group's.

This superficial survey tends to support the traditionally held view that the subsidiary of a UK business treats the advice offered by the corporate personnel department with a degree of caution. The reasons are clear. Firstly, the subsidiary is profit-responsible and with that responsibility comes authority. Secondly, the corporate personnel department is often not aware of the detailed strategy guiding the actions of the organization's subsidiaries. And thirdly, the corporate personnel function is often the only central function that the distant subsidiary can ignore and almost for form's sake there must be a temptation to exercise this right.

In a recent study of the role of the centre in large UK businesses (Goold and Campbell 1987), there is mention of no activity that could reasonably be ascribed to a corporate HRM function. It is interesting to compare this with a case study in the same book which deals with Matsushita. Matsushita was not one of the companies researched by the authors but its activities are culled from published sources to provide an international comparison. Paradoxically, while the research discovers no role for a corporate HRM function in the strategy process for UK companies, for Matsushita, the HRM function is arguably dominant.

Of course, nobody has suggested that the corporate HRM functions in such companies as Cadbury Schweppes and BOC do not do useful things. However, on the evidence of this research, they appear to continue to be separated from the strategy process. And yet, there are still many relatively large corporate HRM departments (Sisson and Scullion 1985). Perhaps the only conclusion to draw is that size and strategic influence are not related.

Guidelines for the Role of the Corporate Human Resource Function

This brief analysis suggests that a situation identified and discussed more than a decade ago (Legge 1978) still persists. It remains the case, however, that the generic functions we have briefly discussed, where they are linked to the organization's corporate strategy, should be undertaken by a specialist corporate function. With this in mind, and taking account of the dangers posed by 'role ambiguity' what functions should the corporate function figure for?

There are three areas which are the unique domain of the corporate HRM department (in the sense that they do not sit easily within a finance or legal department's domain) and which must be addressed as an adjunct to the organization's corporate strategy (Miller 1989):

1 the management of the organiztion's identity to employees;
2 the development and reward systems which attach to the organization's most senior executives;
3 the management of the organization's structure to match its strategy.

Many HRM specialists will perhaps not recognize that one of their key roles is the management of the corporation's identity. Yet this is the most obvious explanation for the recent phenomenon to which several commentators have alluded, namely the devolution of collective bargaining.

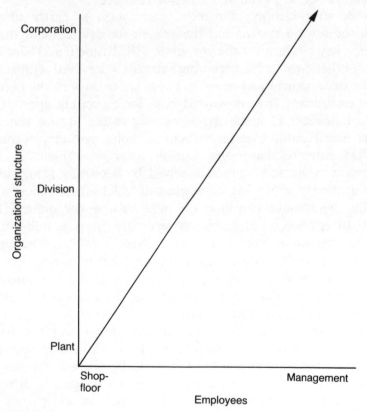

Figure 8.2 Corporate HRM. Strategically managing the problem of identification (*Source*: Miller 1987)

Figure 8.2 indicates the general problem of identity. It suggests that there is a tension to be managed for most organizations between shop-floor employees seeking to identify with the corporation as a whole (because this is likely to be the 'richest' organizational unit) and the corporation itself which seeks to have this group identify solely with their place of work. In other words, if shop-floor employees identify with the corporation as a whole, their remuneration aspirations are likely to be a reflection of other than their own efforts. It makes sound strategic sense therefore to encourage identification with the employing unit. Conversely, the corporation's most senior executives managing the divisional units are likely to identify very closely with the unit they are managing and the task of the corporation is to have them, additionally, identify with the corporation as a whole. Only in this way will the corporation's strategic objectives be realized and only in this way will be most senior executives be a genuine corporate resource.

It is because identity, for most employees, is partly filtered through the reward system and the system for development that it becomes a key concern for the corporate HRM function. There are, however, other reasons for becoming intimately involved with senior executive development and reward. These are to do with the need to have an established and recognized base for exercising appropriate strategic influence. In much the same way as the finance function exercises guardianship over investment in capital projects, so should the HRM function have guardianship over investment in HR development. Role ambiguity is resolved by becoming firmly identified with the range of what we might call 'chief officer functions'.

Finally, we should consider the role of the corporate HRM function in relation to organization structure. It is a well-known axiom that 'structure follows strategy' (Chandler 1962). The structural choices available to the organization are not numerous but the primary structure should support and not hinder the attainment of strategic objectives. The ultimate choice may be a functional, multi-divisional, holding company, matrix or Strategic Business Unit (SBU) structure; the determinants of that choice and the issues associated with making a change should be features of the role performed by the corporate HRM function. The reasons for this are associated with the fact that the behaviour of managers is in many ways determined by the organizational structure in which they are located. Thus, although we recognize that reward and development will mould and influence, we also recognize that structural influences will very often mask the positive effects of an otherwise successful development programme.

For example, the influence of a hierarchical, functional structure on a manager who has been subject to a development process designed to make him a 'team player' will be swift and damaging. It is perhaps an obvious point to make, but the interrelatedness of the key determinants of successful HRM is not something than can easily be ignored.

Conclusions

The linkages between HRM and strategy are poorly developed. There are many reasons for this. The conceptualization of strategy is being reconsidered and many businesses in consultation with academics and consultants are seeking to replace tools and techniques which were appropriate in the 1960s and 1970s but are ill-suited to the 1990s. The development of HRM inevitably lagged behind developments in strategy. Sadly, just as the linkages between HRM and strategy tools such as the Boston Consulting Group (BCG) matrix began to be developed, concepts within the matrix such as 'cash cow' and 'wildcat' became simplistic. To put it at its simplest, the goal-posts were moved.

Now, there is a much closer degree of developmental equality between HRM and strategy; both areas are seeking a new paradigm. It is an ideal opportunity to make significant advances in both HRM and strategy – in an integrated way.

References

Andrews, K. 1971: *The Concept of Corporate Strategy*. Homewood, Ill.: Dow Jones Irwin.

Ansoff, H.I. 1965: *Corporate Strategy*. New York: McGraw-Hill.

CBI 1989: *Evaluating your Training: matching outcomes to needs*. London: CBI.

Chandler, A.D. 1962: *Strategy and Structure: chapters in the history of industrial enterprise*. Cambridge, Mass.: MIT Press.

Fletcher, C., Johnson, C. and Saville, P. 1989: A test by any other name. *Personnel Management*, March, 46–51.

Fombrun C., Tichy N.M. and Devanna, M.A. 1984: *Strategic Human Resource Management*. Chichester: John Wiley.

Galbraith, J. and Nathanson, D. 1978: *Strategy Implementation: the role of structure and process.* St Paul, Minn.: West Publishing.

Goold, M. and Campbell, A. 1987: *Strategies and Styles: the role of the centre in managing diversified corporations.* Oxford: Blackwell.

Guest, D. 1990: Human resource management and the American dream. *Journal of Management Studies*, 27(4), 377–97.

Hofer, C.W. and Schendel, D. 1978: *Strategy Formulation: analytical concepts.* St Paul, Minn.: West Publishing.

Keep, E. and Mayhew, K. 1987: The assessment: education training and economic performance. *Oxford Review of Economic Policy*, 4(3), 219–30.

Legge, K. 1978: *Power, Innovation and Problem Solving in Personnel Mangement.* Maidenhead: McGraw-Hill.

Miles, R. and Snow, C. 1978: *Organisational Strategy, Structure and Process.* New York: McGraw-Hill.

Miller, P. 1987: Strategic industrial relations and human resource management – distinction, definition and recognition. *Journal of Management Studies*, 24(4), 347–61.

Miller, P. 1989: Managing corporate identity in the diversified business. *Personnel Management*, March, 36–9.

Miller, P. and Norburn, D. 1981: Strategy and executive reward: the mismatch in the strategic process. *Journal of General Management*, 6(4), 17–27.

Mintzberg H. 1990: The design school: reconsidering the basic premises of strategic management. *Strategic Management Journal*, 11(3), 171–96.

Pearce, J.A., Freeman, E.B. and Robinson, R.B. 1987: The tenuous link between formal strategic planning and financial performance. *Academy of Management Review*, 12(4), 658–75.

Porter, M.E. 1990: *The Competitive Advantage of Nations.* London: Macmillan.

Purcell, J. 1985: Is anyone listening to the corporate personnel department? *Personnel Management*, September, 28–31.

Quinn, J.B. 1980: *Strategies for Change: logical incrementalism.* Homewood, Ill.: Irwin.

Schuller, T. 1989: Financial participation. In J. Storey (ed.), *New Perspectives on Human Resource Mangement*, London: Routledge, 126–36.

Sisson, K. and Scullion, H. 1985: Putting the corporate personnel department in its place. *Personnel Management*, December, 36–9.

Storey, J. (ed.) 1989: *New Perspectives on Human Resource Management.* London: Routledge.

Thune, S. and House, R. 1970: Where long range planning pays off. *Business Horizons*, August, 81–7.

9

Selection

GORDON ANDERSON

Introduction

Selection and performance appraisal, the subjects of this and the following chapter, have for long been seen as central aspects of human resource management (HRM). Although many of the methods have become well established and accepted in organizations, new challenges have emerged.

Major factors affecting both selection and performance appraisal include the changing nature of modern organizations, and the greater emphasis being placed on HRM. Handy (1989), for example, has identified a number of trends in the design and operation of modern organizations, all of which have important implications for selection and performance appraisal. These trends include:

- flatter organizations, with fewer levels in organizational hierarchies;
- greater numbers of 'knowledge-based' employees with fewer jobs for holders of traditional skills.

Handy also discusses more profound shifts in organizations, brought about by discontinuous as opposed to incremental change. 'Continuous (incremental) change is comfortable change. The past is then the guide to the future. . . . Discontinuous change is not part of a pattern . . . it is confusing and disturbing' (1989:3,5). Essentially Handy is arguing that it is not only the increased pace of change, but the magnitude of discontinuous changes that is calling for radical rethinking about the nature of organizations of the future, and the kind of people required to work in them. Handy's 'shamrock' model (named after the shamrock, the Irish national emblem, a small clover-like plant with three leaves) shows modern organizations made up of three separate, though interacting elements:

1 the core employees – likely to consist mainly of qualified professionals, technicians and managers;
2 the contractual fringe – made up of both individuals and organizations, who are paid for results in fees, and not for time in wages;
3 the flexible labour force – consisting of part-time workers and temporary workers, the growth of this form of employment being a reflection partly of the continuing growth of the service sector in most economies, and partly of change and the need to adapt swiftly to different competitive markets.

Not surprisingly, the jobs within organizations are also subject increasingly to change. Kanter (1989) has identified many new, and often conflicting demands, on employees in general, and on managerial employees in particular, in modern organizations. According to Kanter, 'the mad rush to improve performance and to pursue excellence has multiplied the number of demands on employees' (1989:20–1).

These demands, according to Kanter, include the need to:

• think strategically and invest in the future but keep the numbers up today;
• be entrepreneurial and take risks, but do not cost the organization anything by failing;
• continue to do everything that is currently being done even better, but also spend more time communicating with employees, serving on teams, and launching new projects;
• know every detail, but delegate more responsibility to others;
• become passionately dedicated to 'visions', but be flexible, responsive and able to change direction quickly.

The emergence of these changes implies the need for the careful definition of jobs and job objectives, and increasingly for revised definitions, in considering the selection of employees.

Selection and performance appraisal are also being influenced by the increased emphasis on HRM in many organizations. While Guest (1989) rightly points out that the term 'human resource management' can mean different things to different people, there appears to be consensus thinking that there is, or should be, increased emphasis on a more strategic and integrated approach to HRM. This implies that HRM considerations, including notably selection and performance appraisal, should be part of the process of formulating corporate strategy, given greater recognition, as pointed out by Sisson (1989), that the management of people is a key, if not the key element in the strategic planning of any business – and not just a series of implementation responses to strategic decisions dominated by financial and marketing considerations.

Selection: The Challenges

The recruitment process involves organizations in communicating with persons who might be realistic candidates for job vacancies. The selection process is concerned with the evaluation of candidates, and the development of systems, procedures and methods to ensure that sound selection decisions are made, to ensure that high-quality personnel are brought into organizations.

Torrington and Hall (1987) recommend that the term 'employment decision' should be used instead of 'selection decision' on the grounds that the latter implies a one-way decision-making process in which organizations evaluate groups of candidates and make decisions about whom to offer jobs. In reality, there is a two-way decision-making process in which candidates are involved in decision-making, in that if offered a job, a candidate has the right to decide whether to accept it or reject it. It is increasingly important for organizations to recognize this fact when the labour market for particular skills is characterized by an excess of demand over supply. Under such conditions, organizations with vacancies to fill must devote considerable attention to particular aspects of the selection process:

- presenting the organization and the job in a way that should prove attractive to candidates;
- reaching decisions, not only in terms of whom they wish to appoint, but rather deciding which of a group of candidates are appointable;
- placing them in rank order, recognizing that the first, second or third-ranked of the candidates may reject a job offer and give preference to an alternative offer or to an improved offer with their current employers.

Good examples of 'tight' labour markets with demand for certain skills outrunning supply are to be found in Hong Kong, where the 'brain-drain' problem has accelerated in recent years, with many skill categories experiencing high emigration rates in anticipation of the political changes of 1997, leading to labour shortages.

Of the various decisions made in organizations, selection decisions are among the most important, for a variety of reasons. They can lead to new opportunities for corporate strategy and tactics, and to competitive advantage by injecting new human resources into the organization, or by giving existing personnel fresh opportunities to display their talents, for example, if one or more hierarchical layers in the organization structure are removed and job responsibilities are redefined and increased.

In addition, selection decisions represent a deceptively large investment in human capital. If, for instance, an organization offers an individual aged 30 years a job at £20,000 per year, a simple calculation would suggest that, assuming that person works for 30 years, the selection decision represents an investment in human capital of around £600,000. This calculation underestimates the economic magnitude of the decision, because it ignores the indirect costs of employing an individual, for example national insurance and pension contributions, and the additional costs of salary rises and fringe benefits.

Selection decisions are much harder to reverse if errors occur, compared with many other corporate decisions. By contrast, decisions concerned with investment in capital assets can often be readily reversed by selling the capital assets. Selection decisions in many countries are increasingly difficult to reverse because of legislation concerned with unfair dismissal. Bad selection decisions can have major damaging effects, in terms of harm to the business and to interpersonal relations, as well as potential negative impacts on public image if corrective action, such as demotion or dismissal, has to occur.

Selection Objectives

The principal objective of the selection process is to help organizations make decisions about individuals whose characteristics most closely match the requirements of vacancies to be filled. As previously noted, candidates, too, have decisions to make. They have, for instance, the right to withdraw during the selection process, if information emerges which either reduces their interest in the vacancy or shows that they are unsuited for the position.

If a candidate is offered a job, he or she has to decide whether to accept or reject the job offer, or to try to negotiate more favourable terms and conditions. It is in the interests not only of the candidates, but also of the organization, that candidates should be in a position to make sound rational decisions. A second major objective of the selection process, therefore, is to ensure candidates receive adequate information about the job, and the organization, to enable them to decide if they really want the job.

The third major objective emerges from the inevitable fact that in the selection process a narrowing of the field of candidates takes place, finally leading to the making of a job offer to one person or to a small number of candidates. A proportion, possibly a large proportion, of candidates will be rejected. The third objective of the selection process is therefore to ensure that candidates feel they have been courteously and fairly treated during the selection process.

The importance of this third objective lies in the fact that an organization can never predict when it will be in contact again with unsuccessful candidates. They may present themselves at some future date as candidates for a different vacancy for which they are better suited. They may take up employment with a supplier or with a client organization. These possibilities help to demonstrate how important it is to create a positive image of both the organization and the fairness of its selection process, leaving them with the feeling, even if unsuccessful: 'What a good organization – I wish I could have worked for it.'

Selection Procedures

While selection procedures must satisfy a number of requirements, according to Roe and Greuter (1989), it is important that they fulfil four main functions:

1 *Information gathering.* This involves generating information about the organization, the job, career paths, employment conditions on the one hand; and, on the other, about candidates, including their experience, qualifications and personal characteristics.
2 *Prediction.* Using information on past and present candidate characteristics as a basis for making predictions about candidates' future behaviour.
3 *Decision-making.* Using the predictions about candidates' future behaviour as a basis for making decisions about whom to accept or reject.
4 *Information supply.* Providing information, on the one hand, about the organization, the job, and employment conditions to candidates, and, on the other, providing information about the results of the selection process to the various parties involved – line managers, personnel specialists, etc.

While many options are available to organizations in designing and developing selection procedures, an important consideration is that all of the four functions should be adequately carried out. Other considerations that will shape the design of selection procedures include:

- *The availability of managerial and specialist skills.* Selection procedures must be developed in a way such that they can be implemented by available managers and specialist staff (e.g. personnel specialists).
- *Cost/benefit factors.* The quality and soundness of selection procedures must be balanced against the costs involved.

Selection Methods

Organizations can choose among a number of options in developing selection methods for jobs. These include application forms and letters of application, selection interviews, tests, references and group selection methods. Assessment centres, which incorporate some of these methods, are used increasingly for selection, as well as for other purposes, such as identifying training and development needs, and future potential.

Application forms

The application form, or letter of application, is an extremely important element in the selection process. While the other methods, especially the interview, have a strong influence over final selection decisions, the application form or letter of application is particularly important in the early stages of the selection process when decisions have to be made to reduce substantially the number of applicants under consideration. An application form usually requires the candidate to provide such basic factual information as:

- personal details – marital status, address, telephone number;
- education and training – details of qualifications and dates of attainment;
- work history – details of employment including summary of duties with present and former employers;
- leisure interests.

Some application forms, more ambitiously, invite applicants to make statements concerning:

- how they achieve job satisfaction;
- why they are applying for the job in question;
- how they perceive their ambitions and career plans.

A well-designed, comprehensive application form brings several advantages to the selection process:

- it provides sufficient data to permit initial screening decisions on candidate suitability to be made;
- it permits selectors to compare one candidate with another;
- it provides a basis for interview preparation for those candidates who are short-listed;
- by eliciting relevant factual information, it permits the selection interviewer to concentrate upon the interpretation of the candidate's background.

However, because of poor design and layout, the benefits of using standard application forms are not being fully realized (Muir 1988). Often too little information is sought, headings are too vague, and a lack of space under key headings encourages superficial responses.

A good application form should therefore ensure that candidates are not impeded from expressing themselves fully. Much can be gained in assessing candidates' responses in a well-designed application form – the power of description, clarity and precision in presenting information. In addition, it is often retained as the initial document in the successful candidate's personal file, providing an indication of possible training and development requirements.

Many smaller organizations invite candidates to submit letters of application together with copies of their curriculum vitae. Although there is always greater difficulty in comparing candidates who may have adopted different approaches in composing their letters of application and in designing their curricula vitae, highly motivated candidates are likely to put sufficient effort into the preparation of these documents so that the organization obtains considerable relevant information about their backgrounds. There is always the danger, however, that even the most well-intentioned candidate does not provide information to answer the questions uppermost in the selectors' minds.

The selection interview

Mixed results have emerged in a number of research studies concerning the reliability and validity of the selection interview.

The analysis of some researchers (see e.g. Hunter and Hunter 1984) suggests that the validity of the selection interview seldom rises above 0.20. Nevertheless, Gill (1980) and Robertson and Makin (1986), in surveys of selection methods, have concluded that the selection interview continues to be considered as the central and most important selection method in the great majority of organizations.

Lewis (1984) suggests that this paradox can be resolved in various ways:

- The selection interview is valid, in so far as it provides a sample of behaviour which illustrates sociability, interactions with others, and verbal fluency.
- The selection interview may not be valid, but practical considerations make it a realistic choice, especially in situations where the number of applications is too small to justify more elaborate procedures.
- The selection interview is not valid, but interviewers maintain a high level of faith and confidence in their judgement and ability to make sound selection decisions.
- The selection interview is not valid, but it does provide an opportunity of both selling the job and explaining the job to applicants.

The theme, implicit in these four options, is that the versatility of the selection interview explains its popularity, and its high level of usage. The face-to-face encounter of the selection interview provides an opportunity to communicate the benefits of both the job and the organization to applicants. It also provides an opportunity for candidates to clarify their information needs, and to ask for, and receive, additional information.

The impressions conveyed by representatives of the organization in the selection interview are likely to count heavily with candidates. Harn and Thornton (1985) found that the behaviour of interviewers towards them had some influence on whether candidates decided to accept or reject job offers.

Heriott (1989) has advocated that the role of the selection interview should be redefined, largely in terms of the second and third selection objectives listed previously, to assist decision-making by candidates and to communicate a positive image of the organization. He has argued that the importance of the selection interview can be justified when viewed as a social encounter in which information is exchanged and mutual trust is built up. His argument is based on the idea that the psychological contract between the individual and the organization begins during the recruitment and selection process, and principally at the selection interview, and not after the employment contract has been agreed.

The interaction between interviewers and candidates at the selection interview provides opportunities, in addition, for checking candidates' perceptions (e.g. of the job and the organization), for negotiating with candidates on job responsibilities as well as terms and conditions of employment, counselling candidates on how any negative perceptions they may hold about the job and/or the organization can be overcome, and persuading them to look favourably on the benefits. The importance of these aspects of the selection interview will depend on the seniority of the job being filled, and the level of flexibility and discretion associated with selection decisions.

Selection tests

Testing in some form is used by many organizations as part of their selection procedures. Beach (1980:229) defines a test as a 'systematic procedure for sampling human behaviour'. Livy (1988) uses an alternative explanation in describing a test as an example of scientific method applied to human behaviour, from which statements can be made about future performance and behaviour. For selection purposes, tests are normally given under standardized and controlled conditions. Beach reports that tests are widely used for employee selection, citing a survey involving 473 American Organizations, with from 250 to over 5000 employees, which found that selection tests were used by over 80 per cent. British experience is different, the survey evidence of Robertson and Makin (1986) indicating that 64 per cent of British organizations never used personality tests when selecting managers, and 74 per cent never used cognitive tests.

Testing concepts
The central concepts underlying all forms of testing are reliability and validity. Before any test is used for selection, the organization should be satisfied as to its reliability and validity.

Reliability
The reliability of a test is the consistency with which it produces the same score through a series of measurements. In other words, if we ask the same person to take the same test on a number of separate occasions, approximately the same score should emerge each time,

both in absolute terms and relative to others who have undergone the test.

Validity

Validity refers to the extent to which a test measures what it is intended to measure. This presupposes that fundamental questions concerning the criteria of job behaviour expected of candidates, and the constituents of successful performance have been answered, so that there is a sound basis against which test results can be evaluated.

There are various types of validity:

1 *Face validity*. This means a test must give the impression of measuring relevant characteristics. If the face validity is low, no matter what redeeming features the test possesses, candidates are likely to feel alienated and disinclined to co-operate, and will not form a positive view of the selection process.
2 *Concurrent validity*. This refers to the extent to which the scores of a test relate to the performance of employees currently undertaking the kind of work for which candidates are being evaluated.
3 *Predictive validity*. This refers to the extent to which the scores of a test relate to some future measure of performance.

Both concurrent validity and predictive validity imply the need for some kind of criterion, or criteria, developed from job analysis, against which test scores can be correlated.

Correlation

Correlation is a statistical concept which provides a measure of the relationship between two series of numbers. Measures of correlation are used to assess the reliability and validity of selection tests. Correlation coefficients are calculated on a scale from 0, as one limit indicating no reliability or validity at one extreme, to $+1.0$ indicating total reliability or complete validity, which is unrealistic to expect. Depending on the kind of test, a reliability of 0.65 or upwards should normally be acceptable. In the case of validity, a measure of between 0.4 and 0.6 often occurs, and is likely to be acceptable. If the measure of validity for a test is 0.5, this means that the test is measuring, and is able to explain, 0.5^2 or 0.25 (25 per cent) of the relationship between the test scores and the criterion being used as an indicator of job performance. Other factors that are either unknown or else cannot be measured by the test account for 75 per cent of the relationship. It should be stressed that correlation does not necessarily imply a causal relationship.

Types of tests

A wide range of types of tests can be used in selection. The choice includes:

1 *aptitude tests* – measuring the potential to do something, provided proper training is received;
2 *achievement tests* – measuring skills or knowledge that have been acquired;
3 *vocational interest tests* – measuring preferences for different types of work;
4 *situation tests* – evaluating candidates in a situation that resembles some aspect of the job to be filled;
5 *personality tests* – measuring characteristics of candidates, such as emotional maturity, conformity, extro/introversion.

The use of tests

Tests are normally used as a supplement to other selection methods, and not in place of them. In this respect, they can often make a valuable contribution to the selection process, by revealing dimensions of behaviour, character, ability and achievement that would not normally be discovered by other means. Tests are often of value in selecting a smaller group of candidates from a larger group, but are less helpful in identifying the particular individual who will perform best on the job. Tests are likely to predict future behaviour more accurately than selection interviews, in those areas covered by tests.

Ethical considerations involve clarifying for candidates who will have access to test data, and offering to provide some form of feedback of test results. Legal considerations require that tests must comply with equal opportunities legislation. Tests must therefore be scrutinized for the possibility of unfair discrimination.

References

Organizations frequently use references to assist with selection, normally in support of other methods. While references can take a variety of approaches, the essential purpose is to obtain information from a third party, with a view to providing a factual check on the candidates' qualifications and experience, and/or receiving an assessment of the candidates' suitability for the job in question.

Some of the options the organization must consider in obtaining references are:

• whether the reference should be obtained orally, or in writing;

- if in writing, how the reference should be structured, and what information should be asked for;
- how the reference should be used in the selection process. For instance, it may be used before other parts of the selection procedures are implemented, in parallel with other selection methods, or at the end of the selection process, to provide confirmation of provisional decisions about candidates.

Written references give the referees greater time to reflect on questions, on the wording of answers, and on information provided about the job vacancy. Although there is no empirical research work to support this, it could be assumed this will assist the reliability and validity of references. On the negative side, referees may be reluctant to commit adverse comment about candidates in writing.

Oral references obtained, for example, by telephone, may encourage referees to be more candid and open in expressing views. Further, a verbal exchange gives the selector the opportunity to question and probe views expressed by the referee, to see how well supported they are. As pointed out by Dobson (1989), oral references are likely to take up more time and resources than written ones, and so can probably be justified primarily in the case of senior appointments or situations where selection decision-making is proving difficult either because of problems in discriminating among candidates or of mixed, conflicting evidence being gathered from other sources about candidates' suitability.

The structure of reference reports will be influenced by the extent to which specific factual information is sought, and how far evaluative comment is requested.

At one extreme unstructured approaches can be used, where letters are sent to referees asking them for any factual information or evaluative comment they feel will help the selection process. At the other extreme, reference forms may include rating scales and forced choice questions, aimed at assessing specific attributes.

Some studies (e.g. Reilly and Chao 1982) have indicated disappointing results regarding the reliability and validity of references. Jones and Harrison (1982) have suggested, based on their research, that the validity of references can be improved by obtaining from referees, within a structured format, samples of characteristic candidate behaviour relevant to criteria based on job analysis.

References have the potential for making a useful contribution to the selection process. Dobson (1989) provides some guidelines for ensuring that referee information is gained in a reliable and error-free way:

- base questions on job analyses;
- if possible, interview the referee;
- solicit facts and behaviours, rather than evaluations;
- when personality traits have to be measured, define them, and ask for specific examples;
- identify the opportunities the referee has had to observe candidates;
- provide the referee with relevant information about the job vacancy.

Group selection methods

Group tasks are used in some organizations, as a selection method, usually for supervisory and managerial positions. The case for using group selection methods is that information not readily obtainable from other selection methods can be gained about a range of candidates' abilities.

Group selection methods can take a variety of forms. Plumbley (1985) has identified the following classification of group selection methods:

1 *Leaderless groups*. A group of usually 5–10 candidates, with no appointed leader or chairman, is asked to discuss a particular topic for a given period of time, often for half to three-quarters of an hour, observed by selectors. This topic may be job-related, or drawn broadly from current affairs.
2 *Command or executive exercises*. Applicants receive individual briefings, usually relating to a wider problem or issue. After a given time for individual preparation, each candidate puts forward a recommended course of action or solution, to defend and debate with the other candidates in the group.
3 *Group problem-solving exercises*. In this situation the group is required to analyse a problem and develop solutions within a given time period. This involves the group in organizing its own resources, and working collectively on a common or shared set of tasks under time pressure.

Organizations using such methods are likely to place emphasis on assessing:

- *social skills* – friendliness, co-operation, getting on with others;
- *influencing skills* – assertiveness, resolving conflict, persuasion;
- *communication skills* – clear expression, use of forceful argument, summarizing skills;

- *intellectual skills* – applying knowledge and past experience, thinking analytically and logically, evaluating the arguments of others;
- *attitudes* – political, economic, racial; views towards business, government, authority;
- *personality* – role adopted in group situations; level of activity in group; leadership qualities exhibited.

Normally group selection activities are evaluated by several selectors or assessors. Important questions therefore concern the extent to which the assessors receive training in observing and scoring candidates, and how far their ratings of candidates agree.

Positive findings about the use of group selection methods were reported by the British Civil Service (1976). This study reported a high validity correlation between assessments and subsequent job grades achieved. The case for using group selection methods is probably strongest in dealing with young candidates, e.g. college graduates or school-leavers, with little experience to probe in interviews.

On the negative side, group selection methods may give rise to problems of interpretation, and to misleading results. Candidates, aware that they are being observed, and in competition with others, may indulge in attention-seeking behaviour. Some may find the whole experience so stressful that they fail to reveal positive aspects of themselves.

Another important question raised by Livy (1988) is the question of the criterion variable. In other words, what are group selection methods actually measuring? Turnage and Muchinsky (1984) indicate that these methods may reveal long-term potential, but not necessarily job performance. Livy, therefore, has a sound point to make when he suggests that group selection methods may reflect the right type of organizational person in the minds of assessors, so that the results become a self-fulfilling prophesy!

Assessment centres

The assessment centre (AC), or multiple assessment approach, has made a major contribution to the selection of employees, especially at managerial levels in many organizations. An AC can be defined as the 'assessment of a group of individuals by a team of judges using a comprehensive and integrated series of techniques' (Fletcher 1982:42). While the term 'assessment centre' is American, the method of multidimensional assessment was pioneered by the British War Office Selection Board during the Second World War, to cope with the problem of identifying and selecting officers. Later, ACs were adopted by the British Civil Service and by a few large British companies. It was in the USA, however, that the major developments in ACs took place, with AT&T being a pioneer in setting up its programme in the mid-1950s. Other major users have included IBM, Mobil, Digital and Standard Telephones and Cables.

An AC does not imply a physical centre, but rather a particular approach or philosophy which recognizes the benefits of a multiple techniques approach, which can incorporate interviews, group selection methods and psychological testing, to permit the evaluation of a range of dimensions that are seen as relevant to the job vacancy.

Characteristics of assessment centres
While the format and design may vary substantially, a good AC should normally include the following:

1 a variety of assessment techniques;
2 several candidates, usually six to eight in number;
3 several assessors/observers involved;
4 assessment made on a number of dimensions.

The success of assessment centres
A number of validation studies have been carried out, mainly in the USA. The results on the whole, are positive. For example, a study of 5493 people who participated in ACs at AT&T displayed a highly significant relationship between assessment ratings and progress in management (see Mosel and Byham 1977).

Steps in introducing an assessment centre
These include:

1 *Defining requirements*. Once the target job/jobs have been analysed, the results can be classified to provide a list of criteria or competencies around which the AC should be designed.
2 *Identification and design of assessment instruments*. Once the criteria, or dimensions to be measured, have been identified, assessment instruments, consisting of a number of activities must be designed (or bought off the shelf) and organized, to ensure that there are a sufficient number of the right type of activities to measure all the relevant dimensions.
3 *Design and organization of the programme*. The timetable should be drawn

up; the number and names of participants finalized; the number and roles of assessors decided; plans for the provision of feedback agreed.

4 *Selection and training of assessors.* Assessors must understand the principles underlying the programme, the activities, the dimensions to be assessed, the techniques of assessment, scoring methods, and the principles and techniques of providing feedback.

Selection: Summary and Conclusions

The evolving concepts of HRM, stressing the linkages between HR policies and corporate strategy, have led to increased emphasis on recruitment and selection. The importance of selecting the right people has been stressed by influential management books such as *In Search of Excellence* (Peters and Waterman 1982), reinforcing the notion that 'people make the place' (Schneider 1987).

A range of factors – the changing nature of organization structures, new, often conflicting pressures on employees in general and managers in particular, together with changing demographic patterns and changing patterns of work – combine to create a new environment and new challenges for recruitment and selection.

At first sight it may appear that little progress has been made with regard to recruitment and selection methods and techniques. In the case of selection, organizations still place reliance on the traditional methods of application forms and selection interviews.

Recent developments have not highlighted revolutionary new methods but have been concerned more with reassessing and refining the use of established methods. More thought and care are devoted to the design of application forms. Organizations are developing rejoinders to the many studies in the literature that have highlighted low reliability and low validity findings for the selection interview by focusing on the philosophy that it is primarily a social encounter and flexible mechanism for two-way communication between candidates and interviewers, often assisting candidates more than interviewers in reaching decisions about whether their abilities match the vacancy.

The way forward for producing sound selection decisions appears to lie in developing greater understanding of the role and contribution of the various selection methods available, and to design selection procedures that draw upon a number of techniques. This is particularly true in the case of testing, given the importance of defining exactly how any selection test will be used and for what purpose, as well as considering how it will supplement data derived from other selection methods in helping to facilitate sound selection decisions.

This trend towards multi-method approaches culminates in the greater recognition, and use of ACs. Although they can be considerably more expensive, in terms of both set-up and operating costs, than simpler, more conventional procedures, there is evidence to suggest they lead to better selection decisions. As well as being used to assist with selection decisions, ACs are being increasingly used to identify employee potential and employee development needs.

Much of the literature dwells on matching individuals to jobs and can be criticized as being too mechanistic. Increasingly both in the literature (see e.g. Bergwerk 1988) and in practice, greater recognition is being given to adapting recruitment and selection practices to permit the assessment of candidates in terms of their suitability for the corporate culture as opposed to a specific job. Although apparently less specific and more subjective, this consideration is likely to weigh more heavily in selection decisions of the future, especially as the life-span of particular jobs and skills becomes shorter.

Another important trend, likely to gain in significance in the future, concerns the increased emphasis on fairness and avoidance of excessive bias in the selection process, together with greater recognition of candidates' rights. Some European countries, particulary Sweden, the Netherlands and Germany (see e.g. Ekvall 1980) are leading the way in considering the importance of candidates' rights. Ekvall reports that in Sweden employee representatives are present when psychologists report on the results of testing, and an applicant who undergoes psychological testing is allowed to be informed of the results before the potential employing organization is informed. Furthermore, the applicant has the option of having the test results destroyed, if he or she wishes to withdraw. While in some countries these might appear excessive measures to protect candidate interests, they do draw attention to the important fact that in the UK, and indeed many other countries, there may still be a tendency to focus exclusively on the organization's perspective in making selection decisions and to neglect the increasingly important aspects of how candidates make decisions, in deciding whether to accept job offers or not.

References

Beach, D.S. 1980: *Personnel: the management of people at work*. New York: Macmillan.

Bergwerk, J. 1988: Recruitment and selection for company culture. *Journal of Managerial Psychology*, 3, 9–15.

Civil Service Department: Behavioural Sciences Research Division 1976: *Civil Service Administrators: a long term follow-up*. BSRD Report 31.

Dobson, P. 1989: Reference reports. In P. Heriott (ed.), *Assessment and Selection in Organisations*, John Wiley, 455–68.

Ekvall, G. 1980: Industrial psychology in Sweden. In X. Zamek-Gliszezynska (ed.), *Work Psychology in Europe*, Warsaw: Polish Scientific Publishers.

Fletcher, C. 1982: Assessment centres. In D.M. Davey and M. Harris (eds), *Judging People*, McGraw-Hill, 42–54.

Gill, D. 1980: *Selecting Managers: how British industry recruits*. London: IPM, BIM.

Guest, D.E. 1989: Personnel and HRM: can you tell the difference? *Personnel Management*, January, 48–51.

Handy, C. 1989: *The Age of Unreason*. London: Business Books.

Harn, T.J. and Thornton, G.C. 1985: Recruiter counselling behaviours and application impressions. *Journal of Occupational Psychology*, 54, 165–73.

Heriott, P. 1989: Selection as a social process. In M. Smith and I.T. Robertson (eds), *Advances in Assessment and Selection*, New York: Wiley.

Hunter, J.E. and Hunter, R.F. 1984: Validity and utility of alternative predictors of job performance. *Psychological Bulletin*, 96, 72–98.

Jones, A. and Harrison, E. 1982: Prediction of performance in initial officer training using reference reports. *Journal of Occupational Psychology*, 55, 35–42.

Kanter, R.M. 1989: *When Giants Learn to Dance*. London: Simon & Schuster.

Lewis, C. 1984: What's new in selection. *Personnel Management*, London, January.

Livy, B. 1988: *Corporate Personnel Management*. Pitman.

Mosel, J.L. and Byham, W.C. 1977: *Applying the Assessment Centre Method*. Pergamon.

Muir, J. 1988: *Recruitment and Selection*. Management Services.

Peters, T. and Waterman, R. 1982: *In Search of Excellence*. New York: Harper & Row.

Plumbley, P.R. 1985: *Recruitment and Selection*. London: IPM.

Reilly, R.R. and Chao, G.T. 1982: Validity and fairness of some alternative employee selection procedures. *Personnel Psychology*, 33, 1–62.

Robertson, I.T. and Makin, P.J. 1986: Management selection in Britain: a survey and critique. *Journal of Occupational Psychology*, 59, 45–57.

Roe, R.A. and Greuter, M.J.M. 1989: Developments in personnel selection methodology. In R.K. Hambleton and J. Zaal (eds), *Advances in Testing*, Deventer: Kluwer.

Schneider, B. 1987: The people make the place. *Personnel Psychology*, 40, 437–53.

Sisson, K. (ed.) 1989: *Personnel Management in Britain*. Oxford: Blackwell.

Torrington, D. and Hall, L. 1987: *Personnel Management: a new approach*. London: Prentice-Hall.

Turnage, J.J. and Muchinsky, P.M. 1984: A comparison of the predictive validity of assessment centre evaluations versus traditional measures. *Journal of Applied Psychology*, 69.

10
Performance Appraisal

GORDON ANDERSON

Introduction

In recent years there has been considerable growth of interest in performance appraisal, and the great majority of organizations now operate some type of performance appraisal scheme. Long (1986), reporting the results of a major survey of performance appraisal practice in the UK, estimates that around 82 per cent of all organizations in the UK have a performance appraisal scheme. While traditionally performance appraisal was applied primarily to managers and supervisors, Long indicates that it is increasingly being extended to cover clerical and even manual workers. The Institute of Personnel Management (IPM) study also dispels the myth that performance appraisal is confined only to large organizations; 79 per cent of the companies with under 500 employees who participated in the survey indicated that they operated a system of performance appraisal.

In the USA, performance appraisal is commonly used in all sectors of industry and commerce. The Bureau of National Affairs (1983), analysing the results of a survey of 244 organizations, revealed that, in addition to the appraisal of managers, 91 per cent of appraisal schemes covered first line supervisors, 88 per cent professional and office employees, and 63 per cent skilled manual workers.

While, as discussed in the next section, important objectives can be set and achieved, many difficulties in implementing performance appraisal have been highlighted. Haimann and Scott (1974) have summarized the major difficulties as follows:

1 the difficulty of measuring the quality of performance of employees because each is an individual with different capacities;

2 the complicated problems of measurement brought about by the dynamic changes that take place within an individual as he or she grows in years and experience;

3 the problem of formulating standards for employee performance.

A number of writers, especially during the 1970s, expressed pessimistic views about the future of performance appraisal schemes, and the assumptions on which they are based. Some have tended to write off conventional versions of performance appraisal as backward, simplistic and even counter-productive, arguing that conventional appraisal processes often lead both the manager and employee to approach the performance review with dysfunctional role stereotypes. The employee expects to hear what is wrong with his or her performance, while the manager expects to have to sell the evaluation to a reluctant and possibly hostile member of staff.

Farnsworth (1974) asserts that the history of appraisal systems is one of confrontation and conflict, of poisoned relationships and frustrated hopes. Disagreements about performance, according to Farnsworth, are a major factor in employee turnover, and even when an employee does not leave he or she is frequently embittered by the experience. Levinson (1970) believes that performance appraisal, especially when results-oriented approaches are used, is inherently self-defeating in the long run because it is based on a reward–punishment psychology that serves to intensify pressure on the individual. As long ago as 1957, McGregor expressed the view that managers are often reluctant to carry out appraisals, and Levinson reinforces this opinion by stating that managers perceive their appraisal of others as a hostile, aggressive act which, unconsciously, is felt to be hurting or destroying the other person.

Some, though not necessarily all, of these criticisms have been overcome by the precise specification of appraisal objectives, and wide consultation in the design process, together with considerable attention to ensure that implementation is carefully planned. Lingering doubts about the concept remain in some quarters, despite more widespread usage.

Appraisal Objectives

Performance appraisal is increasingly viewed as central to good human resource management (HRM). This is highlighted in Cumming's classification of performance appraisal objectives. According to

Cummings and Schwab (1973), the objectives of performance appraisal schemes can be categorized as either evaluative or developmental. The evaluative purposes have a historical dimension and are concerned primarily with looking back at how employees have actually performed over a given time period, compared with required standards of performance. In this respect, performance appraisal carries out a useful auditing function for HRM in providing a mechanism for periodically reviewing the effectiveness of employee performance.

The developmental, or future-oriented purposes of performance appraisal, are concerned for example with the identification of employees' training and development needs, and the setting of new targets. There is evidence that performance appraisal schemes are more likely to be effective, credible and sustainable, when the developmental and evaluative functions are balanced, or where, if anything, the emphasis is more on the developmental aspects.

Brinkerhoff and Kanter (1980) identify a third, overarching purpose of performance appraisal, namely that it serves the useful function of encouraging managers to think carefully and objectively about the performance of their staff, and factors influencing it.

Performance appraisal has close links with other important areas of HRM – in particular with selection, motivation, succession planning and the training of employees.

Performance appraisal data provide relevant information required for validating selection methods, in assessing whether selection methods are bringing high performers into the organization. Performance appraisal is likely to lead to the identification of the training and development needs of employees. Indeed it can be argued that without an appraisal scheme, it would be only accidental that training and development efforts would be aimed in the right direction (Anderson 1980). Performance appraisal provides feedback to employees on job performance, and provides a basis for improvement and development. A key feature of any appraisal system, according to Cameron (1982), is to create a learning experience.

Performance appraisal is centrally linked to the motivation of employees, in that performance appraisal provides some of the essential components of effective motivational strategies, in particular, feedback that permits an employee to learn how well he or she is performing, goal or objective-setting that specifies what the person should be doing, team-building that allows the employee to participate with peers and their managers in solving problems that

Table 10.1 Main purposes of performance appraisal schemes (%)

	1977	*1985*
To assess training needs	96	97
To improve current performance	92	97
To review past performance	91	98
To assess future potential	87	71
To assist career planning decisions	81	75
To set performance objectives	57	81
To assess salary increases	39	40

Source: Long (1986)

impede their productivity, and monetary incentives that reward good performance (see Latham and Wexley 1981).

Long (1986), reporting survey data of the IPM, identifies the main purposes of performance appraisal in UK organizations (see table 10.1). These data highlight that organizations typically view their performance appraisal schemes as having a range of purposes, the most frequently mentioned being the assessment of training and development needs, the improvement of employees' current performance and the review of their past performance.

The major change indicated suggests that many more UK organizations are introducing or adapting performance appraisal schemes to focus on performance objectives. Two of the more controversial issues concern the fourth and seventh entries in table 10.1, the assessment of employees' future potential and the use of appraisal schemes to determine increases or new levels of salary.

A number of writers and researchers have argued that some of the purposes are conflicting. Randall et al. (1984), for example, have argued the need for the separation of the assessment of potential, rewards and performance, advocating three separate review meetings. Concern about conflicts of this nature extends back many years in the literature. Meyer et al. (1965) concluded that managers find it difficult to combine the roles of judge and counsellor.

The case for separating the consideration of employee potential from performance appraisal can be largely summarized as follows:

• Supervisors and managers who use appraisals may be unable to make more than a very subjective guess about the long-term potential of their staff.

- Adverse ratings and/or comment about potential could have damaging effects on employee morale and motivation, especially if the employee is currently performing well (though this issue could be resolved by keeping this part of the appraisal report confidential – see later comments in 'Openness').
- Some supervisors and managers may feel that they are being asked to 'play God' in assessing the future potential of their staff, and may feel disinclined to do so.
- Other mechanisms, e.g. assessment centres (ACs), can provide more comprehensive, objective assessments of employee potential.

Many organizations, however, as can be seen from table 10.1, still include the assessment of employee potential as an objective of their appraisal schemes, often on the grounds that the immediate manager's view, even if subjective, is a useful measure, and can be considered alongside the results of ACs.

Performance Appraisal and Pay

One of the key performance appraisal issues concerns linkages with pay and rewards. Although Long (1986) found that only 40 per cent of the UK organizations surveyed by the IPM used their appraisal schemes for determining pay increases or new salary levels, in the USA comparable survey data show that American organizations place much more emphasis on a direct relationship between performance appraisal and pay. In a study whose findings are not dissimilar to others, Eichel and Bender (1984) found that 90 per cent of the organizations surveyed cited pay and reward decisions as the main purpose of performance appraisal.

Research evidence, especially of Lawler (1981) and Prince and Lawler (1986), suggests that there are strong reasons for relating performance appraisal to pay decisions. Furthermore, recent organizational practice in many countries appears to be following the American pattern in this direction.

Summarizing the conclusions of Lawler, and Prince and Lawler, the positive advantages in linking performance appraisal and pay are:

- All parties, appraisers, appraisees and reviewers, take performance appraisal more seriously.
- Many individuals feel that, for reasons of fairness, there should be a close link between performance appraisal and pay.
- Organizations are likely to develop performance-oriented cultures, in

which high performers are seen to receive extra rewards, and lower performers receive lower rewards.

Their researches, however, also identify negative factors:

- When pay and performance appraisal are closely linked, the pay issue may overshadow all the other purposes of performance appraisal.
- There may well be a tendency for employees to withhold negative information about performance, leading to a less than frank appraisal discussion.
- Employees may try to influence appraisers, in seeking to set lower, more conservative goals.
- Employees may adapt their behaviour to target on receiving good ratings, rather than genuinely improve their overall performance.

None of the above problems are necessarily insurmountable but they do indicate clearly that, while there are definite advantages to be gained, the linkages with pay and reward decisions add extra pressures and stresses to any performance appraisal scheme.

Organizations must therefore be fully aware of the risks and issues involved before linking pay and reward decisions to performance appraisal. The advantages all presuppose that a valid performance appraisal system operates. If invalid data emerge from the appraisal system, the damaging effects in terms of loss of motivation and feelings of employee grievance could be substantial. Job design is another important factor. Pay-related performance appraisal is likely to be effective only in organizations where jobs are designed in such a way that allows individual performance to be measured. In situations characterized by high interaction among jobs in achieving results, group-related pay systems may be more appropriate.

Who Conducts Appraisals?

A question of great importance in any performance appraisal scheme concerns who should conduct performance appraisals. Not surprisingly, one of the questions of major interest to the average employee – possibly the most important for many – is quite simply 'Who will be my appraiser?' The answer to this question will impact on individual feelings about the likely fairness of the appraisal process. Managers, too, will have a keen interest in this question, in finding out for how many employees they will be expected to appraise. Answering the question of who should conduct appraisals often forces companies to clarify any ambiguities that may exist in the organization's structure.

There are number of options as to who should conduct appraisals, and these are discussed in the following sections.

The immediate manager

This is overwhelmingly the popular choice in the great majority of organizations. Long (1986) reports that among organizations located in the UK 98 per cent usually entrust the task of conducting appraisals to the person with direct line management responsibility for the employee being appraised.

The essential argument, long emphasized by American organizations, is that since performance appraisal is an integral part of the managerial role it should be undertaken by the person with immediate management accountability.

The manager's manager

A more traditional approach, formerly used by the British Civil Service, is for the manager's manager to carry out appraisals. This approach is still used by some organizations, with 20 per cent of organizations indicating some applications, according to Long, describing the IPM's UK study. The argument in favour of this approach is that it leads to more objective appraisal since the manager's manager should be better able to take a broader, impartial view of an employee's performance. The difficulties are that this approach tends to erode the position of the intermediate manager, and that the manager's manager may not have a detailed familiarity with the employee's work.

The more common modern approach is for the immediate manager to be the appraiser, with the manager's manager being the reviewer. The role of reviewer, if actively carried out, is extremely important in ensuring consistency of standards and valid performance appraisal data.

Self-appraisal

Self-appraisal by the individual is not usually a totally separate option, and can, for example, be readily combined with either of the first two examples. One of the major trends in recent years has been the inclusion of self-assessment into the performance appraisal schemes of many organizations. Typically this leads to the development of an extra stage in the appraisal process, with the employee initiating the appraisal through the completion of a self-assessment document, which is then conveyed to the appraiser. The appraiser is then in a responding situation, commenting on the views of the appraisee, as well as providing independent input.

A number of choices must be made by an organization when utilizing self-appraisal. For example, if the employee's self-assessment is submitted in advance to the appraiser, it becomes one of the inputs into the appraiser's preparation and into the initial formulation of an appraisal report. Alternatively, the appraisee may exchange his or her self-appraisal with the appraiser's draft report at, or just before, the appraisal interview.

Although this latter approach avoids the possibility of a contamination effect, in that the employee's self-assessment cannot have any distortion or undesirable influence on the appraiser's evaluation, it can lead to a more difficult and unpredictable situation for the appraiser to handle. Most organizations seem to prefer the first to the two options described, giving appraisers the opportunity to study, and consider carefully, the self-evaluations made by employees in advance of appraisal interviews.

Multi-appraisal

The limitations of conventional performance appraisal in placing considerable, and sometimes total, emphasis on the judgement of the employee's manager, have been identified and discussed by a number of writers on the subject. A pioneering study carried out a number of years ago in Gulf Oil, and described by Stinson and Stokes (1980), highlights an alternative, multi-rater method which overcomes a number of the deficiencies of conventional, manager-oriented appraisal. Gulf Oil based its multi-rater appraisal scheme on the concept of the job network, i.e. on those individuals, at more senior or more junior levels, or at the same level in the organization (but excluding the immediate manager in the line reporting relationship) on whom the performance of the employee being appraised has principal impact.

In the Gulf Oil scheme, which was confined to senior managers, those being appraised were invited to nominate between five and eight persons in their job network. These individuals were then asked to complete a rating form, evaluating the manager being appraised using a number of dimensions of managerial behaviour. A collated summary of their ratings was prepared by the human resource department, and passed to both the employee and his or her immediate manager. Anonymity was considered important, in encouraging candid and honest ratings, so nothing on the summary feedback sheet could be traced back to any individual. Those being appraised were then asked to complete a self-evaluation, which was also passed to the immediate manager. The immediate manager, equipped with both the summary feedback from the members of the job network, and the employee's self-evaluation, then prepared the company's official appraisal document and conducted an appraisal interview.

Although clearly a resource-intensive approach to administer, it led to very specific, constructive feedback emerging from the members of the job network and helped to distinguish between organizational and individual factors which affect performance.

Peer appraisal

Several studies (see e.g. Latham and Wexley 1981) have come to positive conclusions about the value of peer appraisal, which has for long been used by a number of professional organizations, for example university teachers. Difficulties with this method can lie in the reluctance of individuals to appraise peers. In addition, peer appraisal is likely to be effective only if the nature of the organization is such that peers work closely together and are well acquainted with one another's work.

Subordinate appraisal

Those who work for a supervisor or manager have a unique perspective of that person, and of some aspects of that person's work performance and contribution to the organization. Some organizations are therefore showing an interest in subordinate assessments as part of the appraisal process.

Who should be Appraised?

An important and fundamental question concerns which employees in an organization should be covered by performance appraisal.

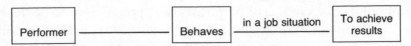

Figure 10.1 Components of performance
(*Source*: Mohrman et al. 1989)

Increasingly, the answer seems to be 'everyone', and Long (1986) indicates that while past practice has been to confine performance appraisal to managers and supervisors, there is evidence that most organizations are extending their schemes to include not only secretarial and clerical but also, in some cases, manual workers. Interestingly, Long also reports evidence of extension of coverage in the upper echelons of organizations, to include directors.

Appraisal Methods

A wide range of methods and criteria for appraising performance is used by organizations. The various ways of measuring performance stem directly from the different components of performance (see figure 10.1).

In many early performance appraisal schemes (and still to be found in some) the emphasis was placed on the left-hand side of figure 10.1, the performer, in using personality traits (e.g. judgement, reliability, initiative) as the basis for assessment. Dissatisfaction with this approach has grown over the years, because of difficulties in arriving at common definitions of personality traits and avoiding very subjective judgements.

There has been a shift towards the right of figure 10.1, with an increasing number of organizations reviewing performance against pre-set objectives. This trend has emerged from the philosophy of 'management by objectives' popularized by writers such as Drucker (1954). Objectives as far as possible should be specific and measurable, and should be challenging to employees, though achievable. The effectiveness of objective-setting or results-oriented appraisal depends to a substantial extent on employee participation in the goal-setting process, since shared goal-setting generally leads to higher feelings of employee commitment to achieve goals that have been jointly agreed.

As it becomes more common practice to extend performance appraisal to all organizational levels, there is increased recognition that a number of variants of performance appraisal need to be developed. For instance, objective-setting approaches, defining results to be achieved, are often considered to be more appropriate for managerial than for non-managerial employees.

At non-managerial levels, mechanisms focusing on the central part of figure 10.1, the assessment of behaviour, may be more appropriate. The appraisal of job behaviours or competencies implies that these characteristics should be derived from detailed job analysis, to determine the most important dimensions for appraisal purposes.

Examples of behaviours or competencies used for assessment could include, for example, communications skills, counselling skills, analystical ability, willingness to introduce and accept change.

One behaviourial approach, popular in the USA, is called BARS (behaviourially anchored rating scales). This method is an improvement over simple rating scales, in that it provides a set of behavioural descriptions at each point on a rating scale. For example, if a scale measures performance quality, then a set of statements is used describing the behaviour associated with the worst quality at one extreme, and the best quality at the other, with intermediate statements in between.

Openness in the appraisal process

There has been clear evidence of a trend in recent years towards greater openness in the appraisal process, with the appraisal report and its contents being freely shown to the employee being appraised.

The trend towards openness has been encouraged by a number of factors, the three principal ones being identified as:

1 the increased use of results-orientated methods of appraisal stemming from management-by-objectives philosophy;
2 the changing social climate, emphasizing participation and feedback as a basis for development;
3 the growing influence of white-collar unions, stressing the need for mutual trust.

It would be difficult for an organization to operate a results-orientated performance appraisal system without openness, since this type of approach requires the superior and subordinate to identify and set goals that are seen by both parties as being realistic for the subordinate; these agreed goals, where possible translated into measurable objectives, become the basis for the subsequent assessment of

Table 10.2 Openness of appraisal reports

	% of organizations	
	1977	*1986*
All parts of appraisal reports disclosed	39	64
Some parts not disclosed	35	28
Reports not disclosed	26	8
	100	100
Base	236	250

Source: Long (1986)

the subordinate's performance. Traditional, trait-oriented schemes, by contrast, were often closed to employees.

Table 10.2 shows the changes in this aspect of performance appraisal practice that took place between 1977 and 1986. It highlights that only 8 per cent of organizations in the 1986 survey operated closed appraisal systems in which the individual was not allowed to see the completed performance appraisal report, compared with 26 per cent in 1977.

This evidence indicates that an increasing number of organizations recognize the desirability of open communications between appraiser and appraisee in the performance appraisal process. This recognition of the value of openness applies mainly, however, to those aspects that deal with current performance. The undisclosed parts relate mainly, as previously mentioned, to the evaluation of employees' future potential.

The legal dimension also has to be considered, and this will vary from country to country. In the UK, for example, the Data Protection Act of 1984 gives individual employees the legal right of access to personal data, such as information about them contained in appraisal documents, if it is held on computer. Personnel data, as defined by the Act, cover both factual and evaluative information, implying that employees could have access to opinions about them expressed in appraisal documents.

Any indication of intentions such as intention to promote, is outside the scope of the Act. This law does not apply to appraisal documents held in manual systems.

Formal and Informal Appraisal

An area that has often been neglected in the literature about performance appraisal has been consideration of the links between formal appraisal, i.e. the processes of the organization's performance appraisal system, and informal appraisal which should be part of the day-to-day management. And yet there is evidence from a variety of sources (see e.g. Fletcher and Williams 1985) to suggest that this is a vital linkage for appraisal to be effective, and for the organization's official scheme to yield maximum benefits.

One point that has often been stressed by researchers and practitioners is that there should be no surprises at the time of the formal appraisal – when the appraisal interview is held and the appraisal documentation is completed. This implies that those who are appraisers must display a range of skills in their day-to-day management of employees. At least four sets of managerial skills which interact with one another can be identified, to ensure informal appraisal takes place throughout the year, and to provide a sound foundation for the formal appraisal process. These managerial skills are discussed in the following sections.

Diagnostic skills

The ability and interest to investigate reasons for specific items of good and bad performance, and changes of trend in performance. This implies a range of skills in focusing on the individual and exploring a number of factors through observation, talking with other managers and users of the employee's services, that explain performance and changes in performance.

Skills in giving, and receiving, feedback

Any appraiser requires the ability to give employees feedback on specific work items, for example in giving praise and recognition for a task successfully completed and constructive criticism on failure to achieve specific tasks, activities or targets. Thus the formal appraisal should be analogous to a stocktaking or auditing situation, dealing with the overall performance of the individual.

Counselling skills

Although there is likely to be a counselling element in appraisal interviews, in discussing career progression and possibly personal problems with appraisees, appraisers should display a willingness and interest, as well as appropriate skills, in conducting counselling sessions with appraisees, whenever the need arises. Willingness to recognize and deal with personal issues that may be affecting employee's performance as and when they occur is more likely to create a situation where the focus can be on performance issues at appraisal interviews.

Coaching skills

An appraiser's coaching skills are important in ensuring adequate follow-up after formal appraisals. This is particularly the case where objective-setting or target-setting methods of formal appraisal are used. Coaching skills are required to support employees, on an ongoing basis, as they attempt to achieve the targets or objectives agreed in their formal appraisal sessions. These coaching skills involve a number of techniques – e.g. holding informal mid-term reviews, assisting employees to develop self-evaluation mechanisms, and providing on-the-job training. Another aspect of coaching – possibly even more important – is attitudinal, in investing time and effort in coaching employees and taking a continuing interest in their progress and achievements.

The Appraisal Interview

The appraisal interview is seen by most organizations as the key feature which will determine the success or failure of the performance appraisal scheme. Most appraisal schemes include provision for the holding of appraisal interviews which provide an opportunity for managers to inform employees about their performance and to develop plans for the future.

The appraisal interview is one of the most difficult forms of interview which a manager is asked to undertake because:

- The interview can be extremely unpredictable, especially over matters relating to areas of deficient performance and the weaknesses of the individual.

- The manager must display a wide range of interpersonal skills in conducting effective appraisal interviews.
- Appraisal interview skills cannot be readily learned from watching other managers in action. Because of the confidential nature of the appraisal interview, it is unlikely that a manager will witness anyone else in the role of the interviewer except his or her own superior relationships.

Objectives of the appraisal interview

The appraisal interview can serve a number of objectives. They should relate to the overall objectives which the organization expects its performance appraisal scheme as a whole to achieve and are likely to include:

- letting the employee know where he or she stands;
- providing an opportunity for a discussion about the employee's job performance over the period under review;
- agreeing action to improve the performance of the employee, including the setting of objectives.

Characteristics of effective appraisal interviews

An examination of the literature suggests that attention has largely focused on the following characteristics of the appraisal interview.

Employee participation
Studies, for example by Wexley (1986), show that the more the employee participates in the appraisal interview, the greater the feelings of satisfaction on the part of the employee towards the interview and the interviewer.

Interviewer support
In general, the more supportive the interviewer, in terms of, for example, showing an appreciation of the employee's point of view, and adopting a constructive approach to problems, the greater the chance that the employee will accept the results of the appraisal and make changes based on feedback.

Identifying and solving problems affecting the employee's job performance
The greater the extent to which emphasis is placed on identifying and solving problems affecting job performance, the greater the likelihood that the employee's behaviour and performance will

change in a positive way, compared with situations where appraisers impose solutions. This coincides with Maier's (1976) famous classification of appraisal interviewing styles, in which he advocates problem-solving styles, as opposed to 'tell and sell' and 'tell and listen' approaches.

Emphasizing performance rather than personality
Following on from the above, where there is a greater emphasis on job performance rather than on the personality of the employee, more satisfaction with the interview is likely to be generated.

Goal-setting
The setting of specific goals which the employee will seek to attain has been shown to have a more powerful effect on subsequent performance than a general discussion about goals.

Limited criticism
Effective appraisal interviews contain a minimum of criticism. Mohrman et al. (1989), on the grounds that criticism builds up defence mechanisms, advocates a 'four-to-one' principle – four positive comments for every piece of criticism!

Proportion of time spoken by the employee
The greater the opportunity the employee has to speak, the more likely that he or she will feel satisfied with the appraisal interview. This measure may be an indicator of the level of employee influence on the appraisal process. Anderson and Watt (1988) discovered, however, that appraisers and employees may have very different recollections of the proportion of time spoken by each party in appraisal interviews.

Interview processes and outcomes

Anderson and Barnett (1987), studying appraisal interviews and other aspects of the appraisal process for 317 nursing staff, concluded that while on the whole, positive findings towards appraisal interviews were reported, on the basis of the dimensions described above, results were much more mixed, and generally poorer, in terms of employee's recognition of the importance of making changes, and translating the results of the appraisal interview discussions into improved job performance. This suggests that organizations have to face a two-stage challenge – developing, firstly, sound interview processes, and then, secondly, generating linkages between the interview processes and subsequent outcomes, especially in terms of improvements in job performance.

Problems of Performance Appraisal

Although many organizations have devoted a great deal of time, effort and resources to the setting up of performance appraisal schemes, the results have often been disappointing. While there has been considerable progress in improving the instruments of perform-ance appraisal systems, especially by shifting from the more sub-jective, often simplistic methods to more sophisticated, objectively based approaches, the implementation of performance appraisal still tends to be resisted, if not avoided, by many managers.

One difficulty is the face-to-face situation of the appraisal inter-view, where the appraiser sits down with the appraisee and reviews his or her performance. When situations are full of positive com-ments appraisal is easy. When performance and potential are good, when superior and subordinate have an open relationship, when promotions or salary increases are abundant, when there is plenty of time for preparation and discussion – in short, whenever it is a pleasure – performance appraisal is easy to do.

Most of the time, however, and particularly when it is most needed and most difficult to do, when deficiencies in performance are being addressed, performance appraisal refuses to run properly. Beer (1981) suggests three main sources of difficulty:

1 the quality of the relationship between appraiser and appraisee;
2 the manner and skill with which the interview is conducted;
3 the appraisal system itself, namely the objectives the organization expects it to achieve, the methodology, the documents and procedures that make up the system.

The underlying quality of the superior–subordinate relationship has a major impact, since the appraisal process is part of a broader set of interactions between the appraiser and appraisee. Unless there is good mutual trust and understanding, the appraisee is likely to view appraisal discussions with apprehension and suspicion. The appraiser, in turn, is likely to view appraisal time as a daunting experience where employee hostility and resistance are likely to emerge.

If regular informal appraisal takes place as previously advocated, the problems of hoarding up points to deal with at appraisal interview and of springing surprises on employees should be avoided.

The appraisal interview is a most difficult type of interview for any manager to undertake, as previously noted. Managers often experience feelings of unease at the prospect of entering a situation with staff in which a more candid and personal set of exchanges are likely to take place than probably at any other time. In addition, the manager may be exposing himself or herself to criticism. If the interview is not well handled, the downside risks are considerable, in terms of potential damage that can be done to self-image, motivation and working relationships.

Other problems may relate to the way the design process and implementation of performance appraisal have been handled in the organization.

Designing and Implementing Appraisal Schemes

Many options are open to an organization in designing and implementing an appraisal scheme. Decisions must be made on a range of important issues, some of which have already been discussed. The following is a summary of major questions which an organization must address in designing or redesigning its system of performance appraisal:

- What categories of employees should be covered by performance appraisal?
- Should any employees be excluded because of organizational status (e.g. through membership of the lowest or highest echelons in the organization structure) or on the grounds of age (e.g. closeness to retirement age)?
- What criteria should be used to evaluate an employee's contribution to the organization?
- What kind of documentation should be used?
- Who should be the appraisers? Should it be the employee's immediate superior, or someone at a more senior level in the organizational hierarchy?
- Should employees be given an opportunity to make an input to their own appraisal, e.g. through a self-assessment document or through the inclusion of employee comments in the official appraisal documentation.
- Should the individual's potential, as well as current performance, be evaluated?

- Should the contents of performance appraisal reports be freely divulged to employees?
- What review and appeals mechanisms need to be established?

Finally, and of paramount importance, what purposes should performance appraisal serve, and what use should be made of the data generated through appraisal documentation?

The list illustrates the many choices and decisions that must be made, not surprisingly giving rise to substantial variations in practice.

Many organizations experience difficulty in grappling with the problems of deciding what kind of performance appraisal system to adopt, or how to improve an ineffective system.

Because performance appraisal is, or should be, a central part of the management process, it is of vital importance that all managers in the organization, and indeed, it could be argued all employees, should have feelings of ownership over the performance appraisal scheme, and should recognize that their whole-hearted involvement is central to its success. One of the key conditions for successful performance appraisal, design and implementation is consultation. Consultation at the design stage with groups – including directors, senior and middle managers, supervisors, employees, trade unions – should not only help to alleviate anxieties and generate interest and commitment but also stimulate innovative ideas about appraisal methods and implementation procedures which help to ensure that the scheme is effectively tailored to the organization's requirements.

Top management support

The commitment of top management is crucially important, especially as many of the benefits of performance appraisal relate to the medium and long term. The support and interest of top management will encourage managers at other levels to devote care and attention to the implementation of performance appraisal, especially if it is made clear to managers that how objectively and how effectively they appraise their staff will impact on their own appraisals.

Training appraisers

The training of managers and supervisors in appraisal methodology and in the skills of appraisal interviewing is essential for effective appraisal. As Mohrman et al. (1989) point out, performance appraisal is not something that most individuals are genetically or culturally programmed to do well. In fact some cultural norms work counter to good appraisals.

As performance appraisal systems become more participative, it becomes just as important to train and brief appraisees. This is particularly true in the case of the increasing number of appraisal systems which, as previously noted, involve self-appraisal. Our educational institutions, Fletcher (1984) stresses, do not normally equip people with the skills of self-assessment. Assessment is something that is handed down from above by others throughout the educational system. Thus it is also important to educate and train employees in the skills of self-assessment.

Summary and Conclusions

It is important to stress that there is no such thing as the universal performance appraisal system. What works well in one organization may work badly in another. Appraisal systems must be designed to suit the culture and requirements of an organization. Increasingly, however, the relationship between appraisal and culture is two-way, with organizations expecting their appraisal schemes to contribute to a change in corporate culture that is seen as relevant to the achievement of corporate objectives.

Appraisal systems do not operate in isolation; they generate data that can contribute to other HRM systems – for example to succession planning and manpower planning.

Despite the desirable objectives that a well-run appraisal scheme can achieve, many problems can readily emerge that can impede their achievements. In addition, it must be recognized that there are risks attached to any system of performance appraisal that is introduced. The benefits apply to the employee being appraised, in terms of feedback on performance, strengths and weaknesses, an opportunity to clarify training and development needs, and clarification of what is expected in the future; and to appraisers, in providing both a better understanding of the employee perspective on a range of issues as well as a mechanism to monitor and evaluate performance, providing a basis for actions that will improve employee effectiveness and contribute to corporate performance.

The costs and downside risks are numerous and include negative, defensive employee attitudes towards criticism, a failure by both parties to face up to difficult issues generating bland appraisals that bear little relationship to actual work performance and, most serious of all, an attitude problem which leads to appraisals being seen as an unpleasant chore, to be gone through as fast as possible, with minimal effort and input.

Such problems must be kept in context; increasingly organizations, recognizing the expensiveness of the time and resource commitment to performance appraisal, are taking steps both to train appraisers and brief appraisees, and generally to monitor more effectively their appraisal systems, so that problems can be quickly identified with corrective action introduced.

References

Anderson, G.C. 1980: *Performance Appraisal in Theory and Practice.* Working Paper 8002, Strathclyde Business School, University of Strathclyde, Glasgow.

Anderson, G.C. and Barnett, J.G. 1987: The characteristics of effective appraisal interviews. *Personnel Review*, 16(4), 18–25.

Anderson, G.C. and Watt, E. 1988: A new context for performance appraisal. *Health Care management*, 3(1), 27–32.

Beer, M. 1981: Performance appraisal: dilemmas and possibilities. *Organisational Dynamics*, Winter, 24–36.

Brinkerhoff, D.W. and Kanter, R.M. 1980: Appraising the performance of performance appraisal. *Sloan Management Review*, 21, 3–16.

Bureau of National Affairs 1983: *Performance Appraisal Programmes.* Personnel Policies Forum Survey 135. Washington DC: The Bureau.

Cameron, D. 1982: Performance appraisal and review. In A.M. Bowey (ed.), *Handbook of Wage and Salary Systems*, London: Gower, 197–233.

Cummings, L.L. and Schwab, D. 1973: *Performance in Organisations: determinants and appraisals.* Glenview, Ill.: Scott, Foresman.

Drucker, P. 1954: *The Practice of Management.* London: Harper & Row.

Eichel, E. and Bender, H.E. 1984: *Performance Appraisal: a study of current techniques.* New York: American Management Association.

Farnsworth, T. 1974: Appraising the appraisals. *Management Today*, November, 103–12.

Fletcher, C. 1984: *What's new in performance appraisal. Personnel Management*, February, 20–2.

Fletcher, C. and Williams, R. 1985: *Performance Appraisal and Career Development.* London: Hutchinson.

Haimann, T. and Scott W.G. 1974: *Management in the Modern Organisation.* Boston: Houghton Mifflin.

Latham, G.P. and Wexley, K.N. 1981: *Increasing Productivity through Performance Appraisal.* Reading, Mass.: Addison-Wesley.

Lawler, E.E. 1981: *Pay and Organisational Development.* Reading, Mass.: Addison-Wesley.

Levinson, H. 1970: Management by whose objectives? *Harvard Business Review*, 48(4), 134.

Long, P. 1986: *Performance Appraisal Revisited.* London: IPM.

McGregor, D. 1957: An uneasy look at performance appraisal. *Harvard Business Review*, 35(3), 89–94.

Maier, N.R.F. 1976: *The Appraisal Interview.* New York: University Associates.

Meyer, H.H., Kay, E. and French, J.P.R. 1965: Split roles in performance appraisal. *Harvard Business Review*, 43, 123–9.

Mohrman, A.M., Resnick-West, S.M. and Lawler, E.E. 1989: *Designing Performance Appraisal Systems.* San Francisco: Jossey-Bass.

Prince, J.B. and Lawler, E.E. 1986: Does salary discussion hurt the developmental performance appraisal? *Organisational Behaviour and Human Decision Processes*, 37, 357–75.

Randall, G., Packard, P. and Slater, J. 1984: *Staff Appraisal: a first step to effective leadership*, 3rd edn. London: IPM.

Stinson, J. and Stokes J. 1980: How to multi-appraise. *Management Today*, June, 43–53.

Wexley, K.N. 1986: Appraisal interview. In R. Berk (ed.), *Performance Assessment: methods and applications*, Baltimore: Johns Hopkins Press.

11
Commitment and Involvement

HARVIE RAMSAY

There can be no question that the 1980s saw a shift in the flavour and substance of discussions of employee participation in the workplace. A number of aspects of this shift may be identified:

- A change in political climate, which led to a de-emphasizing of 'hard' or power-centred forms of participation (such as information disclosure, works councils, extended bargaining rights, or worker directors); and towards 'softer' – in power terms at least – and more managerial techniques for engendering employee commitment (such as profit-sharing and employee share ownership, communications and briefing systems, or quality circles (QCs)).
- A similar and related change in the industrial climate, diverting union attention from demands for industrial democracy rights to survival and defence of employment, often requiring them to accept more market-oriented and co-operative views of relations with management.
- A more confident management approach to initiatives in employee relations, including the emphasis of managerial objectives for 'employee involvement' rather than damage-limitation offers of 'participation' concessions. In line with government views, the approach shifted to the introduction of techniques aiming to achieve managerial objectives such as employee commitment and motivation.
- Growing emphasis on strategic approaches to business matters, this extending progressively to the area of human resource management (HRM), and so to the role of employee involvement within this.

It should be remembered that the 1990s already promise a somewhat different flavour again – not a return to the 1970s, perhaps, but certainly with a greater emphasis in political circles especially thus far on employee rights and so industrial democracy (ID) rather than employee involvement (EI) approaches to participation. The main engine of this to date is the Social Charter proposed by the European

Commission and agreed in outline by the member states (except the UK) in December 1989. We will consider the implications of these developments at the end of this chapter.

The Importance of Involvement

As figures quoted throughout the discussion of various forms of EI in this chapter will make clear, it is a widespread and prominent management practice in the UK. The evidence suggests an increasing incidence and variety of schemes over the course of the 1980s. Thus while the Workplace Industrial Relations Survey of 1980 (WIRS1 – see Daniel and Millward 1983) found 24 per cent of managements reporting recent initiatives in EI, the 1984 survey (WIRS2 – see Millward and Stevens 1986) reports that 35 per cent made a similar claim by that time. A CBI survey at the very end of the decade (CBI 1990), though not strictly comparable with WIRS, records levels of incidence that imply a continuation of innovation over the decade, as does the monitoring of company reports by the Department of Employment (1987, 1988).

It has been suggested that this has a number of sources, varying in importance according to sector and organization, but including labour market pressures, the imperative to improve cost competitiveness, the need to gain co-operation with the introduction of new technology, and the need for enhanced competitiveness through flexibility and quality standards. Each of these is said to require that management pay greater attention to winning the acquiescence or even active support of some or all employees; and EI is seen as an important means to this end.

The most popular forms of participation have included some which are often more engaged with union organization than management might prefer in an ideal world (though some companies take a more positive view of union involvement than others). These include health and safety committees, pension fund trusteeships and consultative committees. Only the last of these receive detailed attention in this chapter.

The areas of most active innovation in the 1980s have undoubtedly been ones where union involvement is low, however. The most popular experiments here have included team briefings, QCs and latterly total quality management (TQM) programmes, and various forms of financial participation. All of these are analysed in the following pages. In the government's most recent publication on the subject, *People and Involvement* (Dept of Employment 1989), it is no coincidence that these types of schemes are dominant among those exemplified in the 25 case studies provided. In contrast, trade unions are mentioned in only four of the reports (though they are in fact involved quite actively to the author's knowledge in a number of the other companies cited).

The importance of EI is stressed in a number of studies of management attitudes in recent years. In a 1985 CBI survey, it was rated second only to management skill and commitment to industrial relations as a source of improvement in employee relations, well ahead of legislation or government approach, for instance (MacInnes 1987). Similar findings were reported by Edwards (1987), who also found that some form of involvement or communication was seen as the key feature of personnel policy in 46 per cent of establishments he surveyed. This last figure is echoed in turn in Batstone's survey (1984), where he reports that 47 per cent of personnel managers regard involvement as the major factor in changing employee relations policy over the previous four years.

The topic of EI, therefore, is one that has preoccupied management a good deal in the 1980s or earlier. The next question concerns what they hope to achieve from it, followed by a consideration of whether they are likely to realize their aspirations.

The Objectives of Involvement

Firstly let us consider the main aims which management might entertain for EI, where they are able to exert control over the type and content of schemes which see the light of organizational day. Table 11.1 provides a list, by no means exhaustive, of the kinds of goals which may be sought through EI policies. This catalogue of possible objectives highlights a number of things, including:

- the complexity and range of the subject;
- the need for careful definition of objectives. Vague and general terms like 'improved attitudes' or 'greater incentive' are inadequate for effective targeting and, subsequently, monitoring;
- the potential for objectives to conflict, or at least have a certain strain between them.

To exemplify this last point, a general sense of unity and belonging may sit poorly with the need to sharpen individual competition and incentive, and it may be advisable to use distinct kinds of scheme to

Table 11.1 Possible management objectives for employee involvement

Attitudes	Improve morale
	Increase loyalty and commitment
	Enhance sense of belonging/involvement
	Increase support for management
Business awareness	Better, more accurately informed: stops rumour/'grapevine'
	Greater interest
	Improve knowledge and understanding of the reasons for management actions
	Support for/reduced resistance to management action
Incentive/ motivation	*Passive*:
	Accept changing work practices
	Accept mobility across jobs
	Accept new technology
	Accept supervisor/management authority
	Active:
	Improve quality/reliability
	Increase productivity/effort
	Reduce costs
	Identify and solve problems
	Enhance co-operation and team spirit
	Personal:
	Greater job interest
	Greater job satisfaction
	Employee development
Employee influence/ ownership	Increase job control
	Increase employee suggestions for improvements and their implementation
	Increase employee influence on personnel/social/business matters
	Create/increase employee ownership in the company
	Increase employee ties to company performance and profitability

achieve each if both require enhancement. Alternatively, aims may have to be prioritized (e.g. between the incentive-oriented but elitist and possibly divisive executive share option scheme, and the more diffuse but integrative all-employee schemes).

Most research on managerial objectives suggests that what may seem less substantial aims at general attitude change are widely sought rather than more concrete-seeming ones such as direct

Table 11.1 Cont.

Trade unions	*Anti-union*:
	Win hearts and minds of employees from union influence
	Fulfil rewards and benefits needs outside union channel
	Fulfil representative needs outside union channel
	Restrict scope of union dealings and influence
	Keep union out of company
	With union:
	Get union co-operation
	Draw on union advice
	Restrain union demands
	'Microcorporatism': win over local union representatives (shop stewards, etc.) to management views, detach from national union (where separate)

Source: Extract from Strathclyde University Open Learning MBA Module in Management of Human Resources, Unit 8: Employee Involvement, prepared by the author. Permission to reproduce this table is gratefully acknowledged.

incentive or motivational effects. To some extent this reflects a poor definition of goals in many companies – a point taken up at the end of this chapter in looking at 'strategic' approaches to the subject, and sometimes also reflected in a 'catch-all' listing of what schemes are meant to achieve. It may also be a realistic assessment of most types of schemes, however, in that they may be thought unlikely to have a direct and strong enough impact to create a more dramatic effect. Clearly, though, the kinds of objectives stressed, and the extent to which they might be thought effective in more demonstrable and measurable ways, will vary with the type of scheme under consideration. We therefore need first to identify the main types of scheme.

Types of Schemes

It is possible to construct a detailed typology of involvement and participation schemes, in which managerial approaches such as those concentrated on in this chapter are shadowed by labour-oriented ('industrial democracy') initiatives and controls. For our present purposes, though, a few simple parameters will suffice.

Firstly, it is useful to identify the level at which involvement takes place. A focus on the individual or task level includes initiatives like job enrichment, job enlargement and other work reforms. The work group or department may also experience collective work rearrangements, through some form of group autonomy including that proposed in Japanese-inspired teamworking systems; or the group activity may be more a matter of communication and discussion, as in QCs or briefing sessions. Higher levels of involvement than this typically entail the election of representatives rather than direct participation for everyone, obvious examples being forms of consultative committee or works council. It is also possible that this representation will be installed at the apex of the organization, through the appointment of employee directors; but in orthodox, private-sector British companies this is almost unheard of (a study carried out in the late 1970s uncovered just seven such schemes – see Towers et al. 1987).

The concept of levels is not particularly helpful in distinguishing some types of scheme, however. Communications schemes may be designed to cascade through all levels, for instance (as in team briefings), or to cover all at once (through company magazines or newsletters perhaps). Financial participation, too, can be a pervasive all-employee arrangement, or a group-targeted value-added scheme, or a selective (usually executive) provision for share options. These are schemes which do not allow for decision-making or active involvement by employees, but instead typically entail a passive receipt of information or a profit share (though this may be hoped to provoke some positive, motivational response), and so are not located in the same identifiable way at one level.

This makes it apparent that the subject of involvement must be identified. The employee may be offered what amounts to a feeling-state, a sense of belonging; or information about the organization and its environment may be provided; or some financial reward made; or some share in decisions facilitated. In the last case, the topic of involvement must be further specified. It is helpful to distinguish the general themes of work organization, including such matters as task controls, the implementation of technical change, or labour utilization patterns in the workshop or office; personnel issues, dealing with pay, conditions, staffing levels and employee disciplinary and control questions and the like; social matters, such as welfare policy and company facilities; and business matters, which include more policy-oriented decisions on technology, work system or, most ambitiously, marketing, investment and employment strategies.

Set alongside the list of management objectives provided earlier, these distinctions will allow us to classify a variety of types of involvement scheme. In this chapter, separate sections will focus on four broad types of scheme, assessing each in turn:

1 task and work group involvement;
2 communications and briefing systems;
3 consultative arrangements;
4 financial participation.

The aim throughout will be to summarize the major developments, and to assess the available evidence on the impact of schemes. The position adopted here is that there is at least as much to be learned from problems as from glistening success stories, so the common practice of providing simplistic recipes or uncritical plaudits for involvement will not be adopted. The chapter will close with a resume of the main practical findings, and some observations on future developments, including the emergence of strategic approaches to HRM and EI.

Task and Work Group Involvement

Innovations at individual task and at work group levels have a long history in the management tradition, largely deriving from the human relations experiments of the 1920s onwards. After the Second World War, the emphasis shifted increasingly from simple leadership style and the need of the individual to belong, to the need for employees to face challenges and have the opportunity to use and develop their abilities.

In the 1960s, individualistic policies pushed for job enlargement and, most ambitiously, job enrichment (the introduction of elements of responsibility into the work task). The pace in group innovations was made chiefly in Scandinavia from the late 1960s onwards, where the idea of the semi-autonomous work group was elaborated, the most publicized examples being in Volvo and Saab. In fact the pioneering developments here had their origins in the work of the UK-based Tavistock Institute of Human Relations from the 1950s. By the mid-1970s, innovations were being promoted, often with the encouragement of governments (e.g. the Work Research

Unit of the Department of Employment, attached to ACAS since the mid-1980s), in most European countries and also in the USA. Labour militancy and difficult labour market conditions promoted a 'quality of working life', an ID as much as EI-oriented tone to these innovations.

The Japanese tradition of work group activity was somewhat different, also taking off in the early 1960s (and also initially as a response in part to tight labour market conditions) but concentrating on the concept of quality, an approach which was to attract the enthusiastic attention of companies in the West from the late 1970s onwards.

Job redesign developments

In the 1980s, with the receding pressure from below and the easing of labour markets, management attention shifted to the need to compete in a changing and difficult product market environment. Attention to the success of Japan, as noted above, diverted attention from 'de-alienating' the worker, and towards finding some means to improve their performance, above all in terms of quality and flexibility. Enhancement of work experience and of skill was often claimed as a by-product of this, or even as a means to achieve it in some cases, but job reform *per se* ceased to be the main impetus of change.

None the less quite extensive claims were made that reductions in demarcation and extended task flexibility were under way in the 1980s. One study found that 9 in 10 companies were attempting such changes in 1985 (NEDO 1986), while an ACAS study two years later found a quarter of companies claimed some success (ACAS 1988). However, other observers have commented that the evidence of major changes in work content, or of significant enskilling in work patterns for a large part of the UK workforce, is at best weak (Pollert 1988; Marginson 1989). The popularity of 'just-in-time' and other methods for ensuring that work is more continuous for many employees, together with other evidence on labour utilization in the 1980s, suggests that intensification of work may be more common than a genuine break with Taylorism (Elger 1990).

Explicit attempts to reform work in a progressive or humanistic way appear to have been rare in the 1980s. None are included in the examples of EI in *People and Companies* (Dept of Employment 1989), and in a 1985 survey only 3 per cent of companies reported undertaking 'job enlargement/enrichment schemes' (Baddon et al. 1989). Batstone, too, was moved to comment on the absence of individual work reorganization from the initiatives on EI reported by management in recent years (1989:107–8). This may well reflect the relative lack of success and durability of some of the more prominent job enrichment experiments of the 1970s, and the decision to emulate Japanese practice and focus more on the work group or team.

Quality circles

The idea of QCs is commonly attributed to the Japanese, but closer attention to history reveals that the Japanese innovation was an adaptation of ideas on quality management originating from the visits of two American consultants in the late 1940s and early 1950s. The first QCs in Japan appeared in 1962, but by the late 1980s optimistic estimates suggested there were 1 million QCs there, with all told about 10 million participants.

In the UK, the late 1970s and early 1980s saw an explosion of management interest in QCs. Two surveys at the time found an incidence of 63 per cent (WIRS1 in 1980) and 55 per cent (CBI in 1981) respectively. There are strong signs that the popularity of these schemes was already in decline by the mid-1980s, with two studies reporting 19 per cent incidence (Batstone 1984 and the Warwick multi-establishment firm study in 1985 – see Marginson et al. 1988) and another just 10 per cent (Baddon et al. 1989). The latest CBI survey in 1989 reports 24 per cent incidence, a marked reduction from their own earlier figure. One researcher who traced the performance of QCs throughout the 1980s has observed that by the last years of the decade 'circles were obviously reaching the end of their lives' (Hill 1991:545).

What, then, happened to QCs? Why did they become so immensely popular – and then go into decline?

The popularity of QCs arose from the range of benefits they were claimed to offer. Meetings typically of 6–10 employees, led by their supervisor, would address job-related problems, would if all went to plan:

- find means to improve the quality and reliability of the product or service concerned;
- make cost savings;

- increase employee interest and commitment towards their jobs;
- encourage an aware and flexible response to problems;
- enhance supervisory authority and leadership skills.

For this to be achieved, however, it was necessary to do far more than just call a group of employees together to talk over production problems. Research on attempts to put QCs into practice revealed the importance of top management support, of having a facilitator appointed to promote and sustain the programme, and of appointing a steering committee to maintain monitoring and management involvement. In addition to these requirements, it had to be recognized that such a programme incurs significant costs if it is to be made workable. Management and employee time spent in running the system must be augmented by training time and expenses, if the participants are to be equipped with a sufficient understanding of the organization to make worthwhile contributions.

In practice, investigations of QCs in their heyday showed a fair rate of success, but also indicated that the likelihood of at least some circle failures in any organization was high. Collard and Dale (1989) report that almost one-third of programmes had been entirely suspended within three years of initial start-up, while individual QC failures were typical in the others. The overall failure rate none the less compared favourably with those reported from Japan and the USA. Other studies have been somewhat more critical of QC achievements on balance (Hill 1986; Bradley and Hill 1987; Wilson 1989).

A number of factors appear to be crucial in the success or failure of QC programmes. These include, in addition to the management support and facilitator role noted above:

- *Middle management attitudes.* Often it is at this level that the greatest threat is perceived from QC changes, and if support is not fostered at an early stage it is all too possible for passive or even active sabotage of the programme to occur.
- *Trade union attitudes.* Again, if support for a QC programme is sought at an early stage here, and unions are reassured that there is no undermining of their position, the result may be positive. But if unions are established, there is no evidence that QCs can attract employee support away from them, but rather that they will follow a line of hostile suspicion.
- *Loss of momentum.* Many QCs appear to start vigorously, dealing with long-persistent sources of aggravation, but then run out of steam. The

need for a refuelling of enthusiasm, and regeneration of agendas, then rests with management.

● *Non-application*. One source of disillusionment with particularly rapid impact is a failure of QCs to see their recommendations have any effect. A meticulous attempt to apply as many proposals as possible, and to give good reasons on those not taken up, will be seen as one major indicator of management commitment.

● *Training*. As noted earlier, training QC members as well as leaders to give them the necessary knowledge and skills will also convey commitment; a failure to do so, and to renew training as necessary (or on the request of QCs who identify new problems but do not feel equipped to tackle them) will be taken as a signal that management do not take seriously the efforts they ask of employees, and are seeking only to obtain employee commitment with minimum interference.

The decline of QCs may, therefore, be seen as occasioned by the eventual dominance of these problems over the reported advantages of such schemes. The cynical will see this as one of the familiar life-and-death cycles of fads and fashions in the world of EI, and see the decline as a general feature of EI rather than due to anything specific about QCs.

A more enthusiastic view would be that companies have simply moved on, having learned from QCs, to more ambitious and inte-grated programmes. In particular, it has been argued that to confine quality or other job-related problem-solving to a specific institution is to misconceive the lessons of Japanese experience, which requires that quality consciousness must suffuse the attitudes of the organiza-tion, not just be dealt with in isolation. This, it is argued, explains the developments outlined below.

Recent developments

The most prominent innovations of recent years are again largely inspired by the Japanese example. On the one hand, they involve an extension of group innovations back into the work activity itself. On the other, they entail a revamping of the whole approach to quality.

Teamworking
This has its origins in the practices of companies like Komatsu, Hitachi and Nissan, all of whom have operations in the UK. The ideas involved bear some resemblance to the Scandinavian experi-ments mentioned earlier, but their problem-solving agenda is shaped

far more by management than quality of working life or ID considerations at root. Teamworking is seen as a vehicle for greater task flexibility and co-operation, as well as for extending the drive for quality.

Companies which were experimenting with TEAMS by the late 1980s were still few and far between (IDS 1988) but included Cummins Engines, Cadburys, Birds Eye Wall's, and Albright & Wilson. Team sizes are typically 7–10, though some are much larger. Task flexibility and job rotation are sometimes limited, partly by the sheer range of tasks, and partly by the nature of the skills involved. Even with this caveat, the companies undertaking teamworking programmes tend to regard major training programmes as a necessary accompaniment. There is also a tendency to remove or redefine the supervisory role, and to appoint team leaders, both of which create potential dangers as well as savings.

As yet it is too soon to assess the merits and demerits of teamworking, and to conclude whether it marks a significant advance on other group-oriented EI techniques. Claims of spectacular benefits abound, but this is nothing new in the EI game. An early study by Cross (1989) claims the average productivity improvements from a number of sources in the team activities at 20 per cent. Cross warns, however, that the production system often constrains the degree of autonomy that can be accorded to a team, and that adequate systems for training, rewards, responsibility and performance are all required for success. Gapper (1990) also cautions that management time saved in traditional supervision and control may well be reabsorbed by the need to give adequate support to individuals and groups.

Total quality management
These programmes derive from a growing belief in the 1980s that commercial success comes not simply from low cost competitiveness but from high and reliable quality, and through this a welding of more stable and mutual relationships between suppliers and customers. This philosophy is seen as unrealizable without the commitment and customer awareness of employees all the way through the organization, including 'internal' customers in the company who will use a department's output. The stated aim in pursuit of this is to create a culture of 'continuous improvement'. Companies operating such systems for several years already include Motorola and Xerox, and more recently programmes have been initiated at ICI, Unilever, Black & Decker and British Telecom.

Typically TQM purports to subsume QCs or teamwork arrangements into a more integrated approach. At the same time, it is generally acknowledged that it is marketing and/or image led, rather than being driven primarily by EI itself. The goals also tend to be 'harder' than for other programmes, emphasizing performance far more and employee satisfaction or development rather less. In consequence, there are signs that the whole approach places more emphasis on the entire management chain, and to some extent rather less on the involvement and efforts of ordinary employees.

The reports to date of TQM in action are generally positive in their assessments (Hill 1991; IDS 1990a; Wilkinson et al. 1990), but there remains ground for some scepticism as to whether it will pass the test of time where other approaches that were 'really different' have failed to do so. Similar pressures and potential problems to those identified above for teamwork persist, with the added challenge of maintaining the necessary integration of business strategy, employee support and the institutions through which TQM is realized. There is also a question mark against the workability of such a system in a context of low morale and poor organizational performance which, though a common problem for most EI arrangements, may be intensified by the totality of the approach itself, particularly in a situation of job rationalization and cutbacks.

Communications and Briefing Systems

Good communication has been accepted as an undeniable touchstone of the effective management of employee relations throughout the living memory of all today's managers. The classical human relations school developed the awareness of the importance of giving employees appropriate information to avoid rumour and secure commitment. It was sometimes argued that management paid little more than lip-service to genuine communication, however, and a CBI survey as late as the mid-1970s found that 80 per cent of employees felt that they were not kept informed of corporate developments (CBI 1976 quoted in Townley 1989:329).

Despite this, some companies have long used numerous communication methods to reach employees. ICI began their staff magazine almost as soon as the company was formed in 1927, for instance. Notice-boards, newspapers, letters to employees, employee meetings addressed by management, suggestion schemes and numerous other channels were widespread by the 1970s, and have continued to proliferate. By 1984, WIRS2 found only 12 per cent of establishments had no communication arrangements at all (Millward and Stevens 1986:152), while just over half of the companies responding to the CBI's 1989 survey claimed to have a formal communications policy.

Communication may be divided into two characteristic forms: written and oral (though the use of videos partly bridges this gap). Written communication can be shaped and controlled from the top, highly professional in presentation, and is cheap in terms of its cost of management time. It may not be a good way of getting employee attention, however, particularly in this era of 'junk mail' dropping through the letter-box at home. According to one recent survey of 400 companies (Vesta Communications, reported in IRS *Employment Trends* no. 448, 28.9.89), management themselves rated notice-boards and memos as relatively poor methods of communicating, yet used them more than anything else.

Approaches such as team briefing, employee opinion surveys and development and appraisal systems were rated as far more effective. On the other hand, most of these methods rely on oral communication and are time-consuming. One such, team briefing, saw the most rapid growth of all in the 1980s, and will be examined a little more closely in the next section. In terms of objectives, communications policies will typically be directed at the ambient, attitudinal aspects of personnel policy, with their content depending on whether the primary intent is, for example, to give information *per se*, to create business awareness, to generate a spirit of community, to promote involvement, or to ease the acceptance of change and draw forth ideas from employees. Ascertaining which need is greatest, and how to target it, is one of the key preparatory tasks for any communications policy.

Many companies have started providing employee reports, a parallel document to shareholder reports, which provide information on the state of the company. Townley (1989) charts increasing use of this method from the late 1970s, peaking around three-fifths of surveyed organizations in the early 1980s (though the 1989 CBI survey suggests only 38 per cent were using this means of communication). All surveys confirm that this method is characteristic above all of larger companies.

Section 1 of the 1982 Employment Act required that companies should also make a statement in their annual reports detailing their policy and fresh initiatives in the preceding year on the E1 front. This in itself was expected to promote company action, including readiness to communicate with their own employees. Surveys of subsequent reporting have been carried out by the Department of Employment and the Institute of Personnel Management (IPM), with similar findings. They show that a minority of companies, again particularly the larger ones, complied with all aspects of the requirements, but that most early reports were either deficient or non-existent. Later surveys suggest a high incidence of replication of paragraphs from one year to the next, and so a rather token response by many companies, so that the overall result of the legislation has been somewhat disappointing for advocates of involvement.

Team briefings

Briefing systems are not new in British business – 51 per cent of respondents to a 1975 British Institute of Management survey reported that they had such an arrangement (Townley 1989:331). During the 1980s, however, a carefully formulated cascade briefing group system was promoted by the Industrial Society with considerable success. Presentations had to be relevant to those receiving them, with only 30 per cent of information relating to wider corporate matters. Groups were to be typically from 5 to 15 members in size.

Team briefing systems were consistently found in just under two-fifths of companies in a series of surveys from the mid-1980s (Baddon et al. 1989; WIRS2; Marginson et al. 1988; CBI 1990). By and large companies report a high degree of satisfaction with their arrangements, but as this has been the case with other techniques (such as QCs) there is a need for caution in taking this at face value.

Team briefing is claimed to produce a number of benefits, including increased commitment, avoidance of misunderstanding, promoting acceptance of change, and reinforcing management through the process of information provision. The 1989 CBI survey found that 2 per cent of establishments rated their scheme highly effective, 41 per cent effective, and only 29 per cent said it was ineffective or needed improving.

As yet the vast majority of reports on the working of briefings are by managers involved or based almost entirely on management accounts, but a recent study by Marchington et al. (1989) reported three independently researched case studies. The authors found that while benefits were claimed for team briefings, they should not be exaggerated, that a number of difficulties could be identified, and that success depended on context to a significant extent. Briefings were in practice always likely to be seen as disposable in times of pressure (such as the Christmas rush in a retail organization), so that timing could become irregular and undermine the commitment to holding them at all. Irregularity tended to reduce credibility of the system with employees, and in any case briefing by itself was unlikely to transform employee attitudes, let alone alter behaviour in ways contrary to their immediate interests. Management scepticism was a sure basis for the sabotage of the arrangements, and this played a major part in the problems experienced in the NHS location studied. Attempts to bypass or weaken the unions might be effective to some degree, but only if other factors were already sapping the union hold on its members, and where the unions were strong and hostile this was more likely to be to the detriment of the briefing system itself (a conclusion familiar already from the research on QCs reported above).

Two-way communication

Team briefings are designed as predominantly one-way com-munications systems. It is widely accepted, however, that employee commitment and involvement will be greater, and the climate of employee relations generally far more positive, if communication works in both directions. A number of methods may be employed to this end, including attitude surveys, appraisal systems, open door and 'speaking out' policies, suggestion schemes, and policies of hav-ing senior executives 'walking the floor' to be seen and to listen. This may also be the primary objective of QCs and similar arrangements, though like suggestion schemes they may also have a useful efficiency and cost savings yield.

Two-way communications initiatives were by some way the most popular reported type of initiative in the WIRS2 survey, with 12 per cent of managers saying they had been introduced within the last four years (though, rather less positively, only 6 per cent of manual and 7 per cent of non-manual representatives reported such an intiative). Once more large firms, and particularly ones which were foreign-owned, were most likely to report such initiatives. 'Walking the floor' was reported by 65 per cent of companies in the

1989 CBI survey, while 19 per cent (65 per cent of large companies) indicated that they had employee attitude surveys or audits.

While the importance of this type of initiative is widely acknowledged, and many companies have sought to move forward in listening as well as telling, the effectiveness of these schemes is again hard to judge, and is likely to be heavily contingent on the general atmosphere of employee relations into which it is introduced. A climate of high trust is likely to be a prerequisite for open speaking from below, creating something of a catch-22 situation, and the problems of maintaining momentum in both directions are likely to be formidable.

Problems and lessons

A number of observations on challenges to communications practice in business, each with self-evident implications, may be identified. These include:

- loss of momentum after initial enthusiasm;
- too little information – or too much;
- too much 'tell and sell' by management provoking employee mistrust of the reality of involvement, especially where most news is bad news, and accompanied by calls for belt-tightening and restraint;
- backfire from attempts to undermine or circumvent a trade union;
- lack of training, of presenters and of recipients of information;
- over-formality. The 1989 CBI survey found that typically informal employee–manager contact was regarded as more effective than any institutional system.

Consultative Arrangements

Joint consultation has been an established channel for employee participation for many decades, with a history stretching back into the nineteenth century and a period of massive popularity in the years immediately following the Second World War, when some surveys suggested that perhaps three-quarters of manufacturing companies had such bodies. During the 1960s, the conventional wisdom (echoed in the Donovan Report and elsewhere) was that consultation was withering, displaced by the growing momentum of shop steward organization and plant bargaining. The 1970s saw evidence of a revival, however, with many joint consultative committees (JCCs) now having shop stewards in the role of representatives, leading to arguments that consultation not only could coexist with plant bargaining but that it could act as a lubricant for a constructive approach thereto.

Available evidence suggests that JCCs survived in the conditions of the 1980s also. Two representative samples taken in the mid-1980s (WIRS2; Baddon et al. 1989) both suggested that one in three companies had formal consultation machinery, as with most other forms of involvement this being more likely the larger the company. The 1989 CBI survey indicated that 47 per cent of their respondents had such a body. The evidence also confirms the prominence of union representation in JCCs, and though there are some signs of a decline in this practice over the decade (see e.g. Joyce and Woods 1984; Millward and Stevens 1986:145), the 1989 CBI survey still found just 43 per cent of committees where unions appointed none of the members.

Apart from these general consultative committees, on which we will focus here, other similar bodies with more specific remits may exist: *ad hoc* bodies to deal with particular issues as they arise; health and safety committees; and productivity committees, to give examples. In Germany and indeed most other European countries similar bodies, usually known as works councils, are established by statute or, occasionally (as in Sweden) by national union–employer agreement. The German legislation on this subject grants employees through the council a series of rights to information, to be consulted, and on certain matters of particular direct relevance to employees, the right to co-determination (e.g. on payment and recruitment systems, discipline, working hours and work study). In the UK there are no such obligations either to have a committee, or to grant it any particular rights – and the likelihood that such a requirement might be one result of the European Commission's Social Charter has caused much bristling in British managerial circles.

Where management defines objectives for consultation, these may take a number of forms, including:

- straightforward augmentation of communication channels;
- more active co-operation and support in meeting challenges to the organization;
- restricting the scope of the union and collective bargaining, or helping to keep unions outside the company altogether;
- enlisting the union into a more constructive relationship. One variant

may seek to win over shop stewards, perhaps against the national union's wishes;
- offering token participation. It should be recalled that this remains a possible, and in some ways a perfectly valid management tactic to head off challenges.

Clearly the form and allotted capacities of a JCC will be expected to vary to reflect these objectives. Though management may not be able to fashion the constitution and substance of JCC activity in complete freedom, it is normally the case that the initiative will lie primarily with them.

As with other forms of EI, reports of the working of JCCs are usually favourable. Applying our established need for caution in making a balanced assessment allows us to identify a number of possible outcomes, however. Success may entail achieving any of the above objectives, but three characteristic variants involve the attainment of active co-operation and support, the marginalization or exclusion of unions from employee representation, or the complementary operation of consultation and collective bargaining side by side.

On the other hand, there are also three plausible types of failure. In two, the committee has little impact on employee relations, either because it deals only with trivial issues (the 'tea, towels and toilets' syndrome), or because it remains powerless and so attracts little employee interest, even when dealing with important matters. The third possibility involves a breakdown of the JCC, either because of the severity of the problems it attempts to deal with, or because of conflicting expectations from the two sides (typically with management seeking discussion and co-operation, while employees seek settlement of grievances and an element of bargaining and influence on important matters). This instability can, in exceptional cases, make labour–management relations worse than before the committee was established.

One review of independent case studies of JCCs (Ramsay 1990) found that problems tended to prevail, in particular triviality or powerlessness, leaving the JCC with a marginal role in labour–management relations. Others are more optimistic (e.g. Marchington 1987), seeing complementary and co-operative outcomes as more likely. It is clear, none the less, that difficulties are not uncommon – judgements on the operation of works councils in Europe vary also, but frequently identify similar problems of marginality. At the best, schemes may need regular review and revamping if vitality is to be maintained. A number of other comments on approaches to consultation can be added, assuming here that the intention is not simply to make a token concession:

- Consultation needs to be genuinely in advance of decisions being settled, or the exercise may be seen as a manipulative one.
- An ambitious remit is needed to ensure that the JCC does not lose momentum.
- Resourcing is important, including proper research and secretarial backing for employee representatives.
- Full and effective reporting back to constituents is necessary if the JCC is not to become detached from and irrelevant to most employees.
- Training of members on both sides is again a necessity.
- Management representation must be sufficiently senior to carry weight, able to put managerial views authoritatively, and to convince employee representatives that the company takes the process seriously.
- Action on agreed proposals should be swift, avoiding the classic weak response of the chairperson agreeing to 'look into things'; rejection of JCC ideas or proposals should not be without good reason, and seen to be so.
- It is wise to keep the union informed even if they are not directly involved in the JCC, unless the intention is openly to sideline them; such a strategy carries heavy risks.

Financial Participation

The startling rise in popularity of financial participation in its various forms since the late 1970s has sometimes obscured the fact that it is not a new idea. The Involvement and Participation Association (as it is now called) was in fact founded in 1884, primarily to promote such schemes among business, and the idea goes back at least to the early part of the nineteenth century. Karl Marx is to be found in 1858 strenuously attacking the idea as a pernicious trick played by employers on their labourers, for instance (a view which prevailed in the labour movement well into the twentieth century, and has not altogether vanished today).

Financial participation takes two chief forms: employee share ownership (ESO), in which employees gain a direct stake in (usually) the company they work for, and profit-sharing, which provides instead a cash bonus from the revenue surplus. While these schemes are often regarded chiefly as aspects of remuneration (and in the case of executive share schemes this may well be a true reflection of their role), research shows that for most managements that introduce them the main objectives are concerned with involvement, commitment and related attitudinal effects (Baddon et al. 1989). It is this aspect of their intended role that is considered here.

Financial participation, particularly ESO, has been massively stimulated by government encouragement and tax incentives since 1978. Special relief was initially given to schemes for all employees which placed shares donated by the company into a trust for seven (later five) years, i.e. approved deferred share trust (ADST) schemes. In 1980 relief was also given for schemes which involved employees making a savings commitment over the years, at the end of which they could take shares at the offer price made initially, or if preferable the lump sum of savings plus interest – save as you earn (SAYE) schemes. Later share-based methods granted this special tax relief status include discretionary or executive schemes, and most recently, in the 1989 Finance Act, employee share ownership plans (ESOPs) in which all shares are retained in a trust and cannot be sold outside the company at any stage. Other share option schemes exist which, for various reasons, are not eligible for tax relief. The largest obstacles are for smaller, unquoted companies, especially when they wish to avoid any danger of ownership and control slipping out of management hands.

Profit-sharing schemes making a cash payment are also widespread in the UK. Few of these are at present eligible for any tax relief, the exceptions being the profit-related pay arrangements approved under the terms laid down by the 1987 Finance Act, with up to one-fifth of pay being variable in a specified relationship to company profits. Many employers have objected to the restrictive definitions in this legislation, preferring for instance to vary wages with what they see as a more relevant, value-added measure of employee performance.

Survey information suggests that a large proportion of the workforce in the UK are covered by at least one form of financial participation. Two major surveys taken in the mid-1980s confirm this. The Glasgow/Strathclyde study (Baddon et al. 1989) found that 65 per cent of all respondent companies had some kind of scheme. The most popular form was cash-based profit-sharing, which represented almost one in three of all schemes (including value-added and non-individual incentive systems, which accounted for a third of all cash schemes reported). This was followed by executive schemes, which after one year already accounted for almost a quarter of reported schemes. Most of the remaining schemes were one of the approved Inland Revenue types (ADST or SAYE), though other share-based schemes still survived in significant numbers. This pattern is roughly confirmed by the Department of Employment survey (Smith 1986; Poole 1988), though the overall incidence of schemes (which are more restrictively defined) is put lower, at 31 per cent of companies. One in five companies in this survey operated an all-employee scheme. Finally, the 1989 CBI survey confirms that cash schemes remain most popular (27 per cent of surveyed companies declaring them), but indicates continuing take-up of various share schemes. In interpreting all these figures, it should be noted that it is quite common in many large companies especially to operate more than one type of scheme.

Both surveys confirm that publicly quoted, larger companies were markedly more likely to operate share schemes than smaller ones (unless they were foreign-owned, this creating other obvious problems for share distribution), but in contrast cash-based schemes were found not to vary significantly in incidence by size of organization. In short, cash schemes remain more feasible and manageable for small business than share schemes, despite the inducements offered for the latter. The more recent profit-related pay provisions were slower in taking off (IDS 1987), though the 1989 CBI survey suggests that they were becoming more widespread on the threshold of the 1990s.

Despite this widespread preference for cash schemes, the take-up of government share schemes has continued to rise, more than doubling since the mid-1980s, and Inland Revenue figures give the total of approved all-employee schemes as 890 for ADST and 891 for SAYE (IDS 1990b), though the selective executive schemes had soared in numbers to almost 4000 by the end of the 1980s (Ramsay et al. 1990). This apparent enthusiasm for self-rewarding by senior management has caused added scepticism in union circles, and some distress among business advocates of greater unity and common treatment at work.

Objectives

As we noted above, attitudinal change is the main objective expressed by managers as their reason for promoting financial participation.

Incentive aims may be indicated, but it is generally accepted that schemes of this sort are too weakly linked to employee performance and too far from employee control to have a meaningful effect on behaviour in any direct way. Cash-based schemes may have some greater role in this respect than share schemes.

Other aims have been more prominent, at times in the past particularly. Anti-unionism was an explicit intention of many of the schemes in the late nineteenth and early twentieth centuries in the UK. While some employers have still sought to use schemes as a disincentive to strike, with penalties built into the cash or share distribution in the event of industrial action (e.g. Hotpoint, Southern Newspapers, British Telecom), this is no longer a common feature, and most companies are at pains to emphasize that their schemes have nothing to do with industrial relations (especially as the last thing they want is for them to become subject to collective bargaining).

The promotion of employee ownership in itself is an important facet of Conservative Party political philosophy, but does not seem to be prominent in employer circles. The idea of co-partnership developed in some paternalistic business circles from the late nineteenth century continues to embrace the idea of employees sharing in the benefits of successful business as a means to make society more just in some circles, and companies like the John Lewis Partnership or Scott Bader have gone so far as to put all ownership into an employee trust in pursuit of this, but for most managements the call of such an ideology is less strong.

Employee influence over business is also sometimes represented as a goal of financial participation. By and large, however, the link is at most a weak one, and the spheres of sharing in profits and sharing in decisions are seen by both sides as unconnected. Companies operating financial participation schemes are more likely to operate other forms of involvement too (Baddon et al. 1989; Poole 1988), but the link is more one of stylistic inclination (i.e. managements that see a need for one are also favourable towards experimenting with the other) than conscious and connected strategy.

In pursuit of a general atmosphere of employee trust, loyalty, commitment, identity and belonging, it would appear that all-employee share schemes have a stronger logic than cash-based ones. Arguably an ADST type of scheme, in which the company gives shares, will be most effective. On the other hand, if enhanced business awareness is the primary intention, an SAYE scheme involving employees' own funds might be expected to generate a stronger sense of linked prosperity. The combination of both types of scheme clearly makes a fair amount of sense. However, it should be remembered that take-up rates on SAYE schemes run at around 20 per cent (IDS 1990b; Baddon et al. 1989), with manual workers typically falling well below the average (Baddon et al. 1989:64; Ramsay et al. 1990), so there may be some danger of divisions emerging.

Performance

The general view of managements operating financial participation schemes is, as with other types of involvement, typically favourable (Baddon et al. 1989; Jenkins and Poole 1990; CBI 1990). Many of the claims made are based on general impressions and faith rather than evidence (which is particularly hard to generate for the objectives we have identified), and take a rather vague and hopeful rather than definite form, however. There is clear evidence, moreover, that in practice financial participation, whether share or cash-based, may have rather an indirect and dilute influence on employee attitudes.

Cash schemes, in particular, run the risk of being seen as a fancy (though not unwelcome) hand-out, fairly quickly taken for granted, rather than becoming a source of identification and commitment. Share schemes ensure a longer-term link, especially if the five-year trust minimum for Inland Revenue schemes is operative, and may at least ensure some curiosity about business performance through the medium of share price.

This conclusion appears to be contradicted by several studies showing that most employees approve strongly of share schemes, and sizeable proportions express the view that they make people work harder, give them greater awareness of management problems, make them more cost conscious and so forth (see Bell and Hanson 1984, 1987; Fogarty and White 1988; Jenkins and Poole 1990; Baddon et al. 1989). Not only are these findings some way from describing actual behaviour, however, but they also leave out results indicating less positive views of such schemes (see Ramsay et al. 1986, for a commentary). Thus more respondents agree than disagree that financial participation is 'just another bonus', and that 'there are better ways of improving benefits', while there is strong agreement that it has nothing to do with worker participation (Baddon et al. 1989; Fogarty and White 1988). Moreover, a detailed study of attitudes both to general issues and to specific perceptions of their employer found that participants and non-participants in SAYE schemes differed only marginally in their outlook (Ramsay et al. 1990). The chief distinguishing feature of the two groups was whether or not they had had money to take up the savings option in the first place.

Observations

The findings reported above suggest a number of conclusions concerning financial participation schemes:

- Careful consideration needs to be given to the objectives sought in selecting schemes. Ones which maximize incentive and are discriminating between groups or individuals may well be at odds with those which stress shared identity and co-operation, for instance.
- A grace and favour system making payments at management discretion will not only not attract tax relief to become a more efficient form of remuneration, but may also generate a sense of arbitrary management decisions, so working contrary to the intended effect.
- Financial participation 'on the cheap' will be most likely to get dismissed as such. But even considerable pay-outs may come to be seen as welcome bonuses, yet have little meaning beyond this.
- Financial participation is unlikely to be particularly effective in isolation. It may have a stronger effect on attitudes if it is part of a wider, coherent approach to EI than in isolation (though in practice this is quite rare).
- Overall, perhaps, not too much should be expected from an approach which remains somewhat remote from employee performance and effort, or from their everyday experience.

Concluding Remarks: Lessons and Strategies

In the course of this chapter, a number of issues have arisen repeatedly with regard to different approaches to EI, and emerge as broader guidelines for the operation of schemes:

- Management commitment should run further than just initiation; many schemes can be costly in management time if they are to be properly run.
- Support for EI must be ensured throughout the management system, in preparation for any initiative; one repeated source of failure is lack of support below the top level, especially where (as with workshop or office

task-based or briefing schemes) middle- and lower-level managers are pivotal to the implementation of the scheme.

- Proper consideration of objectives in advance is a necessary preparation for a convincing approach which avoids potential confusion or conflict between schemes.
- Training of all involved, among both management and participants, is an essential investment, partly to show commitment, and partly to ensure competence rather than disillusionment.
- Adequate and impartial monitoring of schemes is also essential wherever possible, and against measuring sticks set by specified objectives, to avoid the prevalence of 'professions of faith' and a public relations image of performance.
- Problems and shortcomings are not exceptional, but typical in EI. The mistake (all too common) is to be misled by the prevalence of public relations accounts into believing in panaceas. In particular, the impact of most schemes on employee attitudes and behaviour may be far less profound, and even less permanent, than is usually supposed.
- Attempts to bypass or undermine established trade unions by means of EI schemes are likely to fail, and may even backfire and founder on union hostility. In non-union companies, this danger recedes, but this does not erase the other problems of sustaining significant changes in employee responses.

Table 11.1 charts the range of possible objectives. Specific objectives such as incentives to greater efforts and efficiency, co-operation in achieving change and flexibility, or the pursuit of the ever more prominent goal of quality, may all be present in different schemes. The objective of achieving employee commitment and related shifts in attitudes figures most prominently in the profile of management priorities in establishing involvement schemes, however. Other benefits are likely to flow more indirectly from the hoped-for change in the attitude climate in the enterprise.

But what of the strategic aspect of EI policy? The requirement of 'strategy' in business has become almost axiomatic today. In its pursuit, an integration of objectives and planned action is expected throughout the organization: HR strategy must be an integral part of business strategy, with labour utilization approaches reflecting production and marketing priorities, for instance. Employee involvement in turn must fit with HRM strategy. More than this, in most 'progressive' management thinking, it is accepted (outwardly at least) that involvement is one key to the sort of workforce performance that is essential for achieving a competitive edge.

Within the sphere of EI itself, this requires that various types of scheme are not merely initiated in an *ad hoc* and disconnected manner, but are part of a coherent and linked programme of involvement. It may well be thought that financial participation schemes will only have an impact where they form part of a strategy of EI including other, more direct forms of engaging employee support and commitment, for instance. Similarly, the often repeated message that the success of Japanese methods is rooted not in any one technique but in their connection as an HRM philosophy leads to a strategic approach.

Research on strategy in HRM is relatively recent, but such as it is it suggests that claims to be strategic are often more image than reality. While many large companies in particular operate a battery of EI schemes, connected planning of different initiatives with reference to a guiding philosophy, tied further to other elements of business strategy, is a rarity according to one recent study (Baddon et al. 1989: ch. 5), a view confirmed privately by most seasoned observers of the business community. Whether this will change in the remainder of the twentieth century remains to be seen. Meanwhile, EI has become an integral element in many companies' HRM strategies. The assessments in this chapter suggest that it should be seen as a range of innovation options, but that these should not be regarded as a panacea for all organizational ills.

None the less, the future does promise significant changes on the EI front. There are signs that change will be impelled by another shift of climate: the effects of the Social Charter associated with the completion of the Single Market of the European Community planned for 31 December 1992. The Charter proposes a series of employee rights, including payment levels, bargaining rights, union membership, and on information, participation and consultation. This approach runs counter to that prevailing in the UK and in British government policy throughout the 1980s, which emphasized involvement in forms and degrees determined by management. Moreover, participation has been described by the President of the EC, Jaques Delors, as the most important element of the Charter.

This and other changes (including the partial resurgence and regrouping of the unions on new platforms) may create a fresh pressure from below more in the traditions of the ID debate of the 1970s. The complication of thinking on employee participation is potentially considerable; it certainly implies that strategic thinking can no longer proceed as if employees themselves had no part in shaping it.

References

ACAS (Advisory, Conciliation and Arbitration Service) 1988: *Labour Flexibility in Britain: the 1987 ACAS Survey*. London: ACAS.

Baddon, Hunter, L.C., Hyman, J., Leopold, J. and Ramsay, H. 1989: *People's Capitalism: a critical analysis of profit and employee share ownership*. London: Routledge.

Batstone, E. 1984: *Working Order*. Oxford: Blackwell.

Batstone, E. 1989: New forms of work organization in Britain. In P. Grootings et al. (eds), *New Forms of Work Organization in Europe*, New Brunswick: Transaction.

Bell, D. W. and Hanson, C. 1984: *Profit Sharing and Employee Shareholding Attitude Survey*. London: Industrial Participation Association.

Bell, D. W. and Hanson, C. 1987: *Profit-Sharing and Profitability*. London: Kogan Page.

Bradley, K. and Hill, S. 1987: Quality circles and managerial interests. *Industrial Relations*, 26, 68–82.

CBI (Confederation of British Industry) 1990: *Employee Involvement – Shaping the Future for Business*. Study by KPMG Peat Marwick Management Consultants. London: CBI.

Collard, R. and Dale, B. 1989: Quality circles. In K. Sisson (ed.), *Personnel Management in Britain*, Oxford: Blackwell 356–77.

Cross, M. 1989: Implementing a teamwork philosophy within an existing site. Paper to City University Business School, London, conference on Teamwork, Oct. 1989 (summarized in IRS *Employment Trends*, 451, 7.11.89).

Daniel, W.W. and Millward, N. 1983: *Workplace Industrial Relations in Britain*. London: Heinemann.

Department of Employment 1987: Involving the staff. *Employment Gazette*, March, 147–9.

Department of Employment, 1988: Employee involvement. *Employment Gazette*, October, 573–5.

Department of Employment 1989: *People and Companies: employee involvement in Britain*. London: HMSO.

Edwards, P. 1987: *Managing the Factory* Oxford: Blackwell.

Elger, A. 1990: Technical innovation and work reorganisation in British manufacturing in the 1980s: continuity, intensification or transformation? *Work, Employment and Society*, special issue, May, 67–101.

Fogarty, M. and White, M. 1988: *Share Schemes – As Workers See Them*. London: Policy Studies Institute.

Gapper, J. 1990: At the end of the honeymoon. *Financial Times*, 10.1.90.

Hill, F.M. 1986: Quality circles in the UK: a longitudinal study. *Personnel Review*, 15(3), 25–34.

Hill, S. 1991: Why quality circles failed but total quality might succeed.

British Journal of Industrial Relations, 29(4), December, 541–68.

IDS (Incomes Data Services) 1987: *PRP and Profit Sharing*. Study no. 397, April.

IDS 1988: *Teamworking*. Study no. 419, October.

IDS 1990a: *Total Quality Management*. Study no. 457, May.

IDS 1990b: *Profit Sharing and Share Options*. Study no. 468, October.

Jenkins, G. and Poole, M. 1990: *The Impact of Economic Democracy*. London: Routledge.

Joyce, P. and Woods, A. 1984: Joint consultation in Britain: results of a survey during the recession. *Employee Relations*, 6(3), 2–7.

MacInnes, J. 1987: *Thatcherism at Work*. Milton Keynes: Open University Press.

Marchington, M. 1987: A review and critique of recent research into joint consultation. *British Journal of Industrial Relations*, 25(3), November, 339–52.

Marchington, M., Parker, P. and Prestwich, A. 1989: Problems with team briefing in practice. *Employee Relations*, 11(4), 21–30.

Marginson, P. 1989: Employment flexibility in large companies: change and continuity. *Industrial Relations Journal*, 20(2), Summer, 101–9.

Marginson, P, Edwards, P.K., Martin, R., Purcell, J. and Sisson, K. 1988: *Beyond the Workplace: managing industrial relations in the multi-establishment enterprise*. Oxford: Blackwell.

Millward, N. and Stevens, M. 1986: *British Workplace Industrial Relations 1980–1984*. Aldershot: Gower.

NEDO 1986: *Changing Working Patterns: how companies achieve flexibility to meet new needs*. Report by the Institute for Manpower Studies for the National Economic Development Office in association with the Department of Employment. London: NEDO.

Pollert, A. 1988: The 'flexible firm': fixation or fact? *Work, Employment and Society*, 2(3), September, 281–316.

Poole, M. 1988: Factors affecting the development of employee financial participation in contemporary Britain: evidence from a national survey. *British Journal of Industrial Relations*, 26(1), March, 21–36.

Ramsay, H. 1990: The joint consultation debate: soft soap and hard cases. Discussion paper no. 17, Centre for Research on Industrial Democracy and Participation, University of Glasgow.

Ramsay, H., Hyman, J., Baddon, L., Hunter, L. and Leopold, J. 1990: Options for workers: owner or employee? In J. Jenkins and M. Poole (eds), *New Forms of Ownership: management and employment*, London: Routledge, 183–204.

Ramsay, H., Leopold, J. and Hyman, J. 1986: Profit-sharing and employee share ownership: an initial assessment. *Employee Relations*, 8(1), 23–6.

Smith, G.R. 1986: Profit-sharing and employee share ownership in Britain. *Employment Gazette*, 94(8), September, 380–5.

Towers, B., Cox, D. and Chell, E. 1987: *Worker Directors in Private Manufacturing Industry in Great Britain*. Research paper no. 29. London: Department of Employment.

Townley, B. 1989: Employee communication programmes. In K. Sisson (ed.), *Personnel Management in Britain*, Oxford: Blackwell, 329–55.

Wilkinson, A., Snape, E. and Allen, P. 1990: TQM and the management of labour. *Employee Relations*, 13(1), 24–31.

Wilson, F. 1989: Productive efficiency and the employment relationship – the case of quality circles. *Employee Relations*, 11(1), 27–32.

12
Pay, Performance and Reward

CLIFF LOCKYER

Introduction

Pay, effort or performance and reward have been central issues in the employment relationship since the earliest days, as such a wealth of literature has preceded the current interest in payment techniques within human resource management (HRM). Arguably, HRM – in its haste to promote the commitment and involvement of the employee to the organization and often away from the trade union – has ignored much of the knowledge and wisdom of the past. Frequently the operationalization of HRM payment schemes is flawed by internal confusion, contradiction, superficiality, and an ignorance of those factors, both internal and external to the organization, on which appropriateness and effectiveness of payment systems depend.

This chapter firstly reviews the history and development of payment systems, illustrating the links between traditional and HRM systems. This leads to a typology of payment systems, and a categorization of those factors which have traditionally influenced the appropriateness and effectiveness of particular schemes. Secondly, a review of the objectives and concerns of HRM leads to an analysis of HRM-related payment schemes. The chapter concludes with an assessment of the extent to which HRM payment schemes meet the essential criteria for effective payment schemes and hence are likely to become significant features of the employment landscape.

As the ACAS guide to payment systems notes, 'Payment systems are an integral part of industrial relations, and they can have a considerable effect, for good or ill, both on the efficient running of an enterprise and on management–employee relations' (ACAS 1985:2). Pay and work measurement are elements of the control and motivation of people at work. Conflicts inevitably arise as employers seek to use labour as efficiently as possible and seek to promote efficiency through the payment systems. Much of management and industrial relations/personnel literature has been directed at the merits and disadvantages of differing motivational schemes and their associated payment methods in differing market, technological and production conditions.

The Development of Payment Systems

How much an employee should be able to do, and how to motivate the employee have been two basic issues facing management since earliest days. Knowles (1952) cites Exodus, in the Old Testament, as containing the first example of a strike, a dispute over effort between Egyptian masters and their Jewish bricklayers. The first reference to measured day work can be found in the printing trade in the fourteenth century. Master printers were expected to produce sufficient sheets of paper which, when stacked, would reach a predetermined mark, a 'day werk', on a wall. By the 1600s published tables of 'day werkes' (how much work an agricultural labourer could be expected to complete under different conditions) were available for landowners as an early form of manpower planning and labour costing. Clearly the introduction of clock time, and more latterly time and motion study, offered a solution to many of the problems of defining possible 'effort' or reasonable 'performance' by employees. The development of payment systems, focusing on incentive schemes, were less successful solutions to the problems of low levels of employee commitment and co-operation. Nevertheless, today more than 40 per cent of employees have some element of their pay determined by their performance or effort.

Gospel's (1983) account of the history of payment systems provides a valuable account of the relationship of pay to production methods. With the onset of the Industrial Revolution employers faced major problems in motivating and controlling employees. The traditional alliances between master and servant seemed ill-suited to the new methods and pace of work, and the problems of generating and maintaining a sense of co-operation appeared harder, especially with the formation of trade unions.

Initially many employers, after abandoning experiments with model villages, turned to the putting-out system. The employer provided raw materials and sometimes tools to a dispersed labour force. This cheap system of production avoided the need for the conventional factory; it reduced capital investment and spread the risk of production. Secondly, it was a flexible system of production. The employer could vary production by varying both the amounts of materials put to outworkers and by varying the numbers of out-workers. Thirdly, production efficiency was partially assured through the rational economic assumptions of motivation.

Homeworking is the contemporary version of the putting-out system. Employees or self-employed work at home on stocks delivered and collected by the employer. It flourishes in sectors such as: clothing, light and low value assembly work, maintenance, data inputting and areas of computer programming. When linked to assumptions of employee motivation which stress the discretion of the individual to plan and schedule their own work and the freedom of working at home, it becomes a respectable HRM technique. It can be an efficient technique as its flexibility enables rapid readjustment to changed levels of demand, and it reduces long-term non-wage labour costs. In many respects it parallels the practices of large firms of interlocking subcontractors to their production.

Large-scale production and a need to reduce the costs associated with stocks of work in progress favoured the factory system of production. Gospel (1983) notes that as work became located within the factory different methods of group payment systems emerged including: the butty system, gang working and subcontracting. These schemes, which emerged in the early part of the nineteenth century, contain within them many of the elements of modern motivation theory.

All, to some varying extent, stressed elements of both economic incentives (scientific management) and social needs (human relations). In the construction industries the management of labour was devolved to a subcontractor who had the responsibility of hiring, supervising the work and controlling the labour, and who would be paid a lump sum to complete a task. Alternatively, a group of employees would be paid a lump sum to complete a task. In some industries, for example mining, housebuilding, and to a lesser extent engineering, the group itself would decide the membership of the group, allocation of tasks and the size of payment to individual group members. Such schemes provided a clear incentive to work efficiently and to ensure a control on all members of the group to work. A variation existed in shipbuilding where craftsmen paid the wages of their helpers.

In addition to the motivational benefits these schemes placed the onus of efficiency and resolution of production problems on employees (frequently the skilled workers or gang boss). Such schemes tended to operate best where there was a high manual skill, low level of mechanization or non-standard or non-recurring tasks. As production became integrated and more sophisticated a greater degree of planning and hence control was necessary.

Technological advances such as mechanization and much of automation necessitated routine regular tasks which were unsuited to the freedom and variable pacing of such group production methods. Nevertheless, more recent technological and organizational developments in a number of industries have enabled firms to return to such concepts, within an HRM framework, to organize their production around group production concepts for motivational reasons associated with productivity and quality; for example, job enlargement, autonomous work groups and cellular production schemes.

By the mid nineteenth century employers in the textile industries had lists of piece-work prices for work; these spread to common lists for towns and then to district rates. The rise of such town and district rates gave an important role for employers' associations. Additionally, the impact of piece-work led to trade unionism and attempts to reduce the worst effects of exploitation.

In the nineteenth century other systems of payment tended to fade in the face of payments by results schemes, the introduction of the foreman and more direct systems of control. By the turn of the century pressures to improve efficiency led to the introduction of work, or time and motion, study to establish the most efficient methods of work and the time necessary to complete standard tasks.

Payments by results and work study became the symbolic payments methods and work measurement techniques of the Industrial Revolution. By the end of the nineteenth century they had spread to much of engineering. Despite all the criticisms of incentive schemes and advances in motivational theory, incentive payments remain the most common form of motivation in employment.

A Typology of Payment Systems

Payment systems are traditionally classified by either one, or a combination, of the following (IDS 1980):

1 The degree to which pay relates to output: for example, salary grades, measured day work, and time or flat rate systems are examples of payment schemes based on the number of hours spent at work. There is no clear relationship between effort and reward.

   Piece-work, payment by results, merit schemes, bonus schemes, share ownership, profit-related pay and performance-related pay are the main payment methods with some relationship between reward and effort.

2 Pay schemes which relate pay to effort or output can be further classified by the extent to which pay varies directly or remotely to individual effort. Piece-work and payments by results schemes are methods with a direct and close link between individual effort and the size of the reward. Conversely, share ownership, profit-related pay and establishment-wide bonus schemes have only a remote relationship between individual effort and the size of the reward.

3 Less interestingly for the purposes of this chapter, payment schemes can be classified according to the immediacy of payment. Frequency of payment traditionally indicated the status of the employee and the extent of non-monetary rewards and conditions. Calculating pay per hour or day indicated manual status, whereas payment per week or per month indicated staff status.

Time-based, non-incentive related payment schemes

Time rates – either hourly, weekly, monthly or yearly – are popular in smaller organizations and/or where the work is varied or non-standard and hence difficult and/or costly for work study. In these schemes the employee receives a fixed payment. Typically the method has been used for non-productive employees, for example salaried staff, maintenance and other craft workers.

Time or flat rate systems illustrate many of the requirements for a successful payments scheme. They are simple and cheap to operate, and are easily understood by all. While the stability of pay, which is a feature of time rates, is generally appreciated by employees the method offers little in terms of financial incentives to improve efficiency and productivity. Furthermore as Brown (1989) notes, trade union pressure and the need to respond to changing circumstances tend to lessen the simplicity (see Sisson 1989:259).

Measured day work (MDW) systems are those where:

the pay of the employee is fixed on the understanding that he will maintain a specified level of performance, but the pay does not fluctuate in the short term with his actual performance. This arrangement relies on some form of work measurement or assessment, as a means of both defining the required level of performance and of monitoring the output level (Office of Manpower Economics 1973, quoted in Burchill 1976:74).

Measured day work schemes are appropriate when output is machine or process controlled, operations are closely linked and when management seeks high consistent production from a rigid sequence of operations. It is based on detailed work study.

In the UK MDW was seen as a payment system which overcomes many of the industrial relations' difficulties associated with payment by results (PBR) schemes. It was claimed that it would lead to an improved flexibility of labour and higher productivity (National Board for Prices and Incomes 1967; IDS 1979), hence it was sometimes described as a 'high day rate system of payment'. While it generally led to fewer disputes over pay rates, these were replaced by more disputes over effort and 'manning levels'. In reality the gains were often less and the problems greater. The schemes relied on work study arrangements which were often complex and difficult to understand. In MDW schemes there is no incentive to improve output. Rather employees would receive the same rate of pay for the minimum acceptable effort. Furthermore, there was no incentive for production employees to endeavour to maintain production, or to assume responsibility to undertake minor maintenance. To generate the claimed flexibility required a greater commitment to training and the development of a greater sense of co-operation between management and employees. Above all the scheme required a much greater degree of competency among management to programme work efficiently, to maintain sufficient levels of stocks and components and to organize adequately to reach and maintain satisfactory production schedules.

Incentive-related payment schemes

Piece-work is the oldest and simplest form of wage incentive. Operators are paid according to the number of pieces they produce, pay is proportional to effort, the more produced the larger the reward. Clearly the scheme rests on 'rational economic' assumptions as to motivation, and as such invokes a degree of criticism from the human relations tradition. However, there are clear parallels between piece-work and the newer forms of performance-related pay. It is easy to argue that performance-related pay is the 'behavioural' piece-work for white-collar and managerial staff.

In practice the simplicity and some of the motivational value are lost for four reasons. Firstly, the scheme needs some method of determining an acceptable level of work. This usually implies the introduction of some form of work study. Secondly, notions of fairness, equity and expectancy demand that the techniques should ensure that workers of similar skills and economic value should earn approximately the same (ACAS 1983). Thirdly, the need for some security of earnings imposes a need for a minimum level or fallback rate. This can range from 30 to 70 per cent. So most schemes tend to have a form of guaranteed earnings when operators cannot work for lack of materials, machine breakdown, etc. Fourthly, there is much evidence that employees endeavour to work to informal limits and thus artifically restrict their pace of work.

Payment by results may be broadly defined as:

> Any system of wages and salaries under which payment is related to factors in a worker's performance other than time spent at his employer's disposal. The term is most commonly applied to payment systems which attempt to establish a formal relationship between pay and output or effort. Such systems have one underlying assumption: namely, that where the worker can vary his output according to the effort he puts into his work, and this can be related to his earnings in a way he can understand, the prospect of increased earnings will induce him to work harder (National Board for Prices and Incomes 1968a: para. 8).

Most payment by results schemes are work-measured schemes. A set time is allowed to complete a task. The bonus depends upon the difference between the actual time taken and the allowed time, i.e. the amount of time saved. The standard time allowed is generated by averaging a series of timings of actual time taken with a series of allowances for fatigue and rest pauses, etc. Such standard times can be established by actually measuring the task or by the use of previously established measurements (synthetic times). The incentive element can be varied in four ways. Firstly, proportionally where the bonus increases in direct proportion to output. Secondly, progressively where the bonus increases at a faster rate above a particular level. Thirdly, regressively where the bonus increases at a slower rate than output. Finally, variably where the relationship between payment and output differs at different levels of output.

Schemes can seek to reward quality and other items as well as output. For employers, piece-work systems put the onus for efficiency on to operators and are a well-proven system of motivation. However, such schemes tend not to provide short-term control over production levels or wages. Incentive schemes can have an adverse effect on the quality of work. Where trade unions are recognized and play an important role in wage determination, incentive schemes can lead to considerable negotiation over changes to methods, materials and volumes of output and their effects on earnings. The ability of piece-workers to increase output as compared with those under time systems of pay has led to issues of relativities and differentials becoming issues of dispute. When there is a high demand for labour, piece-work schemes can lead to increases in labour costs as employees seek to maintain average earnings when new times, methods or materials are introduced.

Piece-work can offer employees an ability to exert some control over the pace of work. Notwithstanding fears of rate cutting, piece-work offers employees the opportunity by increasing effort to increase rewards. However, earnings can vary for reasons outwith the control of employees and frequently the price of incentive schemes can be a loss of variety of work.

Traditionally bonus payments have been introduced to encourage employees to maintain or improve on standard production. These can be either a fixed payment or a scheme in which the payment varies according to sustained changes in achievement levels. While such schemes appear to introduce a degree of incentive they tend to become more complex and costly to administer. Significantly, there is little evidence to suggest that such bonus schemes have a measurable motivational impact.

There is considerable variation in such schemes. A popular form is that of the suggestion scheme which offers some economic reward for schemes which aid production. The reward can be made to the employee making the suggestion or be added to the bonus scheme paid to all staff. Plant- or enterprise-wide schemes have been advocated by human relations writers who stress the collaborative and co-operative atmosphere which can be engendered by schemes which encourage all employees to contribute to improving performance/reducing costs and hence share in some reward.

In its simplest form such schemes lead to a bonus for all employees

Table 12.1 The context of pay

Factors internal to the organization	Factors external to the organization
Need to control labour costs	Need to relate pay to the labour market
Equity between the worth of jobs	Trade union policies and industry practices
Equity in terms of rewarding differing contributions	
Personnel management policies	Legislation as to payment, equal pay and opportunity
Technology and organization of production constraints	Industry patterns
Product cycles and changes	Product markets and competition

General principles
Inexpensive to administer and cost-effective
Easy to operate
Easy to understand
Perceived as fair, does not exacerbate employee relations
Effective in achieving aims

based directly on the total volume of output, or the sales value of goods produced in a given period. Other schemes have been based around ideas of reducing costs as well as increasing output.

Typically a bonus will be paid when production exceeds a predetermined level. The bonus can increase when further production and/or quality targets are reached. The advantages of such schemes echo much of the human relations literature: increased employee involvement; enhanced teamwork; more co-operative and collaborative atmosphere to use employees' knowledge and skills to reduce costs, improve efficiency and lead to an increased sense of unity of purpose.

Where there is a gradually rising demand and a slow rate of product and technical change such schemes can have an influence. However, the direct incentive effect on the individual is weak because the individual employee cannot see any clear relationship between his or her work, the overall performance and bonus. Drawing on expectancy theory we can see how an employee may feel increased resentment because increased effort has not resulted in an increase of the bonus. There is little evidence of sustained success of such schemes in large organizations.

The review of early and conventional payment systems indicates that to be effective a system needs to relate to a number of factors. These are illustrated in table 12.1. There is evidence that a number of HRM payment schemes have ignored several of these basic considerations in their concern to increase the commitment of the individual.

Human Resource Management and Pay

Intellectually HRM, with its humanistic image of the employee, derives largely from human relations and neo-human relations. As such it draws on concepts of the work group, leadership styles, communication and job content to generate a range of motivational techniques and associated payment and reward systems to improve and reward enhanced performance. This element of HRM focuses on the behavioural elements as a basis of pay systems.

Human resources strategy is: 'The expanded utilisation of human resources primarily through measures for enhancing motivation, tapping shop floor knowledge of production and corresponding measures for training and work organisation' (Jurgens et al. 1986:259).

The logic in developing a behavioural, more human, or individual-centred approach largely based on a reworking of a number of 1940s to 1960s ideas is to generate efficiency. Efficiency underlies the second strand of HRM, namely a focus on employees as the human assets of the firm and an increased focus on the costs of employees. In contemporary HRM literature we note the concern and investment in 'core' employees and the simultaneous search for more effective 'flexible' patterns of employment. This leads to a number of contradictions. On the one hand HRM presents itself as developing payment systems which link individual performance to career development and salary advancement, yet at the same time it debates the cost benefits of flexibility of working hours (e.g. annual hours, flexible rostering). Simultaneously it is concerned with developing reward and payment techniques to overcome the problems of motivating part-time or fixed contract staff.

With its focus on increasing employee performance and commitment, HRM has to be seen as part of a wider strategy which includes:

1 a strategy to reduce labour costs through more efficient and flexible patterns of work organization and division;
2 a technology strategy associated with the introduction of more flexible and efficient forms of mechanization and automation;
3 by attempts to recover and increase the effective control of work, generate employee commitment rather than merely compliance;
4 a move from collective to individual workplace relations.

Thus the HRM techniques of pay and rewards can only be understood from this wider, and not always internally consistent, set of objectives.

Strangely HRM, like much of human relations, neglects much of the historical development and analysis of pay, effort and rewards discussed earlier. This neglect leads to relatively arid and superficial debate which focuses largely on payment techniques and ignores both the context of the payment system and most of the alternative explanations of worker reaction and behaviour to motivation and payment systems.

Goodrich (1922) provides us with a further, critical understanding of pay and work to HRM. Work is an effort–reward relationship in which employees calculatingly respond to employer initiatives and seek to extend their control of work. Goodrich's concept of the frontiers of control envisages work as a continual struggle in which the employers seek new schemes of motivation and work measurement to extend their control. Employees respond by a variety of collective acts – organization, collective action and restrictions of output – to assert their control.

The response of HRM to the collectivization of work is to seek to reassert the unitary perspective. Crucial to the view of pay is a direct relationship between the individual and the organization. Individual pay rates, frequently related to some management assessment of performance and/or behaviour, reinforce this link and act to reduce the sense of collective action among employees. Within the public sector there are examples in health, transport and local government of the introduction of performance-related payment schemes associated with a simultaneous ending of established collective bargaining arrangements.

The response of HRM to the issue of control of work is to seek a set of techniques which reduces the gap between employee performance and potential, which increases employer control of the employee (Townley 1990). Control can be achieved by motivational methods, as in payment schemes, by leadership styles, through new

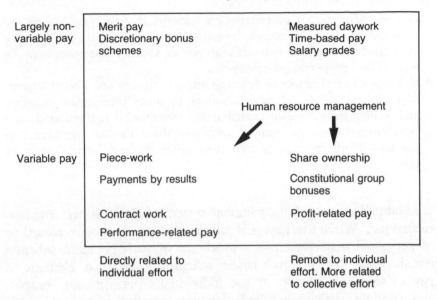

Figure 12.1 The contrasts between traditional and HRM payment systems

work organization and communication methods stressing the work group, or by using technologically advanced forms of work monitoring and control. Frequently in strategic HRM it is the interaction of a number of these aspects. It is in this sense we can understand Peters and Waterman's (1982) contribution to HRM as an attempt to alert management to the potential performance of employees.

The contrasts between traditional and HRM payment systems can be shown in figure 12.1. The logic of HRM is to move from the top right quadrant, the essentially collectively based, non-individual effort-based payment schemes. The direction can vary. Firms pursuing a policy of encouraging a sense of participation among employees may seek to move to the bottom right quadrant, stressing financial links with the organization. More commonly the move is towards performance-related pay – variable payments directly related to individual effort.

But in HRM pay and performance can be elements in a number of potentially contradictory policies. Pay can be a means to:

- Individualize the employment relationship and possibly to be a component of a non-union strategy. Yet it may relate to schemes designed to strengthen teamwork and intra-group collaboration.
- Increase productivity and efficiency by relating reward to a combina-

tion of either output or behavioural patterns thought valuable by the organization. But the search for efficiency leads to schemes to vary employment status and potentially to reduce security of employment for a significant proportion of employees.

• Relate pay to techniques designed to improve the quality of work experience, either through job enrichment or by other involvement schemes and to increase individual contribution. However, it is predicated on a search to increase organization control over the individual employee, and the underlying rationale is increasing efficiency and intensification of effort.

Undoubtedly the symbolic payment system of HRM is performance-related pay. While this payment scheme has a high priority according to personnel management the incidence of such payment schemes remains low. Performance-based schemes linking an element of pay to some assessment of the individual's performance (output) and conduct (behaviour) have become popular in recent years. These developments have been associated with a move away from an emphasis on personal qualities inherent in conventional merit rating towards an assessment of performance against managerially established objectives.

Fowler (1988) identifies three elements in a move towards performance-related pay: a move towards rewarding output rather than input and an increasing use of qualitative rather than quantitive judgements in assessing individual performance; a concern towards assessing performance in terms of working objectives rather than personal qualities; and the abandonment of general, annual pay increases for all towards schemes in which all increases are decided on an individual performance basis.

Undoubtedly a major element in the popularity of performance-related pay has been its widespread introduction in the public sector. During the 1980s the British government has endeavoured to move away from the traditional wage and salary principles that all government employees doing the same job should receive the same pay (elements of the traditional arguments for equity of treatment). The trend has been to inject a more managerialist/commercial approach. Putting performance pay into the civil service and nationalized industries has been as much an act of political will as new employment policy.

More generally four reasons are most frequently cited to explain the spread of performance-related pay:

1 It is seen as an element in a wider strategy of changing employee attitudes towards those which stress high performance and a new corporate culture. It can be coupled with more sophisticated and complex performance appraisal schemes and constitute a central element in a policy for training and development.
2 In terms of expectancy theory it stresses the link between individual performance and reward. The basis for expectations for reward change from those of cost of living, comparability and other factors external to the organization, to the individual's own efforts and the success of the organization.
3 Relating to employees on an individual basis is seen as contributing to a reduction in the influence of trade unionism and collective bargaining. It underpins a unitarist view of the enterprise and a teamwork approach to management.
4 It can minimize increases in labour costs since it replaces annual increases for all employees to a system of targeting increases to those employees who contribute more, in some way, to the organization.

But the success of such schemes depends upon: sustained low inflation (Fowler 1988); management trust, commitment and ability (IPM 1990; Kinnie and Lowe 1990); simplicity (Fowler 1988 cites the example of a scheme which had a 34-page management manual and required the completion of a six page appraisal form for each employee); being an integral part of the company's total reward strategy (IPM 1990); an acceptable means to translate appraisal into pay (Kinnie and Lowe 1990); considerable preparation and revision (IDS 1988b).

When accompanied by policies of target-setting (management by objectives) performance-related pay schemes relate closely to the motivational approaches of the neo-human relations school. It is worth while reconsidering the strengths and weaknesses of such motivational approaches of this school and relating these to performance-related pay:

1 The real problems of measurement.
2 What do such schemes do for the majority of staff on whom the organization relies?
3 Is pay a real motivator for those who are already motivated? It is more likely that bad pay decisions are excellent demotivators.
4 Pay cannot be established solely by criteria internal to the firm – it must relate to the local labour market and the demands for specific skills. The declining labour supplies and the need to recruit new groups may well lead to situations where the facilities provided might be seen as

more important in retaining staff and overcoming staff shortages than performance-related pay.

Performance-related pay schemes have often been associated with moves towards integrated pay or single-status arrangements; this is often termed 'harmonization of conditions'. Policies of common treatment for managerial and hourly rated staff reflect human relations concepts and are justified in terms of promoting a teamwork, or common interest approach (Price in Sisson 1989:279–92).

The response of HRM has been to look to organizational and involvement schemes to reinforce monetary-based schemes. The emphasis on the integrated work group, possible introduction of quality circles (QCs) and briefing groups along with a range of other involvement schemes have been used to buttress MDW schemes.

These have tended to replace the old human relations schemes which stressed the adoption of plant- or enterprise-wide schemes. The human relations theories of motivation and of the value in developing a sense of teamwork, or, to use the more modern terminology 'a corporate culture', led to the emergence of schemes which seek to improve overall performance and engender a sense of working together.

In recent years there has been a limited growth of schemes which seek to strengthen the collaborative and co-operative links between management and employees by reinforcing the link between pay and the fortunes, or profits, of the business (IDS 1981, 1987).

Recent changes to Inland Revenue provisions have led to a growing interest in profit-related payment schemes. The British government has argued that profit-related pay and share ownership schemes reinforce the link between employee and employer, by making a portion of pay vary with the fortunes of the business. Again as figure 12.1 illustrates, this only creates a remote link between individual effort and reward, but is a move away from a collective relationship to work.

To a degree the value of such schemes depends upon the extent to which it is perceived to be available equally for all employees or whether it operates at the discretion of management. Such schemes indicate a new issue, that of a need to endeavour to retain key staff. Share option schemes can contribute to the retention of staff since to minimize exposure to tax liability can require the shares be held for a number of years.

Summary and Conclusions

It is clear from the earlier discussion as summarized in figure 12.1 that there is not one best payment system – the suitability of a payment system depends upon the technology of production, the characteristics of the labour market, the extent and nature of competition and the attitudes that employees bring to work (Lupton and Gowler 1969). The history of payment schemes should lead us to be cautious of the claims of motivational theorists, as there is little evidence from the past that motivational schemes, apart from those based to a large degree on economic rewards, have been successful. However, clearly pay, the amount, relativities and pay differentials between individuals or between groups are of major importance in issues of motivation and satisfaction (National Board for Prices and Incomes 1968b). Equally, any motivation scheme must be cheap and easy to administer – a requirement which disqualifies many of the more modern schemes. Additionally, we have focused on the immediate economic rewards of work; attention should be given to the other economic incentives – bonuses, facilities, 'perks', pensions, etc. all of which constitute an element in the employee's assessment of the economic rewards of work.

Furthermore, any payment system must not only be simple, cheap to manage and effective, it must also relate to the methods of production and to labour market conditions. The concern of HRM for greater control of employees has created payment schemes with a tremendously long administrative tail. The time to complete the appraisal system well, especially if the scheme is linked to other personnel policies such as development and training, to allow for meaningful dialogue between appraiser and appraisee, may well be regarded as excessive by line management. As such the scheme may fall into disregard.

Employees relate to work in complex and often contradictory ways. Assessing the relative importance of monetary and non-monetary rewards and incentives has proved problematic. It is unclear as to the relative stress employees put on high money rewards at the expense of long-term security of earnings. Such uncertainties question the effectiveness of schemes which relate an element of pay to profit or share ownership.

Notwithstanding these considerations, it is clear that the success of any payment system depends, in part, on effective management control over wages and wage costs. Furthermore, the application of proper work standards and monitoring is essential for effective control to be assured.

Most payment systems tend to lose their effectiveness and stimulus through time, due to the changing composition of the labour force, advance of automation, and residual inequalities in the system (Royal Commission on Trade Unions and Employers' Associations 1968). For example, output incentives lead to problems of inequitable relationships among different groups. The frequent use of allowances and other agreed payments to compensate those excluded from the operation of such schemes, high rates of wage drift, and the problems of advancing technology all contribute to the undermining of such schemes.

Similarly the scope for cost reduction schemes, with their emphasis on co-operation and teamwork, cannot in themselves create a willingness to co-operate or a management capable of exploiting this. Often it proves difficult to establish reliable and equitable norms for calculating the bonuses to be paid. It is questionable whether such schemes should be introduced to get a job done that management can do on its own. In a tight labour market a management may well find itself paying bonuses for the elimination of practices which could have been bought out by management, or could have been removed by technological change, methods realignment or other actions of management. Furthermore the company may be tied to a historic norm which might not reflect the current competitive environment in which the firm operates.

The choice of scheme is dependent upon the technology and organization of work. The contradictions and complexities of production do not lead to the easy identification of the symbolic payment scheme of HRM. Schemes stressing individual effort sit uneasily with group- and plant-wide schemes. Often there appears to be little difference between the Victorian incentive schemes and more modern versions of performance-related pay. The contradictions in HRM over pay make it difficult to evaluate the efficacy of the 'new' payment systems. Any cursory review of the personnel journals leaves the impression that the new schemes are frequently promoted with more of an evangelical zeal than logical argument (Brewster and Connock 1985).

These contradictions and the neglect of technological contexts have meant that developments in payment and reward schemes have operated, for the majority of firms, more at the level of rhetoric than of substantial changes. There have been considerable developments in the introduction of performance-related payment schemes (IDS 1988a,b) and in some industries the interrelationship of pay to new organizational structures and new policies towards trade unions. But for the majority of employers the costs and uncertainties of the new payment methods have meant a preference and reliance on the more traditional systems of payment and effort measurement.

References

ACAS 1983: *Job Evaluation*. Advisory Booklet no. 1. ACAS, HMSO.

ACAS 1985: *Introduction to Payment Systems*. Advisory Booklet no. 2. ACAS, HMSO.

Brewster, C. and Connock, S. 1985: *Industrial Relations: cost-effective strategies*. London: Hutchinson.

Brown, W. 1989: Managing remuneration. In K. Sisson (ed.), *Personnel Management in Britain*, Oxford: Blackwell.

Burchill, F. 1976: *Introduction to Pay Systems and Pay Structures with a Note on Productivity*. P881 Industrial Relations Course, the Open University Press, Milton Keynes.

Fowler, A. 1988: New directions in performance related pay. *Personnel Management*, November, 30–4.

Goodrich, C.L. 1922: *The Frontier of Control*. London: Bell (republished 1975 by Pluto Press).

Gospel, H. 1983: The development of management organisation in industrial relations: a historical perspective. In K. Thurley and S. Wood (eds), *Industrial Relations and Management Strategy*, CUP. 91–110.

Hendry, C. et al. 1988: Changing patterns of human resource management. *Personnel Management*, November, 37–41.

IDS (Incomes Data Services) 1979: *Guide to Job Evaluation*. London: IDS.

IDS 1980: *Guide to Incentive Payment Systems*. London: IDS.

IDS 1981: *Guide to Profit Sharing*. London: IDS.

IDS 1985: *Improving Productivity*. Study 331. London: IDS.

IDS 1987: *PRP and Profit Sharing*. Study 397. London: IDS.

IDS 1988a: *Integrated Pay*. Study 411. London: IDS.

IDS 1988b: *Paying for Performance*. Top Pay Unit. London: IDS July.

IPM (Institute of Personnel Management) 1990: *Performance Related Pay*. Personnel Management Fact Sheet no. 30, June.

Jurgens, U., Dohse, K. and Malsch, T. 1986: New production concepts in West German car plants. In S. Tolliday and J. Zeitlin (eds), *The Automobile Industry and its Workers*, Cambridge: Polity Press.

Kessler, I. 1991: Workplace industrial relations in local government. *Employee Relations*, 13(2).

Kinnie, N. and Lowe, D. 1990: Performance related pay on the shop floor. *Personnel Management*, November, 45–9.

Knowles, K.G.J.C. 1952: *Strikes: a study in industrial conflict.* Oxford: Blackwell.

Livy, B. (ed.) 1988: *Corporate Personnel Management.* London: Pitman.

Lupton, T. and Gowler, D. 1969: *Selecting a Wage Payment System.* London: Routledge & Kegan Paul.

National Board for Prices and Incomes 1967: *Productivity Agreements.* Report no. 36. London: HMSO.

National Board for Prices and Incomes 1968a: *Payment by Results.* Report no. 65. London: HMSO.

National Board for Prices and Incomes 1968b: *Job Evaluation.* Report no. 83. London: HMSO.

Office of Manpower Economics 1973: *Measured Daywork.* London: HMSO.

Peters, T.J. and Waterman, R.H. 1982: *In Search of Excellence: lessons from America's best run companies.* New York: Harper & Row.

Royal Commission on Trade Unions and Employers' Associations 1968: Research paper no. 11. London: HMSO.

Sisson, K. (ed.) 1989: *Personnel Management in Britain.* Oxford: Blackwell.

Townley, B. 1990: Foucault. Power/knowledge and its relevance for HRM. Paper presented at a Conference on Employee Relations in the Enterprise Culture. Cardiff Business School, September 1990.

13

Training and Development

JEFF HYMAN

Introduction

The trickle of publications which announced the arrival of the 'human resource' dimension to management has swollen into a flood. No edition of *Personnel Management* (or more surprising, perhaps, *Employment Gazette*) would be complete without details of some success story of organizational change promoted, initiated and executed by an eager senior 'manager of human resources' as part of an integrated corporate strategy to meet and overcome competition, improve work flexibility, enhance quality and boost productivity and profits.

Academic commentators, while energetically expanding their research interest, output and publications into management and specifically, the HRM phenomenon, have tended to be somewhat more circumspect about actual developments. Most would agree that the broader environment within which organizations operate has been undergoing considerable change, particularly over the 1980s. Advances in technology, increased competition, the climate of enterprise engendered by the Conservative government and its compound ramifications in terms of industrial restructuring, union decline and influx of overseas operations have collectively and individually presented domestic organizations with a complex of challenges and opportunities. The immediate prospect of the Single European Market in 1992 and the longer-term effects of the revolutionary changes in Eastern Europe also heighten commercial uncertainty.

These manifold changes have helped to stimulate closer interest by researchers into the processes, strategies and practices of management and in particular the management of employment relations under conditions of turbulence. It appears that changed circumstances do not lead to uniform responses by employers; indeed, we can note considerable variation in the actions of managers in response to circumstances facing the organizations for which they are held accountable. Some attempts to manipulate the employment relationship have been allocated somewhat arbitrarily into either the 'hard' or 'soft' manifestations of HRM, the former calculative and based upon rational deployment of organizational assets, both human and capital, to serve immediate organizational ends. In contrast, the 'soft' approach, with its emphasis on motivation through communication and consultation, can trace its immediate ancestry to the human relations traditions espoused by Mayo and adopted, more recently, by Hertzberg, Argyris and others. Implicit to the soft approach is recognition of a long-term mutual commitment between employer and employees, a relationship which is lacking in the hard-edged version of HRM.

Though it would be difficult to embrace these somewhat diverse trends within a universal model of HRM, there are common features. Both promote the supremacy of individual employee relationships over the collective, either implicitly or through overt emphasis; both link employee management with broader operational directions to be taken by companies; accordingly, each stresses the need for an appropriate organizational culture ('corporate mission') in which these features can flourish. Researchers differ, though, over interpretations of the extent or depth to which migration towards either (or both) of these HRM poles has occurred. In particular, doubts linger as to the nature and extent of change in contemporary employment relations. For instance, commentators have questioned whether specific and embracing personnel policies are actually enacted beneath the superficial highly polished HRM gloss (Marginson et al. 1988). Flexibility, a key component of either approach to HRM, seems to be rather more elusive in its functional form than suggested by proponents for a multi-skilling revolution (MacInnes 1987:113–24), and initiatives in terms of part-time and short-term contractual employment are possibly not as widespread as originally asserted in early accounts (MacInnes 1987:115–17). Training and development form a special case owing to their centrality in changing the performance potential of employees and managers; this importance is testified by the gathering attention afforded to them in recent years by government (see White Paper 1988), practitioner bodies

such as the British Institute of Management, management consultants and increasingly, by academic researchers.

Until recently, however, training held little attraction for employers in the UK. Following publication of a succession of damning
comparative studies of UK industrial performance, realization has
hardened that British workers not only lack the skills of their
Continental, American and Japanese counterparts (NIESR 1989),
but that managers in the UK are sadly deficient in the qualities
found in abundance elsewhere and that little is done by their employers to help in the acquisition of qualifications and competence to
enable them to manage better (Handy et al. 1988; Constable and
McCormick 1987; Mangham and Silver 1986).

As employers are consistently failing to train their staff and
managers, it is difficult to see how they can be realistically pursuing
an HRM approach which is dependent upon learning as the vital
route to effective work and organizational performance. At the
conceptual level, Thurley's (1990:55) point that 'the HRM model
tends to focus on skill development' confirms the centrality of
training to HRM but fails to address the sort of model we are left
with if opportunities for skill development are not offered in practice. The assumed links between HRM, training and performance
again appear prominently in the diagrammatic representation of the
HRM process presented by Storey (1989:7). Even in its 'hard'
manifestation, short-term market forces would lead rational employers to train for immediate job requirements in the apparent
absence of alternative sources of labour. There is some evidence that
limited training opportunities are being offered by employers for that
reason (Training Agency 1989). Nevertheless, limited is the key
word; the same report points out that two-thirds of economically
active people aged between 19 and 59 claimed not to have received
any formal training over the previous three years. Moreover, many of
the respondents held scant expectations of receiving training, and
reflecting the 'anti-learning' cultural context typified by so many
organizations in the UK, pathetically few saw any point in seeking it
for the future.

The Failure to Train

But why do British employers fail to train and develop their staff,
when ample evidence exists that to do so offers them clear benefits?

In an illuminating article Keep identifies a number of barriers which must be surmounted if a genuine training climate is to be adopted. One problem is that the surmounting needs to be performed by personnel and training specialists, neither of whom have been well equipped for such activity. Moreover, the barriers are substantial; only a minority of senior managers are educated to levels enjoyed by their overseas counterparts and few have been recipients of sustained developmental programmes (Keep 1989:118). Consequently, training for their employees has not received high priority. Corporate objectives have tended to be short term with strategies defined by short-term profit and financial criteria, thereby constraining any longer-term developmental aspirations held by personnel specialists for their employees while encouraging the acquisition of required skills through poaching (Keep 1989:121). Indirectly related to the immediacy of domestic commercial activity, the continuing attachment by British managers to informality in their employment practices mitigates against the adoption of HRM, which, moreover, could jeopardize the authority (and conceivably, the jobs) of poorly equipped managerial staff by widening the scope of tasks performed by the subordinates. For this reason, resistance by line managers to some manifestations of HRM might be anticipated.

Somewhat understated in Keep's classification are the effects of government policy, though this is an essential influence upon employer orientations towards training. Traditionally voluntarist in direction, government policy in the UK eschews legislation or other formal incentives for employers to train their workforces systematically. Voluntarism has culminated in the market-led approach which has dominated the Conservative period of office which began in 1979, with training provision passed exclusively to employers to allocate on the basis of market need. The result has been that the imperatives of market uncertainty have, in combination with the other factors outlined above, conspired to loosen employer commitment to long-term training (*A Challenge to Complacency*, Coopers and Lybrand Associates 1985:7). This approach is in great contrast to the directions taken by the UK's leading trading partners: *A Challenge to Complacency* demonstrates that economically successful 'training countries' have real controls, legal, cultural or both, on training provision. Here, other than regular doses of exhortation, regulation is largely absent, and company executives feel little sustained pressure to change their ways.

If neither senior executives nor line managers can be relied upon to undertake responsibility for creating a positive environment for the development of employees, what is the scope for a personnel specialist presumably more sensitive to long-term consequences of such negligence? While personnel may wish for a stronger developmental orientation (and many personnel managers would be schooled in the corporate advantages to be gained from policy-making openly formulated and consistently implemented) they frequently find themselves in a less than strategic position to push their preferences. We have seen that many organizations adopt limited time horizons for the realization of their objectives, leading to the managerial ascendancy of the financial specialist and supremacy of cost controls as the mainspring of management action. And as Armstrong has pointed out, accountants experience severe difficulty in accounting for investments in people; one consequence is that training expenditure is regulated very much according to cost rather than developmental investment criteria. Further, personnel would find it difficult to justify training expenditure owing to the acknowledged difficulties in measuring its return in financial terms (Armstrong 1989:160). Not surprisingly, training evaluation beyond that of measuring its near-immediate impact upon individual recipients is rarely undertaken even in the most training-conscious organizations (Hussey 1988). The Training Agency (1989) which arrived at its conclusions through the careful aggregation of survey data, was nevertheless forced to rely largely upon anecdotal material to illuminate the benefical effects of training, an approach which, by neglecting to highlight failures, quantify effects or illustrate trends, represents an easy target for the corporate accountant intent upon cost reduction exercises.

Compounding the institutional weakness of personnel are its associations with employee welfare, its range of superficial and un-related activities and, until recently, a uniformly inferior position within the managerial hierarchy. A high proportion of personnel practitioners appear to lack professional and relevant qualifications, itself an interesting observation, bearing in mind that the same people would be expected to act as the prime organizational advocates for the benefits of education, training and qualifications for employees. Equally seriously, recent survey work indicates that formal and professional qualifications are held by limited numbers of training specialists. Moreover, the limited priority afforded to training was demonstrated in the survey by the high proportion (two-thirds) of designated training specialists who were reported to spend less than one-tenth of their time on training activities (Hyman and Bell 1989).

Opportunities for Training

The analysis so far makes sombre reading for the personnel specialist convinced of the value of systematic development policies for the workforce and wishing to convert, confirm or increase an organization's commitment to this vital activity. At this point, we can state that all is not gloom and there are a number of favourable signs; indeed, it could be argued that a combination of factors have currently converged to provide a more highly favourable context for promoting employee development than has been evident for some years, providing the personnel (or human resource!) practitioner with scope to apply the specialized 'expert' skills associated with the function (Torrington 1989) in this direction.

As we shall see, these favourable signs are clearly interrelated, but for purposes of analysis, can be located within structural and occupational categories. The structural factors include the following: impending problem of skill shortages and the need to recruit, 'grow', retain and motivate key employees; the increasing sophistication of technology; pressures of competition; quality of products and services; with these combining to ensure a need for greater employee flexibility, participation and adaptability. Positive occupational indicators derive from an increasing recognition by senior management of the relevance of personnel in confronting the structural challenges outlined above. This is seen by the growing acknowledgement of the importance of management education and development as expressed through the Management Charter Initiative, the enthusiastic acceptance by many senior managers of responsibilities offered to them to co-ordinate training and enterprise in the government's employer-dominated regional training bodies (see below), rising numbers of personnel specialists with formal occupational qualifications, and the recent apparent growth in personnel managers at senior director level. The trends towards some sophisticated personnel techniques, such as performance appraisal, also point towards a more consistent and integrative approach to employee management. The expanding significance of Europe on employment matters will also reinforce the need for personnel expertise. Personnel should now be considering how they can exploit the favourable tilt in their direction to establish a lasting organizational commitment to employee development. Each of the factors will now be considered in more depth.

Structural Factors

Skill and labour shortages

Two main strands comprise the staffing problem facing, or likely to face, most employers: first, is the projected decline in numbers of young people during the 1990s. Related to this 'demographic time-bomb' are the growing problems posed by general and specific skill shortages in key areas of the economy.

Numbers of 16–19-year-olds in the population are predicted to fall by a quarter between the years 1987 and 1995. Compounding this contraction is a growing pressure and tendency for young people to continue in education. In Scotland, for instance, the proportion of school-leaving higher education entrants has grown from 18 per cent of the age-group in 1982/3 to more than 21 per cent in 1988/9 (*THES* 7.9.90). Government intentions to bring the UK's modest higher education participation rates more into line with other countries is being reflected in the growing numbers of young people continuing with their education (Pearson et al. 1990:1; *THES* 24.8.90). An inevitable consequence of these trends will be a severe shortage of young people available to employers at school-leaving age. As a consequence of these trends, alternative sources of labour may be sought by employers. These would include older unemployed, retraining existing workers, attracting the economically inactive, such as early retirees and in particular, women returners. As Mairi Steele demonstrates in chapter 14, many employers are taking active steps to retain the services of women employees with accumulated skills and to offer training for women in occupations where labour shortages threaten productive efficiency.

The related problem of labour shortages derives directly from the UK's historical and continuing failure to train. We are now in the paradoxical situation of witnessing persistently high levels of unemployment coexisting with critical shortages of essential skills, even in regions with the highest levels of unemployment (see Department of Employment 1990: table 4.3). A recent CBI survey found that one-third of companies estimate that output is being adversely affected by skill shortages. Another study, conducted in Scotland, found that half of nearly 500 companies were experiencing difficulties in attracting appropriate labour, especially for professional, technical and skilled manual occupations (*Fraser of Allander Quarterly Economic Commentary* 1987). These problems could well be exacerbated when the Single European Market increases the mobility of valuable skills across national boundaries; the signs are that more qualified people will be enticed to work on mainland Europe than will be attracted to come and work in the UK. Employers are beginning to realize the gravity of the situation and personnel specialists are in a unique position to push claims for an integrated personnel policy offering high priority to employee development. The fact that most young graduates who leave their first positions after less than two years' service, do so through lack of fulfilment and opportunities for self-development provides personnel with valuable ammunition. The scope, and challenge, currently facing personnel is demonstrated by a survey reported recently in which over one-quarter of graduate recruits considered that their organizations did not show interest in their careers. Even worse, over one-third replied that their managers had not been trained to look after graduates, while a further 55 per cent were unable to say whether their managers had received this training (see *Personnel Management Plus* 1990:4).

New technology

The potential impact of new technology on work has been much examined in recent years (see e.g. Cooley 1987; Daniel 1987; Webster 1990) and is highly pertinent to the skills shortage issue outlined above in that the full productive capacities of new technology cannot be fully exploited in the absence of skills to operate and service it. Without the required familiarity, employers will either shrink from introducing technology, or if introduced, only part of the potential of new technology will be realized. In either case, the consequence will be a lack of competitive edge. The NIESR study into the manufacture of kitchen furniture in the UK and Germany provides startling evidence of how a highly skilled workforce interacts with technology to produce high quality and wide choice of output without compromise over productivity. Needless to say that this represented the German rather than British workforce; in the former, nine out every ten manual employees were qualified skilled craft workers, in contrast to the one in ten found in the British factories (Steedman and Wagner 1987).

If British employers are to move away from the 'low added value–low skills equilibrium' ascribed to them so appropriately by Finegold and Soskice (1988:22), technology must be embraced and the skills to operate and manage it must accompany its introduction and development. Evidence shows that most workforces readily accept new technology and that introduction is most successful when the human implications of its introduction in terms of participation, communication, security of employment through training and safety are given full and open consideration by management (McLoughlin and Clark 1988:72–4; Fogarty and Brooks 1986:9). The personnel specialist must, therefore, be familiar with technology and be in a position to insist to line colleagues and superiors that these 'human' conditions be fulfilled prior and subsequent to the implementation of technology. Managers, who generally speaking, are themselves not technologically literate should receive new technology training as an integral part of their own development: a survey by Brown/Coopers and Lybrand in 1988 disclosed that while two-thirds of managers had access to a computer, only two-fifths used a computer on a regular basis. Over half of the managers surveyed had received no training at all in the application of computer technology.

Pressures of competition

Competition can take many forms. Traditionally, product or service competition is based on cost to the consumer; *ceteris paribus*, in a competitive market, the least expensive product or service will prevail. In reality, of course, products serving the same market can vary considerably in terms of cost but in other factors as well. Quality of produce can vary, so that output from some sources or countries is automatically associated with value and quality, such as Marks and Spencer, or Japan as a quality producer country. Conversely, other products can be tarnished with the tag of poor quality or reliability (e.g. in 'finish' or in attention to detail). Availability is another potential source of difference, coupled with punctuality in delivery times and after-sales service. As we saw with the kitchen furniture example cited above, choice available in terms of model range or services offered is also likely to influence consumer behaviour.

Product competition between companies and between producer

countries is becoming more heated with anticipation of the Single European Market and the rise of developing countries to challenge the dominance of established producers. A major plank of the Conservative government's economic strategy to ensure economic stability has been to introduce or strengthen the operation of market forces in the public sector through privatization, compulsory competitive tendering, and more generally, through liberalizing the labour market and by providing the impetus behind the enterprise economy.

The disciplines of competition are forcing organizations to examine closely their methods of manufacture, quality, service and customer relations as key components of their service to consumers. Publications such as *In Search of Excellence* (Peters and Waterman 1982) stress the value of a service and quality-based corporate culture. While technical innovation will be a major feature in ensuring quality, choice and output, this must be combined with the required human inputs along the entire chain of production. Effort, attention to quality, adaptability and cost-effectiveness will be the necessary components of the productive mix. These demand not merely a level of technical competence, but also the commitment of all employees concerned and the challenge to the employer of retaining that commitment over time.

In these situations, training, in the broad sense of encouraging continuing positive orientations to the organization, becomes crucial, for this should help to establish and reinforce the crucial value-system base upon which the development of commitment can be built. But positive orientations do not, and will not, simply emerge from the organizational infrastructure; they need to be planned for and systematically implemented throughout the workforce. No greater contrast with earlier images of training restricted to a tiny minority of skilled craftsmen or the rare management course offered 'when conditions allow' could be envisaged.

The drive for quality

We saw above that competition is expressed strongly through attention to quality. A number of factors have contributed to this concentration on quality; first, new technology for production and services is able to perform consistently to the highest standards. Consumers now expect these standards to be met or exceeded.

Second, higher levels of disposable income mean that consumers are more concerned with quality than with price alone. The quality expectations of people grow in line with ever-improving standards and the publicity given to these through publications such as *Which* and growing numbers of televised consumer programmes.

Third, low-cost production can take place where labour is relatively inexpensive as in some developing countries and the emergent countries of Eastern Europe. Advanced economies cannot easily compete on labour cost criteria and aim to seek out appropriate market opportunities, possibly requiring smaller batch production at high quality and supported by continuing product innovation. Fourth, production and provision of services are now heavily internationalized. Developments made in the parent country can rapidly be reproduced in satellite operations, requiring competing producers to respond with equivalent or superior innovations, thereby stimulating further competitive reaction.

The emphasis given to quality in production and in service provision has clear implications for provider organizations in their approaches to employee management and in particular to training and development programmes. Hence, following the example set by Japanese producers, many organizations are now experimenting with built-in quality programmes such as 'zero defect' and 'right-first-time' manufacture. The infusive effect of this approach throughout the workforce can be seen from the account given by Peter Wickens (1987) of the Nissan production system. In a chapter entitled 'Quality – above all', Wickens makes reference to the commitment given to quality in the company's 'philosophy statement': 'We aim to build profitably the highest quality car sold in Europe.' He stresses that the positive commitment to quality permeates all levels of the company, and especially in management whose attitudes and knowledge derive from 'their education level, the seniority system, continuous in-house training, development and rotation and sheer dedication' (p. 63).

Encouraging employees to become their own quality controllers, implementing quality circles, team-building and associated groups or introducing and sustaining a 'quality culture' into the organization have far-reaching implications for the training and development of the entire workforce, particularly as it is almost impossible to impose quality requirements on employees. As Wickens points out, concern for quality must emerge from the relationship between employee and product. Hence, training for quality consciousness needs to be a continuous and inclusive part of the work of each employee, of each manager, and should be integral to the relationship between them.

Management style

If a concern for quality cannot be coerced into employees who are expected to assume greater responsibility for their work, there are additional implications for the employee–management relationship. In these conditions, managers need to learn to co-ordinate and advance the talents and skills of specialized staff. Key employees need to be encouraged to use their own discretion in arriving at speedy and effective solutions to problems surfacing in their spheres of activity. They need, though, access to the resources, informational and physical, required in order to resolve these issues. This approach to management calls for a 'high-trust' (to quote Fox 1985) relationship between the parties. Such a response cannot be forced from employees, but needs to be part of an agreed equation, in which management are willingly prepared to share information with subordinates, to delegate work and share responsibility (and rewards) while maintaining their overall authority on the basis of applied knowledge and organizational contribution rather than through titular status.

Participative management cannot take place within a vacuum. It requires to be adopted as part of an overall philosophy endorsed and applied throughout the organization. Many managers have an understandable fear of releasing valuable information to colleagues (let alone subordinates) fearing that to do so will dilute their responsibility or deprive them of authority. As Keep has pointed out, the prospects of greater employee self-reliance can be threatening to an under-educated and potentially vulnerable management team (1989:123). Training can help managers to overcome these fears, as well as offering them the opportunity to develop their own abilities for closer involvement in managerial affairs.

Practically, in the participative organization, managers will need to learn how to disclose and share information, possibly through formal consultation or communication networks; they will need to learn how to provide opportunities for individuals and groups to use their talents, and to encourage their development through appraisal and reward systems. These are not easy changes to contemplate for managers accustomed to a culture of protective secrecy, anxious to safeguard existing command structures for fear of losing face or status. Change of this sort can only be considered when senior management itself is prepared to take the lead in adapting its management style rather than concentrate on relying upon the artificial and self-defeating protections of hierarchy and secrecy.

The personnel and training function can provide a catalytic service in helping to bring about a more participative management style. Nevertheless, fears of sharing can only be genuinely dispelled when the sharers know that the consequences (there might be genuine fears that jobs are at risk from redundancy as organizations remove tiers in the organization structure through 'de-layering' – see 'Cutting out the middle manager', *Personnel Maragement Plus* 1990) to them will not be unfavourable. Managers can learn, but the organization must prepare secure ground for learning to take place.

Other factors also pointing to the importance of management style include the considerable changes occurring to the framework of organizations. Though the directions and extent of structural modification have varied, they are linked by a common strand in that change has been sought as a direct or indirect response to market pressures. Changes include moves to flexibility through subcontracting variable activities to external agencies, thereby helping to minimize otherwise fixed labour costs; decentralization of activities into product or geographical divisions (multidivisional or 'M' form); development of 'organic' structures to respond to market and process change; decentralized decision-making accompanied by devolution of bargaining arrangements to enterprise-, division- or establishment-level bargaining in organizations that recognize trade unions.

Second, is the move, in some organizations, at least, towards forms of work flexibility (ACAS 1988). Functional flexibility is associated with more responsibility. Employees gain increased discretion over their work, and in so doing become more valuable to the organization, which may introduce techniques such as performance appraisal and performance-related pay in order to monitor and stimulate work performance. Deficiencies can be remedied by supplementary training; high performers should receive regular opportunities to develop and extend their capabilities through training and development. It should also be added that appraisers will almost certainly require training in order to assess the work of subordinates systematically and fairly.

Our review of the shifts taking place within the broader context in which organizations operate and the complementary developments taking place within organizations themselves have clear implications both for personnel management generally and specifically for training and development, until now the least advanced and most neglected of all personnel activities.

However we define and describe HRM, it is clear that these changes are leading to re-evaluation by managers of employment relationships within a broad framework which gives priority to the attainment of organizational objectives. A significant outcome for managers and employees has been the rise in performance appraisal, new pay and bargaining arrangements and other significant changes to terms and conditions of employment. Nevertheless, if this re-evaluation is going to engage fully with the challenges facing organizations, it is imperative that full weight be given to training and development to accompany these initiatives. Further neglect will not only increase the distance between ourselves and competitor nations, but rapidly bring into question the motives of management towards restructuring employment relationships; the costs of change will have been borne by employees through job loss and continuing insecurity and the benefits, in terms of subsequent mutual commitment between the parties, largely illusory.

Occupational Factors

Personnel is going to have to fight its own corner in converting the potential noted above into developmental reality for managers and employees. But at least, they will be so engaged at a time when conditions for advance are relatively favourable. We can point to at least six areas which engage with the structural changes noted earlier which could place personnel specialists in a more favourable position to promote their case for continuing investment in employees and managers. First, we can note the positive reception by employers to the wide-ranging criticisms contained in the Handy and Constable and McCormick reports (1987) into management education, development and training. Positive action emerged quickly through the establishment of the Management Charter Initiative to which increasing numbers of employers have committed their organizations to follow a charter of good practice for their managerial employees. By early 1990, 600 organizations, employing nearly one in three of the UK's managers and in excess of 7 million people, had committed themselves to the Charter (*THES* 6.4.90).

A second sign of senior management endorsement of the links between training and performance has been the enthusiastic reception and initial involvement by senior executives as members of almost 100 Training and Enterprise Councils (TECs, Local Enterprise Companies (LECs) in Scotland) established by the government to assess, co-ordinate and deliver training on a regional basis throughout the country.

A third factor concerns the status of personnel, reflected in specialist contributions to management and relatedly, to its place within the managerial hierarchy. At the beginning of the 1980s Daniel and Millward (1983) noted that many personnel practitioners were not specialists in the function. Only about one-quarter had occupational personnel qualifications and only an equivalent proportion worked exclusively in personnel. Some recent signs indicate that personnel managers are becoming better qualified both in terms of basic education and occupational qualifications (Torrington 1989:57,63; Whittaker 1989). While personnel is unlikely to establish the credentials usually associated with professional status (see e.g. Sisson 1989:13), greater specialization demonstrated through occupational qualifications should allow personnel specialists more scope to offer 'expert' employment management authority in its relations with their line, other functional and senior management counterparts.

Also emerging from the 1980 WIRS survey was the minority (42 per cent) of establishments with specialist personnel practitioners represented at board level, where they might be in a position both to influence organization-wide issues and to incorporate personnel matters for consideration at the highest organization levels. A subsequent WIRS survey conducted at the height of the recession and amid high unemployment in 1984 provided a stable figure of 43 per cent main board personnel or industrial relations representation (Millward and Stevens 1986:35). However, in a large-scale survey conducted in the winter of 1989, a rather more favourable picture emerges: over 60 per cent of 'heads of personnel' were reported to have a place on the main board of directors, and in organizations with more than 5000 employees, this proportion rose to three-quarters (Price Waterhouse 1990).

Fourth, though as yet signs of a more profound approach to training and development by employers are limited, there are indications of change in related aspects of employee management which should provide some leverage for personnel specialists, especially those with strategic and board responsibilities, to link these changes with employee development. Performance appraisal, with its intent to change individual behaviour at work (Randell 1989:159) and employee development are clearly closely related, particularly as one strand to the purpose of appraisal is geared towards identifying and furthering employee potential. Performance appraisal unaccompanied by formal and implemented training opportunities will rapidly signal to employees the 'contractual' as opposed to commitment (or 'social'; see Streek 1988) orientation to their relations with managers.

A fifth factor concerns the moves taking place towards European integration. Thurley has suggested that tension between the competition implied by the Single European Market and the requirement that member states compete on equal terms within an agreed structure of employment regulation could lead to the development of a 'European model' of personnel management. This model would encompass the principles of employee rights and obligations as laid down in the Social Charter overlaid with a respect for cultural and national differences and values. Achieving this balance in the management of the international enterprise emphasizes key roles for education and staff development: 'European integration will result in the demand for new international education and training courses to develop specialists to help shape the policies that will make such international firms actually work' (Thurley 1990:57).

Finally, we return to our earlier observation that training and development are central to an HRM approach to employee management. We also pointed out that organizations which purported to recognize their staff as assets, but then failed to invest in these assets, could scarcely be following an HRM approach. The apparently high levels of disaffection expressed by graduate recruits regarding their advancement prospects would seem to confirm the presence of a gap between organizational intent and practice. Conversely, there are companies with expressed policies which fit the 'committed' HRM profile and for which training and development form an inclusive part of both organizational philosophy and practice. It is perhaps not surprising that many of these organizations show senior management commitment to training, expressed possibly through subscription to the Management Charter Initiative and have energetic and influential personnel departments to pursue the training ideal.

Concluding Comments

Evidence from diverse sources shows that changes are taking place to and within organizations; size, differentiation of structure, control systems, allocation of responsibilities are all under corporate scrutiny as organizations, in the public and private sector alike, face up to the implications of a threatening and uncertain economic climate. In these circumstances, particularly with signs of world recession all too apparent, domestic inflation and interest rates at uncomfortably high levels, and prompted by financial advisers intent on preserving shareholder dividends, managers may be tempted to seek cost cuts as their primary route to survival; already there are signs that physical investment is being cut back in response to current market signals. If physical investment is at risk, what might be the fate of human investment through development, an area continously neglected by UK managers in this country, even under favourable conditions?

An alternative response to the developments taking place at present concerns the need to plan, or to invest, for the future, an aspect of management totally at odds with the short time-span approach seeking immediate shareholder gratification. Companies which operate in countries with supportive financial institutions and which are consequently under less threat from corporate predators, can plan their activities according to more distant horizons, diversify their activities and seek out new markets in the confidence that their managers and workforces are capable of adapting to new conditions. The evidence shows that British managers persist with their shrinking world, successively cutting back those areas where developmental costs might be incurred even though competition has to be faced, in terms of quality, productivity and service. Yet, despite constant publicity and governmental exhortations, there have been few signs that companies are training and developing their employees at the levels and depths necessary to meet these challenges.

Training and development, therefore, should not be seen simply as a desirable component of HRM, but as evidence from comparative studies show, as an essential contributor to organizational objectives. The fact that it is difficult to identify a specific contribution should not deter the personnel specialist from pressing claims for investment in employee development; as stated above, many successful organizations integrate their developmental activities within a broader personnel perspective such that making an attempt at evaluation of training's contribution in isolation from these other factors (and from the effects of technological investments) becomes a highly questionable exercise. It is interesting that in Japan, the level of integration of training into management processes makes for difficulty in estimating training budgets, which tend to exclude major indirect expenditure items (Dore and Sako 1989:81).

For too long, British employers have rejected training and development, but through a conjunction of relatively favourable structural and occupational factors personnel is now in a stronger position to press the case for human investment as a concomitant to physical investment. Whether this is undertaken as part of an explicit HRM orientation or independently as an expression of effective management of people towards securing organizational objectives is immaterial. After many years in which training companies faced and had to contend with poaching from non-trainers, we are beginning to move into a 'reverse-poaching' direction in that non-training companies, albeit those that pay well, may risk losing valuable staff to the minority of organizations which offer career prospects and full opportunities for advancement to men and women.

References

ACAS 1988: *Labour Flexibility in Britain*. Occasional Paper no. 41. London: ACAS.

Armstrong, P. 1989: Limits and possibilities for HRM in an age of management accountancy. In J. Storey (ed.), *New Perspectives on Human Resource Management*, London: Routledge, 154–66.

Brown, R. and Coopers and Lybrand 1988: *Managers and Information Technology Competence*. BIM.

Constable. J, and McCormick, R. 1987: *The Making of British Managers*. BIM/CBI.

Cooley, M. 1987: *Architect or Bee?* Hogarth.

Coopers and Lybrand Associates 1985: *A Challenge to Complacency*. MSC/NEDO.

Daniel, W.W. 1987: *Workplace Industrial Relations and Technical Change*. Frances Pinter/PSI.

Daniel, W.W. and Millward, N. 1983: *Workplace Industrial Relations in Britain*. London: Heinemann.

Department of Employment 1990: *Labour Market and Skill Trends 1991/92*.

Dore, R.P. and Sako, M. 1989: *How the Japanese Learn to Work*. Routledge.

Finegold, D. and Soskice, D. 1988: The failure of training in Britain: analysis and prescription. *Oxford Review of Economic Policy*, 4(3), Autumn, 21–53.

Fogarty, M. and Brooks, D. 1986: *Trade Unions and British Industrial Development*. PSI.

Fox, A. 1985: *Man Mismanagement*, 2nd edn. Hutchinson.

Fraser of Allender Quarterly Economic Commentary 1987: 13(2), November, 62–7.

Handy, C. et al. 1988: *Making Managers*. Pitman.

Hussey, D. 1988: *Management Training and Corporate Strategy*. Pergamon.

Hyman, J. and Bell, K.R. 1989: *A Training Revolution? The Experience of Scotland*. University of Strathclyde, Discussion Paper no. 1.

Keep, E. 1989: Corporate training strategies: the vital component? In J. Storey (ed.), *New Perspectives on Human Resource Management*, London: Routledge, 109–25.

MacInnes, J. 1987: *Thatcherism at Work*. Milton Keynes: Open University Press.

McLoughlin, I. and Clark, J. 1988: *Technological Change at Work*. Open University Press.

Mangham, I. and Silver, M.S. 1986: *Management Training: context and practice*. ESRC.

Marginson, P. et al. 1988: *Beyond the Workplace*. Oxford: Blackwell.

Millward, N. and Stevens, M. 1986: *British Workplace Industrial Relations 1980–1984*. Aldershot: Gower.

NIESR (National Institute of Economic and Social Research) 1989: *Productivity, Education and Training*.

Pearson, R. et al. 1990: How many graduates in the twenty-first century? Summarised in *IMS Report* no. 177.

Personnel Management Plus 1990: 1(3), September.

Peters, T. and Waterman, R. 1982: *In Search of Excellence*. New York: Harper & Row.

Price Waterhouse/Cranfield 1990: *Project on International Strategic Human Resource Management, Report*.

Randell, G. 1989: Employee appraisal. In K. Sisson (ed.), *Personnel Management in Britain*, Oxford: Blackwell, 149–76.

Sisson, K. 1989: Personnel management in perspective. In K. Sisson (ed.), *Personnel Management in Britain*, Oxford: Blackwell.

Steedman, H. and Wagner, K. 1987: A second look at productivity, machinery and skills in Britain and Germany. *National Institute Economic Review*, no. 122, November, 84–96.

Storey, J. 1989: Introduction. In J. Storey (ed.), *New Perspectives on Human Resource Management*, London: Routledge.

Streek, W. 1988: The uncertainties of management in the management of uncertainty. *Work, Employment and Society*, 3(1), 281–308.

Thurley, K. 1990: Towards a European approach to personnel management. *Personnel Management*, September, 54–7.

Torrington, D. 1989: Human resource management and the personnel function. In J. Storey (ed.), *New Perspectives on Human Resource Management*, London: Routledge, 56–66.

Training Agency, 1989: *Training in Britain*. Main Report. HMSO.

Webster, J. 1990: *Office Automation*. Harvester Wheatsheaf.

White Paper 1988: *Employment for the 1990s*. Cm 540, December.

Whittaker, J. 1989: Institute membership – passport or profession? *Personnel Management*, August, 30–5.

Wickens, P. 1987: *The Road to Nissan*. London: Macmillan.

14

Human Resource Management: an Opportunity for Women?

MAIRI STEELE

Introduction

The opportunities and problems for women returning to and staying active in the labour market have received much attention recently both in academic and management circles and in the media generally. This interest is largely due to concern over existing skill shortages in certain sectors and locations (Employment Department Group 1991) and over predicted labour shortages arising from a reduction in the number of young entrants into the labour market – the so-called 'demographic time bomb' (NEDO/TC 1988). How employers should rise to these challenges has also taken up considerable space in practitioner journals and the media. Recent reports from, among others, the Institute of Manpower Studies (IMS), illustrate this concern; *The Under-Utilisation of Women in the Labour Market* (Metcalf and Leighton 1989); *Good Practices in the Employment of Women Returners* (Rajan and van Eupen 1990) and *Retaining Women Employees* (Metcalf 1990). The Institute of Personnel Management (IPM) has also turned its attention towards '"carer-friendly employment practices" for effective human resourcing' (Berry-Lound 1990).

Dickens (1989:168) suggests (in an edition of the *Industrial Relations Journal* devoted entirely to women in employment) that women are in the process of being rediscovered as a valuable resource and that if employers are to cope with changes in the labour market they

> will need to plan their human resource needs in a strategic way: considering new patterns of recruitment, exploring new sources of

Table 14.1 Women of working age in employment working full-time and part-time, Great Britain

	1979		1984		1989		Change 1979–89
	000	*%*	*000*	*%*	*000*	*%*	*(000)*
In employment[a]	9,030		9,202		10,705		+1,675
Full-time	5,603	62	5,221	56	6,063	57	+460
Part-time	3,426	38	3,945	43	4,460	42	+1,034

[a] Includes those who did not state whether they worked full-time or part-time.
Source: Employment Gazette (1990b: table 2).

recruits and/or a reshaping of the jobs to which people are recruited; considering better ways of retaining and fully utilising existing employees with re-skilling and training to aid redeployment.

Thus it would seem apposite to devote a chapter to the question of women at work in a textbook on human resource management (HRM). In this chapter the changing position of women in the labour market will be considered, as will the constraints which hinder women's participation in the labour market and the various employer initiatives and strategies designed to recruit and retain female employees. If HRM is about developing the skills and capabilities of individuals then it would seem to be a golden opportunity for women to improve their position and terms and conditions at work, assuming of course that women, as resources, are treated equally regardless of sex or marital status. This may, unfortunately, be rather a large assumption to make.

The Changing Position of Women in the Labour Market

Today more and more women are going out to work and they make up an increasing proportion of the British labour force, currently 43 per cent (EOC 1991). More women are working full-time than in the past although a significant proportion of women, particularly married women, work part-time (table 14.1).

It is estimated that both the numbers and the proportion of women in the labour force will continue to increase throughout the

Table 14.2 UK civilian labour force aged 16 and over, 1981–2000

	Thousands			*Percentage changes*	
	1981	*1988*	*2000*	*1981–8*	*1988–2000*
All	26,883	28,275	29,334	4.5	3.7
Women	10,845	12,041	12,999	9.9	7.9
Men	16,038	16,233	16,335	0.8	0.6

Source: Employment Gazette (1990a).

1990s (table 14.2). Some estimate they will represent 47 per cent by the year 2000 (*Employment Gazette* 1989b) while others (Henley Centre) suggest that this could be as high as 50 per cent (Berry-Lound 1990:19). The employment prospects for women in the next decade will be enhanced by the much debated decline in the number of young people entering the labour market (NEDO/TA 1989; NEDO/TC 1988) as employers are being urged to seek alternative sources of labour and adopt non-traditional recruitment practices to meet this shortfall.

While participation rates for women in the UK labour force are already high, the employment of women continues to be concentrated in certain sectors and occupations, notably in non-manual jobs and in the service sector (table 14.3).

In addition, within these occupations women are less likely to be in higher-level jobs and women who work part-time are more likely to be in lower-skilled jobs. Metcalf and Leighton argue that this indicates a significant underutilization of women's capabilities and that 'human capital is being wasted' (1989:38). Indeed, because of dependant care and family responsibilities and the related need to work part-time, returning to the labour market can mean a step down for women in terms of jobs, grading, pay and occupational status (Dex 1987). However, given that the service sector and part-time working are predicted to expand in the next decade (IER 1989) this would appear to augur well for the employment of women.

Overall then, the trend in the post-war period has been for more women to be in paid employment. The reasons for this are both complex and interrelated:

Table 14.3 Occupational analysis of people in employment aged 16 and over, by sex, 1990[a] (%)

	Male	*Female*
All occupations	56.6	43.4
Managerial and professional	62.3	37.7
Clerical and related	19.3	80.7
Other non-manual occupations	46.7	53.3
Craft and similar occupations including foremen in processing production repairing, etc.	89.7	10.3
General labourers	91.2	8.8
Other manual occupations	54.8	45.2

[a] Preliminary 1990 LFS estimates.
Source: Employment Gazette, April 1991.

- growth in sectors and occupations which traditionally employ large numbers of women;
- financial reasons, although these are complex depending on whether the woman has a husband in employment; whether the woman has a high financial dependence on work; on wider economic and political factors which influence household budgets; short- and long-term financial needs;
- social reasons;
- dissatisfaction with domestic life and work;
- career reasons;
- changing attitudes towards working mothers.

However, the lifetime working patterns of women vary considerably and are related to whether they are married or not and whether they have children (or other dependant care responsibilities) and what age the children are. For the majority of women the birth of the first child is associated with a break from the labour market and the trend is for this to be a shorter break. Returning to work is also related to the number of children, for although some 14 per cent return to work within six months of the birth of their first child only 3 per cent of women return within six months after subsequent births (Martin and Roberts 1984:125). However, these figures disguise an underlying trend. Increasing proportions of women are returning to work after childbirth. The proportion of women returning to work within six months of their first child being born is also increasing but this is largely dependent on occupation and level of qualification

(McRae 1991). Women with higher-level qualifications (A level and above) and non-manual intermediate occupations are more likely to return to work within six months and are more likely to return to full-time employment. A number of factors influence this decision:

- Women with higher-level qualifications/occupations may be established in a career that they do not wish to interrupt and indeed may be under pressure to return or else lose status or position within the career structure.
- They are more likely to be in better paid jobs and therefore suffer greater economic loss by not returning.
- The conditions on returning to work attached to enhanced maternity pay and leave may be influential. For example, an employer may require a woman to return for a specified period, say at least three months, after her maternity leave or she may be liable to pay back some maternity pay.

In addition, it was found that unsupported mothers are particularly likely to return to work straight after the birth of the first child despite being in low-level occupations.

While women's motivations to work and working patterns may be complex they raise clear issues for the human resource (HR) specialist:

- Motivation and commitment to work vary during different phases in their working life.
- Part-time work is often attractive to women with children even if they are not fully utilizing their skills and abilities. This is a waste of resources.
- The longer a woman is out of the labour market the greater the difficulties she will encounter when returning in terms of confidence and skill requirements.

Women, then, are an underutilized and valuable resource regardless of demographic or skills pressures prominent at present (Rajan and van Eupen 1990). There are, however, several factors which make it difficult for women to participate fully in the world of work and realize their full potential.

Despite the increase in female activity rates in the labour market, there remain some 6 million women who are not in paid employment. Obviously not all these women are either able or willing to work but estimates from the 1988 *Labour Force Survey* suggest that nearly 900,000 were keen to return to work but were unable to do so (unpublished data; see Berry-Lound 1990:21). There are a number of related factors which deter women from returning to or staying active in the labour market:

- dependant care responsibilities;
- financial considerations;
- employment practices;
- discrimination;
- access to training.

The aim of the second part of this chapter is to examine these constraints and to consider some of the initiatives designed to enable women to return or stay active in the labour market. However, public policy developments should not be overlooked as they set the framework in which these initiatives are introduced.

Dependant Care

The lack of appropriate and affordable dependant care is often cited as the most important constraining factor on women's employment and it is one which has received considerable attention recently, Metcalf and Leighton (1989) estimate that in the UK there are 2.7 million women with children and 964,000 women caring for the elderly and infirm who are not in paid employment. Scott (1989a) in her study *Families and Under Fives in Strathclyde* found that 63 per cent of non-working mothers would choose to work if suitable child care was available (47 per cent of those would choose to work part-time).

There are several major issues related to dependant care which make returning to work less attractive, reduce female participation in the labour market and determine the nature of employment they return to. These include:

- cost of dependant care and effect on net earnings – varies according to the age and number of children;
- availability of dependant care (including travel considerations);
- quality of available dependant care provision;
- employment opportunities are restricted due to the hours women are not available to work and times of year when child care becomes problematic (e.g. school holidays).

Dependant care is not only a constraint for those women wishing to return to or stay active in the labour market but it is also a constraining factor for women who wish to train, retrain or enter further education (Scott 1989b).

The provision of child care in the UK is inadequate and compares unfavourably with other European countries. The EOC (1991) estimates that in Scotland and England there are day nursery places for only 2 per cent of under-fives, while the figure for Wales is 1 per cent. Cohen (1988) argues that the provision of child care in the UK is piecemeal, relies heavily on private and voluntary providers and that the provision for working parents has been the most neglected area. One consequence of this is that the UK has one of the lowest employment rates for mothers of pre-fives in Europe. However, the area of dependant care is one in which positive action can be taken by employers, local authorities and the state.

Financial Reasons

While many women work primarily for financial reasons, the marginal income to be gained from employment can also work as a disincentive to many women (Metcalf and Leighton 1989). Once tax, national insurance and dependant care costs are taken into consideration it may not be financially worth while. Given the current social security structure this is particularly the case if a woman has an unemployed husband or if she is a single parent. In addition, despite legislation on equal pay, gender differences in pay continue although EOC argues that these may be narrowing (EOC 1991).

Employment Practices

There are several ways in which employment practices act as disincentives to women. These are often closely related to the issue of child care but also involve wider questions of equal opportunity policies and practices. There are two main areas in which employer attitudes and practices have a negative effect on women:

- inflexible working time;
- continued discrimination in recruitment, selection and access to training.

In addition to employer practices, deep-seated attitudes towards working women, in particular those who work part-time, remain. Women are seen as being less ambitious, not worth training or promoting because they will only leave to have children, women are unreliable (because of domestic responsibilities) and generally less committed to work than male counterparts. Marriage for a man is seen as stabilizing while for women it is seen in terms of child bearing, maternity costs and the end of her career. These attitudes are still dominant and must act as an underlying constraint.

Flexible Working Arrangements

It has been established that the majority of women with domestic responsibilities who wish to return to the labour market would prefer to work part-time (see for example, Scott 1989a). However, the majority of part-time jobs are low status, low skilled and low paid. At the other end of the spectrum professional posts are often not available on a part-time basis and as a result many women return at a lower status. What is needed is a more balanced approach which recognizes the needs of the business or organization and the needs of employees.

Part-time work has traditionally been offered to women with domestic responsibilities but even the hours in which part-time work is offered may not be suitable. The problem of flexible working also changes according to family circumstances. So, for example, women with school-aged children may need to limit their working time to school hours and may be unable (or it may not be cost-effective) to work during the school holidays. In short, part-time work only goes a little way to encourage female participation in the labour market. Other strategies are also needed such as flexitime, term-time working, job-sharing, school hour and twilight shift working. These are considered in more depth below.

Discrimination

Unfortunately legislation relating to sex (and race) discrimination and to equal pay has not eradicated discrimination in recruitment, selection, promotion and training at work. This is apparent by the continued existence of job segregation – women are concentrated into a few occupations and into lower-status jobs; the majority of women work in low-paid jobs and inequalities in pay between men and women remain (EOC 1991).

Women are subjected to discrimination on at least two levels:

• in selection and recruitment for jobs which offer promotion and career prospects;

- in work in terms of access to training and, as a result, promotion.

There remains a reluctance to promote or train part-time workers and this of course disproportionately affects women. As a result of continued discrimination at work and prevailing attitudes towards working women, their skills and experience are not being fully utilized in the economy. As Metcalf and Leighton (1989:68) argue, this is 'a waste of human capital and, through reducing intrinsic job interests and pay, a reduction in participation'.

Discrimination in training at work is one dimension but more important for women seeking to return to the labour market are training and education opportunities available to them out of the work environment, such as training to encourage and facilitate re-entry, training to avoid downgrading on returning and training and education to learn new skills. Women encounter various disincentives including gender stereotyping of subjects and courses, the timing of courses and ability to attend and, of course, the persistent problem for the majority of women seeking to return to work, dependant care.

Employer Initiatives

So, what have employers done to try and alleviate these difficulties and deterrents to women's employment and what are the lessons to be learned from these? Three main areas will be considered: dependant care, flexible working practices and equal opportunities.

Dependant care

Despite changing attitudes towards working women and changing attitudes among men themselves regarding their child-care responsibilities, women continue to shoulder much of the responsibility for child and other dependant care. Evidence shows, however, that employer assistance with child care does improve the retention of staff (*IRRR* 1988a,b; IRS 1990) and enhances the company's image when seeking to attract female employees. The issue, however, is complex depending on the age of the children or relative concerned and the various demands made on the employee at different stages in the 'care cycle'. As the care issue is one which presents most difficulties for women it would seem one which the HR manager should tackle. This assistance can take several forms (although these focus almost exclusively on child care), including:

- workplace nurseries;
- buying places in joint venture or private nurseries;
- financial assistance or voucher schemes;
- maintaining a register/network of qualified childminders;
- unpaid leave during school holidays/term-time working;
- school holiday playschemes;
- after-school care assistance;
- time-off/special leave for care of sick dependants;
- improved maternity leave;
- career breaks.

Of these schemes workplace nurseries have probably received most publicity recently, although the actual extent and coverage of such schemes are small (Berry-Lound 1990; NEDO/TA 1989; Craig and Morgan 1989; IRS 1990; Metcalf 1990). Research indicates that workplace child-care initiatives are concentrated in certain sectors (e.g. banking and finance) and are determined by geographic and local labour market conditions. In addition, workplace nurseries are not the cure-all the media or pioneering companies would have us believe and indeed other forms of assistance, such as vouchers or direct financial help, may be more cost-effective and appropriate for both employer and employee. Joint ventures, where several employers combine their resources to provide child care, may be more attractive to employers although these are limited in the number of places each employer can offer to its employees. Alternatively, employers can keep a register of qualified and available childminders while the employee remains responsible for arranging the care.

While there has been a marked increase in employer interest in workplace child care it is unlikely that this approach could ever come close to solving the child-care problem. Indeed it has been argued that in the private sector in particular 'childcare needs will be dictated by commercial advantage, not by the needs of parents and children' (Working for Childcare 1990:20). Many employers would in fact question whether they should be responsible for child-care provision, arguing that this is a matter for government intervention or local authority responsibility. In an effort to widen the debate, the EOC has advocated the introduction of a 'caring tax' whereby employers pay 1–2 per cent of payroll to help meet the costs of national child-care provision. Government and parents would also contribute and funds would be channelled through a National Childcare Development Agency (EOC 1990).

The advantages and disadvantages of workplace nurseries may be listed as follows:

Advantages
- retention of skilled and experienced staff;
- minimize absenteeism and disruption to working day;
- good company image;
- quality care and employee peace of mind;
- equal opportunities.

Disadvantages
- deals with only one phase of child's life cycle;
- cost – set up and running;
- demand exceeding supply;
- travel to work considerations for employee with young children.

Given the wide range of care-related schemes listed above there are a number of ways in which HR specialists can at least go part way to alleviating the dependant care problem for women. Metcalf (1990) found that the most common practice in this area was allowing time-off for the care of sick children, with much of this being given on an informal basis. Formal arrangements were more common in local authorities due to pressure from trade unions and as part of the authority's equal opportunities programme. These arrangements can obviously only go a small way towards dealing with the dependant care problems but should nevertheless be an integral part of any dependant care package.

As part of this package many employers now offer maternity leave and pay above the statutory minimum, and this can involve widening eligibility to those employees who would not normally qualify, extending periods of paid and unpaid maternity leave and increasing levels of maternity pay. Some companies are now going as far as offering financial incentives for a fixed period after a woman returns to work. Abbey National offer an extra £75 a month for two years after maternity leave and Legal and General boost pay by 25 per cent for the first six months after maternity leave (*Financial Times* 17.7.90).

Related to extended maternity leave is the concept of career breaks which offer employees longer periods away from work to devote to child care with the possibility of returning to the same employer at the same grade. Evidence shows an increased interest in such schemes outwith the sectors in which they are already popular, such as banking, insurance and finance (*IRRR* 1989). Brannen (1989) found that women who return to work with the same employer after childbirth are more likely to be promoted or remain at the same grade than those who resigned during maternity leave and moved to another employer. While career breaks are in an experimental phase and their extent is limited it would appear that such schemes are advantageous to women in terms of their occupational mobility and to employers in terms of the utilization of skilled and experienced workers. Career break schemes vary considerably between employers but the main features are:

- an extended period of time away from work, normally to look after children, with regular contact being maintained between employee and employer;
- length of service and other conditions must be met before an employee is eligible (e.g. length of service, satisfactory performance, good career prospects);
- breaks can be complete or the employee may be able to work part-time but return eventually to full-time employment;
- contact maintained during the period off which may include an undertaking to work during specified periods (e.g. to provide holiday cover);
- some employers guarantee a return to the same job and at the same grade while others do not.

The advantages and disadvantages of career breaks may be summarized as follows:

Advantages
- improved recruitment and retention of skilled and experienced staff;
- maintains occupational mobility of staff;
- staff confidence, skills and experience not lost through keep-in-touch schemes;
- provides a pool of temporary, but experienced, labour;
- costs little to organize and operate.

Disadvantages
- eligibility. May only be offered to a limited number of staff and at sole discretion of management;
- jobs may not be guaranteed;
- financial loss to employees.

Flexible working

Closely related to the dependant care issue is the question of flexible working time. The traditional approach to accommodating women's family and work responsibilities has been to offer part-time work. However, part-time work is often poorly paid, of low status and there is an assumption that only certain types of job are suitable. However, these attitudes and practices are changing, particularly among employers faced with labour and skill shortages and recruitment and retention problems, and there have been improvements in the terms and conditions of part-time workers (IDS 1990). The evidence shows that it is now more unusual for part-timers to be paid less than pro rata for doing the same job as a full-timer and that employers are now more willing to improve other terms and conditions of part-timers, such as pension provision, redundancy rights, maternity entitlement, sick pay schemes, profit and share schemes. However, part-time jobs are still concentrated in certain sectors (services, distribution and hotels and catering) and in certain occupations, notably clerical, administrative and sales jobs.

There are, of course, a number of strategies available to the HR manager who seeks to introduce more flexible working time arrangements. These include:

- flexitime;
- job-sharing;
- term-time working/school hours shifts;
- twilight shifts;
- homeworking.

Of these options, flexitime and job-sharing are the most common although increasingly employers are experimenting with alternatives. Boots, Dixons and Thistle Hotels, for example, have introduced term-time working for parents in an effort to ease recruitment and retention difficulties.

Equal opportunities

Essentially the schemes discussed above involve the organization taking remedial action to remedy the effects of past discrimination. Although many employers describe themselves as equal opportunities employers, discrimination on the grounds of sex and marital status persists and women are subjected to deep-seated attitudes towards them as workers and moreover as working mothers. The initiatives discussed above seek to address some of the specific difficulties encountered by women in the world of work. However, if these schemes are not an integral part of a wider commitment to equal opportunities then they will not prove to be the golden opportunity alluded to in the opening paragraphs and the under-utilization of women as a valuable resource will continue. Thus consideration should be given to the benefits (to both men and women) of putting EO polices into practice (EOC 1986):

● better utilization of skills and resources;
● improved motivation and performance, reducing turnover;
● developing people's abilities;
● positive image of the organization;
● improved communications and industrial relations.

Specific attention should be given to recruitment and selection, training (for both employees generally and those involved in the recruitment and selection process), promotion procedures and terms and conditions of employment, including equalizing pay and access to other benefits.

The conclusion to be drawn from the above discussion is that employer initiatives aimed at recruiting and retaining female employees should not be seen in terms of a shopping list. A range of schemes and initiatives which match the needs of the business and the varying needs of the employees needs to be adopted within a framework which seeks to widen equal opportunities.

Human Resource Management and Women

The question remains, is HRM an opportunity for women at work in terms of developing skills and abilities and career prospects? It is a question which so far has been overlooked in the HRM debate and will be difficult to answer here without entering headlong into the problematic area of defining the term HRM (already dealt with in chapter 1 and elsewhere) and how it differs from 'traditional' or 'conventional' personnel management or employee relations. However, it is the intention of this final section to attempt an initial discussion and hopefully raise areas for further debate and analysis. This will be done at three levels: the HRM view of women, the strategic nature of HRM and the role of trade unions and collective bargaining. The HRM debate focuses almost exclusively on a generic view of employees and the exclusion of any analysis of gender. (An exception is Scase and Goffee (1990) although this is limited to women in management.) This sanitized view of employee relations implies that 'human resources' will be treated equally and have equal access to career development and progression. While equal treatment is surely to be welcomed by women (and indeed other groups at work), can HRM deliver and can any gains made as a result of HRM policies be permanent?

Much depends on the organization's view of women; are they viewed as a cost or investment (Hendry and Pettigrew 1990), 'valued asset rather than variable cost' (Storey 1989:8)? The perception of women in the organization and the level of understanding of their specific problems will to a large extent determine the nature of the employers' 'women-friendly' policies and perhaps more importantly, levels of commitment to them. Many of the initiatives discussed in the preceding section are driven by labour market pressures which certainly perceive some women as valuable assets and go some way to acknowledging the specific constraints faced by women. However, there is a tendency for these schemes to be directed at women in higher-level positions who are eligible or can afford to take advantage of child-care facilities, career breaks, job-sharing, etc. But is this a recognition of women as a valued asset to the organization or are these schemes to be viewed merely in terms of a short-term 'man-power tactic' (Atkinson 1984)?

Rajan and van Eupen (1990) argue that schemes directed at en-couraging women returners should first and foremost encompass a clear corporate policy with mechanisms for implementing them. This would appear to square with perceptions and definitions of HRM in terms of commitment to corporate strategy, strategic business policies, long-term planning and a heightened status for the human side of enterprise. This 'hard' version of HRM, seemingly responsive to changes in the market through flexibility and the treatment of employees in a rational and quantitative way, could, in the long term be favourable to women. If organizations are to be successful then the valuable skills and experience of its employees (women and men) cannot continue to be overlooked or underutilized. However, if these initiatives are piecemeal reactions to current skills and labour shortages then the opportunities for women may not be so encour-aging. Short-termism implies that once the immediate rationale for introducing dependant care help or flexible working time is removed then any gains made may be short-lived.

The 'softer' version of HRM, emphasizing motivation, commitment and participation, would appear to be responsive to the constraints women face in their working lives, and employer initiatives to recruit and retain women are quite comfortable within this model and again in the long term favour women. However, tensions exist between both 'hard' and 'soft' versions of HRM and the position of women at work. These tensions are rooted in HRM's treatment of employees as individuals and its underlying unitarist frame of reference. Thus, individual women, particularly those valued by the organization, could benefit from HRM, although the elements of management discretion and eligibility for such benefits mitigate against widespread improvements for women in an HRM scenario. Questions must remain regarding any long-lasting benefits for women as a whole, particularly since there seems to be no place within the HRM model for employees who enter the labour market already disadvantaged.

It would seem that for women to make any permanent gains from labour market and demographic pressures or their 'rediscovery as a valuable resource' these gains have to be consolidated and made widely available to all women at work. This raises the issue of collective bargaining and the role of trade unions, elements again inconsistent with the HRM model of employee relations. However, analysis of recent employer initiatives to attract and retain women indicates that these practices are most common in local authorities, where trade unions have played an active role in their negotiation and implementation. Even where these elements operate in tandem the focus remains firmly on the individual, implying that union structures may be bypassed. So while the dichotomy between trade union recognition and HRM may be oversimplified the issue remains – are equality issues to be part of the bargaining process or do they remain in the domain of managerial prerogatives?

It is not suggested that collective bargaining is a panacea for the improvement of women's position at work. Any improvements need to be firmly rooted in policies which foster and promote equality of opportunity for all at work. Other external factors, such as the legal framework and public policy attitudes towards women at work, will also be significant. The issues which surround discrimination and job segregation predate HRM and will continue after HRM has had its day. However, in light of the above discussion, collective bargaining would appear to offer women more than HRM.

References

Atkinson, J. 1984: Manpower strategies for flexible organisations. *Personnel Management*, August, 28–31.

Berry-Lound, D. 1990: *Work and the Family: carer friendly employment practices*. Wimbledon: IPM.

Brannen, J. 1989: Childbirth and occupational mobility: evidence from a longitudinal study. *Work, Employment and Society*, 3(2), 179–201.

Cohen, B. 1988: *Caring for Children: services and policies for childcare and equal opportunities in the UK*. CEC.

Craig, P. and Morgan, D. 1989: *Workplace Nurseries – Who Cares?* Workplace Nurseries Campaign.

Dex, S. 1987: *Women's Occupational Mobility. A Lifetime Perspective*. Macmillan.

Dickens, L. 1989: Women – a rediscovered resource? *Industrial Relations Journal*, 20(3), 167–75.

Employment Department Group 1991: *Labour Market and Skill Trends 1991/92*. Sheffield: Employment Department Group.

Employment Gazette 1990a: Regional labour force outlook to the year 2000. January, 9–19.

Employment Gazette 1990b: Women in the labour market. Results from the 1989 Labour Force Survey. December, 619–43.

Employment Gazette 1991: 1990 Labour Force Survey preliminary results. April, 175–96.

EOC (Equal Opportunities Commission) 1986: *Guidelines for Equal Opportunities Employers*. Manchester: EOC.

EOC 1990: *The Key to Real Choice – an Action Plan for Child Care*. Manchester, EOC.

EOC 1991: *Men and Women in Britain 1991*. London: HMSO.

Hendry, C. and Pettigrew, A. 1990: Human resource management: an agenda for the 1990s. *International Journal of Human Resource Management*, 1(1), 17–43.

IDS (Incomes Data Services) 1990: *Part-time Workers*. Study 459. London.

IER (Institute for Employment Research) 1989: *Review of the Economy and Employment 1989/90 Occupational Assessment*. Coventry: IER, Warwick University.

IRRR 1988a: *Childcare Provision 1: employers head for the nursery*. 425, 4 October, 2–7.

IRRR 1988b: *Childcare Provision 2: allowances and other benefits*. 428, 15 November, 7–9.

IRRR 1989: *Bridging the Career Break*. 431, 10 January, 6–9.

IRS (Industrial Relations Services) 1990: *Effective Ways of Recruiting and Retaining Women. A Survey of Practice from Recruitment and Development Report*. IRS.

McRae, S. 1991: *Maternity Rights in Britain. The Experience of Women and Employers*. London: Policy Studied Institute.

Martin, J. and Roberts, C. 1984: *Women and Employment: a lifetime perspective*. London: HMSO.

Metcalf, H. 1990: *Retaining Women Employees*. IMS report no. 90. Brighton.

Metcalf, H. and Leighton, P. 1989: *The Under-utilisation of Women in the Labour Market*. IMS report no. 172. Brighton.

NEDO/TA 1989: *Defusing the Demographic Time Bomb*. London: NEDO/TA.

NEDO/TC 1988: *Young People and the Labour Market. A Challenge for the 1990s*. London: NEDO/TC.

Rajan, A. and van Eupen, P. 1990: *Good Practices in the Employment of Women Returners*. IMS report no. 183. Brighton.

Scase, R. and Goffee, R. 1990: Women in management: towards a research agenda. *International Journal of Human Resource Management*, 1(1), 107–25.

Scott, G. 1989a: *Families and Under Fives in Strathclyde*. Strathclyde Regional Council.

Scott, G. 1989b: *Childcare and Access: women in tertiary education in Scotland*. Scottish Adult Education Research Monographs no. 9. Edinburgh: Scottish Institute of Adult and Continuing Education.

Storey, J. (ed.) 1989: *New Perspectives on Human Resource Management*. London: Routledge.

Working for Childcare 1990: *Meeting the Childcare Challenge: can the market provide?* London.

15

The Search for Workforce Flexibility

PAUL BLYTON

Introduction

Over the 1980s and early 1990s the issue of labour flexibility has attracted considerable attention both among national policy-makers and within individual work organizations. In the UK for example, the removal of statutory regulations governing the labour market and the use of legislation and other powers to reduce trade union influence, have been explicitly targeted at increasing flexibility both in the labour market and in employment. In work organizations, practices such as relaxing job boundaries, increasing the number of non-permanent staff, introducing new working time patterns and wage payment systems, extending the use of self-employed and subcontract workers, and establishing closer relations between buying and supplying companies, have all been discussed as potentially important sources of flexibility. In turn, this flexibility is identified as playing an important role in achieving various organizational objectives, including lower labour costs, improved responsiveness to market uncertainties, greater utilization of plant and equipment and higher-quality output. Indeed, the pursuit of greater workforce flexibility is widely regarded as a key policy in the development of human resource management (HRM) and the achievement of a close relationship between business strategy and personnel practice.

In certain respects the breadth of this discussion surrounding the flexibility concept has been useful, both in underlining the links between diverse work arrangements and in identifying the potential contribution of different employment practices to broader organizational objectives. Yet such diversity in the use of a concept also generates its own problems. In terms of flexibility, these lie particularly in the way it has been used as a summary term for a diverse set of developments, and in the assumptions commonly made about the degree of uniformity in the nature, extent, pace and consistency of changes taking place, not to mention the factors bringing those changes about.

If securing greater workforce flexibility remains an important issue for human resource (HR) managers in coming years – and we will argue that this is likely to be the case – it is necessary to look in more detail at assumptions currently underpinning the flexibility concept and assess how these mesh with other issues high on HRM's agenda. This challenging of assumptions has been made all the more necessary by the 'magic charm' status which workforce flexibility has been accorded in some management literature in recent years, which has argued that in greater flexibility lies the potential for achieving a host of organizational objectives. Partly this reflects a tendency to contrast flexibility with rigidity and attribute connotations of adaptability and dynamism to the former and fixed attitudes to the latter.

Yet even a brief examination of the issues and evidence indicates that in extending various forms of flexibility, managers also run certain risks, not least a potential loss of stability, continuity, commitment and quality as well as possibly creating the grounds for considerable workforce and trade union resistance. To assess these issues and more generally to evaluate the current and future significance of workforce flexibility, the remaining sections of this chapter examine the factors creating pressures for greater flexibility; the main dimensions of workforce flexibility; the recent patterns of development of these different forms, as revealed by case study and survey findings; the limits to flexibility as it is currently conceived; and finally, the possible future direction of developments in workforce flexibility.

Factors Encouraging Greater Flexibility

The changes in employment and working practices subsumed under the heading of flexibility represent, in the main, an increase in the pace of activities already occurring rather than something wholly new. This begs the questions, however, of what has given rise to this increase in pace and will these causal factors endure (that is, will the pressure for greater flexibility continue)? In a changing economy it is of course difficult, if not impossible, to measure the relative significance of certain factors compared to others. While acknowledging this, it is nevertheless possible to identify a series of factors encouraging a more intense search for greater workforce flexibility.

First, growing international competition has increased the need among domestic organizations to achieve greater competitiveness. The spread of industrialization into low-labour-cost countries such as Taiwan, Korea, Singapore, Brazil and Mexico; the continued expansion of the Japanese domestic economy and the growth of Japanese multinational activity; the shake-out effect of the early 1980s world recession which reduced the number of less efficient organizations; and the removal of trade barriers within Europe and North America, have all fuelled a search for greater competitiveness through lower costs (including lower labour costs) and higher quality and specification. In both private and public sectors, cost-cutting has been a major initial stimulus to attempts to increase workforce flexibility. Further, with the pressures of increased competition has come greater market uncertainty, partly because particular market segments more rapidly approach staturation due to higher total output, and partly because home markets are becoming increasingly subject to international competition as the search for markets intensifies. Organizational flexibility (particularly the ability to innovate and diversify) is thus seen as increasingly important and within that, manpower flexibility represents a major contributor to overall organizational flexibility.

These two influences of competition and market uncertainty have exerted a particular impact in recent years through the greater prominence of multinational organizations, particularly those originating in Japan. In the UK and elsewhere, Japanese companies have demonstrated an ability to organize more effectively than most of their competitors within the host economy. This is also evident in the Japanese multinationals' ability to establish and maintain a higher degree of workforce flexibility than typifies the majority of domestic organizations. The Nissan plant in Sunderland, for example, established a wide-ranging flexibility agreement in its early period of operations, which has since acted as a spur to achieving greater flexibility in other car plants in the UK (Wickens 1987).

In some contexts, greater workforce flexibility has also been encouraged by the introduction of new technologies. The ability to reprogram and retool computer numerically controlled (CNC) and other computer-aided equipment rapidly, can allow batch sizes to be reduced and a greater variety of work to be undertaken, thereby giving those organizations enhanced scope for responding to particular market trends and changes. Further, advanced equipment can often fulfil in a single sequence what was formerly a series of discrete tasks. Hence, not only may some new technology require those working with it to extend their range of competences, it can also act to undermine previous occupational structures and give rise to new ones. In this respect, the current generation of technologies is no different from its predecessors in overnight making certain jobs obsolete and giving rise to a series of new ones. Overall, a period of rapid technological change encourages, if not predicates, a greater flexibility both among a workforce and within the organization as a whole, to achieve synergy between operator and machine, output and market.

Also significant in accounting for the growth in flexibility are various political, economic and social factors. Though not restricted to the UK, several of these factors have been prominent in this country. For example, government policies towards privatization and competitive tendering in the public services have led to a growth in the amount of non-standard and 'external' workers in the public sector. Further, the weakening of trade unions in the 1980s through such means as greater legislative circumscription, reduced the possibility of resistance to changes in employment and working practices which, in earlier periods, had frequently been opposed by the unions (e.g. in relation to the removal of demarcations and the use of temporary workers and contractors). Further, the creation of a large-scale youth training scheme, based on a comparatively low wage paid to those participating, has acted to deliver a major source of temporary and inexpensive labour to the market-place. This is part of a broader point in that high levels of unemployment in the 1980s created conditions which allowed employers to expand their use of temporary workers, in the absence of competing job opportunities in the labour market.

Labour supply factors have also facilitated the growth of flexibility. The increased desire among many women with children to find paid employment, coupled with continuing inequalities in domestic responsibilities, have resulted in many women seeking part-time rather than full-time employment. These same domestic commitments also play a part in a preparedness to work 'twilight' and weekend shifts when a partner can assume the domestic responsibilities. Thus, increasing demand by employers for a labour force not comprised solely of full-time employees, has been matched by a growth in supply of labour who are not seeking full-time work. With the decline in the number of young people leaving school, future increases in the labour force are likely to be achieved by attracting more women on to and back to the labour market. If this is the case, it suggests that increased flexibility, via greater part-time working, will not be unduly hampered by the nature of labour supply.

Taking this last point a little further, in some regions employers are already experiencing severe shortages of labour and as a result are making greater efforts to attract more women into employment. As part of 'returner' and other schemes, employers are offering working arrangements which fit with outside commitments. Hence, different labour market conditions are giving rise to different flexibility patterns: where labour markets are slack, employers are able to shift all market uncertainty on to labour via practices such as temporary employment contracts. In tight labour market situations, however, flexibility is again being encouraged, but this time a version which is designed to be attractive to prospective employees.

What this discussion indicates is that the list of factors encouraging greater workforce flexibility is varied and that in different contexts, particular factors can exert influence in different ways. What is more, at least some of the factors (level of competition, rate of technological change, level of market uncertainty) show no signs of declining; indeed if anything they are likely to intensify in coming years. As a result, pressures to continue searching for lower costs and greater flexibility are also likely to remain for the foreseeable future.

The Concept of Flexibility

At its simplest, flexibility denotes pliability, adaptability and a responsiveness to pressure. Its opposite is inflexibility, rigidity and sclerosis. Though the term was not applied to any great extent before the 1980s, the ideas underpinning the notion of labour flexibility are far from new. Casual forms of employment, by the hour or the day, typified many industries in the past (and continue in some cases today). These provided employers with considerable scope to match the volume of labour with the level of demand. In dockworking, for example, men were engaged to load or unload a ship and were likely to be laid off on completion of the task. Overtime, shift-work and short-time working are other long-established sources of flexibility, enabling employers to extend or contract the working day as changes in demand warrant. Yet while employers have long recognized the importance of labour flexibility, what marks out the present from earlier periods is the added significance being placed on various forms of flexibility as sources of greater organizational efficiency. This greater value is reflected in the range of work patterns and practices being subject to review, and an increased pace of change in at least some aspects of workforce flexibility (Hakim 1990).

Much of the recent discussion on flexibility stems from the work of Atkinson (1984) and his identification of a trend towards the 'flexible firm', comprised of different groups of 'core' and 'periphery' workers. According to this model, at the centre of organizations is a primary or 'core' workforce of full-time, permanent employees who possess key (and scarce) skills, and as a result enjoy relatively high-status positions with good prospects of security and promotion. These core workers are seen to be supported by groups of secondary or 'periphery' workers who are more usually semi- or unskilled and whose jobs are likely to be less stable, with many on temporary and part-time contracts and with few prospects of advancement. In this model these latter groups of workers are identified as the major buffer against changes in demand. When pressures on output rise, the peripheral workforce is expanded via recruitment from the external labour market. When demand recedes the periphery work-force is reduced.

The notion of the flexible firm has a number of similarities to earlier analyses of 'primary' and 'secondary' labour markets which highlighted the extent to which labour markets were segmented, to the general disadvantage of particular groups, notably women, ethnic minorities and youth (Wilkinson 1981). In the current debate, the flexible firm model has been useful in signalling possible areas in which change is taking place, and how different types of flexibility may be associated with different work groups; it also has merit as a check-list of a range of developments which could be found within an organization. The flexible firm model has also attracted consid-erable criticism, however, including the view that the core/periphery distinction is over-simplistic and can be misleading in terms of the role and contribution of different work groups within the enterprise. Some organizations, for example, rely heavily on a part-time work-force, and others on contract workers. In these situations, such groups are often of central rather than peripheral importance to the organizations (see e.g. Malloch 1991). Similarly it is evident that in many cases, ostensibly 'core' groups of skilled workers do not necessarily enjoy the status suggested by the model (O'Connell Davidson 1991). In addition is the argument that evidence of flexibility among 'peripheral' groups has been gathered indiscriminately without sufficient attention being paid to its appropriateness as an index of flexibility. The growth of part-time working, for example, has been highlighted by some as an indication of increased flexibility; yet for others it reflects only the continued growth in service sector employment (where part-time working is more common), with little or no sign of employers switching from full-time to part-time labour to increase flexibility (Pollert 1988). There also appears a general lack of appreciation of the continuities also present in the way workforces are hired, deployed and rewarded, and a lack of recognition too that various aspects of the flexible firm model, such as forms of temporary working, have long existed.

In practice it would seem that while critics are correct in pointing to the conceptual and empirical shortcomings of the original model, nevertheless considerable changes have been and are occurring in a large number of work organizations in areas such as patterns of employment, working arrangements and practices, the nature of reward systems and industrial relations, the use of various types of contract labour and the general organization of production, including relations with suppliers and customers (Blyton and Morris 1991). While the evidence suggests that in many areas (such as multi-skilling, or closer relations with suppliers) developments to date have fallen well short of the 'ideals' of flexibility as expounded in the management literature, nevertheless the picture is one of widespread change in employment patterns and working practices, aimed at securing lower labour costs, tighter manning levels, higher machine utilization, greater staff mobility and fewer interruptions and bottle-necks in production.

To disaggregate the developments taking place, it is useful to examine the different forms of flexibility separately. Here we focus on four: functional or task flexibility; numerical flexibility; temporal flexibility and financial flexibility. Having done this, it will be the task of later sections to identify the extent of their development, the links and potential conflicts between these different forms, and their relationship to other organizational and HR strategies, such as improving levels of commitment and achieving higher quality.

Task or functional flexibility

This concerns the versatility of employees to undertake a range of tasks. This can involve either the horizontal integration of tasks (those formerly undertaken by other employees at the same level) or vertical integration (tasks formerly carried out by employees at higher or lower levels). Much of the discussion on functional flexibility has centred on skilled manual work and the degree to which traditional demarcations are being eroded, to be replaced by 'cross-trade' working and 'multi-skilling'. As we discuss below, the replacement of craft boundaries by multi-skilled workers remains the exception rather than the rule, though limited movements in this general direction are widespread. More common, however, appear to be developments taking place away from the skilled groups, involving both production workers and non-manual employees. Among production groups, one sign of this has been widespread reductions in the number of job grades within organizations, which in turn facilitates greater mobility and transfer across job boundaries. Among white-collar staff, functional flexibility has been stimulated partly by developments in information technology which cut across previous job classifications such as filing clerk and typist, through the development of electronic equipment designed to input, store, retrieve and transmit information.

Numerical flexibility

This refers to an ability to vary the amount of labour in response to fluctuating levels of demand. This is achievable through such means as the use of temporary and short-term contract workers, and 'hire and fire' policies. Also relevant here is what some writers have termed 'distancing', whereby firms use subcontracting partly as a means of responding to demand fluctuations. While the general evidence indicates a widespread growth in subcontracting, both for ancillary activities and certain aspects of production, the trend in temporary working is more ambivalent, partly because of a lack of data on the level of temporary working prior to the 1980–2 recession (Casey 1988). Numerical flexibility appears to have attracted more interest in the UK compared to some other European countries such as Sweden, where the emphasis has been placed more strongly on achieving greater task flexibility (Brunhes 1989).

Temporal flexibility

This is linked to numerical flexibility and many writers have discussed the two together, as aspects of the volume of labour. In the present argument, however, it is useful to distinguish the particular contribution of temporal or working time flexibility since there are signs that this aspect is likely to become increasingly important in many work organizations in coming years. From a management perspective, temporal flexibility refers to the adaptability of working time patterns to reflect patterns of work pressure. As we noted above, shift-working, overtime and short-time working have traditionally been used in this way (Blyton 1985). In recent years, however, new working time patterns have been devised to reflect specific patterns of demand. For example, part-time schedules have been introduced in retailing and elsewhere to cater for peaks in customer activity. In addition, as pressures build up for further reductions in the working week, increasing attention is being given to the arrangement of working hours as well as their overall duration (Blyton 1989). Further, employers' interest in attracting new entrants, particularly women, on to the labour market is forcing greater consideration of working time arrangements (such as part-time schedules and flexitime arrangements) which allow work commitments to be meshed with outside responsibilities.

Financial flexibility

This involves a shift away from single and uniform payment systems towards more individualized and variable systems. Among other things these seek to establish a closer relationship between performance and reward, through such means as performance-related pay, profit-sharing schemes and fee-for-service payments. In the UK and elsewhere, financial flexibility in the 1980s also entailed an ability to pay lower wages to groups such as young workers. This ability was secured partly by state action to weaken trade union power, partly by establishing youth employment schemes which reinforced low wage retes and partly by removing certain conditions (e.g. Fair Wages Resolutions) and introducing others (e.g. competitive tendering/privatization of services in the public sector) which further encouraged relatively low wage rates in various sectors and occupational groups.

It is clear, therefore, that flexibility covers a diverse range of developments. Faced with such diversity, a common tendency has been to assume a high degree of uniformity: that the various developments are occurring at more or less the same pace, in the same places, for similar reasons and with similar outcomes. In practice, however, this is far from the case. Closer examination reveals a much more fragmented and unevenly paced set of developments, borne out of a heterogeneous mix of causal pressures. Indeed, at least some aspects of flexibility potentially contradict others, and could clash with other organizational objectives. It is to an examination of this evidence that we now turn.

Evidence of Developments

In regard to workforce flexibility, one of the most contentious issues remains its extent: how much flexibility is there and what trends can be distinguished? From this flow a series of supplementary questions: has flexibility developed in some sectors and occupations more than others? Do different forms of flexibility act as alternatives or do they develop in parallel or in sequence? To what extent does flexibility represent part of broader organizational strategies or an isolated development? Do current concerns with flexibility represent a real break with the past or merely a redefining of longer-established trends? Despite problems such as a lack of agreement on what constitutes flexibility, a dearth of longitudinal studies, and a frequent absence of precision on the extent and depth of changes, a view across several studies suggests that:

- There has been a growth in various forms of flexibility in the 1980s and early 1990s, in both public and private sectors and in manufacturing and services.
- The extent and pace of this growth are uneven both in terms of industrial sector and form(s) of flexibility.
- Different types of flexibility are prominent in different sectors, and similar forms are being pursued for a variety of reasons.
- While flexibility agreements have played an important role, many of the changes have been introduced by unilateral management action.

Functional Flexibility

Summarizing the available evidence, it is evident that the 1980s witnessed a widespread relaxation in demarcations between crafts and between production and craft workers, but that in the vast majority of cases these distinctions and job boundaries remain. Change appears widespread but in most cases relatively shallow: for example, minor maintenance work being undertaken by production workers, some overall blurring at the margins between crafts, and a greater integration of closely related skills, such as instrument mechanic and electrician. Two further points need making, however. First, in a significant number of organizations, the changes introduced have been more far-reaching than the general picture indicates. This is particularly true (though is not confined to) greenfield sites where flexible working practices have been secured partly through extensive selection and recruitment procedures (see below).

Second, many of the changes have involved the broadening of non-skilled jobs. A key management aim behind this has been to operate at lower manning levels and cover tasks by broadening job responsibilities. This is equally evident in service industries (such as ancillary workers in hospitals) as in the manufacturing sector. Compared to those involving skilled workers, however, these changes in working practices have received less attention. Partly this may reflect the interest generated around the notion of 'multi-skilling' which has focused attention on craft workers. In addition, the relaxation of craft demarcations have tended to be more subject to formal agreement in the collective bargaining sphere (Marsden and Thompson 1990), while the enlargement of jobs among semi- and unskilled workers has been less subject to formal union–management agreement.

Turning to studies of functional flexibility, one is struck by the difficulty of gauging the extent of change across a diverse range of organizations. What may be judged a major change in working practices in organization A (perhaps due to previously rigidly defended lines of demarcation), could be viewed as a relatively minor change in organization B (possibly because an atmosphere of change has characterized this latter organization for some time). This imprecision is partially compensated, however, by the extent of study on this issue in recent years. A national ACAS survey involving almost 600 establishments collected a broad range of information on flexibility in mid-1987 (ACAS 1988). This has been supplemented by more recent surveys, together with various case studies. On functional flexibility, the ACAS survey gathered data on the relaxation of:

1 demarcations to allow production workers to undertake routine maintenance work;
2 demarcations between different crafts;
3 demarcations between manual, technical and clerical grades.

Overall, one-quarter of the establishments had introduced one or more of these changes among at least some of its workforce during the previous three years. In all three areas, the changes were far more evident in larger establishments than in smaller ones. However, some care must be exercised in interpreting this last finding since it may reflect demarcations already more relaxed in smaller establishments, leaving less scope for further reduction. What the ACAS survey suffers from, however, is an inability adequately to reflect the depth of changes taking place. In a separate study specifically targeted at working practices, Michael Cross (1988) has shown that over the 1980s the development of anything approaching 'multi-skilling' has been limited. More common has been the restricted reform of demarcations, with changes tending to occur at the margins of jobs rather than involving far-reaching reforms of occupational structures.

Among companies cited as being in the vanguard of pursuing functional flexibility, this has often been developed in conjunction with a 'teamworking' concept, whereby craft workers are typically removed from separate maintenance departments and integrated into production-oriented teams. In Continental Can, for example, the former craftsman's role has been turned into that of 'production technician' who operates on the line, ensuring maintenance is carried out and machine downtimes are minimized (IDS 1988). Similar arrangements operate elsewhere, for example the drive-shaft manufacturer, Hardy Spicer, where production teams contain 'systems technicians' who carry out tasks such as machine set-up and basic maintenance, as well as bearing responsibility for loading, quality and output (Hendry and Pettigrew 1988). Likewise Ind Coope in Burton have devised a teamwork arrangement using 'operator craftsmen' who undertake this twin role formerly demarcated between skilled and production workers. Many other organizations have similarly introduced various forms of teamworking over the past five years, including Cammell Laird, Cummins Engines, Birds Eye Wall's, Shell Chemicals and Cadbury Schweppes (*IRRR* 1989).

Among the most highly developed are those operating in Japanese plants in the UK – notably Nissan, Komatsu and Sony – where an ability to work in teams is an important component in recruitment decisions.

In this area of functional flexibility and teamworking, a notable case is that of British Steel. Throughout its history, the iron and steel industry has been characterized by a rigid demarcation of steelworkers' occupations into promotion lines, in which seniority represented the key principle for advancement up the line (a line being for example, 5th, 4th, 3rd, 2nd and 1st melter, or rollerman) (Bowen 1976). Just as production work was rigidly demarcated into work crews, so too a diversity of craft grades was maintained. In recent years there have been moves to transform this pattern. In a number of plants this is being pursued by a relaxation of demarcations and the introduction of single craft apprenticeships to establish single mechanical and single electrical craft disciplines. In individual cases, however, notably parts of the Teesside complex, flexibility is being taken further with the establishment of teamworking, based on common training modules and reinforced by an agreement that advancement to team leader will be on the basis of training undertaken and demonstrated competences, rather than seniority. Teamworking in British Steel is aimed at focusing more explicitly on the tasks to be completed in a particular area, utilizing self-contained teams of workers responsible for all activities (production, maintenance and technical activities) and supported where necessary by a pool of mobile specialist teams. Among the main aspects of this work structure is the integration of skilled workers into teams of process operators, with time-served craftsmen undertaking production jobs for at least part of their time (Blyton 1990).

There are a number of possible reasons why functional flexibility has not been pursued further in the majority of organizations. Some of these we address in a later section when we consider the limits of flexibility, but among the factors which might usefully be raised here is the provision of training. Functional flexibility rests on an assumption that adequate training is provided for workers (either craft or non-craft) to undertake a broader range of tasks. It would seem that in many situations, the full implications of this in terms of training requirements, have not been calculated. The size of the issue can be seen from the example of one steel plant in the UK in 1989 where over 1000 craftsmen each had 38 days of retraining (though this reflects not only a move to greater flexibility but also the need to achieve competence in working with new technology) (Blyton 1990). This need for greater training to develop functional flexibility is arising in a context where (1) in the past, UK employers have been criticized for their lack of training provision compared to their major international competitors (see chapter 13), and (2) there are tighter financial constraints due to high interest charges and other economic difficulties, making additional funding for extra training facilities difficult to secure. A second factor limiting functional flexibility among skilled workers has been the resistance among craftsmen themselves to giving up time-honoured job definitions. This was clearly demonstrated in a dispute involving Ford UK in 1988 when one of the points at greatest dispute was the craftsmen's unwillingness to undertake production work (Wilkinson and Oliver 1990).

Numerical Flexibility

In many respects, the development of numerical flexibility is more straightforward to track than functional flexibility since it is dealing with more readily measurable issues: for example, whether the amount of temporary working, fixed-term contracts, subcontracting and so on changed over a given time period. In addition, there is evidence that compared to other forms, numerical flexibility has been pursued more strongly by some employers who have been motivated principally by the cost-cutting potential of particular aspects of numerical flexibility.

Various national surveys including the annual Labour Force Survey (LFS), ELUS (Employers' Labour Use Survey) and the ACAS survey have sought information on aspects of numerical flexibility. The overall picture is one of a modest increase in a number of aspects of numerical flexibility, with some (such as subcontracting) showing a greater growth than others. The ACAS survey, for example, found three-fifths of organizations using temporary workers (ACAS 1988). Just over two in five of these had increased their use of temporary working in the previous three years, compared to 13 per cent who had decreased their reliance on temporary workers; the remaining organizations in the survey reported no change. The corresponding figures for the use of outside contractors was 77 per cent of establishments using contractors, with 40 per cent recording an increase in use in the previous three years, 7 per cent recording a decrease and 52 per cent remaining unchanged.

Outside contractors were particularly evident in manufacturing (where nine-tenths of responding organizations were using contractors) and in larger establishments (nine-tenths of firms with between 500 and 1500 employees reported using contractors). The three most common functions for which contractors were used were maintenance, cleaning and transport, followed by catering, computer services and security. Public organizations currently pursuing greater numerical flexibility include the Civil Service and the National Health Service. In health, one of the most visible aspects of numerical flexibility is the use of agency staff to provide cover for nursing shortages. This not only reflects the use of temporary staff to cover for absences or extraordinary demands, but also indicates current difficulties in some areas in recruiting and retraining suitably qualified staff in the National Health Service (Ursell 1991).

Use of certain other forms of numerical flexibility (e.g. short-term fixed contracts and homeworking) is much less widespread; the ACAS survey found 16 per cent of workplaces using fixed-term contracts and 6 per cent employing homeworkers. In both of these cases, however, the trend is similar to those outlined above, with much higher proportions reporting an increase than a decrease in their use. Turning to part-time working, the ACAS survey identified 70 per cent of establishments employing part-timers. Almost three in every ten reported an increase in their use of part-timers over the previous three years compared to 15 per cent reporting a decrease and 56 per cent unchanged. As in the case of the other employment practices, however, while this reveals something of the extent of part-time working and some general indication of the pattern of change, it is not sensitive enough to reveal the depth or scale of changes taking place: for example, whether employers are replacing full-time jobs with part-time ones. One practice which could cast some light on this last point is the development of job-sharing whereby the responsibilities of a full-time job are shared by two people. Different surveys have suggested that as many as one in six organizations operate some form of job-sharing (IDS 1989). Accuracy is difficult, however, since some organizations clearly operate a much looser definition of job-sharing than others. What is clear is that in organizations with job-sharing, the practice is generally restricted to a handful of positions. A more evident change, however, is that until recent years, job-sharing had been almost totally confined to the public sector. With growing concern over the recruitment and retention of women employees in some areas, job-sharing is starting to figure a little more within private-sector organizations, including Boots, BP and the Halifax Building Society, as well as former public corporations such as BT and British Gas. While useful for purposes of discussion, it is important to recognize that in practice several of these aspects of numerical flexibility are closely interlinked. For example, in the expanded contracting sector, it is common for a high proportion of workers to be engaged on a part-time or casual basis, often with no written contract of employment (Coyle 1986; Fevre 1986).

Temporal Flexibility

The available evidence suggests that only limited new developments in working hours arrangements have taken place to date. We noted above how various aspects of temporal flexibility are well established – notably overtime, shift-working, and short-time working. We noted too that part-time working is often being used in retailing and elsewhere as a means of temporal flexibility, allowing work schedules to be created and modified to match peaks of demand in the working day or working week. In addition, it is evident that significant amounts of informal time flexibility exist in many work arrangements. In the main, however, previous discussions on working time have focused more on issues of duration than on the arrangement of working hours. There are signs, though, that this is changing. As the working week becomes shorter the issue of the effective use of working time becomes correspondingly more significant. Further, as the costs of capital equipment rise and its rate of obsolescence accelerates, the importance of working time patterns to maximize machine utilization increases. Also, as labour shortages in particular areas become increasingly acute, interest in flexitime and other time options is being revived as a means of attracting and retaining valued staff.

Some examples will serve to indicate developments beginning to be more evident. The linking of reduced hours to greater temporal flexibility was the source of the prominent 'flexible rostering' dispute in British Rail in 1982, in which a management offer of a pay rise and reduced working week was contingent on drivers abandoning the fixed eight-hour day and accepting rosters varying from seven to nine hours, to allow for more effective matching of drivers' working time with train movements (Ferner 1985). A similar issue was voiced in the 1989–90 engineering dispute in the UK over a shorter working week. However, while during the dispute various references were made by employers to increasing the scope for varying weekly working hours, in practice most subsequent agreements have left this issue unspecified. Where working time has been specifically referred to in these settlements, it has been in relation to 'bell to bell' working and reductions in the number of tea-breaks in return for a shorter working week (IDS 1990a). This pattern varies somewhat with developments in the West German engineering industry where reductions in the working week (from 40 to 38.5 in 1984, to 37 in 1989, 36 in 1993 and 35 by 1995) have been associated with an increase in managerial power to introduce variation in weekly hours depending on the volume of work, provided an average is achieved over a six-month period (IDS 1990a). Other developments in working time in Western Europe also indicate greater consideration being given to the link between working time patterns and operating times. In the Netherlands, for example, a widespread practice in engineering over the past decade has been to translate agreed reductions in working time not into shorter weekly hours but into additional free days for employees, so as to maintain operating times at former levels (the free days being rostered into the shift pattern and thus covered by other employees) (Blyton 1988). A number of Dutch enterprises have gone further, operating shift systems which are longer in periods of heavy demand and shorter during quieter periods. Further, organizations such as the steelmaker Hoogovens operate a shift system with longer shifts in the summer to cover for employees on vacation, and shorter shifts during the rest of the year to meet the agreed average working week (Blyton 1988).

These Dutch examples have elements of what is sometimes referred to as 'annual hours' systems. These were much discussed in the UK in the 1980s and a number of schemes have been introduced, though they are confined largely to process industries (Lynch 1985). Under these systems, agreement over working time is made in relation to the total hours to be worked annually. This gives management greater scope to vary the hours in any given period to match demand. Overall however, annual hours systems have been adopted by only a small minority of organizations; in the ACAS survey, only 3 per cent of organizations had introduced annual hours working for any of their workforce (ACAS 1988).

An example of an organization altering working time patterns to increase machine utilization is British Coal (BC). In its pursuit of six-day working (which involves producing coal on six rather than five days, leaving Sunday for essential maintenance and safety work) BC has argued that a principal objective is to increase returns from the capital equipment tied up in new pits, particularly in the face of increased exposure to competition from imports of foreign coal (Hill et al. 1989). Outside the coal industry, one of the most significant developments linking changes in working time to increased plant utilization is the 1990 agreement at the Rover Longbridge plant which ties a shorter working week to round-the-clock production. The agreement provides for a basic 37-hour week on conventional day and night shifts, an average 36-hour week on a three-shift rotation and 31.5 hours on a seven-day pattern of continental shifts (IDS 1990b). This is the first car plant in the UK to introduce 24-hour production, and could set a precedent for similar agreements in other plants.

During the 1970s many employers introduced 'flexitime' arrangements, allowing employees to vary their start and finish times within certain limits, provided that an agreed 'core' period is worked and that hours worked equated with the agreed working week over a given settlement period. These systems were partly introduced to attract and retain staff and by 1980 it was estimated that 8 per cent of employees in the UK were involved in flexitime arrangement (Blyton 1985). Overwhelmingly, flexitime has been confined to non-manual employees, although at least one researcher has identified ways in which flexitime can be incorporated into a shift system for production workers (McEwan Young 1978). For employers, these schemes potentially offer added benefits of a greater degree of 'self-supervision' over timekeeping, and reducing the number of minor absences. Despite these potential benefits, however, there was only limited further expansion of flexitime arrangements throughout the first half of the 1980s. More recently the development of flexitime appears to have revived to some extent. The ACAS survey found that 14 per cent of responding organizations had introduced or extended its use of flexitime between 1984 and 1987, and a further 11 per cent planned to extend its use in the following year (ACAS 1988). Labour shortages and a desire to recruit and retain women workers appear to be a major reason for this revived interest.

Factors such as reductions in weekly working hours, the increased proportion of part-timers in the workforce and increasing pressures on utilizing plant and equipment are likely to stimulate further managerial efforts to secure greater temporal flexibility. As we discuss in a later section, however, the success of new working arrangements is likely to depend in important part on the extent to which they meet employee preferences over working hours patterns and are consistent with a large body of research evidence on the harmful effects of certain working time patterns.

Financial Flexibility

As noted earlier, financial flexibility entails a move away from standardized and collectively agreed payment systems towards more variable and individualized systems, which seek a closer relationship between individual performance and reward. This has been pursued in a number of ways. For example, in the UK, the state has played an important role in reducing 'obstacles' to financial flexibility, through reducing trade union power, weakening Wages Councils, removing Fair Wages Resolutions and so on. The decentralization of collective bargaining has also acted to reduce the prominence of national pay agreements, and increase the importance of more locally based settlements. Further, management's introduction of new elements in reward, including merit or performance-related pay, profit-sharing, and share option schemes, has contributed to greater financial flexibility. The extent of such developments has not been fully recorded and there are indications that management discussions and advocacy of financial flexibility are running significantly ahead of practice. Nevertheless, in the ACAS survey over a quarter of organizations had introduced profit-sharing over the previous three years and almost as many had introduced some form of merit pay (ACAS 1988).

The signs are that aspects of financial flexibility will develop further in coming years. Firstly, the extension of other forms of flexibility will bring about a greater diversity in organizational payment systems. Much subcontracting, for example, is undertaken on a fee-for-service basis. Further, as organizations continue to modify their structures around the notion of local profit centres, the emphasis on decentralizing collective bargaining systems is likely to remain, as managers seek to achieve greater local control over labour costs.

The Limits of Flexibility

Workforce flexibility has been identified as an important component of broader organizational flexibility which in turn is widely viewed as a major ingredient in achieving and maintaining organizational success. Yet flexibility is not the only characteristic regarded as important to that success. The 1980s 'excellence' literature, for example, also emphasized the importance of organizational cultures which embodied commitment and pursuit of quality as important goals (Peters and Waterman 1982). Similar arguments have been put forward in subsequent HRM texts. Yet if numerical flexibility is pursued via high levels of temporary working, this is unlikely also to produce sustained levels of commitment and quality output. There is a fundamental inconsistency between the simultaneous pursuit of 'dependable' and 'disposable' labour (Legge 1990). Commitment can be secured by a variety of means but important elements in this are usually high salary, job security and/or access to promotion; most temporary workers have none of these. In addition, the very nature of temporary working would normally preclude anything other than minimal training, which could further hinder the achievement of high-quality output. An additional clash of objectives could be the pursuit of harmonization and single status with the maintenance of diverse employment contracts, some permanent, others embodying different degrees of temporariness.

Guy Standing (1986) has remarked that another possible pitfall of flexibility is that it may undermine stability and continuity within organizations. The short-term nature of fixed contracts, for example, contrasts with the continuity embodied in more permanent employment relationships. These potential clashes with other organizational processes and objectives relate particularly to numerical flexibility. Many numerically flexible strategies have been pursued for their cost-cutting and control potential rather than for any deeper contribution to the organization. However, if continued heavy reliance on numerical flexibility impedes the achievement of other objectives and runs contrary to managerial thinking regarding employee development, teamworking, etc., we may anticipate less emphasis on numerical flexibility in the future and more on other forms of flexibility.

In principle, there is potential for areas of common interest between management and workforce in achieving greater flexibility (this is an issue which was largely unaddressed in the 1980s, reflecting the weakness of trade unions and workers' position in the overall labour market). On working practices, for example, broader training and the attainment of greater competences could not only improve levels of job satisfaction but also employees' earnings potential in the external labour market. In addition, new working time schedules could represent a means for existing employees to achieve a better match between work and non-work commitments. There is considerable evidence, for example, that many workers would prefer a time schedule which offers more free days (as in the Dutch example quoted above) than one which translates any reduction in hours into a slightly shorter working day (Blyton 1985). For management too this potentially offers greater flexibility since it ensures the maintenance of longer operating times.

If managers' pursuit of time flexibility translates into more extensive shift-working, it will be important that the research is taken into account which highlights the dysfunctions of some forms of shift-working. In particular, the social, psychological and medical problems associated with night-working are well documented (see e.g. Carpentier and Cazamian 1977). Not only do workers function much below their optimum during night shifts, but the extent to which they adjust over time is limited, if at all. On top of this are the marked social and family disruptions which can be caused by shift-working. The overall implication is that while round-the-clock working may look at first sight an extremely efficient use of resources, there are considerable drawbacks, which were a major reason for the general reductions in the 1960s and 1970s in the proportion of shifts containing night-working (NBPI 1970; Bosworth and Dawkins 1980).

Summary and Conclusion

Various aspects of workforce flexibility have been pursued in recent years, though to varying extents and at different rates. Managerial arguments in favour of increasing flexibility have focused largely on its potential contribution to lowering labour costs, increasing responsiveness to change and improving utilization of new equipment.

In the UK in particular, flexibility has developed within a particular set of circumstances (e.g. weak unions and labour markets and an inadequate training 'infrastructure'), and as a result has given rise to forms of flexibility which have emphasized primarily the cost-cutting and control aspects of numerical flexibility. If flexibility is to become part of a long-term strategy, however, rather than reflect short-term opportunism, it will be necessary for management to address the possible inconsistencies arising between flexibility strategies and other HR objectives, and also to accept the need for greater investment in flexibility (in training, enhanced payment for skills, and communications, for example). It will be important too that greater recognition is given to employee interests in the creation of new working arrangements and practices. Failing this, flexibility is likely to become a progressively more marginal, rather than remain a central, aspect of HRM policy in the 1990s.

References

ACAS (Advisory, Conciliation and Arbitration Service) 1988: *Labour Flexibility in Britain: the 1987 ACAS survey*. Occasional paper 41. London: ACAS.

Atkinson, J. 1984: Manpower strategies for flexible organisations. *Personnel Management*, August, 28–31.

Blyton, P. 1985: *Changes in Working Time: an international review*. London: Croom Helm.

Blyton, P. 1988: *Labour Flexibility in the EEC: the growth of new working time patterns*. Report for the European Commission. Available from the author.

Blyton, P. 1989: Time and labour relations. In P. Blyton, J. Hassard, S. Hill and K. Starkey, *Time, Work and Organization*, London: Routledge, 105–31.

Blyton, P. 1990: Steel: a classic case of industrial relations change in the 1980s. Paper presented to a conference on Employment Relations in the Enterprise Culture, Cardiff, September. Available from the author.

Blyton, P. and Morris, J. 1991: A flexible future: aspects of the flexibility debates and some unresolved issues. In P. Blyton and J. Morris (eds), *A Flexible Future? Prospects for Employment and Organization*, Berlin: de Gruyter, 1–21.

Bosworth, D.L. and Dawkins, P.J. 1980: Shiftworking and unsocial hours. *Industrial Relations Journal*, 11(1), 32–40.

Bowen, P. 1976: *Social Control in Industrial Organisations*. London: Routledge & Kegan Paul.

Brunhes, B. 1989: Labour flexibility in enterprises: a comparison of firms in four European countries. In Organization for Economic Co-operation and Development, *Labour Market Flexibility: trends in enterprises*, Paris: OECD, 11–36.

Carpentier, J. and Cazamian, P. 1977: *Nightwork*. Geneva: International

Labour Office.

Casey, B. 1988: *Temporary Employment: practices and policies in Britain.* London: Policy Studies Institute.

Coyle, A. 1986: Going private. In Feminist Review (eds), *Waged Work: a reader*, London: Virago, 222–37.

Cross, M. 1988: Changes in working practices in UK manufacturing 1981–1988. *Industrial Relations Review and Report*, no. 415, May, 2–10.

Ferner, A. 1985: Political constraints and management strategies: the case of working practices in British Rail. *British Journal of Industrial Relations*, 23(1), 47–70.

Fevre, R. 1986: Contract work in the recession. In K. Purcell, S. Wood, A. Watson and S. Allen (eds), *The Changing Experience of Employment*, London: Macmillan, 18–34.

Hakim, C. 1990: Core and periphery in employers' workforce strategies: evidence from the 1987 ELUS survey. *Work, Employment and Society*, 4, 157–88.

Hendry, C. and Pettigrew, A. 1988: Multiskilling in the round. *Personnel Management*, April, 36–43.

Hill, S., Blyton, P. and Gorham, A. 1989: The economics of manpower flexibility. *The Royal Bank of Scotland Review*, no. 163, 15–26.

IDS (Incomes Data Services) 1988: *Teamworking.* Study no. 419. London: IDS.

IDS 1989: *Job Sharing.* Study 440. London: IDS.

IDS 1990a: *The Shorter Working Week.* Study 461. London: IDS.

IDS 1990b: *Report no. 574.* London: IDS.

IRRR (Industrial Relations Review and Report) 1989: Labour Flexibility reassessed. *Industrial Relations Review and Report*, November, 7–10.

Legge, K. 1990: Employment relations in the enterprise culture. Paper presented at Employment Research Unit Conference, Cardiff, September.

Lynch, P. 1985: Annual hours: an idea whose time has come. *Personnel Management*, November, 46–50.

McEwan Young, W. 1978: Flexible working arrangements in continuous shift production. *Personnel Review*, 7, 12–19.

Malloch, H. 1991: Strategic management and the decision to subcontract. In P. Blyton and J. Morris (eds), *A Flexible Future? Prospects for Employment and Organization*, Berlin: de Gruyter, 191–210.

Marsden, D. and Thompson, M. 1990: Flexibility agreements and their significance in the increase in productivity in British manufacturing since 1980. *Work, Employment and Society*, 4, 83–104.

NBPI (National Board for Prices and Incomes) 1970: *Hours of Work, Overtime and Shiftworking.* Report no. 161, Cmnd 4554. London: HMSO.

O'Connell Davidson, J. 1991: Subcontract, flexibility and changing employment relations in the water industry. In P. Blyton and J. Morris (eds), *A Flexible Future? Prospects for Employment and Organization*, Berlin: de Gruyter, 241–58.

Peters, T. and Waterman, R. 1982: *In Search of Excellence*. New York: Harper & Row.

Pollert, A. 1988: The flexible firm: fixation or fact. *Work, Employment and Society*, 2, 281–316.

Standing, G. 1986: *Unemployment and Labour Market Flexibility: the United Kingdom*. Geneva: International Labour Organization.

Ursell, G. 1991: Human resource management and labour flexibility. In P. Blyton and J. Morris (eds), *A Flexible Future? Prospects for Employment and Organisation*, Berlin: de Gruyter, 311–27.

Wickens, P. 1987: *The Road to Nissan*. London: Macmillan.

Wilkinson, B. and Oliver, N. 1990: Obstacles to Japanisation: the case of Ford UK. *Employee Relations*, 12, 17–22.

Wilkinson, F. (ed.) 1981: *The Dynamics of Labour Market Segmentation*. London: Academic Press.

Part III

Cases

16
Human Resource Management and Personnel Management: the Case of Ford Motor Company

KEN STARKEY AND ALAN McKINLAY

Introduction

Guest (1987:503) argues that if the term 'human resource management' (HRM) is to have any social scientific value 'it should be defined in such a way as to differentiate it from traditional personnel management'. He then proposes that HRM constitutes one of four models of best personnel practice, that few UK organizations practise HRM, but that there might be a slow trend in the direction of HRM as evidenced by the increasing adoption of HRM policies such as employee involvement. The definition of HRM is a set of policies designed to maximize organizational integration, employee commitment, flexibility and quality of work. The HRM model is characterized as being people-oriented with an emphasis on the maximization of individual talent and consultation with the workforce. The only companies cited as practising this model in the UK are IBM and Hewlett-Packard.

The three other major personnel models Guest describes are:

1 the *paternalist welfare* model, characterized by careful selection, training and treatment of staff, with a strong customer focus, a prime example of which is Marks and Spencer;
2 the *production model*, based on tough, consistent industrial relations practice, focusing on the maintenance of efficient continuity of production, exemplified by Ford Motor Company;
3 the *professional model*, which emphasizes professionalism in four core activities of selection, training, pay and industrial relations. Firms such as

ICI, Unilever and some of the major oil companies are cited as examples of this model.

This approach to HRM, which is far from atypical, has at its core a contingency view of personnel practices. The effective adoption of the different models depends on the appropriateness of particular practices to particular industrial settings.

Guest suggests that the HRM model is significantly different from traditional personnel practice, which has more in common with the elements of the other three models. In this chapter we critically examine these distinctions in an analysis of personnel practices in Ford Motor Company, a paradigmatic example of Guest's 'production model' of personnel management. We argue that if one adopts a longitudinal perspective it is possible to discover key points in company evolution in personnel practices where the traditional model of personnel management becomes inadequate for the changing strategic situation of the company, and the changing strategic needs of the company make HRM practices more attractive. We also argue that it is possible to identify elements of more than one model coexisting more or less comfortably in the same company setting. The nature of this coexistence raises the issue of whether or not the presence of apparently contrasting models of personnel practice constitutes a transitory phase and, if it is such a transitory phase, whether the next evolutionary step in personnel practice will involve a return to traditional models, as, for instance, 'cycles of control' theorists such as Ramsay (1983) would argue, or whether we are witnessing the evolution towards a new general model of personnel practice based on the HRM model.

Pressures for Change in Personnel Practice

A central premiss of Torrington's analysis of the relationship between HRM and personnel management is that the nature of HRM is 'not yet clear' (Torrington 1989:60). By this he seems to mean that the functional implications of the uptake of HRM principles by the personnel function, often with a retitling of the function as a symbol of its changing orientation, are not yet clear. The pressures driving such changes as do exist, however, do seem clear. A key policy goal underpinning HRM practice is to 'maximize organizational integration' (Guest 1987:503). The goal of such integration is most clear in the principle of 'strategic integration' which 'refers to the ability of the organization to integrate HRM issues into its strategic plans' (Guest 1989:42); HRM assumes strategic importance when the need for employee commitment becomes central to the implementation of corporate strategy, for example, commitment to strategic goals concerning efficiency, quality and innovation. The management of the human resource becomes a key factor in the search for competitive advantage (Porter 1987).

The increased attention paid to the human factor in the 1980s can be traced to three main issues: the success of Japanese firms in the West, the publication of Peters and Waterman's *In Search of Excellence* and ensuing debates concerning the nature of excellence, and the growing awareness of the importance of the management of the human resource in strategy implementation. In the USA interest in HRM was also generated by the 1981 launch of the HRM module as a compulsory subject in the Harvard Business School Master of Business Administration degree course.

The debate about the roots of Japanese success has focused on a variety of factors that are seen as distinguishing the Japanese enterprise from the Western. The key sources of Japanese success have variously been seen as:

1 The Japanese ability to redefine the nature of industrial markets through product price, reflecting their efficiency, quality of product and innovation. The Japanese have proved themselves able to resolve the 'innovation–efficiency' dilemma (Lawrence and Dyer 1983) and achieve both while, in the West, we have concentrated on efficiency in the strategy of large-scale production of standardized products (i.e. in Porter's terminology a cost leadership generic strategy). This is now outmoded. It has led to inflexibility and, ironically, inefficiency (Abernathy et al. 1981).

2 The Japanese strategy of production flexibility to match a marketing strategy of product differentiation, as seen, for example, in the fragmentation of the market for standard cars into a set of distinct sub-markets, to generate a more diverse range, updated more often. This production flexibility is sustained by the skilled use of new manufacturing technologies, product development based on simultaneous engineering, with product design and manufacturing working in tandem rather than the sequential functional specialization of the West, and the integration of suppliers into just-in-time (JIT) relationships to facilitate the prompt response to fluctuation in demand.

3 The Japanese social organization of production based on teamwork, job rotation, learning by doing, skill flexibility, the use of workers'

tacit knowledge, culture, trust, respect, long-term employment, self-management and the philosophy of continuous improvement. Broader job definitions have a major impact in terms of reducing the need for indirect workers to support production and self-certification of quality and self-control require fewer tiers of lower-level managers to monitor and discipline.

4 Japanese industrial structure as evidenced by Japanese avoidance of the vertical integration of Western companies. Japanese strength lies in quasi-integration, networks of firms established in long-term co-operative relationships (the *keiretsu*), rather than in conglomerates.

5 The role of the Japanese government in supporting key industries through the Ministry of International Trade and Industry (MITI).

All of these factors obviously have some effect on the competitiveness of Japanese firms and analysts are divided in giving any one factor priority. From the HRM perspective it is the social organization of production that has proved most influential. There have been strong claims, backed by empirical research, that it is its management of its human resource that is the key factor in understanding Japanese success (Abernathy et al. 1981). Certainly this view is at the root of the phenomenon of Japanization, the attempt to emulate Japanese production practices in the West, an approach that has proved successful in companies like Xerox (Giles and Starkey 1988). The core of the argument is, according to Deming, a key protagonist in teaching the Japanese how to manufacture quality products, the stress on purpose at work and worker self-respect as sources of competitiveness. The conventional Western approach, in comparison with the new competition, creates obstacles so that 'the hourly worker is deprived of his right to do good work and to be proud of himself'. This, according to Deming, 'may be the single most important contribution of management to poor quality and loss of market' (Deming 1982:166). The main theme of the critique of the conventional Western approach based on scientific management is that people need identity and meaning in work and that work arrangements should, therefore, emphasize trust, teamwork and the opportunities to develop creative, problem-solving and co-operative capabilities. The alternative to scientific management is to create, as in Japan, opportunities for the pursuit of meaning in work (Best 1990:161).

Peters and Waterman were also crucial in bringing human resources (HR) concerns to the forefront of the management agenda with their *In Search of Excellence*. Their '7-S framework' has as its central idea the claim that organizational effectiveness stems from the interaction of not just strategy and structure, the traditional concerns in organization design (Chandler 1962), but also from the relationship between systems, management style, as seen in an organization's culture, the organization's skills base, its staff and its superordinate goals. Excellence is equated with HRM. The latter also emerges as a key concern in the strategic management literature in:

- the view of strategy as a process to be managed rather than an exercise in rational planning and execution (Quinn et al. 1988);
- the view of strategic management as a form of organizational learning;
- the increasing awareness in strategic management of the problems of strategy implementation and actually 'making it happen' (Harvey-Jones 1988) and the importance in strategy implementation of continuous attention to the fine-tuning of detail as strategies evolve incrementally;
- the emphasis on leveraging resources and the development of core competences as the essence of strategy (Beer et al. 1984; Hamel and Prahalad 1989; Prahalad and Hamel 1990).

Guest (1988:10) also suggests that embracing HRM principles might have significant effects for a company's image: 'A company seen to be in the forefront of the management of human resources may gain advantages in the market place. Firstly it may attract sales through an image of social responsibility and quality. Secondly it may attract a pool of high quality recruits.' Announcements by the former chairman of Jaguar about inefficient working practices, outmoded job demarcations and out-of-date plant reminiscent of the antiquated factories of the Soviet bloc, however true, are unlikely to be warmly received by those responsible for making, marketing and selling the company's product in a market where its success depends heavily on its high-quality 'state of the art' image! In a job market of limited high-quality skilled potential employees a reputation for HRM policies and practices is likely to have a significant effect on attracting and retaining appropriate recruits.

From Traditional Personnel Management to Human Resource Management

Guest (1987) contrasts HRM with a 'production model' approach to personnel management. In this section we examine changes in personnel practice in Ford Motor Company both in the USA and in Europe. Ford is Guest's ideal-typical example of the production model approach which is based on tough, consistent industrial relations practice, focusing on the maintenance of efficient continuity of production. This approach has much in common with Purcell and Gray's (1986) 'traditional/consultative' style of employee relations in which 'labour is viewed as a factor of production and employee subordination is assumed to be part of the "natural order" of the employment relationship'. According to this view unions are accepted as inevitable, employee relations policies centre on the need for stability, control and the institutionalization of conflict, management prerogatives are defended through highly specific collective agreements and careful implementation is paid to the administration of agreements at the point of production. The importance of management control is constantly emphasized with the aim of minimizing or neutralizing union constraints on both operational (line) and strategic (corporate) management decisions. To support such an approach there is a strong emphasis on the central personnel control function (Purcell and Gray 1986:214–15).

In crucial respects, the 'production/traditional/consultative' approach to personnel management differs fundamentally from that espoused in the HRM perspective. The HRM model is characterized as being people-oriented with an emphasis on the maximization of individual skills and motivation through consultation with the workforce so as to produce high levels of commitment to company strategic goals. Labour is more than a factor of production to be minimized. It is an asset to be invested in. The emphasis is on the fostering of working conditions that encourage 'responsible autonomy' rather than the need for 'direct control'. Labour provides potential not constraint. It is a resource to be used to its fullest capacity. The traditional 'production model' is based on the negotiation and enforcement of collective agreements, an emphasis on the need for closed managerial definition of the nature of work and forms of control that support this definition and behaviours that conform to it, employee compliance rather than commitment, and relationships of low trust between management and labour (Fox 1973).

Under the 'production' paradigm of personnel management, order and stability are seen as key issues in producing for stable markets. When markets change so does the emphasis in management:

the need to meet rapid and continuing change in markets shift the emphasis away from formality, and the imperatives of juridification (Storey 1989) and arbitration (Littler 1987), as the focus of employment management. This [change] does indeed require a difference of emphasis and skills among personnel professionals (Kochan and Capelli 1984) and is why top management has seemingly begun to take an active interest in HRM (Hendry and Pettigrew 1990:36).

Ford Motor company in the 1980s provides an excellent example of major changes in personnel practice. We choose to concentrate on Ford for two reasons: (1) because of its paradigmatic importance as progenitor of the traditional 'production' approach; and (2) because of the magnitude of the changes it initiated during the 1980s which reflected a critical re-evaluation of the production approach and a significant move in the direction of HRM for strategic reasons.

Ford is synonymous with the creation of a particular management style – Fordism – based on hierarchical decision-making with strict functional specialization and tightly defined job design and specialized machinery to mass produce a standard product for mass markets (Starkey and McKinlay 1989). A conjunction of market and technological factors stimulated Ford's current efforts to redesign jobs, mode of organization and its prevailing culture. The organizational model for its rethinking of its approach to personnel management was, in part, Japanese-inspired. The company had its close links with Mazda, in which it owns a 25 per cent stake, to serve as a source of competitive bench-marking. This bench-marking formed the basis of its long-term strategy. The pre-existing Fordist system provided important elements of continuity:

> The attempt to reconcile Ford's short- and long-term objectives has meant that the company is currently negotiating a major transition period; on the one hand, striving to introduce aspects of 'Japan-like' industrial organisation in preparation for future strategic change, whilst, on the other hand, maintaining established managerial practices and work organisation patterns essential to current competitiveness (Starkey and McKinlay 1989:94)

The changes of the 1980s in the UK had their origins partly in the recognition that structural reforms of internal bargaining procedures were insufficient to generate the magnitude of organizational change that problems of declining productivity presented, and partly in the response to change initiatives emanating from the American parent company. The primary impetus to change arose from growing recognition of the magnitude of the Japanese threat, actual in the USA, and imminent in the UK with the establishment of the Nissan plant in the north-east of England. The new competition posed the threat of radically new standards of efficiency, quality and design. The problems for Ford UK on the manufacturing side were exacerbated by its poor performance relative not only to the new Japanese competition but also to Ford's factories in Europe. The major challenge Ford management has set itself is to develop a co-operative industrial relations environment which will improve its capacity for strategic change. The move is towards HRM policies and practices in a firm and industry that have been synonymous with conflictual relations between management and employees.

In the USA a key role in Ford's return from the brink of disaster at the end of the 1970s was played by the Employee Development Strategy and Planning Office which was responsible for developing HRM policies based on principles of participative management (PM) and employee involvement (EI) in support of the company's most pressing strategic issues – improved quality of design and manufacture. In 1979, this group was instrumental in developing a policy letter that sanctioned EI. It became the policy of the company to encourage and enable all employees to become involved in and contribute to the success of the company. This required a major culture change in order to develop a work climate in which employees, at all levels, could achieve individual goals and work satisfaction by directing their talents and energies towards clearly defined company goals. This policy was also sanctioned in a letter of understanding with the United Auto Workers (UAW). Over the years EI came to play a central role in the improvement in quality of the company's products and also contributed to other major changes of central strategic importance (Johnson 1988:194–5).

Employee involvement is defined as 'the processes by which employees at all levels have the opportunities to participate actively in the key managerial processes affecting job-related matters' (Banas 1984:2). The processes offering opportunities for participation include consulation (to maximize information and commitment), collaboration (based on a norm of consensus) and delegation (the manager assigns responsibility for an agreed outcome to an individual or group). The joint aim of management and unions was to make work a more satisfying experience, improve the overall work environment, enhance creativity, contribute to improvements in the workplace, and help achieve quality and efficiency and reduce absenteeism. Participative management, the other side of the coin to EI, is defined as 'the techniques and skills which managers use to provide employees with opportunities to participate actively in key managerial processes affecting job related matters' (Banas 1984:1). Techniques include job redesign, team-building, task forces and problem-solving groups. Skills include contracting (establishing clear expectations) and rewarding and modelling participative skills.

Company strategy is embodied in the 1984 mission statement (statement of mission, values and guiding principles). Ford's mission is to be a world-wide leader in automotive and related products and services and in newer industries such as financial services. Its basic values are described as people, products and profits. The guiding principles form a code of conduct that encapsulates policy towards employees, customers, dealers and suppliers. These guiding principles include commitment to the following: quality in all aspects of the business, customers, continuous improvement, EI and teamwork at all levels, specified levels of competitiveness and return on assets. Ford strategy is underpinned by its strategic vision of being a low-cost producer of the highest-quality products and services which provide the best customer value. All strategic issues such as quality improvement, customer satisfaction and cost reduction have one common denominator:

> they all depend on the capacities, competencies, and commitment of our people. Although marked improvement has been made in changing our corporate culture to capitalize on our human resources through the empowerment of our people, the strategic issue, now and into the future, is how to create and sustain a 'right'-sized, flexible work force with the capacities, competencies, and commitment (including the technical and managerial leadership) that gives us a competitive edge in a turbulent, uncertain world marketplace (Johnson 1988:196).

The marked improvements associated with these changes in the USA in the 1980s include major improvements in earnings, profitability, market share, productivity, product design, quality and customer satisfaction. The company perceives itself as having gone through a major transformation in management style and, with the help of the UAW, with having generated a recognition by employees, unions and management alike that their common interests are best served when there are agreed common goals and mutual benefits (Banas and Sauers 1988). Employee involvement has been embraced as company policy so that managers are expected to act accordingly. The other side of the coin to EI is PM – skills that managers use to provide employees and fellow managers with opportunities to participate in key managerial decision-making processes. A major goal of the change initiative, therefore, was managerial behaviour. The company had accepted Deming's assessment of their quality problems as primarily rooted in management practices and not, as management had previously believed, worker failure to conform to management dictates. A major aim was to tap into 'the competencies (depth), capacities (breadth), and commitment (motivation) of the workforce at all levels'.

> Reduced to its essentials, EI is the process by which employees are provided with the opportunities to contribute their minds, as well as their muscles, and hopefully their hearts, to the attaining of individual and Company goals. Through a variety of techniques – such as problem solving groups, new product launch teams, ad hoc quality and scrap involvement teams – opportunities have been created, for hourly employees to contribute their ideas, their analyses, and their solutions to job-related problems. Since 1979, virtually every hourly employee, either directly or indirectly, has been affected by this process. Today EI is functioning in virtually all major Ford facilities (Banas and Sauers 1989:3).

In the USA the troubles of this time were seen as firmly rooted not just in problems of the business cycle and in the new competition but in lack of trust between management and labour, a lack of clear corporate values and sharply defined goals and in a turbulent history of adversarial labour–management relations. In the UK the moves towards an HRM culture were not the immediate crisis faced in the USA. In fact, Ford of Europe played a key role in providing finances to see the parent company through the troubled years of the early 1980s! In Europe the company was enjoying great success at this time. Ford UK is a wholly owned subsidiary of Ford Motor Company USA. The US parent exercises a certain degree of control, for example, over spending beyond certain limits, but the UK company is responsible for decisions concerning day-to-day operations and for pay bargaining, although the latter needs the formal approval of the parent which usually supports the UK company's judgement on these matters. Two major change personnel management initiatives were launched in Ford UK from 1979 onwards. The first, 'After Japan', had its origins in a trip to Japan by the company's vice-president of manufacturing. 'After Japan' represented the company's acknowledgement of the threat posed by Japan. Its limited success is attributed by senior management to management mistakes in the attempted implementation of some of HRM initiatives proposed, most notably in the unilateral imposition of quality circles, and to union resistance. The second change initiative centred around the HRM policies and practices emanating from the US parent under the EI/PM banner. Formal agreement to this initiative was refused by the blue-collar unions but, for a time, granted by the staff unions.

Central to 'After Japan' was the view that the roots of Japanese success could be traced to a management style that was diametrically opposed to the Fordist model. The essence of the Japanese approach was seen to lie in management by consent rather than control, and the mobilization of commitment rather than the elimination of worker discretion. The need for change was communicated to the workforce with the results of a competitive bench-marking exercise against Japanese productivity standards and strategic targets set in terms of return on investment, market share, efficiency measures and reduction in headcount. The strategic goals were quality, customer satisfaction and cost competitiveness. Elements of the Japanese system of JIT inventory management were introduced as well as a new quality philosophy of 'right first time'. Quality circles were also introduced, the major leaning towards HRM. At the same time the production model of personnel management was refined in the introduction of more rigorous cost control systems (Marsden et al. 1985:188).

Initially, Ford envisaged the introduction of quality circles as the first step in the rapid 'Japanization' of the company, a process that was to include training the workforce in problem-solving and inter-personal skills to enhance teamwork, JIT and more stable relations on a long-term basis with preferred suppliers who could meet the company's exacting design and quality standards. The failure of the quality circle initiative, basically because they were imposed rather than negotiated in their introduction and, thus, came to be seen as a means of subverting traditional bargaining agreements, led the company to the recognition that a gradual, processual approach to modifying a company culture rooted in a long history of adversarial industrial relations was required rather than a quick structural reorganization alone.

The successor to the failed quality circle initiative was the adoption of the American process of EI and PM, and approach to management that has been incorporated into rationalization and pay and working conditions negotiations. Only the staff unions agreed to formal

involvement in this process but the philosophy and practices underlying the process have been diligently pursued by Ford management
informally at the local level. For example, problem-solving work
groups, akin to quality circles, flourish in certain Ford UK facilities.
The 1985 Pay and Working Practices Agreement is seen as a break-
through in this process of informal diffusion with its key elements of
versatility and flexibility, the acquisition of new skills and the
elimination of inefficient demarcation lines in both craft and production work. These elements were reinforced in later pay and
working conditions negotiations which were conducted in an EI/PM
mode.

One of the main goals of PM is the changing of managerial attitudes
and the dismantling of what is now perceived as dysfunctional
hierarchies. Its aims are to simplify managerial control, devolve
authority and break down the barriers between managerial groups
which have their basis in both hierarchy and functional specialization. The key goal is a major culture change so that EI/PM
become not just another change programme but an accepted way of
life. It is symptomatic of the major advance that the company has
made in this direction that it can accept, philosophically, the recent
withdrawal of the staff unions from the formal EI agreement on the
grounds that enough of the principles of the initial programme
have been internalized to make progress in this direction a natural
feature of the current evolution of the Ford management style and
culture. The great success of the recent Employee Development and
Assistance Programme with its introduction of non-pay and non-
job-related benefits in the form of funding for individual personal
development through participation in education courses outside the
company represents the latest outcome of the ongoing 'battle' for
employee hearts and minds, a key element of the HRM agenda.

One should also mention the important role of quality in the
change process. Peter Drucker (1990) argues that the introduction of
statistical quality control (SQC), based on the work of Deming and
Juran, is radically changing thinking about manufacturing management through its impacts on the social organization of the factory.
By aligning information with accountability, Drucker argues, SQC
resolves the apparently irresolvable conflict between 'scientific
management', based on the work of F. W. Taylor and Henry Ford,
and the 'human relations' approach founded by Elton Mayo. Both of
these approaches were aimed at improving quality and productivity
but, according to Drucker, it is only with the advent of SQC that the

management of manufacture becomes truly scientific, the dream of Taylor, and worker pride and knowledge, the key factors in the human relations approach, can be fully capitalized upon:

> without SQC's rigorous methodologies neither scientific management nor the assembly line could actually deliver built-in process control. With all their successes, both scientific management and the assembly line had to fall back on massive inspection, to fix problems rather than eliminate them.
>
> The human-relations approach sees the knowledge and pride of line workers as the greatest resource for controlling and improving quality and productivity. . . . But without the kind of information SQC provides, you cannot readily distinguish productive activity from busy-ness. It is hard to tell whether a proposed modification will truly improve the process (Drucker 1990:96).

Statistical quality control provides the knowledge technology to design both quality and productivity into the manufacturing process by giving responsibility for the process and control of it to the only people who can assure quality – the machine operators. Ford has diligently pursued the introduction of SQC using Deming as a consultant (Pettigrew 1985). Beside its impact on quality itself and productivity, a major by-product of the new emphasis on quality is the establishment of a common language for both management and employees, with mutually acceptable objective definitions of terms, to discuss and negotiate the strategic problems facing the company. The language of quality, therefore, provides an important source of and impetus to consensus.

The legacy of 'After Japan' and the lessons from the US EI/PM initiative is an ongoing dual agenda change strategy: on the one hand, in continuity with the production model, the strong defence of managerial prerogatives and its disciplinary code, for example, in the strict rules concerning suspension if supervisory authority is not accepted pending fuller consultation, while, on the other hand, the pursuit of a more complex, longer-term approach aimed at building more consensual management–labour relations. Exemplifying the latter, rationalization and efficiency measures are no longer pushed through in the traditional top-down style but are negotiated through a gradual process of communication and persuasion without compulsory redundancy. Even as difficult a decision as the relocation of some of its engine capacity to the continent rather than at Bridgend has gained local acceptance.

Conclusion

We started this chapter by looking at one of the more sensitive analyses of recent developments in HRM (Guest 1987). We begin our conclusion by suggesting that Guest has perhaps been too sensitive to distinctions between his four models of personnel management. Such strong distinctions do suggest an either/or choice for management, certainly between the production and the HRM models. In practice, different approaches will tend to coexist, at least during those transition periods when firms move from one model of personnel management to another, as our Ford example illustrates, and even having negotiated such a transition period, elements of previous models might prove worthy of retention. As our Ford example also illustrates, the key personnel problem is to adapt approaches established in a very different competitive environment to the demands of an environment of fast change and unpredictability where principles embedded in previous approaches such as the Fordist paradigm of management no longer apply. To understand the present we have to be sensitive to the constraints rooted in companies' histories. The majority of firms find themselves faced with a complex transition period in which to negotiate and experiment with the exact balance between continuity and change. They cannot afford the luxury of throwing away the rule-book and recommencing *ab initio*. Only firms setting up on greenfield sites start with a *tabula rasa* (Guest 1989) but even in this apparently privileged situation company tradition can make such developments far more problematic than they initially appear, as Ford itself learnt in its attempts to establish a hi-tech electronics components plant in Dundee (Starkey and McKinlay 1989). The starting-points for the present are employee relations and management styles established in very different times, unsuitable for the 'new times' we are now facing (Murray 1988). A change agenda can take up to a generation to work through a company as the 'old guard', the previous vanguard, ages and finally retires. New 'brooms', thrusting charismatic leaders, the latest managerial panacea, founder more often than not on the inertia of existing organizational practices (Williams et al. 1987). Sensitive handling of change involves the reassessment of the existing system for strengths that can still prove useful, experiments with new practices to establish which have the potential for broader dissemination, and the acceptance that, such is the weight of history and tradition, some old practices are too strongly embedded to remove in the short term, particularly those involving major attitude change.

The current growth of interest in HRM reflects past failings of the personnel function – 'a persistent failure of personnel departments to innovate on personnel policy and therefore to contribute to the pursuit of competitive advantage' (Guest 1988:10). What is represented by HRM is a policy agenda, in many cases, of personnel management in search of a new role and even a justification for its continued existence. At the very least, it presents us with a radical rethinking of the function. Legge (1989) argues that HRM has three key features that distinguish it from previous approaches to personnel management. Traditional personnel management was couched in terms of something performed on subordinates by managers; HRM focuses not only on the development of employees but also the development of managers themselves (Legge 1989:27). In the Ford case, a prerequisite for effective employee involvement was the development of participative management. With HRM there is, according to Legge, a far tighter integration of personnel practices into the pursuit of strategic goals. In the Ford case, the mission statement emphasized the symbiotic relationship between strategic goals and human resources. Thirdly, HRM emphasizes the strategic significance of strong culture in promoting a sense of purpose and commitment in the organization. Again, the Ford mission statement illustrates this point. Guest (1988) makes similar points when he answers the question – what is needed to install HRM? – although he is pessimistic about the skill of British firms actually to operationalize the HRM agenda. He argues that much recent change in the UK has focused on cost-cutting but that when the limits of such rationalization are reached we may see stronger moves towards HRM.

Perhaps the key distinguishing feature of HRM is its evolving strategic role. Miller (1989) sees traditional personnel management as non-strategic, separate from the business, reactive, short term and constrained by a limited definition of its role as dealing with unionized and lower-level employees. Personnel management becomes strategic when employees are managed in ways which recognize their key role in strategy implementation and a key goal of employee relations becomes the motivation of employees to fulfil strategic objectives. This view fits with the literature on strategic leadership where the most important top management function is to motivate employees to exceptional effort by fostering a sense of commitment to institutional purpose (Selznick 1957; Wrapp 1967; *Strategic*

Management Journal 1989). Strategic leadership and HRM come together in strategic HRM. For Johnson (1988), reflecting on Ford's employee development programmes in the USA, it is an important task for the personnel specialist

> to better identify where our HR systems impact and support corporate strategic issues . . . to demonstrate its competence in strategic planning and implementation. We need to clearly specify the value-added benefit of the HR function in formulating and implementing business strategy. We need to be able to surface the Human Resources implications of strategic alternatives and provide options for handling HR issues that are directly related to strategic planning issues. . . . In short, we need to evolve the role of Human Resources from an administrative role to a consultant one in running the business (Johnson 1988:199).

Other authors are less sanguine about this possibility. Purcell (1989) claims that the whole thrust of current developments in corporate strategy geared to expansion by acquisition and diversification and/or an emphasis on short-run returns on investment and tight financial controls is inimical to the very principles of an employee-centred HRM. Such an approach to strategy marginalizes employees as stakeholders in weighing strategic issues:

> The criticism of diversified, multi-divisional companies on employee relations presented here is another twist of a familiar story. It is odd, then, that the current wave of interest in human resource management is so optimistic and implies that a major reconsideration of personnel practice is underway. The belief is that corporate executives and line managers have discovered the need to encourage employee involvement, team work, and integrated reward systems . . . as a crucial element of their corporate and business-unit strategies. Changes are, of course, taking place. . . . But in many diversified firms, in Britain at least, the material conditions for these to be translated into long-run strategic decisions placing human resource management as the, or even a, critical function in corporate strategy, do not exist. What ought to happen, as prescribed by the burgeoning literature, is a long way from being realized (Purcell 1989:90).

It is odd that Purcell can reconcile this view of the move towards HRM as being, at best, marginal and yet can also state that the old order is crumbling. Into what, one wonders, if the old verities no longer apply and there is no new paradigm to replace them –

anarchy? It is also odd that in the book in which Purcell's chapter is found examples of HRM practices are drawn from a variety of firms including, Bejam, BMW, British Airways, BP, British Rail, British Steel, Ford, GE, General Motors, Hewlett-Packard, IBM, ICL, Lucas, Jaguar, Komatsu, Matsushita, Mercedes, National Westminster Bank, Nissan, Rover, Shell, Toshiba, Whitbread and Xerox. In another recent overview of the field (Evans et al. 1989), multinational examples of HRM practice include SAS, Peat Marwick, Xerox, Olivetti, ICL, Philips, Unilever, Nissan, Shell, Exxon, Nestlé, Honeywell, BP, IBM, Hewlett-Packard, Volvo and Marks and Spencer. The variety of these companies surely signals a strong trend towards HRM practices. Purcell, though, is correct to the extent that his view counsels against too simplistic an acceptance of the inevitability of HRM in a pure form distinct from previous practice. Hopefully, this chapter has demonstrated that it is by no means an unlikely occurrence, nor, perhaps, an undesirable one, that some aspects of the old order will survive with the new order that is emerging.

References

Abernathy, W.J., Clark, K.B. and Kantrow, A.M. 1981: The new industrial competition. *Harvard Business Review*, September–October, 69–77.

Banas, P. 1984: *The Relationship between Participative Management and Employee Involvement*. Dearborn: Ford Motor Company.

Banas, P. and Sauers, R. 1988: *Participative Management and Employee Involvement. Model and Application*. Dearborn: Ford Motor Company.

Banas, P. and Sauers, R. 1989: *The Relationship between Participative Management and Employee Involvement*. Dearborn: Ford Motor Company.

Beer, M., Spector, B., Lawrence, P.R., Mills, D.O. and Walton, R.E. 1984: *Managing Human Assets*. New York: Free Press.

Best, M.H. 1990: *The New Competition. Institutions of Industrial Restructuring*. Cambridge: Polity Press.

Chandler, A.D. 1962: *Strategy and Structure*. Cambridge, Mass.: MIT Press.

Deming, W.E. 1982: *Quality, Productivity and Competitive Position*. Cambridge, Mass.: MIT Center for Advanced Engineering.

Drucker, P. 1990: The emerging theory of manufacturing. *Harvard Business Review*, May–June, 94–102.

Evans, P., Doz, Y. and Laurent, A. (eds) 1989: *Human Resource Management in International Firms*. London: Macmillan.

Fox, A. 1973: *Beyond Contract. Work, Power and Trust Relations*. London: Faber.

Giles, E. and Starkey, K. 1988: The Japanisation of Xerox. *New Technology, Work and Employment*, 3(2), 125–33.

Guest, D. 1987: Human resource management and industrial relations. *Journal of Management Studies*, 24(5), 503–21.

Guest, D. 1988: 'Human resource management – is it worth taking seriously?' London School of Economics, First Annual Seear Fellowship Lecture.

Guest, D. 1989: Human resource management: its implications for industrial relations and trade unions. In J. Storey (ed.), *New Perspectives on Human Resource Management*, London: Routledge, 41–55.

Hamel, G. and Prahalad, C.K. 1989: Strategic intent. *Harvard Business Review*, May–June, 63–76.

Harvey-Jones, J. 1988: *Making it Happen: reflections on leadership*. London: Collins.

Hendry, C. and Pettigrew, A. 1990: Human resource management: an agenda for the 1990s. *International Journal of Human Resource Management*, 1(1), 1–7.

Johnson, R.H. 1988: How Ford's HR staff supports strategic planning. In Y.K. Shetty and V.M. Buehler (eds), *Competing through Productivity and Quality*, Cambridge, Mass.: Productivity Press, 189–99.

Kochan, T.A. and Capelli, P. 1984: The transformation of the industrial relations and personnel function. In P. Osterman (ed.), *Internal Labor Markets*, Cambridge, Mass.: MIT Press, 133–62.

Lawrence, P.R. and Dyer, R. 1983: *Renewing American Industry*. New York: Free Press.

Legge, K. 1989: Human resource management: a critical analysis. In J. Storey (ed.), *New Perspectives on Human Resource Management*, London: Routledge, 19–40.

Littler, C.R. 1987: The social and economic relations of work. *Labour and Industry*, 1(1), 1–7.

Marsden, D., Morris, T., Willman, P. and Woods, S. 1985: *The Car Industry*. London: Tavistock.

Miller, P. 1989: Strategic industrial relations and human resource management – distinction, definition and recognition. *Journal of Management Studies*, 24(4), 347–61.

Murray, R. 1988: Life after Henry (Ford). *Marxism Today*, October, 8–13.

Peters, T. and Waterman, R.H. 1982: *In Search of Excellence*. New York: Harper & Row.

Pettigrew, T.J. 1985: Process quality control: the new approach to the management of quality in Ford. *Quality Assurance*, 11(3), 81–8.

Porter, M. 1987: From competitive advantage to corporate strategy. *Harvard Business Review*, May–June, 43–59.

Prahalad, C.K. and Hamel, G. 1990: The core competence of the corporation. *Harvard Business Review*, May–June, 79–91.

Purcell, J. 1989: The impact of corporate strategy on human resource management. In J. Storey (ed.), *New Perspectives on Human Resource Management*, London: Routledge, 67–91

Purcell, J. and Gray, A. 1986: Corporate personnel departments and the management of industrial relations: two case studies in ambiguity. *Journal of Management Studies*, 23(2), 205–23.

Quinn, J.B., Mintzberg, H. and James, R.M. 1988: *The Strategy Process*. Englewood Cliffs: Prentice-Hall.

Ramsay, H. 1983: Evolution or cycle? Worker participation in the 1970s and 1980s. In C. Crouch and F.A. Heller (eds), *Organizational Democracy and Political Processes*, Vol. 1, Chichester: Wiley, 203–26.

Selznick, A. 1957: *Leadership in Administration*. New York: Harper & Row.

Starkey K. and McKinlay, A. 1989: Beyond Fordism? Strategic choice and labour relations in Ford UK. *Industrial Relations Journal*, 20(2), 93–100.

Storey, J. (ed.) 1989: *New Perspectives on Human Resource Management*. London: Routledge.

Strategic Management Journal 1989: Special issue. On strategic leadership. 10(1–3).

Torrington, D. 1989: Human resource management and the personnel function. In J. Storey (ed.), *New Perspectives on Human Resource Management*, London: Routledge, 56–66.

Williams, K., Williams, J. and Haslam, C. 1987: *The Breakdown of Austin Rover*. Leamington Spa: Berg.

Wrapp, H.E. 1967: Good managers don't make policy decisions. *Harvard Business Review*, September–October, 91–9.

17

Management Values and Change: the Case of Tioxide UK

HEDLEY MALLOCH

Introduction

The case study is mainly located in the Cleveland operations of the Pigment Division of Tioxide UK, a major multinational producer of pigment. It traces the principal strategic changes which took place between 1983 and 1986, with a postscript which outlines key developments from 1986 to 1990. The Pigment Division made pigment, a light-dispersant material used in the manufacture of paint, paper, fabrics, textiles and toothpaste. The company began production of pigment in the UK in 1934 in Cleveland. The company had two factories in the UK, one at Grimsby and a second at Greatham in Cleveland: the Greatham factory opened in 1971 and had a capacity of 55,000 tonnes per year. In 1985 pigment sales accounted for 95 per cent of the company's UK income. It could be regarded as a one-product company making a mature product.

Tioxide UK recorded losses between 1980 and 1983; this period was dominated by redundancies and a recessed world pigment market. From 1983 onwards its manpower strategies were at the heart of a major turnaround in corporate economic performance. In 1987 Tioxide won the IPM and *Daily Telegraph* Award for Excellence in Personnel Management.

Marketing and Production Strategies

World pigment supply was inelastic; price was thus extremely sensitive to fluctuations in demand. When demand fell in the early

Table 17.1 The sulphate and chloride methods of Tioxide's pigment production compared

Variable	The sulphate process	The chloride process
Date first used	1934	1972
Number of plants	7 in the world	1 at Greatham
Production process	Batch	Interdependent streams
Reliability of plant	High	Low
Means of increasing production	Add plant	De-bottleneck plant
Key production task	Process batches	Recover chlorine
Main health and safety concerns	Waste treatment and disposal	Process management and control

1980s, prices dropped sharply. World markets recovered strongly from 1983 and by 1986 demand for Tioxide's pigment had outstripped supply. Tioxide gave priority to domestic and European markets. A major concern was their inability to supply fully other world markets where premium prices could be obtained. Tioxide produced 17 per cent of total world supply in eight factories throughout the world; the world's largest producer was DuPont who produced 20 per cent. Over the period consumers began to demand the higher-quality pigment produced by the chloride process rather than that made by the sulphate process. Greatham was Tioxide's only chloride process factory, whereas DuPont made all of their pigment by the chloride process.

The sulphate method of pigment production was a relatively simple method of batch production. The chloride process was much more complex involving the chlorination of titanium ores, the distillation of liquid tetrachloride, and an oxidization process in which titanium dioxide crystals were grown in a process lasting less than a second. The chloride process had two advantages over the sulphate process: it gave a better quality product and caused fewer waste disposal problems. The sulphate process produced large quantities of potentially dangerous wastes the dumping of which was controlled by law. It also attracted the attention of environmental pressure groups. In 1985 Greenpeace occupied part of the Grimsby factory. Table 17.1 summarizes the differences between the sulphate and chloride processes.

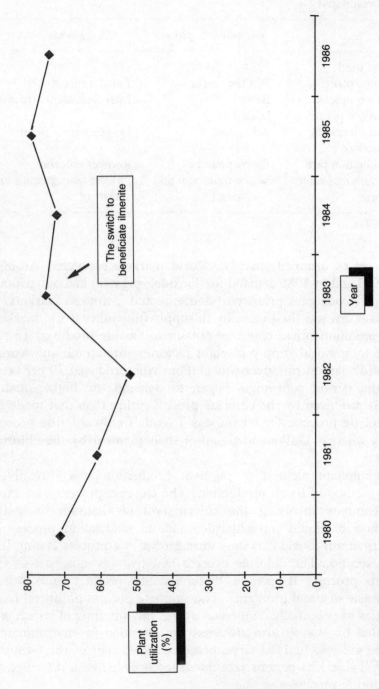

Figure 17.1 Tioxide's Greatham works plant utilization rates, 1980–1986

The chloride process was organized in three interdependent streams. If one part shut down, the others followed. Output was increased by raising temperatures and pressures at key points in the process. For this reason much attention was paid to the engineering problems of 'de-bottlenecking' the plant. The process was difficult to manage. Chlorination and oxidization involved the use of aggressive chemicals and gases at high temperatures and pressures. The plant fabric worked under adverse conditions. Key pieces of equipment often failed. One manager described some of the problems: 'You could get holes appearing in the sides of vessels, you might get the bottom dropping out of reactors and there is the potential for God knows what. It's trying to get over basic engineering problems that is the problem.'

For these reasons Greatham was the location of problem-solving activity focused on production, maintenance and process development. These problems were not fully understood and had to be resolved in a factory rather than a pilot plant. They meant that between 1972 and 1985 Greatham never operated at more than 78 per cent of capacity and were the cause of Greatham's very poor financial performance.

Over the period Tioxide sought to improve the pigment quality. This was partly driven by changing customer requirements, but the main reason was the competitive strategy adopted by new managers promoted to senior appointments during the early 1980s. Like all of Tioxide's managers they were well versed in the management literature, both with long-established writers, and with currently fashionable authors such as Peters and Kanter. They saw the future of the company depending on quality. One commented:

> Once we accept that our product is a commodity we are halfway down the road to death. We strenuously keep our quality image to the forefront; people still are buying pigments on the basis of quality and how well they do in the application, not just on price.... Other manufacturers go for consistency rather than high-performing products.

When demand revived after 1983 Tioxide's priority was to increase production in a cost-effective manner, but the economics and technology of pigment production made this a difficult problem. Large, short-term variations in output were not feasible. Major additions to output were only possible by building new factories. But the world supply of pigment was produced in a small number of plants. New factories meant both big capital outlays and large additions to capacity which would depress prices. The route to profitable production increases was by expanding output in existing plants by improving plant and process to remove bottlenecks to higher levels of production. De-bottlenecking allowed capacity to be expanded at the controlled rate necessary to maintain high prices.

A major economic problem was the inelastic supply of rutile, the most expensive feedstock. The demand for rutile was derived from the demand for pigment. In times of rising demand for pigment there was a commensurate increase in the price of rutile. Therefore one strategic problem for Tioxide was to stop extra profits from being passed on to their rutile suppliers. At Greatham the answer was to use a cheaper, substitute feedstock called beneficiate ilmenite. This decision led to technical difficulties and a fall in production. This is shown in figure 17.1.

Declining output and technical problems intensified conflict between plant managers, maintenance managers and development engineers. Plant managers decided when the plant would be released for maintenance and development work. In a plant whose processes were still being developed, and whose maintenance was a problem, there was both the potential for conflict and the need for co-operation. The development, production and maintenance functions were mutually dependent, but all were separately organized into different departments. There were many conflicts concerning the ownership of the plant and the decision to use beneficiate ilmenite brought them to a head.

Tioxide's Manpower Policies

Managerial jobs were regrouped to obtain better integration of specialist engineering activities. This partly stemmed from the organizational problems following the switch in feedstocks. Development, maintenance and plant engineers were regrouped into area teams. From 1984 decisions on plant management were made by these teams. This was regarded as a major act of decentralization of decision-taking. In addition two linked management bodies, the business improvement council and Juran groups, were established. The business improvement council consisted of senior managers: it identified and examined areas where improvements could be made.

Once areas for improvement had been identified Juran groups, consisting of engineering and production managers, were established to investigate the problem. Juran groups were associated with the ideas of Edward J. Juran (1974): his philosophy drove Tioxide's quality strategy. It gave great stress given to teamwork, quality circles and shop-floor participation in problem-solving. They were described as quality circles for managers. The general manager explained the reason for their introduction:

Juran was something we got into; it's saying that we've got a tremendous wealth of talented people; that we have come nowhere near tapping all of that creative talent; that we have problems that we need to solve and decisions that need to be made. We want to move towards situations where people's accountability and responsibility depends primarily on their ability to contribute to a decision rather than on their position in some kind of hierarchy.

Juran groups analysed problems and their work was often linked to that of shop-floor quality circles. Process improvements were proposed, evaluated and installed. These innovations were seen not merely as devices for technical problem-solving. They were the means for the management of organizational change by decentralizing decision-making and abolishing the separation of planning and execution of work at all levels in the organization. Brainstorming and paired comparisons were used to ensure that a few people could not unilaterally define a problem or set agendas. The Juran groups systematically involved a wide range of people: by the time an answer had been devised there would have been few people who were likely to be concerned in implementing the solution who had not been involved.

The most striking feature of the manpower changes was the widespread introduction of quality circles as part of a strategy to introduce problem-solving methods of participation. They were not seen solely as approaches to raising quality. In 1986 there about 35 quality circles running in Tioxide's Cleveland establishments. Their arrival was associated with the appointment of the new general manager in 1983. He said of their introduction:

It is fair to say that quality circles have nothing whatever to do with the recession problems or any changing environment that we've been in. It has to do with the fact that I passionately, but passionately,

believed that as a company we were getting nowhere really in significant terms with participation and with problem solving. There
were far, far too many examples of our living with chronic losses. We
would have started circles irrespective of what kind of an environment
we'd been in. I can say this with real honesty. I passionately and
strongly believed that we had a fantastic resource in the people who
worked for us. A fund of ideas, of creative talent which we were
nowhere near remotely tapping. People came into the factory and they
hung their brains on the gate and they picked them up again when
they went out. I felt very strongly about that. It was a principle that
we started them. We would have done it anyway. . . . You may say
circles programmes are started up in a recession because things are
looking desperate. Well, not really because redundancies are not a
very good environment for starting circles. You get involved in a
recession and redundancies, then the last thing you are going to be
able to get through easily is a circles programme.

Quality circles were introduced because the organization was seen
to be incapable of responding to suggestions for change made by
the workforce. Their ideas were lost in the bureaucracy of works
suggestion schemes, or dismissed by managers who felt that workers
did not understand the problem. Both the reorganization of managerial work and quality circles were aimed at restructuring work
around teams rather than individuals. Two important supporting
innovations were a distance-learning course leading to City and
Guilds qualifications for chemical plant operators, and the application
of Coverdale training in teamworking skills for plant operators. Both
were intended to underpin the creation of technically competent,
flexible work teams.

The numbers employed at the Greatham factory consistently
increased every year since 1981. Details are charted on figure 17.2.
The decision to increase manning in 1984 was prompted by a
deterioration in plant performance. Plant output, plant utilization
and output in tonnes per head all fell due to problems of the technical reliability of plant. To solve these, the Greatham plant moved
from four-shift to a five-shift system of work.

Four-shift working hindered the development of teamworking.
Spare people to cover for absenteeism, holidays and sickness had to
be built into each shift, making team cohesion more difficult. A
five-shift system removed spares from the shift: holidays and days off
were rostered by shift rather than by individual worker. This was
done to strengthen the team concept.

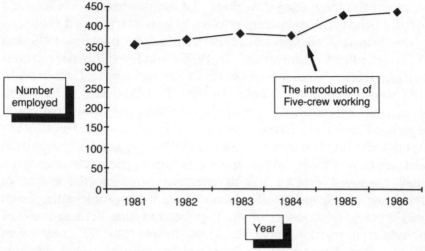

Figure 17.2 Manning levels at Tioxide's Greatham works, 1981–1986

While some work had always been contracted out there was no evidence that Tioxide had sought to intensify its use of contract or part-time workers. Greatham's works manager pointed out the reasons for their reluctance to intensify the use of peripheral workers:

> We don't need them. Even if we did, we would take on permanent staff. We get better quality, better commitment and we can afford to make an investment in them. We are out of the pairs of hands business; we are into the minds business. We would prefer to meet the numbers problem by expanding the capabilities and responsibilities of existing staff.

Over the period Tioxide's management moved from a policy of determining pay and conditions by collective bargaining to one of unilateral determination by managers. This policy was linked to that of harmonizing conditions of employment. In 1980 the terms and conditions of employment of technical staff were negotiated with ASTMS at company level; other white-collar workers' conditions were determined by the company. The pay and conditions of manual workers were settled by the main chemical industry agreement. The unions representing the manual workers were the TGWU, who represented process workers; and the AUEW and the EEPTU, who organized the maintenance workers. All establishments in Cleveland and the Grimsby factory were effectively post-entry closed shops.

The principal changes in industrial relations between 1980 and 1983 can be briefly summarized. In 1980 Tioxide's industrial relations manager left and was not replaced. In the same year Tioxide withdrew recognition from ASTMS. In 1981 Tioxide ceased to be bound by national agreements, arguing that it could not afford nationally negotiated increases. Extra wages would have to come from locally negotiated bonus schemes. After 1981 the control of industrial relations passed from the personnel function to the works managers. They employed process and maintenance workers, the grades of labour for whom industrial relations were most problematic. From 1983 the general manager of the Pigment Division became involved in industrial relations policy-making. From 1981 all negotiations were conducted at plant level. There was no company-level bargaining because of what management saw as technical differences between the plants.

Between 1980 and 1985, differences in conditions between white-collar and manual workers narrowed and by 1985 the principal difference in conditions of employment between them was pensions. A manual worker with full pension entitlement would receive one-half of his pensionable salary, compared with two-thirds for a staff member. In 1982 the manual workers' unions began to press for parity of pensions. Management accepted that pensions should be the same for both groups, but sought to use this as an opportunity to advance their own objectives.

The pensions issue first surfaced at Grimsby and it presented Tioxide's managers with an opportunity to redefine their relations with manual workers. Conditions, including pensions entitlement, would be harmonized, but the manual workers would be required to forgo collective bargaining. The stated reasons for this strategy were cost and flexibility. Equality of pensions would cost an extra 8 per cent of the wage bill. But cash savings were thought to be possible with greater flexibility of labour, less demarcation and better team spirit. Teamworking and quality circles had exposed a number of multi-skilling issues which were a source of concern to the unions. The district committee of the AUEW had opposed the introduction of quality circles. But the managers' perception was that quality circles, devolution and reskilling were popular with manual workers. Management considered that manual workers resented the interference of what the managers saw as a remote trade union bureaucracy in their day-to-day work. They saw an opportunity they could exploit to help them remove collective bargaining.

Managers considered that flexibility was impossible if conditions were negotiated collectively. Changes in working practices would be nominal if the people concerned were not directly involved. Flexibility would be achieved through 'teamworking', that is, where tasks would be allocated to work groups of multi-skilled employees responsible for maintaining and operating plant. Change would be channelled through these teams and it would be implemented by participation, Juran groups, quality circles, communications, and technical and social skills training. To the general manager, this strategy was more effective than collective bargaining at promoting change: 'All the things we were achieving on participation and the change to an organization which was primarily value-driven said: "What do we need all these outside people for?" We're looking for change. We know the road we're going down.'

The pensions issue crystallized these wider issues and concerns first at Grimsby. Here the workforce was older than at Greatham and consequently pensions were a more important issue. The proposal that Tioxide's managers put to the Grimsby's shop stewards was an offer of staff conditions of employment, including membership of the staff pension scheme, in return for forgoing trade union recognition and representation. Grimsby's shop stewards agreed to discuss the matter, to exclude full-time union officers from the negotiations, and to put the offer to a ballot of the workforce at an appropriate time. This was to be when the managers and shop stewards considered that the ballot would command a substantial turnout and at least a two-thirds majority for the offer. During the winter of 1986–7 the Grimsby manual workforce and 47 manual workers employed at a minor non-pigment operation in Cleveland were balloted. Seventy-six per cent of those affected agreed in a 93 per cent poll (Kennedy 1988) to accept a transfer to staff conditions in return for giving up their right to have their trade unions recognized for purposes of either collective bargaining or individual representation.

The offer was not made at Greatham due to opposition from that work's shop stewards. In 1987 the process and maintenance workers at Greatham were the only Tioxide employees in the UK to be covered by collective bargaining. Some managers believed that the move to staff status and the removal of trade unions at Greatham was only a question of time. They argued that the workforce would be driven in this direction by the teamworking initiatives.

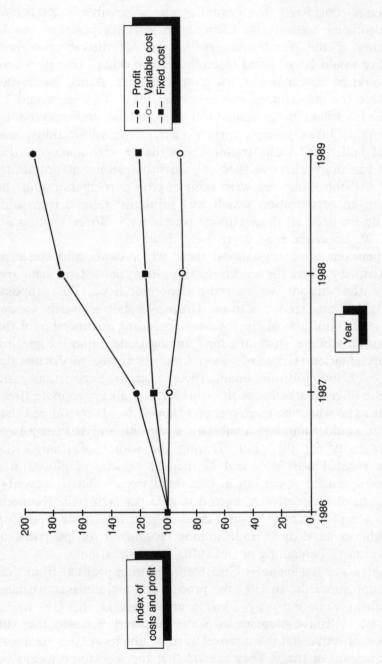

Figure 17.3 Financial performance of Greatham plant, 1986–1989

Table 17.2 The Greatham plant's technical performance: 1986–1989

Parameter	1986	1987	1988	1989
Plant utilization rate (%)	74	75	75	77
Product quality off-specification (%)	15	13	14	5
No. of customer complaints	44	21	15	8
Index of energy consumption	100	100	98	93

Post-1986 Developments

The performance of the Greatham plant between 1986 and 1989 can be seen by an inspection of the key parameters of the plant's financial and technical performance. The plant's financial performance is summarized in figure 17.3. The reduction in variable costs was attributed to better pigment quality, resulting in reduced rework rates; improved plant reliability; reduced energy consumption; and more extensive use of cheaper feedstocks. Table 17.2 gives details of the plant's technical performance.

Over the same period the work of plant operators, maintenance workers and technicians was analysed to identify generic skills and knowledge; and training was reorganized to provide a common development programme aimed at providing generic competences for all who needed them, irrespective of their job titles. One important consequence was that plant workers, maintenance personnel and laboratory technicians received common training: this was seen as supporting the teamworking initiatives. It was regarded as affirming Tioxide's strategy that the competencies of operators, laboratory staff and maintenance workers were the most promising areas of added value for the company. Between 1986 and 1989 training costs more than doubled. In 1989 training accounted for 17 per cent of the manpower budget.

The training manager gave his evaluation of the relative contributions of the many different human resource policies pursued in Tioxide since 1983:

> It's difficult to say – one cannot take particular policies out of context, and everything that we did – Juran, team-working, quality circles, technical training, harmonization, the Business Improvement Council –

all made a valuable contribution in their own right. But if I was pressed I would single out the City and Guilds process plant open learning course mounted by the local technical college for our plant operators. So much of what we did depended upon our people having a good understanding of the plant.

The management of the chloride process was supported by a £30m. programme begun in 1986 aimed at making production more flexible through the development of three independent standby streams which would enable the factory to produce if particular pieces of plant were stopped. This process, called the chloride development stream, was seen as essential to the successful manufacture of chloride pigments. Some 40 employees recruited to the new process were employed on the single-status conditions which were at the centre of union recognition issue. The unions protested; Tioxide's management offered them a representational role on grievance and discipline issues only. In August 1990 management organized a ballot of the new employees on the issue of a union role on grievance and discipline: the balloted employees polled to reject the offer of union involvement.

In 1990 ICI acquired a controlling interest in Tioxide. ICI introduced their own chief executive offer (CEO) into Tioxide and began a comprehensive review of Tioxide's business in relation to that of ICI.

Analysis of the Tioxide Case

The connections between Tioxide's competitive strategy and their human resource management strategy

At the level of strategic analysis Tioxide's strategy was one of growth through new products and new markets. The chloride process offered a superior product, new to Tioxide, but which was the standard offered by their major competitor. They were refusing profitable business in new overseas markets because they did not have the capacity to supply them and they lacked the organizational skill to run a chloride pigment plant at full capacity. Running parallel with these issues were environmental concerns.

An added complication was a weak strategic position with regard to a powerful rutile supplier. Tioxide were unable to harvest the fruits of a potentially profitable pigment market. Their attempts to substitute beneficiate ilmenite in what was an already highly problematic technology triggered a crisis in their production system, which in turn precipitated the manpower strategies outlined in the case. This world of strong suppliers and weak buyers searching for a substitute raw material, in a market-place where large additions to output depressed both prices and profits, provides the stuff of a classic 'five forces' model of competitive analysis (Porter 1980).

At the level of strategic implementation the answers to these problems were the development of the chloride process, de-bottle-necking the plant, and the use of substitute feedstocks. The most important of these was the chloride process. It held the solution to the problems of competing on quality and environmental management. Greatham was Tioxide's only chloride plant at a time when they were opening new plant across the globe. They had to learn to make pigment with this technology. If Tioxide's managers wanted to implement their competitive strategies they would first have to create a learning organization.

These strategies demanded broadly skilled employees exercising problem-solving skills and who were capable of controlling their own operations. The chloride system was fast and error-prone. High plant utilization rates required workers skilled in reading signals and interpreting problematic technical systems. But the deployment of such skills depended upon the creation of a social system where the signals and the functioning of the technology could be interpreted and questioned by operators. There was a clear realization by Tioxide's management that the technical failings of the plant were as much a product of the social system as of hardware failures.

This is the model of employee behaviour which has been advanced in part by Miles and Snow (1978) in their account of the Prospector model of organizational adaptation, and more fully developed by Hirschhorn (1986). It stresses the strategic importance of a work-force who are both informed and enabled to act. The type of management that is required is essentially a participative one (Lawler 1986). It is this model of employee behaviour that explains the developments in Tioxide.

The strategy required rapid intervention and repair when plant failed. Management could not design and run an error-free plant. If they were successful in planning and technical application, then plants could run at full capacity. Such conditions exposed the plants' operating limits and thus made them more likely to fail. Capacity was expanded at the margins by de-bottlenecking, an indeterminate process which ensured that the production system could never be standardized. Successful de-bottlenecking created and exposed new bottlenecks. Here was the paradox: success created new sources of failure and error.

Planning against error was not an alternative: error and failure would occur. Attention was best devoted to the problems of quick intervention. Teams of flexible workers and managers organized around plant were the low-cost solution to problems of rapid intervention. The unpredictability of process production made individual job descriptions difficult to write and costly to operate. Managerial attention focused on work groups as the basis for work allocation, a common work-structuring strategy in process industries (Kelly 1982). Institutions and groups, which represented technical specialism and which could oppose such changes, such as trade unions and functionally orientated managers, had no place in these arrangements.

A further paradox of the case is that Tioxide sought to compete in their product markets on superior quality and reformed the skills of their labour force to support this differentiation strategy. But in so doing they succeeded not just in improving quality, but also in reducing variable costs.

The reasons for these strategic changes

It is tempting to analyse the changes outlined in this case as an inevitable response to changing markets, new technologies, rising employee expectations and a changing legal environment. But none of the problems described in the case were new in 1983. Problems of quality, failing technology, loss-making plant, low levels of employee involvement and skill, a poor competitive position and environmental issues were hardly novel problems in Tioxide in 1983. What drove these changes were the values, judgements and perceptions of key decision-makers who were appointed in the early 1980s. It was with their appointment that new patterns of response to old problems can be observed. As many of them remarked, the changes made in Tioxide over this period were made despite the environment, rather than because of it. These managers construed their organizational world in different terms from their predecessors.

Two aspects of the managers' perceptions of organizational life can be identified and described. First, it was a well-informed view: all Tioxide's managers were well schooled in management thinking.

A high level of staff development had always been undertaken in Tioxide. Management thinking was never allowed to ossify. The key decision-makers were mainly insiders and as such they were both the product of, and the heirs to, a legacy of management development. The evidence in this case refutes the idea that the adoption of new strategies requires new people from outside the organization (Miles and Snow 1978; Grinyer and Spender 1979).

Second, the managers saw the organization in highly unitary terms and aspects of their management education had served to buttress this view. The managers were deeply impressed with the work of Peters and Waterman (1982) and Kanter (1984): these authors' works were obligatory reading for line managers. Their books depict organizations built on employee loyalty to the firm, large-group cohesiveness, total commitment to the employing organization, shared goals and values. Many of the firms cited are anti-union. Unions stress a different focus of loyalty, wider commitments, different goals and values, and membership of a much larger group of people.

Tioxide's Experiences and the Debate on Human Resource Management

Tioxide's experiences inform the HRM debate in four ways. First, there is no evidence that Tioxide's managers were attracted to HRM strategies based on the Institute of Manpower Studies (IMS) model (Atkinson 1984, 1985a,b, 1986; Atkinson and Meager 1986). The reasons for this are easy to discern. Tioxide's problems sprang from an error-prone plant and the necessity to develop new products. The forms of flexibility on offer from the IMS model were irrelevant to them. Indeed, some of its forms, such as temporary work and contract work, would have made them more difficult to resolve as they would have been a source of instability in the workforce. Labour cost minimization was hardly relevant in the context of a capital-intensive operation. The case records increases in manning levels, in order to create teams who could run the plant in a manner consistent with their asset-building strategies. Nor did the values of the managers appear to be consistent with the flexibility on offer by 'the flexible firm'.

Second, the case suggests that there are connections between competitive strategy, the values of the key decision-makers and HRM. Tioxide deployed a competitive strategy of differentiation through quality and an HRM strategy of human asset-building. The data do not demonstrate causality, but they do show concomitance. The case stresses the importance of management values and denies the validity of models of HRM which purport to be solely driven by economics, technology or position on the product life-cycle curve. These structural factors are important, but their meaning is a matter of managerial judgement and interpretation.

Third, the case has important lessons for the implementation of HRM. Change began with the reform of managerial work, and not with manual work. The starting-point was the regrouping of managerial jobs with area teams, and the development of quality-focused integration devices in Juran groups and the business improvement council. These innovations preceded the 'teamwork' initiatives which reformed the jobs of operators and maintenance workers. Tioxide's managers began by first putting their own house in order. This is highly significant. The HRM policies in Tioxide were built on concepts such as teamworking, participation, problem-solving, co-operation, skills development and quality management. If these ideas are relevant to any group of employees, then that group is management. In short, HRM is not something that managers 'do' to manual workers: it is highly relevant to managerial work. The case does not contain any direct evidence on this point, but it is probable that the strategy of first implementing these initiatives with managers gave credibility to later policies aimed at manual workers.

Fourth, the evidence in the case relating to the technical and financial performance of the Greatham plant indicates that, from a management perspective, the HRM strategies described do work. The case supports those who argue that improved corporate performance measured by quality or cost will be achieved by a work-force who work 'smarter', rather than harder or cheaper (Lawler 1986; Buchanan and McCalman 1989). The evidence also suggests that successful HRM need not be a matter of exotic leading-edge solutions. In this case attention to basic operator training in plant knowledge and awareness, and taught by a local technical college, paid Tioxide handsome dividends.

The role of trade unions in Tioxide's human resource management strategies

The evidence in the case suggests the managers saw collective bargaining as increasingly irrelevant to their needs. But this trend began in 1980 with the withdrawal of recognition from ASTMS, implying that the collective bargaining strategy has a deeper, and possibly different taproot from the other manpower changes. The decentralization of industrial relations control from head office to the works managers can be seen as a weakening of collective bonds. Significantly, the control of industrial relations passes from the personnel management function to production management. Over the period Tioxide's industrial relations policy shifted from a model resembling what has been termed 'sophisticated moderns', to one of 'sophisticated paternalism' (Purcell and Sisson 1983). In the former model, unions are recognized and encouraged by employers because of the unions' ability to elicit consent, communicate with the workforce, handle change and promote stability (Fox 1974). They are the means to a more effective management of the workforce and management assess their utility accordingly.

Tioxide's management considered that they had built up their own lines of communication with the workforce through quality circles, the focus on teamwork and other initiatives. In the context of the construction of an organizational culture based on shared values and common loyalties, trade unions were regarded as a source of instability. Management came to regard unions as, at best irrelevant, and at worst obstructive to the achievement of business objectives. The opportunity to abandon collective bargaining presented itself over the pensions issue and they took it. In this sense their actions over pensions were highly opportunistic rather than strategic.

The case contains a most impressive demonstration of the power of managers to fashion employee relations to their own will. About 700 people were removed from the scope of collective bargaining in return for a higher pension offered to them in a wider context of wholesale incorporation. They all worked in highly organized plants; there was no industrial action, nor any involvement by full-time trade union officers. The case points to the price that unions can pay for the weakening of bonds between shop stewards' organizations and their trade union governments.

It raises the speculative question of whether or not trade unions will suffer in the 1990s for the rapid shift to company and plant bargaining which occurred in the previous 30 years. From a union perspective much of this was uncontrolled and under-resourced. At Tioxide it appears to have resulted in key elements of the membership becoming both isolated from the trade union movement and its wider goals and concerns; and to have left them susceptible to the attractive offers which can be made to them by a skilled, subtle and well-informed management. As Atkinson (1986:50) has argued: 'The extent to which they enjoy employment security, merit pay and single-status, and are not subject to authoritarian and hierarchical work discipline, is the extent to which they may abandon collectivism for incorporation.'

Summary and Conclusions

The case has examined the experiences of the Cleveland operations of Tioxide's Pigment Division. It shows how a human asset-building manpower strategy was accomplished in a chemical factory marked by a poor economic and technical performance, but whose products held the key to the company's future competitive ability. The case outlines the apparent economic, marketing and technological imperatives for such a manpower strategy, but concludes that the main motivation were the values and education of key decision-makers in the organization.

Tioxide's manpower strategies with respect to management work, harmonization, collective bargaining, manning and participation are outlined. The main features of these policies include: the regrouping of management work; the extension of staff status to manual workers, conditional upon the removal of collective bargaining; increases in employment; and quality circles backed by technical and social skills training. These initiatives were implemented to support the creation of a flexible, skilled, empowered workforce who could operate a difficult technology, and to enact the values of senior managers.

The case concludes that:

- The IMS model of the 'flexible firm' has no descriptive or analytical value in an appraisal of Tioxide's policies.
- There appear to be connections between Tioxide's competitive strategy and their manpower strategy.
- Tioxide's HRM strategies work when assessed against technical and financial data.
- The manpower strategies raise serious issues for trade unions and collective bargaining.
- The most important driving force in Tioxide's strategic manpower change were the values of their managers.

References

Atkinson, J. 1984: 'Manpower strategies and the flexible firm. *Personnel Management*, August, 28–31.

Atkinson, J. 1985a: *Flexibility, Uncertainty and Manpower Management*. Institute of Manpower Studies Report no. 89.

Atkinson, J. 1985b: The flexible firm. *Manpower Policy and Practice*, 1, Summer, 26–9.

Atkinson, J. 1986: Unions and the flexible workforce: ostriches and opportunists? *Manpower Policy and Practice*, 4, Summer, 50–2.

Atkinson, J. and Meager, N. 1986: *Changing Working Patterns: how companies achieve flexibility to match new needs*. London: National Economic Development Office.

Buchanan, D. and McCalman, J. 1989: *High Performance Work Systems: the Digital experience*. London: Routledge.

Fox, A. 1974: *Beyond Contract: work, power and trust relations*. London: Faber.

Grinyer, P.H. and Spender, J.-C. 1979: *Turnaround – Managerial Recipes for Strategic Success: the fall and rise of the Newton Chambers Group*. London: Associated Business Press.

Hirschhorn, L. 1986: *Beyond Mechanisation*. Cambridge, Mass.: The MIT Press.

Juran, J.M. (ed.) 1974: *The Quality Control Handbook*, 3rd edn. New York: McGraw-Hill.

Kanter, R.M. 1984: *The Change Masters: corporate entrepreneurs at work*. London: George Allen & Unwin.

Kelly, J.E. 1982: *Scientific Management, Job Redesign and Work Performance*. London: Academic Press.

Kennedy, G. 1988: Single status as the key to flexibility. *Personnel Management*, February, 51–3.

Lawler, E.E. III 1986: *High-Involvement Management*. San Francisco, Calif.: Jossey-Bass.

Miles, R.E. and Snow, C.C. 1978: *Organisation Strategy, Structure and Process*. New York: McGraw-Hill.

Peters, T.J. and Waterman, R.H. 1982: *In Search of Excellence: lessons from America's best run companies*. New York: Harper & Row.

Porter, M.E. 1980: *Competitive Strategy: techniques for analysis industries and competitors*. New York: Free Press.

Purcell, J. and Sisson, K. 1983: Strategies and practice in the management of industrial relation. In G.S. Bain (ed.) *Industrial Relations in Britain*, Oxford: Basil Blackwell, 95–120.

18

Human Resource Management and Managing Change: the Case of Rosyth Royal Dockyard

JOHN GENNARD AND JAMES KELLY

Introduction

This case study, based on the Rosyth dockyard in Fife, Scotland, examines the human resource management (HRM) framework established to achieve the objectives of 'contractorization'. Until April 1987, the dockyard was managed by the Ministry of Defence. From that date, its management was contracted to a private company, Babcock Thorn Ltd, with the objective of introducing market discipline to its operations. The chapter is in six parts. The first examines the reasons for contractorization while the second describes how contractorization was achieved. The third analyses the problems faced by Babcock Thorn on entering the dockyard, while the fourth examines the HRM framework established to enable survival in a commercial environment. The fifth section assesses the success to date of contractorization in achieving its anticipated results. The final section considers future threats to securing continued commercial success.

Reasons for Contractorization

Rosyth is both a naval base (i.e. home port to sailors and ships) and a dockyard, the latter servicing and refitting naval ships, ranging from Polaris submarines to minehunters. On the introduction of commercial management, its workforce was 5500 of which 1500 were non-manual, making it Scotland's largest industrial plant. There were a number of reasons for the contractorization of the management of the dockyard.

First, the management structure was highly centralized. Decisions were made in London and Bath (the naval headquarters) and the allocation of refit work between royal dockyards determined centrally by the Ministry of Defence.

Second, the government wished to end the 'cosy' relationship between the dockyard and the navy. The resultant 'soft' product market gave rise to efficiency, economy and effectiveness problems in all areas of management. Quality control problems existed in that management operated in a casual manner over the verification of outstanding work and frequently failed to provide specifications for ship refits. This resulted in poor-quality work.

Third, management budget control systems failed to operate. The Royal Navy sanctioned repair work and paid for whatever work was done at whatever the cost turned out to be. Work was measured in man-hours rather than money.

Fourth, local management had little scope or incentive to resolve their own problems. These were not helped in that the senior management was largely transitory. They did not stay long enough to see through the introduction of new management systems. The Civil Service promotion system often meant a move to Rosyth was a staging post *en route* for a more senior post elsewhere. In one four-year period in the 1980s, Rosyth had seven different production directors. Such turnover made managerial control difficult.

A fifth motive leading to contractorization were the rigidities imposed on management's ability to innovate by the Civil Service industrial relations machinery and procedures. The Ministry of Defence negotiated and consulted with its employees and their organizations through Whitley machinery. Comprehensive national-wide collective agreements covering pay, holidays, hours of work, overtime premium, pensions, incentive schemes and disciplinary procedures, were incorporated into two manuals, the administration and interpretation of which preoccupied management and unions. The disputes procedure, involving five local and two national stages, was highly centralized and often caused grievances and disputes to take many months to resolve.

Conflicts between national agreements and local Rosyth circumstances caused problems which depressed productivity. On occasions the Ministry of Defence would embargo recruitment, due to cash limits, while Rosyth was experiencing recruitment and retention problems. Centralized collective bargaining frequently depressed Rosyth wage rates below those for similar jobs in the local labour market. Constrained by national agreement rigidities, Rosyth managers resolved problems by paying unwarranted extra allowances and permitting unnecessary overtime working, particularly at weekends. These institutionalized practices inflated wage costs.

Incentives from London to improve Dockyard performance all failed. The 1981 Dockyard Efficiency Scheme, based on work measurement, was introduced to give some flexibility to local management but achieved little success. The 1985 Interim Management Measures Initiative which was designed to give additional flexibility to local management also proved ineffective.

The Contractorization Process

The operation of the royal dockyards had concerned governments for two decades (Harte 1988). Although there was consensus that change was needed there was no agreement as to how it might be achieved. However, in February 1984, the Secretary of State for Defence commissioned a report on the dockyards (Levene 1984). It reaffirmed the need to provide greater authority to local managers, to separate the dockyards, as suppliers, from the Royal Navy as a customer, to maximize competition, to improve efficiency and to ensure the Royal Navy knew the true costs of refitting work. The government announced in July 1985 that these objectives could best be achieved by putting the dockyards on a commercial footing outside the Civil Service, but retaining dockyard assets in government ownership for national defence purposes. Subsequently, it introduced the Dockyard Services Bill which received royal assent in July 1984.[1] It enabled the Defence Secretary to transfer the dockyard workforce to a company that would manage the dockyard under contract.

Market discipline would be achieved by ending the system of the Ministry of Defence allocating work between the yards. Post-April 1987, 70 per cent of Rosyth's business would be allocated naval refit work ('core business'). A further 20 per cent could come from navy refit work which it would compete for with other royal dockyards and private ship repairers ('competitive naval work'). A further 10 per cent would be gained from customers outside the navy ('competitive commercial work'). The contractors were to adopt risk pricing and accept full responsibility for profits and losses on contracts. The contract for managing the dockyard was to be for seven years after which it would be put to retender.

A Dockyard Planning Team, established in April 1985, issued an invitation to tender to selected companies asking for a business plan for implementation of contractorization into the royal dockyards. Central place was given to personnel and industrial relations as a criteria for the evaluation of bids. Three groups of companies submitted (i.e. Babcock Power and Thorn EMI, Balfour Beatty with the Weir Group, and Press Offshore in a proposed partnership with Rosyth management) bids to manage the Rosyth royal dockyard. In January 1987, Babcock Thorn was awarded the contract.

Problems Faced by Babcock Thorn

If Babcock Thorn were to gain the confidence of the employees it had to show there was 'a stake for them in the new world' superior to that of the 'old world'. A number of problems had to be overcome for this to be achieved. First, 'core' workloads from the navy were expected to fall while the private ship repair industry was depressed. The workforce feared the company's first decision would be to declare redundancies. Secondly, there were pre-vesting day grievances, particularly the dismissal of seven employees, which were festering and if not handled carefully, would alienate the workforce.

A third problem was that the workforce felt the new management would show the same lack of commitment to the yard as had senior Ministry of Defence managers. Both Babcock and Thorn were large multi-plant companies and there were those among the workforce who thought Rosyth would be a staging post to more senior positions. An additional difficulty was that in the 'old world' a lack of communication between senior management and the employees had existed at all levels. A further difficulty was that the trade unions had been hostile to contractorization. They had pursued a Parliamentary campaign against contractorization, used the courts in an attempt to delay it, and refused to co-operate with potential contractorization companies who had thus found access to the yard to obtain commercial information difficult.

All the above problems meant Babcock Thorn took over a demoralized workforce. It also had employee relations institutional problems in that in the past agreements were negotiated between the

Civil Service and national trade union officials both based in London, assisted, as required, by shop stewards. There were two trade union groups in the yard. One represented non-manual employees among which the former Institute of Professional, Civil Servants (IPCS) was the largest, although the Civil and Public Services Association (CPSA) and the Society of Public and Civil Servants (SCPS) had significant presence. The other represented the industrial Civil Servants among which the Transport and General Workers' Union (TGWU) dominated. Other unions included the Amalgamated Engineering Union (AEU), the Electrical, Electronic, Telecommunication and Plumbing Union (EETPU), the Union of Construction, Allied Trades and Technicians (UCATT), Manufacturing, Science and Finance (MSF), and the General, Municipal, Boilermakers and Allied Trades Union (GMBATU). Both union groups had separate structures and had little contact with each other although single-table bargaining arrangements operated.

Union density was high among both manual and white-collar employees and management encouraged union membership. The workforce was highly skilled and the individual unions jealously guarded their autonomy, job demarcations and informal bargaining over extra allowances. The workforce culture was one of paternalism and militancy. The Civil Service encouraged employee commitment to the navy but the manual unions had an affinity with Fife coal-miners. Their antagonism towards management was exacerbated by perceived inappropriate centralized policies. Conflict between the former Rosyth management and their employees was expressed in individual grievances. Although strikes had occurred they were infrequent and involved small numbers or one union.

The Civil Service industrial relations system was inappropriate for the commercial climate in which the dockyard was now to operate. The institutional arrangements, the national-wide collective agreements and pay structures, needed to be radically changed. This would need careful handling since industrial strife would undermine contractorization objectives and further demoralize the workforce.

Another problem facing Babcock Thorn was that the Ministry of Defence personnel management function at Rosyth was under-developed. Human resource management policies stemmed from the ministry's central civilian management divisions. Rosyth's personnel department had an administrative support role and interpreted a myriad of rules contained in the ministry's manuals. The personnel manager provided a general service to dockyard management. Industrial relations were not recognized by formal designation in the management structure. The approach to HRM had been hindered by a turnover of personnel managers who, on average, changed every three years. One result of this was that shop stewards perceived senior managers and the ministry to be uncommitted to Rosyth.

The organization of the personnel function changed in the 1980s. The Dockyard Efficiency Scheme, the Interim Management Measures and the appointment in 1984 of a personnel and industrial relations director gave greater 'weight' to the HRM function. Pre-April 1987, the function was rule-driven, based on national machinery for consultation and negotiation through a network of committees and sub-committees from national to local level.

The New Human Resource Management Framework

Pre-vesting day grievances

To establish good will Babcock Thorn moved quickly to eliminate pre-vesting day grievances. Two highly sympbolic decisions were made which signalled to the workforce and the unions that a new start was being made and that the new management had a long-term commitment to Rosyth. First, an amnesty on pre-vesting day disciplinary records was announced. This included re-employing seven workers, dismissed in late 1985, for incidents that occurred when a government minister visited the yard. During a mass demonstration stones and verbal abuse were directed at the ministerial party. Second, 138 apprentices completing their training, who had been told by the ministry they would not be retained, were employed. Fifty-five casual employees were also offered permanent employment when their expectation had been otherwise.

Communications policies

Under a new communication policy, the day-to-day flow of information throughout the dockyard became the responsibility of supervisors. In addition, each autumn the managing director and the personnel and finance directors give a state of the company address, followed by a question and answer session to the whole workforce in groups of 250. This exercise signalled the Babcock Thorn commitment to the dockyard. As a part of the 'Way Forward Together' compaign, designed to boost the dockyard's commercial performance, the directors in September 1987 addressed the entire workforce. This was the first time in the dockyard's history that employees had been directly spoken to by senior management. These initiatives were important building blocks in gaining employee commitment.

The company does not view its communication channels as an alternative to those with the trade union representatives. A genuine dual channel system operates. Babcock Thorn communicate directly with individual employees when they consider this necessary but accept the dockyard commercial objectives are less likely to be achieved by competing with the unions in communicating with the workforce.

Collective bargaining arrangements

Babcock Thorn considered its collective bargaining arrangements with the industrial unions. A dockyard collective bargaining forum was established giving recognition to the Rosyth royal dockyard trade unions conveners. The forum considered a number of options including the dockyard coming under the jurisdiction of the Engineering Employers Federation (EEF) and Confederation of Shipbuilding and Engineering Union (CSEU) agreement. This had attractions to Babcock Thorn, given their engineering industry background. However, inter-union difficulties made the option problematic. The TGWU opposed such arrangements. Another option was to establish machinery to negotiate a stand-alone agreement for the dockyard industrial unions. The AEU initially preferred the EEF–CSEU option but it was persuaded to join the other unions in support for a stand-alone agreement. This required delicate handling by management as a company agreement could have divided the unions as it did at Devonport. The dockyard industrial joint council was established in August 1987 to negotiate company-wide agreements. Similar arrangements were subsequently made with the white-collar unions. Shop steward facilities and earnings were improved but the number of full-time union representatives, which included health and safety representatives, was reduced from 36 to 8.

Agreements

The construction of a new employee relations system required grievances and disputes procedures that were designed to resolve problems quickly and as close to the action as possible. To avoid delay, the procedure contains time limits by which each stage must be completed. In May 1988, the dockyard industrial joint council was authorized to call special conferences as the final procedural stage for resolving disputes.

In July 1987, the management and unions, following extensive negotiation, signed an enabling agreement which forms the joint working basis for the commercialization of the dockyard. Its central feature is joint commitment to participation in the development and implementation of change programmes designed to ensure the best use of dockyard resources. The cornerstone of the agreement is the joint desire to secure the dockyard's future. Both parties see the agreement as a major step towards achieving an efficient company capable of competing successfully.

It establishes the agreed common objectives of the company and its trade unions as follows (p. 1):

> Management, trade unions and employees are committed to a common objective to create and maintain an efficient and competitive dockyard with well motivated employees. This will provide the basis for attracting the maximum share of available markets for the benefit of all.
>
> It is accepted that the future of Rosyth Dockyard can best be secured by working together in a spirit of co-operation and participation which recognises the impact of all parties. Towards this end, management have since vesting day, in consultation with the trade unions, taken major initiatives to provide a solid basis for our longer-term working relationship.

The agreement spells out the commitments which management and union enter to achieve this objective. The unions accept employees should co-operate with established rules until changed by negotiation, the setting of correct job times to ensure estimating data are soundly based, continuation of relaxations in working practices, the code of behaviour, the dispute procedures, make more effective use of the working day, reduce absenteeism, improve output performance and contribute, through joint working parties, to the development and implementation of changes intended to utilize the dockyard's resources. The enabling agreement's significance was the philosophy behind it, namely the acceptance and introduction of change to the benefit of all. The agreement was further demonstration that

Babcock Thorn would manage on the basis of communications, participation and joint regulation.

In recognition of the jointly agreed objective, management made a pay offer which was accepted in August 1987. Its major features were a 5 per cent increase payable in two stages – 1 July 1987 and 17 October 1987, the removal of certain long-standing wage anomalies, and the introduction of a profit-related pay scheme. The pay structure was rationalized by consolidating the old dockyard efficiency bonuses within new wage rates. This also improved the workers' holiday and sickness payments and confirmed management's preparedness to accept 'a domestic rate' as the starting-point for negotiations. Under the profit-related pay scheme, payments were to be made to all industrial employees at the rate of £50 per person for each £1m. of pre-tax profit above a threshold level of £2m. The scheme is further company demonstration that a stake for its employees exists in 'the new world' in that they would benefit from the company's success as it became more competitive.

The non-manual structure was also reformed. Eight management grades above foreman level were cut to five. A performance appraisal scheme, applicable to 1600 staff, was introduced, while 120 top managers were put on a risk performance scheme whereby a substantial proportion of their salary is linked to performance.

Agreement was also reached with the industrial unions on changes in working hours, including the introduction of a short Friday and Sunday of five hours each. A policy of flexible working was pursued with secondary skills for craftsmen being well established and further flexibility explored. Zonal management and composite work groups have been increased. Numerical flexibility initiatives involve the use of short-term contracts and subcontractors to cater for short-term peaks in workload.

The conduct of employees

In September 1987, a new code of behaviour entitled 'Working Together' was introduced. It set ground rules for high standards of performance, safety and behaviour. The code outlines the standards expected of employees and what they in turn can expect from the company. Basic requirements from employees are good timekeeping and attendance, conscientious attitude to workmanship, adherence to safety rules and customer care. Employee expectations from the company are a safe and healthy working environment, opportunities for development through training, procedures for dealing with individual and collective grievances and a fair hearing should their conduct or performance be questioned.

The code stresses the role of union representatives in ensuring members receive fair treatment and no procedural delays. It recognizes complaints should be listened to and resolved and the very least response should be an explanation. The code's emphasis is not the implementation of disciplinary procedures but getting managers to use that situation as a last resort. It focuses on achieving work performance standards with counselling to deal with poor performance. The enabling agreement and the code of behaviour are the apex of the HRM framework established by Babcock Thorn and the unions to provide a positive working atmosphere, high individual and collective work standards and a high-quality product to the customer. In short, the HRM contribution to the achievement of the objectives of contractorization.

The change programme

Babcock Thorn recognizes that its aim to make the dockyard a rewarding place to work in could only be achieved by co-operation. The company realized improvements were needed in output, quality and cost. To these ends, a formal change programme was developed based on employee involvement in improving performance in their area of the dockyard. Industrial relations issues are kept separate. By implementing agreed changes, the dockyard hoped to improve its prices, delivery times and quality standards.

The change programme centres on problem-solving. It involves management and seven union representatives working full-time at identifying ways to improve performance. Employee suggestions are processed to 'change committees' who report to a steering committee, chaired by a full-time board director supported by a full-time change manager. The programme is a catalyst to stimulate change on a continuous basis. In 1989, for example, the programme covered 28 projects involving the participation of 500 employees.

Management style

The HRM function had considerable influence in Babcock Thorn's bid and has a strong presence on the Rosyth dockyard board. The director of personnel is one of nine board members. The high status for personnel stems from the Ministry of Defence's sensitivity to the unions' opposition to contractorization and to the background of the Babcock Thorn managers. The management style of co-operation, participation and communication provides the linking mechanism for the different HRM policies, with the personnel department providing consistency across the dockyard. The personnel department is centralized with industrial relations officers monitoring and offering advice to line managers who have responsibility for the personnel aspects of their jobs.

Babcock Thorn does not see a conflict between individual and collective aspects of HRM. It considers that changes are best achieved by working with, and not against, the unions. It promotes togetherness by involvement between management and unions. Togetherness focuses on common long-term strategic interests, eliminating frictions and consulting and negotiating over differences. The unions support this strategy. To quote the chairman of the union side of the dockyard industrial joint committee: 'when I give interviews . . . sometimes I feel embarrassed as I'm unable to say I do not like this or that . . . so I think the members must be saying, he has been bought out'.

The 'togetherness' theme promotes a caring management espousing fair policies and rules within a market constraint. Market pressures and the Babcock Thorn corporate strategy have replaced the Ministry of Defence rule-driven HRM system with one responsive to local circumstances.

Assessment of Progress to Date

The contribution of the HRM framework established at Rosyth following contractorization to the achievement of corporate objectives can only be evaluated after the initial seven-year contract has elapsed. Our efforts to measure its effectiveness over the first three years of its operation were marred by the absence of time-series data. Three major difficulties were encountered in seeking quantitative data. First, prior to contractorization the personnel department gathered information using different statistical methods resulting in few bench-marks against which post-contractorization performance might be measured. In addition, the pre-1987 personnel records were removed by the ministry and were unavailable to Babcock Thorn. Second, Babcock Thorn managers took some 18 months to get their own personnel management records into place. Third, in the light of the unfreezing of the cold war in Europe, the value of these measures has been influenced by defence expenditure cuts which have created uncertainty over the future size of the naval fleet.

Our assessment of the effectiveness of the HRM framework established post-Arpil 1987 in achieving overall corporate objectives, depends on management judgements and perceptions supplemented by crude statistical measures. The Rosyth contract commits Babcock Thorn to secure during its first four years a 5 per cent annual improvement rate in labour costs and 2.5 per cent in the subsequent three years, for all ships refitted of the same class or type. Despite the absence of productivity records Rosyth senior management claim performance has improved by 15 per cent over the period 1987–9 inclusive. Nevertheless, management considers this performance still lags behind that achieved in private ship repair yards over the same period.

Utilization of working day

Pre-April 1987, employee utilization was low. Overtime was worked irrespective of workload and in the period April 1985 to March 1986 averaged 8.2 per cent of normal hours. Post-vesting day management introduced control measures requiring supervisors to plan more effectively within normal hours. A five-hour Friday and Sunday sought to improve attendance and productivity. Management is satisfied with work performance on Sundays but not on Fridays. Since May 1988 overtime has averaged 3.87 hours per employee despite the head count having fallen from 5816 to 5067 although total workload has remained stable.

Since June 1989, Babcock Thorn have provided improved attendance information which measures hours lost as a percentage of hours scheduled to be worked. The results are:

June–November 1989	8.08
December–May 1990	7.68
June–October 1990	8.05

This absence rate is reasonable by heavy industry standards but remains stubbornly stable despite efforts to improve it. Pre-April 1987, hours lost due to absence per employee were 17.7 days.

Non-naval commercial work has increased as a proportion of total workload from 1 per cent in 1987–8 to 5.5 per cent in 1989–90.

This latter figure represents 250,000 man-hours and achieves the figure contained in the business plan submitted by the company to the ministry. Commercial and non-core work over the period has increased from 0 to £14m. in a total 1989–90 turnover of £150m., helping Babcock Thorn achieve a pre-tax profit rate of 5 per cent of turnover.

Continuous change programme – flexible working practices

In the first year of operation of the change programme, union conveners refused to participate in the steering committee, arguing that the introduction of change was management's job. In its second year, however, the conveners participated but at the cost of management accepting the full-time involvement of seven union change representatives.

Given the multi-union organization, the change programme threatened established working practices and inter-union relationships. Employee attitudes varied from enthusiasm among active participants to cynicism among those holding an adverse view of industrial relations. The change programme has had some success but the danger remains that it could consist of bureaucratic committees divorced from mainstream management decisions.

The collective agreements on flexible working challenged sectional work rules. Simplification of the pay structure reduced the number of non-craft grades from 17 to 3, allowing extensive flexibility within and between grades. However, although the craftsmen have accepted some flexibility (e.g. welding), the advent of the multi-skilled craftsman is some way off. At times, craftsmen have resisted performing non-craft work when their own trade is slack. On the other hand, on occasions non-craft grades have resisted flexibility if the use of craft labour on non-craft work threatened their overtime levels. The dockyard's entry to lower-value commercial work (e.g. steel fabrication) requires a much faster work rate if it is to be economic. Dockyard craftsmen are used to performing to the highest standards and have found difficulty in adjusting to acceptable lower-quality standards. As a consequence, they have produced work quality beyond specification and at too high a cost. Notwithstanding these difficulties, the unions are collaborating with composite work groups and zonal management in an effort to secure new orders by being competitive on prices.

Performance-related pay

Babcock Thorn's pay policy is designed to change middle management culture and performance rather than to introduce direct incentive schemes for manual workers. Improved planning and new systems of organization aimed at work reaching manual workers on time were introduced. A performance appraisal scheme, based on job targets, replaced the more subjective Civil Service system.

At the end of the first year of operation, the personnel department reviewed the effectiveness of the appraisal scheme and decided it required tightening up. Too many middle managers were scoring subordinates in the 'satisfactory' category, indicating a reluctance to counsel employees in accordance with the code of behaviour and suggesting reluctance by middle managers to embrace a cost-conscious commercial strategy. To overcome this problem, Babcock Thorn recruited a number of new middle managers from commercial shipbuilding and engineering companies to act as role models to the ex-Civil Servants.

Industrial conflict

Although longitudinal data were unavailable, management reports show that in the two-year period prior to April 1987 strike action was prevalent during the unions' campaign of opposition to contractorization. However, since April 1987, industrial action has virtually disappeared. Since April 1989, company records show a low number of average direct hours lost per month. Over the period April 1989 to March 1990, the average number of hours lost per month was 23.5, while for the period April to October 1990 the figure was 6.9.

Registered employee grievance figures have been low given the size of the Rosyth workforce. Over the period November 1988 to March 1989 the average number of monthly registered grievances was 26, over the period 1989 to March 1990 it was 20 and for the period April to October 1990 inclusive, again 20. During the first year of contractorization the number of accidents in the yard fell by 30 per cent due to major housekeeping operations and safety policies.

Summary and Conclusions

In its first three years of operation contractorization at the Rosyth dockyard has been at best a success and at worst a qualified one.

The explanation of this lies with the introduction of a competent professional management experienced in managing a dynamic competitive environment in which managers can formulate and implement long-term business plans. The values that the Babcock senior managers introduced into the dockyard explain their adopted policy of controlled organizational change. These senior managers, from traditional Scottish engineering backgrounds, were also competent in handling strong trade unions. Previously, Rosyth's managing director, Mr Alan Smith, had been President of the Scottish Engineering Employers' Association and under his leadership, Babcock Power had achieved major changes at its Renfrew plant without undue industrial conflict.

The HRM framework established post-contractorization has also made a contribution to Rosyth's commercial success. The vision of Rosyth's director of personnel, the late Mr Sandy Soutar, embraced the concept of management and employees working together in partnership to improve business performance and employment conditions within a framework of fair and clear rules. His involvement in the writing of policy proposals for the 'contract bid document' established a high status for personnel management in the new company. At company board meetings the personnel director argued from a position of strength based on values and understanding incorporated in the business and HRM plans submitted to the Ministry of Defence at the time of the bid.

At Rosyth, Babcock Thorn adopted a long-term high-trust strategy seeking functional flexibility in the internal labour market. It consciously rejected the adoption of a short-term strategy relying on numerical flexibility to fine-tune labour costs to workloads. The management sought the commitment of existing strong and stable unions to improve commercial performance. The unions, despite their campaign of opposition to contractorization, responded positively. They had feared Babcock Thorn would transfer work from Rosyth to its other plants and create redundancies, but this was defused by the company's determined efforts to secure work from the commercial sector. A positive union response to Babcock Thorn's policies was also helped by the company's decision to improve pay and conditions. More importantly, the company's approach to HRM offered employees and their trade unions a degree of independence and responsibility to volunteer or withhold their co-operation within an acceptance of market logic. In this way, Babcock Thorn's HRM policies have worked hand in hand with changed collective bargaining arrangements as major instruments of institutional and attitudinal change. The HRM policies have been far from manipulative, as is often argued in the case of non-union companies or those companies which wish to reduce significantly the influence of trade unions in their plants.

However, there is an important threat to the continuation of the success of contractorization which will severely test the HRM framework established in the first three years of operation. This threat is the dramatic change in the company's product market following the unfreezing of the cold war which has led the Ministry of Defence to reduce its demand for naval refitting work. Additionally, the ministry has announced the possible closure of the Rosyth naval base with incalculable results for the dockyard. The ministry's decision to abandon the existing refit work at Rosyth on HMS *Churchill* led to employee relations problems. This increased competition in the company's product market is a major unanticipated change. In the light of this, Babcock Thorn and the unions are likely to have to renegotiate the enabling agreement in terms of the joint commitments they entered into to achieve certain commercial objectives. Contractorization is thus entering a second and different phase based on a more difficult product market situation than previously. At this stage, it is impossible to say whether the imaginative HRM framework established in the first three years of contractorization will stand the test of the employee relations difficulties that will arise from an even more competitive product market. However, in the real world product markets are constantly changing and adjusting and competent personnel managers will no doubt be successful in adjusting the existing HRM framework accordingly.

Note

1 The trade unions at the dockyards opposed the introduction of commercial management. They feared job insecurity arising from the abolition of Civil Service status. They did not defend the status quo and accepted the need for greater managerial autonomy to run the dockyards more effectively. However, they believed these changes could be achieved by a trading fund. The unions ran a campaign against the Dockyard Services Bill both within and outside Parliament. They sought to delay the presence of the Bill pending the outcome of the next General Election. Industrial action played a subsidiary role in the campaign and was aimed

at encouraging caution within the Ministry of Defence, deterring potential bidders and as a signal that if private contractors did take over the yard they should understand they would have to deal with strong and stable trade unions. In the final stages of the Bill in the House of Lords, Lord Denning secured the inclusion of a clause to allow the trade unions, if they considered they had not been properly informed or consulted on the proposed change of management, to seek a declaration in the courts. On 30 March 1987, the unions went to court seeking this remedy but lost the case.

References

Harte, M. 1988: The introduction of commercial management into the royal dockyards: Devonport and Rosyth. *Public Administration*, 66, 319–28.
Levene P. 1984: Future of the royal dockyards – preliminary report (mimeo).

19

Culture Change through Training: the Case of Sainsbury

ALLAN WILLIAMS AND PAUL DOBSON

Introduction

Changing the culture of an organization is a fashionable topic in management circles. However, the difficulties involved in changing culture are frequently played down. This makes it a suitable and rewarding topic for a case study. The case to be described below was originally one of 15 cases we studied as part of a research project aimed at identifying the methods organizations used to bring about culture change (Williams et al. 1989). One of the findings to emerge from our study was the ubiquitous role of training in any attempt to change organizational culture. In this chapter we shall summarize some of the findings of the study, and present a case study of an organization which was trying to change aspects of its culture primarily through training. When the case study is used as part of a classroom exercise, students may want to make their own analysis before reading the conclusions.

Concept of Culture

The concept of culture has been enriched by the work of social anthropologists, sociologists, organizational psychologists, management consultants and others. Unfortunately, the variety of meanings given to the term, and the variety of situations in which the term is used, complicate the task of the researcher trying to study culture change. A working definition of organizational culture which we used in our study, and which conforms to some of the more authoritative definitions in the literature, is the following: 'Culture is the commonly held and relatively stable beliefs, attitudes and values that exist within the organization' (Williams et al. 1989:11).

Things to note about this definition include: firstly, to change culture you need to change the beliefs, attitudes and values underlying behaviour; secondly, since it is concerned with commonly held beliefs, the target for change needs to be the organization as a whole or a fairly autonomous part of it; thirdly, the beliefs, attitudes and values associated with a culture will have achieved stability over a long period of time, and therefore are likely to be deep-rooted. If one is prepared to accept these assumptions it follows that planned culture change is an uphill battle requiring leadership, time and plenty of resources!

Methods of Culture Change

Given the potential problems of trying to bring about planned culture change, what methods do we actually find organizations using? Our research indicates the main categories as listed in the headings below.

Changing people

This may be subdivided into two categories: the individual differences approach and the learning approach. The former approach recognizes that some individuals will already hold beliefs close to the desirable ones, while others will not. This approach is reflected in recruitment, selection, transferring employees and releasing them.

The learning approach, on the other hand, recognizes that an individual's beliefs are malleable, and can be changed under appropriate conditions. This approach is reflected in the purposeful use of role models (e.g. using senior managers with participative styles as trainers), of group methods (e.g. quality circles), of formal training programmes and of formal communication channels.

Changing structure

We identified four types of structural changes:

1 restructuring involving changes to the composition of the organization's stakeholders;

2 decentralization;
3 job redesign to increase role flexibility;
4 introducing new structures to cater for new needs (e.g. a new quality unit).

Changing management systems

The two areas where change was most frequent were budgeting and control systems, and HRM systems. Our case studies abounded with examples of the latter. This is not surprising given that HRM systems impinge directly on the beliefs, attitudes and values of employees.

Changing other variables

Although not illustrated by our case studies, it is clear from our knowledge of the literature that changing certain other variables will also have an impact on an organization's culture. For example, a change in an organization's dominant technology from a mechanized office paper system to a computerized information technology system, or a change in the geographical location of a plant from an urban to a rural community, will almost certainly have implications for the type of person employed and therefore for the beliefs, attitudes and values of new recruits.

Dynamics of Culture Change

Knowledge of the methods used by organizations to bring about culture change is only part of the equation for successfully changing beliefs, attitudes and values. To overcome the self-reinforcing properties of culture, any planned change must generate sufficient forces for change, and simultaneously reduce the forces against change. Kurt Lewin's (1951) force-field model is a particularly useful aid in helping one to identify the positive and negative variables which are most likely to result in a pattern of forces conducive to change. On the basis of our research there appear to be three important sources from which forces for culture change are generated:

1 *Some precipitating event or crisis* (e.g. dramatic fall in market share). This condition seems necessary for an organization to question some of the

fundamental beliefs which have influenced the way it has done things in the past.

2 *Organization strategy*. A culture change programme needs to be strategy-led if it is to be integrated with other changes, allocated the required resources to achieve success, and gain the long-term support of the 'dominant coalition' or top management.

3 *Powerful change agents*. To expect external consultants to take on the role of primary change agents is a naïve assumption to make within the context of culture change. Their power base is far too brittle and temporary. What is required is the combined resources of a range of change agents such as the chief executive officer, the personnel director, senior line managers, as well as the specialist expertise of internal or external consultants. Above all it is the chief executive officer who has to take on the role of change agent, because it is he or she who will normally have the most power to influence culture change.

As already mentioned, a successful change programme will attend to forces pushing against change as well as those pushing for change. Useful guidelines in dealing with the former include:

1 The need for change should be recognized by those who will be affected by the change. In our study management attempted to achieve this condition through training, formal communications, and involvement or participation in the decision-making processes associated with the planning and implementation of change.

2 Steps should be undertaken to reduce the uncertainties accompanying change, particularly those threatening the security of jobs and existing rewards. A variety of methods can be employed here, including: training, keeping people informed through effective communications, the direct participation of individual employees in the decision-making processes accompanying change, and where appropriate the early consultation and negotiation with employee representative bodies.

3 Care needs to be taken to ensure that the right behaviours (i.e. those compatible with the desired beliefs, attitudes and values) are being reinforced on the job. It is a well-established fact that the transfer of learning from a formal training course to the job situation is often adversely affected by the lack of appropriate on-the-job reinforcements. Similarly, resistance to change is sometimes the result of traditional, but no longer appropriate, reinforcements being allowed to persist, thus inadvertently continuing to reinforce previously accepted behaviours. The mechanisms through which reinforcements operate include those variables already referred to, that is, role models, organizational structure and management systems.

The Role of Training in Culture Change

From this brief summary of methods used by organizations to bring about culture change, and our knowledge of the conditions conducive to successful change, it will be noticed that training can play an important role. However, training must not be viewed in isolation. It should be clear from the ideas presented above that (1) the processes whereby training is initiated, planned and implemented, and (2) the conditions which are present in the post-training phase, will determine the extent to which training is effective in contributing towards a planned culture change programme. In order to explore the practical implications of these statements, the following case study is presented. It is in two sections: Sainsbury A was researched during May and June 1988 as part of a series of case studies on culture change (Williams et al. 1989), and is presented as written at that time; Sainsbury B reports the results of a follow-up some two and a half years later, in December 1990.

Case Study: Sainsbury A

Background

J. Sainsbury was established as a family business in Drury Lane in 1869 and to this day it retains strong family ties. It is a long-established company with a traditional non-participative management style with clear reporting lines and accountability. Productivity targets are used as a means of management control. While there are exceptions, a typical Sainsbury manager would be described as being primarily task oriented.

The company is one of the largest food retailers in the UK. In 1987, it had 270 supermarkets, 6.5 million customers per week, annual sales exceeding £4000m. and pre-tax profits of £268m. Sainsbury's has over 69,000 staff of whom 40,000 work part-time. The full-time staff include 6500 managers. The majority of the performance indicators suggest that Sainsbury's is a successful company. Profitability, sales, productivity and market share have all increased significantly over the last five years. Over 19,000 jobs have been created over the same period and, in an industry known for its high labour turnover, 12 per cent of the staff have been with the company for over ten years. The organization continues to expand and develop. It has opened 15–17 new stores a year for the past seven years and has branched out into the DIY market through its Homebase subsidiary. There are four associated companies; Savacentre, Brecklands Farms, Haverhill Meat Products and, in the USA, Shaws supermarkets.

The retail operation of Sainsbury's is organized in five geographic areas, each with a training department providing specialist training services to the stores. At the London head office there are training managers who develop and administer the retail training programmes for staff and managers and more general training programmes for managers at head office and in the distribution depots. Each store has a personnel manager who co-ordinates training and a number of store instructors carry out the day-to-day training of sales staff.

Changing culture

The early and middle 1980s saw an increase in customer expectations and competitors began to respond by introducing customer service programmes for staff. Most of these were rather gimmicky short-term 'Smile' and 'Have a nice day' type programmes where there was no attempt to try to change the attitudes of sales staff.

The board recognized that there was a need for Sainsbury's to have a customer service training programme. Six months were spent working by personnel on a proposal for the board. It was realized that ideally such a programme needed the support of management as role models for the change in behaviour. But it was also recognized that a top-down approach would not be acceptable given the existing culture. Consequently, a bottom-up approach was planned. The training department's initiative 'Building better business' (BBB) was thus focused on customer service training for branch sales staff. The board recognized that they were geared to business needs and supported the initiative with the proviso that the training of the checkout and counter staff in such things as bag packing preceded the softer attitudinal training elements. The training was sponsored by the director of branch operations.

Customer Service Training Ltd were brought in as consultant to develop a training package for use in the induction of new staff and the development of existing staff. It was recognized from the outset that the key to changing the behaviour of sales staff was to change their attitudes towards the customer, the job and colleagues. The training had to be aimed at the discretionary part of the job and not the mandatory parts given in job descriptions. That is, the training was required to concentrate on how staff did their job and not on what they did.

Two videos, one called *Out in front* which concentrates on the role of the front-end checkout team, and the other *Counting on service* aimed at counter sales staff, formed the basis of the BBB programme which was piloted in five stores in May 1986. The initial programme was primarily concerned with developing behavioural skills and product knowledge and was less explicitly attitudinal than later developments. After some fine-tuning the programme began to run through all 270 branches, 25–30 branches at a time. This approach kept the resources required to manageable proportions and also served to reinforce and keep the programme alive.

Directors and senior managers were given a one-day course describing BBB. Area trainers were trained in the philosophy and then they ran a two-day course for the branch management team and a three-day course for the store instructors. The latter trained the sales staff who received six hours' off-the-job in-store training.

Each branch was given 12 weeks to get all the sales staff through the programme. This was not difficult in small stores, but in those of 300 staff or more, considerable resources were required. A large number of hours were invested in training and an allowance of 4.5 hours was given to branch managers on their productivity targets. This has created a precedent for more recent initiatives and follow-ups.

In May 1987 a further three videos and a new introductory video began touring the branches. *Look at it this way* puts across the message you only get out what you put in, and encourages positive attitudes towards self, job and colleagues. *You've got what it takes* introduces FRESH – the five essential qualities to make people choose Sainsbury's rather than another store – Friendliness, Responsiveness, Enthusiasm, Sincerity and Helpfulness. *In just three seconds* shows how important are first impressions. It addresses the care that should be taken with presentation – self and store; it looks at body language and explains how to deal with complaints using the three A's – Apologize, Analyse, Act.

The training programme that was developed explicitly explored the nature and significance of attitudes as determinants of behaviour. For example, participants were asked to consider how their attitudes colour their views, how attitudes affect work, and the importance of positive attitudes in determining success. The training methods used are a combination of case study, video presentation, role playing, role modelling and group discussion. The following description of the training programme was given in the Sainsbury's in-house journal in July 1987 (p. 4):

> Building Better Business is not merely a course or a video or an exercise, it's an attitude.
>
> Training for the scheme revolves around six videos which are designed to act as food for thought. Breaks are incorporated into the videos to allow discussion of points raised and participants are encouraged to examine their attitudes to customers and colleagues.
>
> The videos often show the right and the wrong ways of doing things. Participants are asked to use their experience to decide which is the best approach. We all know the difference between getting good and bad responses from people and these videos show how to improve the way you communicate with others.
>
> In addition to taking part in group discussion, each participant completes a booklet which asks questions about his or her working methods; how they deal with customers in a variety of situations, and general attitudes, as well as how things are done in his/her particular department.
>
> The booklet allows staff to stand back and assess themselves and their department in the light of what they are learning.

The BBB initiative has been supported by internal marketing – the BBB logo is given constant exposure in the in-house journal, and in presentations – and by gaining the visible support of the director of branch operations. Monthly reports are made to the board on progress, and BBB is kept on the management agenda. In addition, a number of specific designed activities have been undertaken.

A poster competition was devised where employees were asked to design posters for the BBB programme. The response was so good that a winner and runner-up were selected each month for 12 months. All entrants received a BBB pen or mug and the winners received a £25 cash prize and had their poster professionally printed and circulated on the notice-boards of all branches. The winners also received a 'Certificate of Commendation', signed by the director of branch operations and the senior manager, management training and development.

A Christmas BBB competition was run where entrants had to complete a quiz (designed to test and improve product knowledge), undertake a word search game and a crossword, both closely linked with BBB concepts, and make as many words as possible from the phrase 'BBB training our most valuable asset – you'. Every entrant received a BBB Christmas mug or pen; the first 50 entrants received BBB slimline diaries; and the winner £50 cash, a certificate and an autographed copy of the Sainsbury's *Book of Wines*.

The purpose of these two competitions was to reaffirm and re-inforce the customer service and BBB message. The BBB pro-gramme has now become a vehicle for more than customer service training. Product knowledge, customers with special needs, and telephone training videos have been developed and run under the BBB banner. As it is stated in the Sainsbury's in-house journal (July 1987:5): 'There is no real end to building better business. It is an ongoing training programme which is to be developed for the future and will grow to encompass different areas.'

The product of change

Customer service training was introduced because there was a clear business requirement for it. One of the pilot store managers summed up the effects of the programme in the following way (July 1987:5):

> It was hard work being a forerunner of the scheme. Many people on the administration side were hearing about BBB for the first time. There were lots of feedback sessions to attend. My staff now have more confidence to deal with customer queries and to cope with the jobs they are given. It has created a better working atmosphere. We had a good set up here from the start so it was a case of building on what we already had. Now we have the task of keeping the momentum going and we are doing well on that score.

The programme was targeted at the sales staff, and while the managers are involved in the programme no direct attempt has been made to change their attitudes. Branch managers are required to support the training initiative. They write to all the staff outlining its purpose and attend introductory or summary group discussions. The requirement for managers to adopt a more participative style and discuss such things as being helpful and developing a positive attitude towards colleagues, has had some interesting effects. Branch managers have expressed difficulty in dealing with staff in this way and have requested training in briefing and presentation skills. There is also a rather obvious point of conflict between sales staff who are being asked to become helpful and positive towards customers and colleagues, and the traditional style of the branch manager. The impact of the programme has been variable. In some cases the BBB programme is having a knock-on effect up the the line, while in others the manager's style is inhibiting the impact of the programme. This situation is exacerbated because more senior managers who have not been closely involved in the programme are presenting a traditional role model to their subordinates. While it was initially recognized that a top-down approach was desirable, it was also recognized that in a successful company there is little rationale for changing management style.

Sainsbury B

Background

Sainsbury's success has continued. Group sales have increased to £7.3bn (compared to £4bn in 1987), with sales per square foot increased to £17.26 per week (£15.43); profit before tax has increased to £450m. (£268m.); market share has increased to 11.6 per cent (10.2 per cent); and earning per share has increased to 19.64p (11.34p). Since 1987 the number of employees employed by the group has increased to over 100,000 (62,000 part-time), from 69,000 (40,000 part-time).

The joint presidents of the company remain Lord Sainsbury of Drury Lane and Sir Robert Sainsbury, and the chairman remains Lord Sainsbury of Preston Candover. Of the 19 board directors, 17 were either board or departmental directors in 1987. The two newcomers are both from outside the company, one of them is the personnel directory who was appointed in 1989.

Since 1987 the personnel function has been restructured with the intention of clarifying its roles and responsibilities.

'Building better business' 1990

The original BBB fanfare and supporting competitions and initiatives created a lot of interest among shop staff, and BBB is still a topic of discussion in the stores. However, no new initiatives have been used to support it since its introduction; and more recent training programmes, such as a major programme of retail hygiene (in response to new European legislation on retail hygiene), have not been run under the BBB label. Surveys undertaken by outside consultants indicate that customer service has improved over the years, but it is not possible to determine BBB's contribution to this result.

In general, branch management have been fully committed to the customer service aspect of the BBB programme, and have given it full support. However, some groups felt that it overemphasized the softer attitudinal aspects of customer service training, and encouraged some staff to consider its message as being optional rather than a job requirement. These subjective impressions have led the retail division, with its new director of branch operations, to initiate and develop 'phase 2' version of BBB.

Following concerns expressed by senior management a directive was issued to branch personnel managers in January 1990, setting out the main aspects of the revised approach. Recruiters are now required to assess the customer skills of job applicants during interview. During induction, the employee is allocated a 'guardian' and receives a 30-minute training session on customer skills ('customer care briefing') by the branch manager. This includes a new video and support material entitled 'Building better customer care', or BBCC as the new initiative is known. The video was introduced in 1989, and adopts a more autocratic and hard-hitting style than the previous BBB videos; employees are told what they must and must not do in order to improve customer service. The video is followed by a statement of the importance of the customer to the success of the business, and then by a clear statement of job requirements by the manager:

> Although I am sure that most of you do treat customers correctly, to ensure that EVERY employee operates correctly, I am INSTRUCTING you that from today, everyone must operate to the following minimum requirements: . . . When asking for payment etc., you MUST say 'PLEASE'. . . . If a customer asks where an item is displayed, you MUST offer to take them to the display (Emphasis given in the original material.)

The revised approach is also more formalized than previously: ratings of customer service skill are part of new employee appraisal during the six or ten-week probationary period and adequate performance is a prerequisite to confirmation of employment; managers are required to confirm that the employee has undergone customer skills training; the employee is required to confirm that he or she has received the training; and a formal plan and record of the training are held on personnel files. The original BBB videos are now included as part of post-induction training. Existing staff and management are also required to attend the 30-minute customer care briefing session, and to notify the district manager that they have done so. Managers and supervisors are requested to monitor customer service in stores, and to act as role models in order to 'set a first class example'.

Line management initiated and developed the new programme without involving divisional personnel. The retail division added the programme to the front of the existing BBB training materials. Initially this created some difficulties: there were procedural inaccuracies in the video that tended to undermine its credibility, and its approach was inconsistent with some of the existing videos. Divisional personnel have now been involved, and three of the original BBB videos (*Look at it this way*, *You've got what it takes*, and *In just three seconds*) have been withdrawn, and training revamped to present a more coherent package.

The BBB programme is still running, but in a drastically altered form. The original idea for BBB to act as a vehicle for introducing widespread bottom-up change has disappeared. Its role has been reduced to improving customer service. The training has been shortened, become less participative, and more focused on behaviour rather than attitudes. Greater emphasis has been placed on the monitoring and formal control of training and behaviour. It is too early to tell whether the new approach is going to be more successful than the original at changing customer service behaviour. Certainly it would appear to be more compatible with existing management culture.

Mention has already been made of a major training programme which has been introduced on retail hygiene as a result of European legislation. Two other training initiatives are worth noting: 'Resourcing the business' which is designed to encourage line managers to own their human resource (HR) problems; and there are plans to introduce a programme aimed at developing a more consultative style of management. Compatible with the latter intention was a recently completed job evaluation exercise which had a significant consultative element, and the current consultative approach which the retail division is adopting in arriving at a new uniform.

Conclusions

In this chapter we have summarized the findings derived from a series of case studies concerning the methods of culture change. We have also outlined some of our knowledge relating to successful organizational change. Finally, we have described a case study of culture change which was spearheaded by training. This case study was undertaken at two points in time, and provides us with a 'live' example in which to apply the findings covered earlier in the chapter. A number of issues emerge for discussion, and we should like to conclude by commenting on three of these: culture and customer service; behaviour and attitudes; and culture change.

Culture and customer service

Skilled individuals and efficient management systems provide some of the key elements needed for creating and maintaining competitively superior customer service. If durability for this quality is sought, then the attitudes and values which underlie the behaviour must become an inherent feature of the organization's culture. Only when this process of internalization has taken place will staff feel that it is 'right' and 'normal' to behave towards customers in certain desirable ways.

Improving customer service has become one of the main strategies for enhancing the competitiveness of service organizations in the recent past. The almost evangelical work of individuals such Crosby (1979) under the label of total quality management, have given a significant fillip to this development. It is therefore not surprising to find that many large organizations have been trying to reorientate their culture in order to achieve greater quality in customer care. In common with others Sainsbury's is conforming to this trend, and is using training as the pivotal tool for changing culture.

Behaviour and attitudes

Is improved customer care more likely to be brought about by a training programme which emphasizes changing behaviour or changing attitudes? Phase 1 of the BBB programme emphasized the latter, phase 2 the former. Theoretically, attitudes, values and beliefs underlie much of our behaviour. The main reason why research findings often contradict this relationship, is because behaviour is powerfully influenced by situational factors. Thus, although you may have negative attitudes towards rude customers, you may continue to deal with them in a polite manner in the presence of your supervisor for fear of being reprimanded! The answer therefore is that both behavioural skills and attitudes need to be targeted during training. They will each reinforce one another.

A further reason for attending to attitudes as in the original BBB programme is to do with our understanding of the nature of culture. The culture of Sainsbury is the commonly shared attitudes, values and beliefs of those employed within the company. A subset of those attitudes/values/beliefs relate to customer service. To change this subset means influencing the attitudes of all employees, not just those whose jobs brings them in direct contact with the public. Managers may rarely come into contact with customers, but their attitudes towards customers will be communicated to subordinates who do, either through modelling or through their selective reinforcement of behaviour. Undoubtedly Sainsbury managers will have a positive attitude towards customers, but what they may not be predisposed to do is to encourage staff to give priority to helping a customer find a product as opposed to keeping the shelves fully stocked. It is in these choice situations where priorities have to be determined that attitudes and values often come to the fore, and where cultural cues are exposed. Intentionally or unintentionally managers will have a dominant influence on this aspect of the company's culture. It is therefore important that they should be subjected to the attitudinal training experienced by the sales staff.

Culture change

On the basis of objective information it is not possible to give a categorical answer to the question: has the culture of the retail division changed as a result of the BBB programme? On the basis of our knowledge of the nature of culture and the conditions under which cultural change takes place, it is unlikely that Sainsbury's retail culture has changed. This is not to say that there have not been improvements to the quality of their customer service; only that these observable behaviours may not as yet be reflected in the stable attitudes, values and beliefs which underpin these behaviours and determine their durability.

In analysing the case study in the light of the earlier generalizations made with regard to cultural change, the reader will note that those factors which could be identified as facilitating change include:

- BBB phase 1 targeted attitudes as well as skills;
- it was system-wide, in that managers were introduced to the programme as well as sales staff throughout the country;
- a systematic approach was used in implementing the programme in that senior managers were given a one-day course, trainers were trained and then ran a two-day course for branch management and a three-day course for store instructors, and the latter then trained the sales staff;
- outside experts were used to help in the initial development and implementation of the package, but ownership and responsibility for the main implementation rested with the company;
- the messages communicated in training were reinforced through other media such as house magazines and competitions.

Those factors which may have been inhibiting change include:

- when the programme was initiated the company was a successful business and has remained so, and therefore there was no immediate and strong pressure to change culture;
- the initial phase 1 programme seemed to be more the 'baby' of personnel and training than of the board and line management;
- the traditional 'tell and sell' management style sat uneasily against the softer and more participative style underlying the BBB phase 1 programme.

It is interesting that in the follow-up visit to the company, two noticeable changes have taken place: the programme has been modified so that it sits more comfortably within the traditional management style embedded in the Sainsbury culture; and the current phase 2 version of the programme is the result of an initiative of line management. It is for the reader to surmise whether the company is still on course for a genuine change in its culture.

References

Crosby, P. 1979: *Quality is Free*. New York: McGraw-Hill.
Lewin, K. 1951: *Field Theory in Social Science*. New York: Harper & Row.
Williams, Allan, Dobson, Paul, and Walters, Mike 1989: *Changing Culture: new organisational approaches*. London: IPM.

20

Competitive Strategy, Flexibility and Selection: the Case of Caledonian Paper

P. B. BEAUMONT AND L. C. HUNTER

Introduction

One of the standard jokes about human resource (HRM) researchers in the UK is that they are individuals in search of a subject area. In fact, HRM researchers themselves will typically concede that a relatively 'sophisticated' approach to a 'comprehensive' range of HRM issues will be disproportionately associated with particular types or subcategories of organizations. And when asked to indicate some of the leading, identifiable characteristics of such organizations, the answers will almost invariably make reference of foreign ownership and/or greenfield site status.

In view of the above, any organization with both the characteristics of foreign ownership and greenfield site status should be one in which there was considerable evidence of a relatively well-developed approach towards HRM issues. It is just such an organization which is discussed in this case-study chapter, with the discussion emphasizing the strong linkages between (1) the nature of the organization's competitive strategy, (2) the need for workforce flexibility to help achieve this strategy and (3) the use of an explicit selection approach designed to ensure such workforce flexibility.

An Overview

Caledonian Paper at Irvine New Town in Scotland is a new high-technology operation on a greenfield site. It is a wholly owned subsidiary of the Finnish Kymmene Corporation. The parent company, which specializes in paper production, was established in the late nineteenth century, and currently has some 16,000 employees, with some 3000 of these outside Finland; group turnover in 1989 was approximately £1600m., with production of almost 2 million tonnes of paper, 1.5 million tonnes of pulp end and 1.5 million tonnes of sawn timber, plywood and chipboard. The employees outside Finland work in establishments in Scotland, Germany and France. The paper mill at Irvine is designed to be run on a continuous basis, 24 hours a day, 365 days per year, producing high-quality lightweight coated (LWC) paper for a specialist publishing market, including magazines, catalogues and advertising material. The key dates in the establishment of the mill at Irvine were essentially as follows: in January 1987 the board of the Finnish parent company announced the decision to establish the plant in Scotland, in February the site began to be cleared, from spring 1987 to January 1989 staff were recruited and selected (this was done sequentially from senior management through to production workers), April 1989 was the official start date for production and by October 1989 normal production was under way.

At this early stage any measures of the financial performance of the Irvine plant are not particularly meaningful or valuable. However, it is worth noting that the design capacity of the mill is over 200,000 tonnes per year; at the end of 1990 the target production figure is 140,000 tonnes, rising to 160,000 by the end of 1991, with full production within a further two years. Currently there are some 420 employees of whom less than 300 are shop-floor employees and less than 200 are direct workers. The continuous production process involves a five-crew, three-shift system. This is based on a 20-day module with 3×8 hour shifts per day, averaging 38.77 hours attended per week per worker. Each shift crew has 35 members with its own shift supervisor. Under this work pattern the complete crew, including supervisors, is either at work together or on rest days together. The nature of this operation has resulted in a dual management structure, namely a technical one and a 'man management' one; superintendents are responsible for all machinery and process issues in given areas of the mill, with supervisors being responsible for the personnel in all areas on each shift.

The major items in the employment policy mix at Caledonian Paper are basically as follows. Firstly, a consultative committee, consisting of eight trade union representatives, five management representatives (including three directors), a safety representative

Table 20.1 Principal goals of Caledonian Paper

---

1 *Continuous development of management and personnel*
Using progressive management methods, the company should develop a highly motivated, flexible, professional and cohesive team. Management should create an open and participative environment which encourages the continuous development of the company and its employees.

2 *Effective product development*
A consistent and competitive standard of quality (upper quartile) product should be designed and continuously developed, to meet the present and future market requirements, through co-operation between customer and paper mill.

3 *Application of quality*
The concept that everyone is responsible for the quality of the product as well as for the quality of his/her performance will be applied and developed.

4 *Use of high technology for effective production*
There should be constant review and assessment of 'state of the art' technology in all areas and it should be applied, where appropriate, to ensure the company is among the most effective LWC companies in Europe.

5 *Service and marketing/sales effectiveness*

5.1 Progressive long-term relationships with key customers should be developed for mutual benefit.

5.2 A high standard of service should be established using effective communications.

5.3 The image of a professional paper producer and effective business partner should be developed.

6 *Security of sufficient resources*
The availability of good quality fresh timber should be guaranteed. Availability of all other raw materials and consumables must be guaranteed in all circumstances. A supportive local infrastructure should be developed.

7 *Community relations*
The company should create and maintain a positive environmental image. It should be an attractive and socially responsible employer and community member. Connections with specialist institutions should be made.

---

and two representatives of the non-unionized staff employees, which meets every six weeks to discuss a wide range of issues. Secondly, a negotiating committee, consisting of the three directors and three senior trade union representatives which meets once a year. Thirdly, a safety committee which consists of three safety representatives, the safety officer, the occupational nurse, the production manager and the engineering director. At the shop-floor level there are a number of communication and joint problem-solving arrangements, namely team briefings (which occur on a monthly basis), crew meetings between supervisors and shift members to discuss technical/operational matters, while special trouble-shooting teams are currently being trained and developed to deal with particular technical and production issues. In addition it is a single-status organization with all staff being monthly salaried personnel; the same fringe benefit package (e.g. pension, sick pay) is available to all, there are no clocking-on requirements, and only shop-floor staff are paid for overtime hours.

As regards salaries, the company aims to pay its management personnel at the top end of the UK paper industry, while in the case of the shop-floor staff the intention is to pay at the top end of the range of local area employers; the chemicals and process-orientated industries are particularly important in the latter case. Finally, Caledonian Paper is a unionized establishment, with a single recognition agreement for shop-floor employees having been signed with the EETPU in January 1988; this agreement does not involve closed shop arrangements and does not contain a no-strike clause. Approximately 95 per cent of the eligible shop-floor employees are members of the union.

It has been noted that the attempt to establish an HRM philosophy compatible with overall business strategy is likely to be a feature of the introduction stage of an organizational life cycle (Kochan and Barocci 1985), and certainly a number of new plants or greenfield site operations, in both the UK and the USA, have produced explicit statements of their operating philosophy (Norman 1983). The contents of table 20.1 are in fact an outline of the principal goals which Caledonian Paper has set for itself.

The essence of the 'corporate culture' or 'management style' of Caledonian Paper is, in the words of the personnel director and the employee relations officer, a 'loose–tight' one, a term used very much in the same way as that of Peters and Waterman (1982). That is, there are a relatively small set of largely process-oriented rules and procedures which are very strictly enforced. However, beyond this an essentially loose, open style of management seeks to encourage and develop a mixture of collective and individual attributes. There is, for instance, a great deal of emphasis on teamwork and co-operation but, at the same time, high levels of motivation, initiative, commitment and responsibility are sought and expected from individual employees. The emphasis on individual employee initiative is reflected in the relatively general guidelines which the personnel department issues, for example, to supervisors; detailed, step-by-step procedural manuals are characterized by their essential absence. This strong individual employee orientation, together with the small but very strictly enforced set of process-orientated rules, means that a description of Caledonian Paper as a highly 'paternalistic' employer is not likely to strike a particularly responsive chord with many of its employees.

One of the priorities of senior management at Caledonian Paper is firmly to embed this culture 'in the way of doing things' in the first two years of operation; both induction training and on-the-job practice are among the leading mechanisms designed to achieve this. (The fact that the vast majority of its current employees have been there from the start-up date is clearly relevant here.) This culture, which is viewed as making 'good business sense', reflecting best-practice HRM management and being consistent with the traditions and approach of the Finnish parent company, very much embodies the belief systems and values of senior management à la Ouchi (1981) with the managing director (a Finn), the personnel director and the production director being particularly prominent advocates. The reference to 'making good business sense' above is pursued further in the next section through a discussion of Caledonian Paper's basic competitive strategy and the role that workforce flexibility is held to play in its attainment.

Competitive Strategy and Workforce Flexibility

A recent conceptual paper has identified three basic business or competitive strategies which an organization may adopt, and the associated employee role behaviours and HRM policy mix (Schuler and Jackson 1987). The three competitive strategies identified were:

1 an innovation strategy designed to gain competitive advantage (i.e. develop products or services different from those of competitors);

2 a quality enhancement strategy (i.e. enhance product and/or service quality);

3 a cost-reduction strategy (i.e. be a low-cost producer).

Caledonian Paper's basic competitive strategy is very much a quality enhancement one. It produces LWC paper, largely used in the publication of magazines and brochures, with its targeted market being basically the UK; ultimately it expects to produce 70 per cent for the UK market and 30 per cent for export, although at present there is more of a 50–50 split in this regard. There is not a large customer basis in the UK, as only around 100 organizations have the particular printing machines necessary for using the paper produced at the Irvine plant. Currently more than 50 of these are customers of Caledonian Paper which is (1) seeking to be among the top three producers in Europe in terms of the quality of its product and (2) wants its business to be based on relatively close, longer-term relationships between itself and its customers (i.e. it is seeking regular, repeat business, rather than one-off orders). The achievement of these aims involves a strong emphasis on, firstly, the quality dimension of its product, with product consistency being particularly important in this regard, and secondly, a close customer orientation, as reflected in the ability to customize its product, ensure speed of delivery and provide technical advice, support and back-up to its customers.

The sort of employee role behaviour (e.g. high concern for process, commitment to the goals of the organization) and HRM policies (e.g. high levels of employee participation, a relatively egalitarian treatment of employees, continuous training and development) which Schuler and Jackson (1987) identified as being associated with a quality enhancement strategy are very much features of the set-up at Caledonian Paper. However, at Caledonian it is, above all else, workforce flexibility which is stressed as one of the major routes through which this competitive strategy is to be attained. There are numerous individual indicators or manifestations of the overall emphasis on flexibility in the Caledonian set-up. For example, the number of individual levels of responsibility in the organization structure has been kept to a minimum, use is made of special (temporary) teams, committees or working groups for individual projects, there are no fixed manning levels on any job, and the development of multi-skilling within maintenance crafts and between process and maintenance functions is explicitly written into the original procedural agreement with the EETPU.

However, as a new start-up or greenfield site Caledonian Paper enjoyed a distinct advantage over established, ongoing organizations, in seeking to achieve such levels of workforce flexibility. It has frequently been observed that relatively sophisticated HRM practices are both more common and more successful in greenfield site operations. The reasons for this state of affairs are not hard to find. For example, one US commentator (Lawler 1982:397) has stated that

> new organisations simply have a number of advantages when it comes to creating high involvement systems. They can start with a congruent total system; *they can select people who are compatible*; no one has a vested interest in the *status quo*; and it is possible to do the whole organisation at once so the participative island disease is avoided.

In the particular case of Caledonian Paper it is the use of the selection process to try and build in the maximum possible level of workforce flexibility, in order to, in turn, help achieve the basic competitive strategy of the organization, which we wish to highlight and discuss below.

The Strategic Use of the Selection Stage

The importance attached to the selection stage at Caledonian Paper is nowhere better illustrated than in a parent company background document concerning the plant at Irvine (1987:14):

> The selection and recruitment of personnel is most important since it will form the basis for the whole personnel programme. Psychological tests will be used in the selection in order to test not only trainability and aptitudes, but also the motivation, attitudes and stress endurance of the applicants.

The key elements in the recruitment and selection stage and process at Caledonian Paper were essentially as follows. Firstly, a manpower planning, background exercise involving ideas and information on organizational structure, culture, workforce numbers, attitudes, etc. was undertaken. This was based on experience in Finland and the input of the initially appointed senior management personnel (i.e. the managing director, personnel director and production director) for the plant at Irvine. For example, the target level of manning in the Irvine plant was to some extent based on experience in one of the Finnish plants, although the latter was some 15 years older, involved less sophisticated computer control technology and was part of a much bigger multi-product site. Secondly, the recruitment and selection of managers and superintendents took place in the autumn of 1987, some of whom had background experience in the British paper-making industry. The third phase was the recruitment and selection of supervisors and shop-floor employees, which largely took place in the period January–August 1988.

The latter phase involved more than 10,000 applications with over 2500 individuals being called for interview and testing purposes, which resulted in a final selection figure of approximately 300. To carry out this volume of recruitment and selection, a temporary recruitment–selection department was established which consisted of 10 individuals (including 4 'outsiders', namely 3 psychologists and a personnel consultant) who interviewed and tested approximately 20 people per day for 4 days per week, over an 8-month period of time. All those interviewed (i.e. some 2500 individuals) went through a series of 4 interviews (2 with line management, 1 with personnel, and 1 with the psychologists), lasting approximately half a day, with the other half of the day being given over to psychometric testing (the 16PF test being used prominently here). This was then followed by a review process at which the results of the interviews and tests were put together and a selection decision made.

It is important to note here that none of those interviewed for shop-floor level positions had previously worked in a paper mill. As a consequence, immediate technical skills and relevant industry experience were not the concern of those involved in carrying out the selection process. Instead what was being sought was trainability, willingness and ability to work as part of a team, and flexibility. There were in fact two dimensions involved in the notion of flexibility. The first was a willingness to work in a 'multi-skilled' manner, as set out in the procedural agreement signed with the EETPU. The second was more of a 'mental process', namely an assessment of the individual's willingness and ability to adjust to the demands of the particular system of shift-working; the personality tests and interview by the psychologists were particularly influential in this regard. Table 20.2 indicates in outline the leading psychological aptitudes examined via these tests.

As individuals were selected (while others were still being interviewed and tested), a job-positioning exercise was then carried out to

Table 20.2 Psychological aptitudes: selection process

---

1 *General aptitudes*
  (a) inductive reasoning
  (b) computation
  (c) logical reasoning
  (d) verbal abilities
  (e) conceptual comprehension
  General intelligence
2 *Special skills*
  (a) mechanical comprehension
  (b) technical comprehension
  (c) visuo-spatial abilities
  (d) manual dexterity
  (e) practical problem-solving
3 *Job-related factors*
  (a) stress tolerance
  (b) reaction time
  (c) short-term memory
  (d) vigilance
  (e) visual capacity
  (f) decision-making
4 *Personality dimensions*
  (a) achievement motivation
  (b) orderliness
  (c) autonomy
  (d) affiliation
  (e) dominance
  (f) nurturance
  (g) endurance
  (h) aggressiveness
5 *Inter-social skills*
  6 *Supervisor/managerial aptitude*
  7 *Motivation*

---

identify the specific job they would hold in the organization. This was then followed by the training stage which, typically, involved 10–20 people per week going through a sequence of (1) 4 weeks' induction training, (2) a period of job-related training (e.g. in local area colleges), and (3) production operator training. The latter involved some 70 individuals spending up to a three-month period in Finland, with each person being attached for learning purposes to an equivalent-level person in the Finnish plant (i.e. counterpart training).

The Verdict to Date?

The purpose of this case study has not been to present an argument in favour of the use of psychometric testing at the selection stage. Instead we have essentially sought to illustrate how this particular organization, because of its new start-up status, was able to use the selection process to try and establish a workforce with the aptitudes that would result in a pattern of role behaviour and performance consistent with, and complementary to, their basic way of competing in the market-place. How has it worked out to date? Have senior management's hopes and expectations in this regard been borne out? Given that it is only some 12 months since normal production was commenced it is clearly too soon to provide any hard and fast answers to such questions.

However, the following points are certainly worthy of note at this stage. Firstly, senior management is convinced, on the evidence to date, that they selected a very trainable workforce, which moved very quickly into normal production. Furthermore, in the initial start-up phase (August 1988–April 1989) labour turnover was virtually non-existent. Since then turnover levels have risen quite substantially, having been as high as 10 per cent in some months in 1990 (see table 20.3). This is a source of some concern given that turnover levels are frequently regarded as one of the leading indicators of the impact of high involvement work systems on 'bottom line' performance and that Caledonian Paper itself has targets for turnover of only some 4–6 per cent. Perhaps related to this occurrence, there is some feeling that the nature of the shift system, particularly during the summer months, is making adjustment demands (i.e. somewhat short notice of overtime to cover absences) on some individual employees that are starting to raise questions about the boundaries between acceptable and unacceptable levels of flexibility. Indeed an internal task force has recently been established to investigate such matters. More generally, a workforce opinion survey is under way to examine a range of issues such as employee attitudes to their jobs and the organization as a whole. Finally, as with so many flexible working arrangements, there is some concern about the attitudes and patterns of behaviour at the supervisory

Table 20.3 Some aspects of the employment record to date at Caledonian Paper

Date	Labour build-up	% Turnover	Number of leavers	% Absence	Production level
January 1987	17	0	–	–	–
May 1987	3	0	–	–	–
July 1988	100	0	–	–	–
December 1988	308	0.6	2	n.a.	–
December 1989	403	5.4	22	2 (production) 2 (engineering and others)	50,000
December 1990	412	11.3	44	4 (production) 2 (engineering and others)	140,000

level, particularly among supervisors with some background experience in more traditional paper-manufacturing establishments. This concern is evidenced by the recent establishment of a programme of interpersonal skills training for supervisors, and some conscious senior management initiatives to convince supervisors of their place and role within the management hierarchy of the organization.

Summary and Conclusions

The basic purpose of this case study has been to illustrate how the recruitment/selection process was used to try and facilitate the achievement of an organization's particular competitive objectives. In this particular case the basic competitive strategy was one that stressed high product quality which, in turn, was viewed as requiring high levels of motivation, commitment and flexibility on the part of the workforce. The story here has been very much 'state of the art' use of the recruitment/selection process towards these ends.

The greenfield site status of the plant helps make the important point that the 'natural home' for strategic HRM is likely to be disproportionately associated with such sites, where above average opportunities for change exist. In this sense the 'external validity' of the case is limited, although it is arguably important in two senses. Firstly, it suggests that HRM researchers should increasingly concentrate their attentions on such sites and, secondly, it does provide a useful reference point for cases based in established plants. The point here is that the management desire for increased workforce flexibility is not exclusively confined to greenfield sites. However, in established plants the recruitment/selection route as the major vehicle for achieving this end is not an option. The interesting question then becomes what means or route can they use as a substitute? The answers to this question should be, to say the least, of considerable interest to both HRM practitioners and researchers.

References

Kochan, T.A. and Barocci, T.A. 1985: *Human Resource Management and Industrial Relations*. Boston: Little Brown, 105.

Lawler, E.E. 1982: Increasing worker involvement to enhance organisational effectiveness. In P.S. Goodman (ed.), *Change in Organisations*, San Francisco: Jossey-Bass, 280–315.

Norman, D. 1983: How a new plant made Pilkington reflect on its IR structure. *Personnel Management*, 15(8), August, 21–4.

Ouchi, W. 1981: *Theory Z*. Reading, Mass.: Addison-Wesley.

Peters, T.J. and Waterman, R.H. 1982: *In Search of Excellence*. New York: Harper & Row.

Schuler, R.S. and Jackson, S.E. 1987: Linking competitive strategies with human resource management practices. *Academy of Management Executive*, 1(3), August, 207–19.

21
Human Resource Planning in Eight British Organizations: a Canadian Perspective

TERRY HERCUS

Introduction

This chapter looks at eight British case studies in the practice of human resource (HR) planning but from a Canadian perspective. The eight cases, drawn from the public and private sectors are, in the main, large organizations with international interests and reputations. Their HR planning practices are compared with each other and a conceptual model so that wider lessons and conclusions can be drawn. The chapter, therefore, falls into four parts: an initial overview of HR planning describing its nature in the US and Canadian contexts; a presentation of the conceptual model; an analysis of the case studies using the model; and, in the final part, drawing some general conclusions.

What is Human Resource Planning?

In 1967, Vetter defined HR planning in a way that expressed the basic elements of the process: 'Through planning, management strives to have the right number and right kinds of people at the right places, at the right time, doing the things which result in both the organization and the individual receiving long-run benefit' (Vetter 1967).

In 1971 A. R. Smith the Director of Statistics for the British Civil Service, suggested that HR planning involved three major steps:

1 Demand work. Analysing, reviewing and predicting the quantity and type of manpower needed by an organization to achieve its objectives.

2 Supply work. Predicting the action necessary to ensure that the manpower needed is available.
3 Designing the interaction between demand and supply so that skills are utilized to the best advantage and the legitimate aspirations of the individual are taken into account (Smith in Timperley and Sisson 1989).

In contrast, Bramham distinguishes short-term and long-term HR planning. In the short term, HR planning provides information about current manpower resources and capabilities in order to develop contingency plans to cope with sudden changes. Anticipating the future is the long-term HR planning function based on the manpower environment, information on business plans, goals and knowledge of present manpower resources (Bramham in Timperley and Sisson 1989).

Walker (1980:5) defines it as 'a management process of analyzing an organization's human resource needs under changing conditions and developing the activities necessary to satisfy these needs'. Milkovich et al. (1983:2–4) used a different approach in their definitions: 'An organization can be said to engage in human resource planning to the extent that it uses formalized procedures to make decisions for the future, integrating its human resource decisions and objectives with those of the entire enterprise and with each other and subsequently monitoring the results.'

From these definitions of HR planning proposed by American and British research scholars, it is possible to develop an answer to the original question: 'What is human resource planning?'

It is a management process which involves these dimensions:

1 *Forecasting HR requirements* for an organization to achieve its business plan/objectives.
2 *Forecasting HR available* for meeting these needs, as well as an internal and external environmental scan of the organization.
3 Identifying the gaps between what will be needed and what will be available and develop *HR action plans* involving staffing, appraisal, compensation and development to meet these needs.
4 *Implement and monitor* the HR action plans, regularly evaluating progress at the senior management/board level.

Human Resource Planning in the USA and Canada

In the USA, in a survey of 200 HR planners, Miller and Burack (1981) found that HR planning is integrated with overall enterprise policies, plans and strategies; responsive HR programmes are implemented with a sensitivity to economic and policy needs of the organization. Towers, Perrin, Forster and Crosby (Canada) Ltd (1972) surveyed 200 US firms and found that 63.5 per cent link HR planning to the business-planning cycle. However, Kahalas et al. (1980) in a survey of 87 US firms found that most firms view HR planning as a section of the personnel department and that 50 per cent of the firms limit HR planning to certain types of employees (Kahalas et al. 1980).

In Canada, the Ontario Manpower Commission (1984) conducted a survey of 1796 Ontario firms and found that 66 per cent have HR projections for groups of staff. The projection of the firm's future staff requirements for any or all staff are based on these projections and that the formulation of plans to ensure that the staffing requirements are met is done through actions or programmes. The government of Canada had a survey conducted by R. J. Clifford and Associates (1981) of 154 firms in 15 industrial sectors in 4 provinces and found that 59 out of 90 firms had strategic HR plans, 145 out of 147 include HR planning in operational plans for at least one year. The median length is 2.2 years, and 76 out of 145 firms have sophisticated HR planning processes.

Surveys of HR planning practices have yielded mixed results regarding the degree to which it is seen as a management process. The Ontario Manpower Commission survey of 1796 Ontario firms found that responsibility for HR planning was assigned to administration or personnel most frequently. R. J. Clifford and Associates, in a survey of 154 firms conducted for the government of Canada, found that larger firms (1000+ employees) have human resource planning groups in their corporate planning departments (Ontario Commission 1984; R. J. Clifford and Associates 1981).

Objectives and Outline of the Chapter

The purpose of the chapter is to provide an understanding of what HR planning is; how it is defined by the major authors in the field, and how it is represented in a conceptual model derived from the literature. The model provides a basis for comparing the HR planning practices in eight British organizations. The case studies are compared with the normative model and with each other in order to draw some conclusions about the nature of HR planning practices.

There are some wider lessons and general conclusions drawn from the eight case studies of British organizations.

Starting with the historical definitions of HR planning in both the USA (Vetter 1967) and the UK (Smith 1971 quoted in Timperley and Sisson 1989) the pattern is traced to more contemporary ones in order to provide a clear answer to the question: 'What is human resource planning?'

A brief survey of HR planning practice in the USA and Canada is provided in order to establish that there is a considerable degree of acceptance of this management process in both countries. There are somewhat mixed views as to whether HR planning is a management process or a specialized HR function.

The second section of the chapter is devoted to the conceptual model of HR planning. The origins of the concept are examined based on a review of the literature. Figure 21.1 provides a diagram-matical representation of the HR planning process starting with the business plan. Forecasts of HR requirements are derived from the business plan and forecasts of HR available to meet these needs are determined from an analysis of the internal labour supply and the HR flows through the organization (wastage analysis).

The gap between what will be needed and what will be available is then identified and forms the basis for HR action plans designed to meet these needs. These action plans are implemented by manage-ment covering: external and internal staffing, appraisal, com-pensation and development programmes. Senior management and company boards monitor and evaluate the HR action plans regularly throughout the year to ensure that plan targets are achieved.

Human resource planning has three important linkages. It links the organization with its environment by means of an environmental scan of internal and external conditions (Walker 1980). It links with the business plan at the strategic and/or operational level. It also links the individual with the organization through career planning that is integrated with the HR planning process. It involves the participation of employees in career-planning decisions, linking individual and organizational goals and plans.

Human resource planning involves support systems to facilitate analysis and implementation: HR information systems, skills inventories, performance appraisal and succession plans (Burak and Mathys 1980). It involves systematic formal procedures, articulation, monitoring and evaluation of results (Milkovich et al. 1983).

The third section of the chapter is devoted to the eight case studies

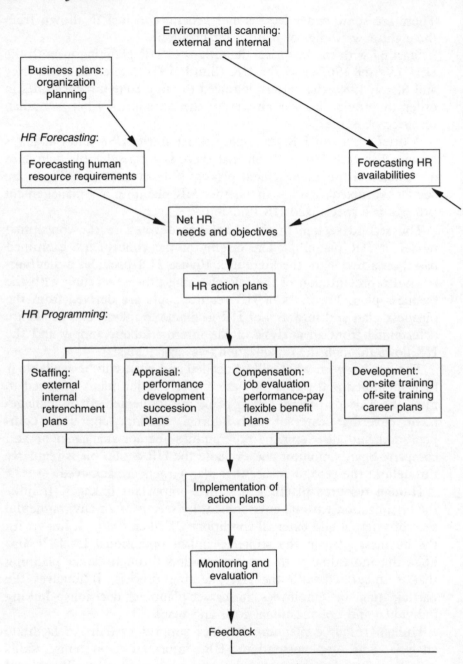

Figure 21.1 Conceptual model of the HR planning process

of British organizations. The research method used in the preparation of these case studies is described; it consists of structured interviews based on research questions developed by Dyer et al. for their study of Corning Glass Works in the USA.

The eight organizations are major international companies which are leaders in their sector of the economy, are drawn from public and private sector, are mainly large firms, and would be readily recognized by an international audience. The HR planning practices of each of the eight organizations are described in the form of a case study.

The cases are compared with the normative model to determine the way in which they are practising HR planning. It was found that two types of planning can be identified: comprehensive and focused. The first type of planning covers all of the employees of the organization, whereas the second type focuses on specific employee groups that are considered to be critically important to the organization.

There are a number of wider lessons and conclusions to be drawn from the analysis of these case studies of British organizations. The value of comparative HR planning is in the exploration of how organizations are using HR planning within their own external environment as a total system. There is valuable learning for students as well as managers working in multinational firms to see how organizations deal with particular national planning populations within their HR planning process.

There is also an opportunity to assess the impact of the external environment on HR planning. The problems of 'housing' staff, transportation, high cost of property, and the prospect of a unified labour market within the EC are all having an impact in terms of strategic business plans and HR planning implications.

A Conceptual Model

Origins from the literature

The conceptual model developed by British author D. J. Bell (1974) in a book called *Planning Corporate Manpower* reflected a practitioner's point of view. He was a member of the Edinburgh group of the Manpower Society, a group of planners who provided mutual assistance and support in their manpower planning corporate activities. Bell identifies five elements of manpower resources:

1 systematic analysis of manpower resources;
2 forecast of manpower requirements;
3 forecast of manpower supply;
4 reconciliation within company constraints;
5 plans for action (utilization, supply, training, personnel policies).

All of these elements are found in the model provided in figure 21.1 in this chapter under somewhat different headings. In particular, the first step is now called environmental scanning of internal and external labour market conditions. In the last step, the action plans now include: staffing, appraisal, compensation and development.

Walker (1980) follows the same basic structure in his conceptual model, using two major headings: needs forecasting and programme planning. The HR forecasting process follows Bell's scheme but adds the forecasting dimension as two separate steps:

- understanding of the environment and organization conditions;
- analysis of current human resource inventory;
- *projected future* human resource supply;
- analysis of current human resource requirements;
- *projected future* requirements;
- needs forecast presentation (recruiting, training, etc.).

Similarly, in the programme planning process, Walker details the action plans under seven headings compared to Bell's four; namely, organization, appraisals, rewards, policies and systems, succession, career opportunities, and individual career planning. In general, Walker adopts a similar conceptual model to that of Bell, but adds much stronger emphasis to the forecasting and programming aspects of the process.

Dyer (in Milkovich et al. 1983) presents a three-step conceptual model of the HR planning process:

1 setting HR planning objectives;
2 planning personnel programmes;
3 evaluation and control.

Within the first step, future staffing needs, and future personnel flows and availabilities are identified and reconciled. Objectives are then set as a basis for the second step, the development of personnel programmes and action plans. Programmes are implemented, evaluated and controlled in the third step. The Dyer model contains similar elements to the Bell and Walker models, but presents a simplified description of the process.

Figure 21.1 explained

The conceptual model of the HR planning process in figure 21.1 provides a composite of the work of the authors cited in the literature. The starting-point, as in their models, is the environmental scanning of internal and external conditions. The organization is linked to its environment by means of this scan.

The forecast of HR availabilities is the next step in the process including an analysis of HR flows through the organization and an analysis of the current HR inventory. This step should provide planners with a projected future HR supply to meet its projected requirements.

The business plan provides a basis for estimating the HR requirements of the firm. These projected future requirements will be forecast, based on managerial estimates, historical trends, job analysis, critical factors or some form of mathematical modelling.

The two forecasts, availabilities and requirements, are reconciled to provide net HR needs. These are the gaps between what will be needed and what will be available. During a period of the scaling down of many organizations in order to reduce costs and increase competitiveness, this gap may, in fact, be a surplus of HR required to achieve the organization objectives. In this case, HR action plans are still required, but will be of a different character than in dealing with a shortage of human resources.

When there is a shortage, HR action plans and programmes are required for the selection, appraisal, rewards and development of HR, including promotions, transfers and reductions in some sectors of the workforce. These action plans are integrated with HR planning in a patterned way. The plans are generally developed by HR specialists with their line management clients on a co-operative basis. The model in figure 21.1 lists a number of possible elements of these action plans which will vary depending upon the organization's specific HR needs at the time. Career plans are identified in the development section because it is essential to involve the active participation of individual employees in work/career planning decisions, linking individual and organizational goals and plans.

The final step in the HR planning process is the implementation of the action plans by line management. In the months that follow, monitoring and evaluation of these action plans by senior management and the board of directors are critically important to ensure that the desired results are achieved. Feedback from this planning cycle is then provided as an input to the next phase of forecasting HR availabilities. The process involves systematic formal procedures: HR information systems, skills inventories, performance appraisals and succession plans. It is a management process that involves future thinking about the HR needs of an organization under changing conditions (Milkovich et al. 1983).

The conceptual model provided in figure 21.1 serves as a normative model against which to evaluate the case studies.

The Case Study Organizations

Research method

The purpose of this series of case studies is to examine how British companies are approaching HR planning; the reasons why they do or do not succeed in their HR planning efforts; and what can be learned that is relevant to senior HR professionals. The conceptual model and research questions were adapted from a set prepared by Dyer et al. for their descriptive case study of Corning Glassworks in the USA.

The sample was chosen with the assistance of faculty members at the universities of Warwick and Strathclyde, based on their knowledge of HR management executives who would be willing to participate in the preparation of case studies on the HR planning practices of their companies. The goal of the study is a comparative case analysis of these British approaches to HR planning using a normative model of HR planning as a management process.

The eight case studies

Case 1: railway transportation
Company 1 has 136,000 employees working in the UK. Its board is appointed by the British government; the personnel director is not a member of the board. The business plan concentrates on six business sectors of the company's operations which are treated separately; they were established to improve business performance (freight, parcel, inter-city, inter-provincial, commuter services and European passenger services). The sixth business was recently set up to run through services to other European countries via the Channel Tunnel starting is June 1993.

Human resource planning is done through a series of planning conferences for each business sector. Planning goals include productivity/service improvement in each sector. Operations and engineering services are managed directly by the business sectors. Each business sector has a personnel director responsible, among other things, for HR planning. The six business directors determine the business goals; HR planning is done to achieve these business plans. It is based on historical trends and covers all employees with greater emphasis on key staff such as train drivers (engineers). Succession plans and career plans are also prepared. Planning conferences provide personnel directors with an opportunity to challenge draft plans and monthly conferences are used to monitor the implementation of HR plans.

The sequence of HR planning starts with market forecasts for the six business sectors. The forecasts use workload approaches (e.g. miles of track per staff; speed and frequency over the track) in order to determine human resource requirements. Business directors can cut levels of maintenance in terms of cost. A heavy investment has been made in cutting total staff numbers (800,000 employees in 1945 to 136,000 in 1991). An employment development department was set up to aid communities to adjust to job losses through consultation at all levels. Union agreements have been reopened with considerable union co-operation; however, strikes in 1982 and 1989 were indirectly linked to job losses.

Human resource planning has been devolved to the business sectors; as a result, the group headquarters personnel department is no longer involved in the details of the planning process. However, it does advise the board on the broad acceptability of business plans. There is still a weak linkage between business plans and HR action plans. Each function forecasts its staffing needs by units and career plans are developed within the unit. Two hundred university graduates are hired each year. Management staff annually discuss their performance objectives which are used as a basis for merit pay. Assessment centres are used to assess training needs and the results are interpreted to the individual. Performance appraisals provide the basis for merit awards based on an management by objectives (MBO) system. Career plans for management staff are developed based on future needs using cross-training and business school courses. Action plans are monitored throughout the system with a periodic review of progress and an annual review of the five-year manpower plan.

The impetus for starting HR planning was the corporate plan

(1960) and the business strategies (1982). It is sustained by pressure on quality of service and the HR climate. Company officials are also anticipating a potential problem of recruitment and retention because of a severe decline in the number of school and college leavers entering the workforce in the UK. While the company is not paying adequate attention to HR planning, company officials believe the devolution of the key responsibility to the business sectors and the removal of the regional tier of management should sharpen its focus on this issue.

Case 2: a confectionery manufacturer

Company 2 employs 4000 employees, a reduction of staff from 10,000 in 1977. The board consists of executive and non-executive members; the personnel director is on the board. The five-year business plan generates the basis for HR planning which reacts to it.

The company is organized into five factories with a personnel manager at each one. Operations are conducted on a decentralized basis. Each function produces a budget and staff needs. The HR plan indicates the additions and retrenchment for each unit and covers all jobs within each functional level. The functional managers are responsible for their own HR planning. The business plan is generated at the board level.

Each department assesses its staff by means of a management audit–skills inventory. Based on potential, succession charts classify all staff in the department. The report is made to the board; managers must take action on major skill shortages. Staff adjustments are made to keep costs down using temporaries and contractors.

Assessment centres are used for key shop jobs with good union acceptance. Appraisals based on MBO reviews are used to assess training needs and review career plans. These appraisals are also done for clerical but not shop-floor staff. Rewards are based on cost of living and achievement of objectives and competencies. Shop-floor wages are set by collective agreements.

A training centre is used, the five plants each being responsible for their own training. The management audit conducted in July monitors the progress of action plans set in November along with meetings held three times a year between personnel managers and factory managers. The audit report goes to the board; two board meetings are devoted to training and development exclusively. Action plans are based on the data collected in the management audits of departments.

The impetus for HR planning was: cost cutting, competition, performance improvement and the introduction of new technology. The major problems were a lack of training of staff when the organization structure was changed and a lack of budget for training in areas of skill shortages.

Case 3: luxury motor cars
Company 3 manufactures luxury cars for world-wide markets, employing 11,000 employees in three integrated plants. The company is organized in a flat structure; decision-making is centralized.

The business plan is drawn up for five years for operating and ten years for product. It covers all units and includes a human resource plan. There is an integrated HR planning process which combines top-down and bottom-up planning. There is a strong line management role in planning and is done three times a year at all levels covering all job categories.

The personnel director is responsible for HR planning in close integration with key executives. Plans are monitored monthly at the board meetings as they are considered to be a significant part of the business plan. Forecasting of demand is based on historical trends, productivity improvements, automation and increased skill of support functions. The forecasts are done for four years ahead in order to fit in with company-run apprenticeship programmes. Forecasting is linked directly to business planning.

Environmental scanning is done regularly by the personnel department. Conflicts in forecasts are resolved by the personnel director and the managers. Each department conducts a training needs analysis; training plans are developed and approved and target dates are set. Training is given line authority. There is an intake of staff once a year: 16-year-olds, 18-year-olds and graduates (21–24) linked directly to training programmes. A co-operative programme is run for university students alternating periods of work and periods of study.

An appraisal system based on performance is used to adjust individual salaries. Training is designed for departments based on their training needs. General upgrading training is available; 25 per cent of the staff are on self-development programmes.

Forecasts and action plans are monitored by results: sales and profits. Action plans are reviewed by department heads at regular meetings. Annual objectives are set with specific targets; MBO is used at management levels.

An HR information system is computerized and is integrated with training. The impetus for HR planning was the lack of skills to achieve product plans. It is sustained by the business growth plan which drives it. The business plan, including the HR plan, has become the central driving force in the corporation.

Case 4: life insurance

The major products of the company are life insurance, pensions and unit trusts. With 6000 employees, it has experienced extremely rapid growth over the last five years in particular. Approximately 2000 employees out of 4000 at head office have less than five years' service. The company is managed by a senior executive team of nine, of whom three are on the board. In other words, the board is essentially a non-executive board. The general manager, personnel, is a member of the senior executive. Company 4 has headquarters and branches in the UK; it also has branches in Canada and Ireland. A certain amount of autonomy is granted to the Canadian operation.

Human resource forecasting is very difficult and is based on business forecasts. However, growth has been very great, creating skill shortages in all categories. This has had a strategic impact on the business plan; there are immense problems in recruiting, training and housing staff. Recruitment and training staff have increased from 6 or 7 some five years ago to now over 40. Experienced staff are required for many of the positions. Line managers are responsible for HR planning. Succession plans and plans for 'fast-trackers' are handled by the executive committee covering the senior group. The most senior group is handled by the managing director. The executive plus the personnel managers serve as an HR planning task force, along with staff from mangement systems.

Careers of professionals such as actuaries, accountants, lawyers, surveyors and general management are reviewed annually. Succession plans for key jobs are handled by the managing director and the general manager, personnel, although it is intended to involve the other members of the senior executive in the immediate future. High potential employees (high fliers) are assessed by managers, career moves and cross-training are then planned for these employees. The firm is aware that staff limitations are a limiting factor to growth.

The bulk of the staff are mainly for clerical functions although up to 100 professional trainees are hired each year. A skills inventory is now being maintained on a computer system. Performance planning and annual reviews (more frequently if required) have been introduced and rewards are increasingly based on actual performance against plan over the previous year with reference to market movements. There is now extensive induction, management skills and professional training at all levels. Human resource planning has moved forward substantially over the last few years. It is now common practice to move middle and senior managers, not just junior managers, from division to division without necessarily involving promotion, as part of their development.

Case 5: financial management
This company of 3250 employees, the smallest one in the study, specializes in financial management and life assurance. The non-executive board meets every four weeks. The head of personnel attends regularly. The company is experiencing a steady growth in business and maintains a headquarters and branches in the UK. Decision-making is centralized.

Career plans are prepared for five years ahead for all staff. Fast-trackers are monitored separately. Human resource planning covers all levels as there is a strong emphasis on HR by both line and staff managers who work closely together.

The corporate plan is presented to managers at a one-day conference; it includes HR plans. The plan is based on areas and volume; targets are set for branch staff based on the forecasted volume of business. Forecasts are linked to action plans through the personnel department.

Careful records are kept on staff in terms of skills, education and potential. Forecasting of HR requirements is co-ordinated with induction and skill training, then on-the-job training with frequent appraisals. High-potential graduate staff are recruited for professional actuarial training to develop professional skills leading to the Fellowship of the Faculty of Actuaries. Appraisals are done annually to set career plans and objectives which are linked to development and rewards. Cash grants are given for training achievements; other rewards are given based on progress through a scale based on performance.

Training is strongly linked to advancement. Team briefings are given to all employees once a month covering a wide range of company-related topics. Quality action teams are established to solicit employee views on company plans and changes in technology.

The personnel manager reports to the board regularly on action plans, for example 5 per cent cut in administrative costs. A skills inventory is kept for high fliers along with succession plans, career plans and appraisals. The impetus for HR planning in this company is the key role of HR to the company's success.

Case 6: wine and spirits

Company 6 is a part of a large holding company. It has 12,000 employees in its world-wide organization with a corporate head-quarters in London, UK. It is engaged in the production and distribution of wine and spirits which are sold through national marketing companies. The company operates on a decentralized basis based on sales orders coming from these national marketing and international brand companies.

Business plans are based on forecasts from marketing and planned productivity improvements; it includes a long-term manpower plan. The business plan is part of a rolling four-year plan covering production, warehousing and distribution. Manpower forecasts are derived from the business plan. Human resource planning covers all units and employee groups. Forecasts are also prepared on a quarterly basis at a divisional level and reviewed with each division head. The personnel director is responsible for HR planning. The HR plan provides the authority to recruit, develop and transfer employees. It is monitored by the managing director in terms of its budgetary impact.

Forecasts of staff demand are based on managerial estimates derived from estimated production and distribution volumes and inventory levels. Forecasts of staff supply are also managerial estimates. Environmental scanning is carried out to ensure a free flow of staff into the system; labour market conditions are surveyed, environmental issues such as EC laws on emissions and quality of water are closely monitored.

There is a strong linkage between the forecasting process and action planning. Recruiting is done to meet the needs identified in the HR plan; performance appraisals provide information on career and training needs, and identify high-potential individuals for a number of possible vacancies. Action plans are then developed on an individual basis. A skills inventory has been established on a world-wide computer program covering education, careers and individual career preferences; it covers the top 200–300 staff in the company. Senior staff in marketing, finance and operations are moved around as part of their development. Merit pay and bonuses are used for senior staff based on company performance and the achievement of their personal job objectives.

The evaluation and monitoring of forecasts are done by means of quarterly reviews and they are continually updated. The executive committee reviews the forecasts and makes any changes required in the business plan. An HR information system, which is updated weekly, provides a computerized data base for human resource planning. It includes all of the basic HR data, including education and training details. A goal-setting appraisal system is used to evaluate job performance, allocate merit pay and develop some individual career plans. The HR planning process is considered essential to the company in signalling HR issues and planning for them. The current issue being addressed is developing a plan for scaling down the company and assisting people to find alternative employment.

Case 7: telecommunications
Company 7 is a major telecommunications organization that employs 200,000 employees. It operates in six divisions: business communications, personal communications, world-wide network, development and procurement, business products, and special businesses. There is a high degree of autonomy within this functional organization which operates in a small number of geographical zones principally in the UK with about 10 per cent of the staff located outside of the UK.

This major reorganization of the company has just been completed, reducing the staff by 5000 managers and 18,000 total employees. The new organization resulted from competition and a 'customer first' focus. The business plan introduced new dimensions to the company with emphasis on world-class standards, expansion in the USA, Canada and Europe; establishment of international networking for business purposes and the development of international managers. The needs of operational people, the impact of competition and effective strategic decision-making were key in determining how HR planning evolves and now functions. A strategic approach has been established covering all employees in the company. The personnel director is responsible for HR planning, working closely with line managers at the divisional level. The general manager settles disputes in the planning process. The sequence of HR planning starts with the identification of operational imperatives in the business plan; the development of enabling personnel strategies results in the HR plan which is carried out at the local level by personnel directors. The HR plan is used for recruiting and release, placement, training, development and promotion, covering a geographic area of company operations.

Staff demand is forecast based on last year's demand, wastage analysis, projects scheduled and changed objectives. It is closely linked to the business plan in terms of the commercial realities faced by the company: cutting complaints and cutting costs. Staff supply is forecast based on a profile of existing staff, skills inventory, estimated wastage, requested transfers, promotions and the need to bring new people into the system. Environmental scanning is done centrally by the manpower planning unit at headquarters; world-wide reports on external factors are submitted to the management board. Feedback from HR planning is an integrated part of business planning and has resulted in changes in the business plan.

Action plans develop directly from the needs of the business plan covering recruiting, training, compensation and industrial relations negotiated changes. The national HR plan is quite general; each geographic unit develops its own separate action plans and retains HR data on a local basis. The action plans are implemented by line managers and monitored by the personnel director on a monthly basis. A summary is presented on a group-wide basis to the monthly board meeting. Monthly reviews of manpower plans also take place at the divisional level by the general manager and the management board.

An HR information system is available on a computerized skills inventory. Individual career plans are developed for the top two groups of executives in British operations based on an executive track system, performance appraisal, superior's assessment, individual's views and succession planning requirements. This process is carried out on an annual cycle; succession plans for each area are also reviewed annually. The problems with HR planning are twofold: data collection and updating; and the demands which keep changing requiring a response to be made. It is sustained by its place as an integral part of the strategic business plan.

Case 8: a computer manufacturer

Company 8 employs 2500 regular employees and a variable number of contractors depending on need. It manufactures computers for Europe, Africa and the Middle East. It is part of a world-wide computer manufacturer and accounts for a significant part of the company's European revenue. The company has a strong human relations philosophy based on respect for the individual, service to the customer and the pursuit of excellence in craftsmanship.

Business planning includes four elements: cost, inventory, space and manpower. The business unit is the basis for the planning process; it includes all four elements in the plan. The planning period is one year, with a five-year strategic plan. The plan is prepared in the autumn and updated frequently. Targets are set in each element; planning is completed and monitored closely; the focus of the plan is one year and covers all units, businesses, all employees and contracted work.

The responsibility for drafting the manpower plan, part of the business plan is shared: personnel, industrial engineering, resource planning and strategic planning managers all contribute. The draft plan is then negotiated with line managers. A manpower committee made up of senior line management and staff is established to monitor the plan and to resolve any disputes. Training is a line responsibility in this company because of the importance of skill planning and developing flexibility in the workforce.

The business plan, including the manpower plan, is used to drive the business. Forecasts of staff demand are derived from the market forecast, volumes of business, productivity improvements and contracted work planned. Forecasts of staff availability are derived from a skills inventory, department heads' inputs on the skill base of their departments, plus an analysis of HR flows (wastage). The environmental scanning of European labour market conditions, as well as social, economic, political and environmental issues, is done annually. Industrial engineering is the driving force behind this forecasting process in the company.

When the forecasting process results in an anticipated surplus of employees, action plans involve a freeze on hiring, natural wastage, early retirements, secondment to other units, volunteers for retirement settlements, lateral transfers and cuts in overtime. When there is a shortfall in required skills, action plans involve external recruitment, internal staffing, job rotation and training plans. Extensive multi-year training programmes are developed to address forecasted skill planning. A flexible workforce is emphasized and opportunities are provided. Contributions are recognized through an appraisal system; there are strong performance rewards and job security. The evaluation and control of the manpower plan involve monitoring the level of activity against the business volumes. Plans are made to redeploy people, to work overtime, etc. in order to adjust the staff levels on both a short-term and long-term basis. Full employment of the company's employees drives this planning process, emphasizing flexibility and skill planning.

The cases compared

The British organizations studied have experienced difficult economic conditions; four of the eight firms have had significant staff reductions. As they emerged from this period, HR planning has been given high priority by a number of these employers because of the shortages of professionals and skilled employees, and corporate goals emphasizing productivity improvement and quality. Human resource planning is generally considered a management process with the active participation of the personnel director and a monitoring role played by senior management and the board of directors. In two cases, however, HR planning is considered the responsibility of the personnel director.

Because of the size of the organizations ranging from 3250 to 200,000 employees, in some cases, the planning population is the business unit, the division or product group with the headquarters acting as consultants or concentrating their planning attention on a smaller group of senior management employees. The demand forecasting methods used are managerial estimates, workload approaches, historical trends and volume of business estimates. The supply forecasting methods vary considerably with some use of computerized HR information systems, skills inventories and succession plans. Environmental scanning is being done by some of the organizations studied.

The linkage between forecasting and action planning is limited in many cases as is the linkage between individual career planning and forecasting. Action plans themselves, however, are quite well integrated, especially staffing, training career plans, appraisal and performance pay systems. Performance appraisal programmes have a central place in six of the organizations. The appraisal information provides the basis for merit pay, career plans, training needs and assessment of potential. Rewards are closely linked to performance, goal achievement, and skill acquisition in six out of eight cases.

Monitoring processes vary widely among the employers. The role of senior management and managing boards meeting monthly with regular reports on HR planning assures top priority to the process and provides the information for evaluating action plans on a continuing basis.

While there were some semantic problems with the research questions, HR planning is in place in these British organizations with linkages to business planning. Planning practices in this study were of two types, comprehensive or focused; they applied to all employees in the first type or they were concentrated on specific groups of key employees in the second type.

Comprehensive planning was being done by employers 1, 3, 5, 6, 7, and 8; these cases provide a strong parallel to the conceptual model of HR planning (figure 21.1). In case 1, the employer's concern for productivity and service improvement in each of six business sectors led to the inclusion of HR planning in their business strategy. It is sustained by pressure on quality of service and anticipated skill shortages in the future. Similar concerns led employer 3 to include HR planning in its business planning process. Improvements in productivity and quality are vital to this employer, along with the need to cope with serious skill shortages through recruiting and apprenticeship training programmes. Employer 5 places high priority on HR because of the corporate value system with the emphasis being placed on individual career plans. Employer 6 considers HR planning is vital to its operations, updates its forecasts quarterly and monitors its action plans closely. In the case of employer 7, HR planning was a central instrument in carrying out a major reorganization of the company and continues its central role in the business plan. For employer 8, a strong human relations philosophy, including job security, is the driving force in HR planning, which is a direct part of the business planning process.

A second group of employers (nos 2 + 4) have focused their HR planning on specific groups of employees that they consider vital to their operations. Employer 2 concentrates attention on an annual management audit and skills inventory to identify major skill shortages. Action plans are then developed for these groups of management and key shop jobs. Employer 4 concentrates planning attention on professional groups: actuaries, accountants, lawyers, surveyors and general management. High fliers, that is, high-potential employees, also receive planning attention in their careers and training.

In several cases, employers have decentralized their operations so that the planning populations are those of a region, division, factory or product group. The head office group acts as internal HR consultants to these divisions and monitors the acceptability of their business and HR plans.

It was found that the greater the emphasis on the business plan and the role played by senior management and board in monitoring the process, the more likely that HR planning would be in place and would be given high priority. This is clearly the case with the employers doing comprehensive planning.

The role of the personnel director as a key corporate player in doing planning with client managers and in linking HR planning with business planning was also evident in these cases. The personnel director appears to play more than a staff role, has some line authority, and certainly has 'influence' in the HR planning and monitoring process at the senior management and board levels.

Conclusions: The Value of Comparative Human Resource Planning

There are a number of lessons to be learned from these case studies of organizations in the UK. There is some risk of picking and choosing individual ideas from the human resource planning practices in other countries. In transferring knowledge across national boundaries, it is important to explore how organizations are using HR planning within their own external environment – as a total system. In this circumstance, case studies provide a good opportunity to demonstrate how organizations are using HR planning; it is a window on the firm, looking at the HR planning process as a central management system.

Case studies are also valuable as teaching materials, providing HR and management students with an overview of the HR planning process within a particular environment. There is also valuable learning for managers working in multinational firms as well. They can see how organizations deal with particular national planning populations within their HR planning process or decentralize the process itself to different national settings.

There is also an opportunity to assess the impact of the external environment on HR planning. For example, the problem of 'housing' staff for a rapidly growing insurance company (case 4) acted as a constraint on its business plans. The high cost of living, especially property costs in the London area, was a serious deterrent to attracting, retaining and compensating professional staff in other cases. The prospects of dealing with the unified market of the EC caused a number of the organizations studied to reorganize their operations, modify strategic business plans and consider the HR planning implications.

The role of senior management and the board, and that of the HR director, appears to be particularly important to the success of the HR planning process in the organizations in the UK which were studied. The board of directors of organizations in the UK is made up chiefly of senior management and includes the HR director in many of the organizations studied. Board-level attention to the monitoring and evaluation of HR planning indicates the importance of HR within these firms. Board meetings in British organizations are held monthly, rather than quarterly; this frequency of meetings allows for more continuous attention to HR plans. As a major corporate player in joint planning with client managers, the HR director links HR planning with business planning by playing a strong staff role with significant influence in the HR planning process in a number of the organizations studied.

References

Bell, D.J. 1974: *Planning Corporate Manpower*. London: Longman.

Burak, E.H. and Mathys N.J. 1980: *Human Resource Planning: a pragmatic approach to manpower staffing and development*. Lakeforest, Ill.: Brace, Park Press.

Dyer, L., Schafer, G. and Regan G. 1982: Human Resource planning at Corning Glassworks – a field study. *Human Resource Planning*. 5(3).

Kahalas, H., Pazer, H., Hoagland, J. and Levitt A. 1980: Human Resource planning activities in U.S. firms. *Human Resource Planning*, 3(2), 53.

Milkovich, G., Dyer, L. and Mahoney, T. 1983: HRM planning. In *Human Resources Management in the 1980's*, Washington, DC: Bureau of National Affairs Inc., ch. 2.

Miller, E. and Burak, E. 1981: A status report on human resource planning from the perspective of human resource planners. *Human Resource Planning*, 4(2), 33.

Ontario Manpower Commission 1984: *An Overview of Human Resource Planning Practices in Ontario*. Toronto.

R.J. Clifford and Associates 1981: *Survey of Manpower Planning Practices in Canada*. Ottawa: Minister of Supply and Services Canada.

Timperley, S. and Sisson, K. 1989: Human resource planning in Britain. In K. Sisson (ed.), *Personnel Management in Britain*, Basil Blackwell, chapter 5.

Towers, Perrin, Forster and Crosby (Canada) Ltd 1972: *Corporate Manpower Planning in Canada*. Toronto, Canada.

Vetter, E.W. 1967: *Manpower Planning for High Talent Personnel*. Ann Arbor: Bureau of Industrial Relations, University of Michigan.

Walker, J.W. 1980: *Human Resource Planning*. New York: McGraw-Hill.

Annotated Further Reading

Books

Baddon, L. et al. 1989: *People's Capitalism: a critical analysis of profit sharing and employee share ownership*. Routledge.
For specialist treatments of the subjects.

Bamber, G.J. and Lansbury, R.D. (eds) 1989: *New Technology: international perspectives on human resources and industrial relations*. Unwin Hyman.
A series of comparative studies on technological and organizational change from Australia, Canada, Denmark, Italy, Sweden, Switzerland, UK and USA.

Bamber, G.J. and Lansbury, R.D. (eds) 1992: *International and Comparative Industrial Relations: a study of developed market economies*, 2nd edn. Sydney: Allen & Unwin.
A complete industrial relations context for HRM in nine advanced industrialized countries: Australia, Canada, France, Germany, Italy, Japan, Sweden, UK and USA.

Batstone, E. Ferner, A. and Terry, M. 1984: *Consensus and Efficiency: labour relations and management strategy in a state enterprise*. Blackwell,
This provides analysis of managerial strategies linking environmental change to employee relations policies.

Bennison, M. and Casson, J. 1984: *The Manpower Planning Handbook*. London: McGraw-Hill.
The authors are members of the (British) Institute of Manpower Studies with extensive experience working with organizations on manpower problems world-wide. The book is intended for manpower planners and human resource managers as a handbook.

Blyton, P. and Morris, J. (eds) 1991: *A Flexible Future? Prospects for Employment and Organisation*. Berlin and New York: de Gruyter.
Many of the 18 chapters in this recent collection report studies which reveal the actual development of flexibility in different industrial and national

locations. The picture is generally one of far greater complexity and variability than is often assumed.

Bramhan, J. 1989: *Human Resource Planning*. London: IPM.

This is a new book by the author of a standard text, *Practical Manpower Planning*, published in 1975. The earlier book was used widely in the UK as a textbook. The current book pursues a number of ideas that related to manpower planning: training and development, organization design, performance and productivity, reward management, and employee relations. The author also attempts to place human resource planning in context.

Brown, W. 1989: Managing remuneration. In K. Sisson (ed.), *Personnel Management in Britain*. Oxford: Blackwell.

This and the book by B. Livy offer more general reviews as to the nature of remuneration in the wage–work relationship. Brown's chapter is especially valuable for the broader, more analytical consideration of the relationship of pay to productivity and to the issue of control and motivation at work.

Buchanan, D. and McCalman, J. 1989: *High Performance Work Systems: the digital experience*, Routledge.

A valuable analysis of how to implement manpower policies aimed at the creation of skilled problem-solving teams.

Cascio, W. (ed.) 1989: *Human Resource Planning, Employment and Placement*. Washington: BNA Books.

A book consisting of eight articles by individual contributors on subjects as diverse as: staffing policies, job analysis and human resource planning, recruitment, recruitment sources, selection, employment tests, placement and career management and outplacement. The article of interest here is 'Job analysis and HR planning' by Ron Page and Dave Van De Bort. The authors use company experience and computer-generated graphics to illustrate the state of the art. Taken together, 'Job analyses' and 'Human resource plans' provide a coherent framework for making staffing and placement decisions to follow.

Cassels, J. 1990: *Britain's Real Skill Shortage*. London: PSI.

A concise and incisive analysis of the failures of British manpower policy and training practices to address the needs of a developed economy competing within an increasingly competitive international environment.

Cooke, William N. 1990: *Labor–Management Co-operation*. Michigan, USA: Upjohn Institute for Employment Research.

Chapter 1 contains a useful summary of the potential benefits and costs to individual employees and unions from employee involvement programmes.

Crompton, R. and Sanderson, K. 1990: *Gendered Jobs and Social Change*. Unwin Hyman, and D.L. Collinson et al. 1990: *Managing to Discriminate*. Routledge.

Useful texts which combine a theoretical analysis of discrimination and job segregation with empirical case studies.

Dunphy, D. and Stace, D. 1990: *Under New Management: Australian organizations in transition*. Sydney: McGraw-Hill.

A path-finding analysis of leadership, organizational change and HRM strategies, which is illustrated with case studies from Australia and other countries.

Edwards, J. et al. 1989: *Manpower Planning*. John Wiley.

This aims to provide the basis for an integrated approach to manpower planning. The chapters include contributions to manpower planning from a wide range of disciplines: economics, mathematics, education and training, industrial relations, and the behavioural sciences. They deal with almost all aspects of manpower planning including qualitative to quantitative approaches.

French, W. and Bell, C. 1990: *Organisation Development*. New Jersey, USA: Prentice-Hall.

A useful and comprehensive text dealing with the various approaches to organizational change.

Fucini, J.J. and Fucini, S. 1990: *Working for the Japanese*. New York: Free Press.

Analyses Mazda's investment in the USA, and describes the experience of work inside the Flat Rock plant.

Gospel, H. 1983: The development of management organisation in industrial relations: a historical perspective. In K. Thurley and S. Wood (eds), *Industrial Relations and Management Strategy*, CUP, 91–110.

This offers competent reviews and analyses of the relationship of pay to the methods and organization of production. Gospel's insightful study of the relationship of payment methods to the development of production provides a timely indication as to the age of some of the 'apparently' modern HRM techniques.

Hirschhorn, L. 1986: *Beyond Mechanisation*. Cambridge, Mass.: MIT Press.

This is a carefully reasoned account of how any technology will fail in unintended and unexpected ways, and of how management can use failure as a source of developmental tension to create a learning organization.

Hyman, J. 1992: *Training at Work*. Routledge.

An examination of training practice through the 1980s demonstrates that a market-driven approach to manpower policy has failed to increase employer commitment to training. Alternative policy approaches are considered.

Kamata, S. 1983: *Japan in the Passing Lane*. Allen & Unwin.

A diary-style account of work inside a Japanese vehicle plant in Japan.

Lane, C. 1989: *Management and Labour in Europe*. Edward Elgar.

An interesting analysis of work organization and employee relations in manufacturing industry in Germany, France and the UK.

Lawler, E.E. 1986: *High Involvement Management*. San Francisco: Jossey-Bass.

This argues that management action in areas like pay and quality circles is a matter of coherent manpower strategy rather than separate policies. Chapter 10 contains a useful discussion of the HRM features and performance of new design plants.

Lawler, E.E. 1990: *Strategic Pay: aligning organizational strategies and pay systems*. San Francisco: Jossey-Bass.

Discusses the advantages and limitations of a wide variety of compensation systems.

Legge, K. 1989: Human resource management: a critical analysis'. In J. Storey (ed.), *New Perspectives on Human Resource Management*, Routledge, 19–40.

A cogent critique of the concept of HRM.

Lewis, C. 1985: *Employee Selection*. Hutchinson.

This book is divided into two parts; the first part considers some dilemmas and controversies facing recruitment and selection, e.g. whether selection is an art or science, and the right to select as opposed to the ability to select. Part 2 contains several chapters on the practice and principles of selection. While it dwells excessively on the recessionary conditions prevailing in the UK at the time of writing, it provides an excellent, all-round introduction, with useful summaries at the end of each chapter.

Livy, B. (ed.) 1988: *Corporate Personnel Management*. London: Pitman.

This offers a general review of the nature of remuneration in the wage–work relationship.

Lupton, T. and Gowler, D. 1969: *Selecting a Company Payment System*. London: Kogan Page.

This is still a valuable contribution to the contemporary debate on payment schemes in terms of the importance of a range of production, as distinct from motivational factors, which affect the suitability of particular payment schemes.

Mintzberg, H. 1989: *Mintzberg on Management: inside our strange world of organisations*. Collier Macmillan.

An easy introduction to Mintzberg's ideas on strategy development and 'training managers not MBAs'.

Nichols, T. 1986: *The British Worker Question*. London: Routledge & Kegan Paul.

This offers one of the most thoughtful and questioning reviews of the relationship of pay to productivity.

Oliver, N. and Wilkinson, B. 1988: *The Japanization of British Industry*. Blackwell.

Describes Japanese industrial practice in Japan, and examines the activities of Japanese manufacturing companies in the UK, and the attempts of indigenous companies to emulate them.

Pascale, R.T. 1990: *Managing on the Edge*. Viking Penguin.

An important book – the *In Search of Excellence* of the 1990s? Sets HRM issues in the broad context of the literature on organization change.

Pascale, R. and Athos, A. 1982: *The Art of Japanese Management*. Penguin.

Describes management practice at Matsushita, with particular reference to HRM practice.

Peters, T. and Austin, Nancy 1985: *A Passion for Excellence: the leadership difference*. Collins.

This testifies to the strength of the managerial imagination in transforming the competitive powers of organizations and their manpower systems, and which warns against the dangers of reifying concepts like 'the product life cycle curve' and 'economies of scale'.

Pieper, R. (ed.) 1990: *Human Resource Management: an international comparison*. Berlin: Walter de Gruyter.

This book brings together the papers presented at a conference, with the same title as the book, held in Gummersback, West Germany in 1989.

The contributors examine HRM in several countries, and the book is an excellent source of cross-cultural comparisons of HRM.

Poole, M. 1986: *Industrial Relations: origins and patterns of national diversity*. Routledge.

An analytical text that cogently explores key themes in employee relations and the importance of the comparative approach itself.

Poole, M. and Jenkins, G. 1990: *The Impact of Economic Democracy*. Routledge.

This book covers the financial participation aspect of 'involvement'.

Porter, M. 1985: *Competitive Advantage: creating and sustaining superior performance*. New York: Free Press.

A discussion (chapters 3 and 4) on how competitive strategy is implemented through the management of the drivers of cost and differentiation – an essential starting-point for anyone wishing to understand the connections between competitive strategy and manpower strategy.

Porter, M.E. 1990: *The Competitive Advantage of Nations*. Macmillan.

A readable, if long, book which seeks to explain why some nations outperform others. Profound implications for the training and development of the UK's population.

Quinn, J.B. Mintzberg, H. and James, R.M. 1988: *The Strategy Process*. Prentice-Hall.

A strategy text that leads the way in developing the process approach to strategic management in which a variety of classic readings highlight the essential link between strategic management and HRM.

Roomkin, M. (ed.) 1990: *Profit Sharing and Gain Sharing*. IMLR Press/ Rutgers University.

A series of articles reviewing the main issues involved in the sharing of profits.

Rowland, K. and Ferris, Gerald (eds) *Research in Personnel and Human Resources Management*. Greenwich, Conn.: JAI Press, various years.

A series of volumes dealing with major issues in personnel and HRM.

Schein, E.H. 1985: *Organization Culture and Leadership*. San Francisco: Jossey-Bass.

An important contribution to the theoretical literature. It also offers useful insights into the difficulties of coping with the concept of culture.

Schuster, F.E. 1986: *The Schuster Report: the proven connection between people and profit*. New York Wiley.

This report is based on the author's empirical study of HRM in a number of large American companies. The survey is systematic and well documented and his conclusions are supported by evidence. Anyone embarking on a similar exercise would find this report particularly useful.

Sisson, K. (ed.) 1989: *Personnel Management in Britain*. Blackwell.

A collection of empirical evidence and useful discussion across the range of personnel and HRM issues (see also T. Watson, below).

Steiner, G.A. and Miner, J.B. 1982: *Management Policy and Strategy*. Collier Macmillan.

A 'traditional' strategy text for those interested in learning more about the subject.

Storey, J. (ed.) 1989: *New Perspectives on Human Resource Management*. London: Routledge.

An interesting set of papers which examine the development of an HRM perspective from different angles giving a comprehensive survey, including a critical assessment of its meaning and progress as practised mainly in the UK. The book is essential reading for students of the subject, but practitioners would also find much that is useful.

Teague, P. 1989: *The European Community: the social dimension*. Kogan Page.

A good overview of the development of EC social policies which provides the context for an interesting last chapter on European collective bargaining.

Walker, J.W. 1980: *Human Resource Planning*. New York: McGraw-Hill.

While this text has not been updated with a second edition, it continues to be a clear, insightful account of the essentials of human resource planning for today.

Walton, R. and Lawrence, Paul (eds) 1985: *Trends and Challenges in Human Resources Management*. Boston: Harvard University Press, An influential collection.

Watson, T. 1989: Recruitment and selection. In K. Sisson (ed.), *Personnel Management in Britain*, Blackwell, 125–49.

This chapter concentrates mainly on the recruitment process, including the drawing up of job descriptions and personnel specifications, and on methods of recruitment, with rather less emphasis on the selection process and selection methods. There is an extensive bibliography.

Wickens, P. 1987: *The Road to Nissan*. Macmillan.

Written by the personnel director of Nissan UK; describes how Nissan developed a blend between Japanese and UK approaches.

Williams, A. Dobson, P. and Walters, M. 1989: *Changing Culture: new organisational approaches*. London: IPM.

A fairly practical book which includes most of the relevant theory, as well as description and analysis of 15 case studies.

Woodruffe, C. 1990: *Assessment Centres*. London: IPM.

An up-to-date, comprehensive introduction to assessment centres. The author stresses, perhaps excessively, the importance of tailoring assessment centres to meet an organization's requirements. It contains some useful chapters on how to determine critical competencies, and how to measure them.

Journals

Abernathy, W.J. Clark, K.B. and Kantrow, A.M. 1981: The new industrial competition. *Harvard Business Review*, September–October, 69–77.

A seminal article examining competing explanations for Japanese success and highlighting the increasing importance of innovation and its HRM implications.

Anderson, N. and Shackleton, V. 1986: Recruitment and selection: a review of developments in the 1980s. *Personnel Review*, 15(4), 19–27.

This article provides a comprehensive review of the literature, and draws on source material from the UK, USA and Europe in considering the recruitment process, self-evaluation, biodata, the interview, testing assessment centres, graphology, references and other developments in selection technology. Although this is an academic article, practitioners should not be deterred; it provides a good summary and update of the literature of recruitment and selection.

Atkinson, J. 1984: Manpower strategies for flexible organisations. *Personnel Management*, August, 28–31.

In this short article Atkinson sets out his 'flexible firm' model and defines the different aspects of flexibility ('functional', 'numerical', etc.) which have since become widely debated.

Crowther, S. 1988: Invitation to Sunderland: corporate power and the local economy. *Industrial Relations Journal*, 19(1), Spring, 51–60.

An interesting discussion of the establishment of the Komatsu plant at Newcastle which highlights the priority attached to the recruitment and selection of production employees.

Drucker, P. 1990: The emerging theory of manufacturing. *Harvard Business Review*, May–June, 94–102.
A recent article by one of the twentieth century's leading management 'gurus'. He focuses on how the quality issue helps resolve some of the tensions of the management–'labour' divide.

Eaton, A.E. 1990: The extent and determinants of local union control of participative programs. *Industrial and Labor Relations Review*, 43(5), July, 604–21.
An interesting empirical study of the influences shaping the way unions at the local level have sought to control employee involvement programmes.

Edwards, C. and Heery, E. 1989: Recession in the public sector: industrial relations in Freightliner 1981–1985. *British Journal of Industrial Relations*, 27(1), March, 57–73.
This contributes to the debate on co-operative versus adversarial industrial relations in securing change through the process of collective bargaining.

Ferner, A. and Colling, T. 1991: Privatisation, regulation and industrial relations. *British Journal of Industrial Relations*, 29(3), September, 391–409.
This article highlights different management styles in employee relations as companies move from public to private sectors.

Guest, D. 1991: Personnel management: the end of orthodoxy? *British Journal of Industrial Relations*, 29(2), June, 149–75.
A detailed analysis of changes in the personnel function in the UK.

Hamel, G. and Prahalad, C.K. 1989: Strategic intent. *Harvard Business Review*, May–June, 63–76.
An important article focusing on how Japanese firms gain their competitive edge by stimulating employee effort through a strong sense of corporate mission.

Kelly, J. 1984: Management strategy and reform of collective bargaining: a case from the British Steel Corporation. *British Journal of Industrial Relations*, 22(2), July, 135–53.
This provides analysis of managerial strategies linking environmental change to employee relations policies.

Kelly, J. 1988: Labour utilisation and industrial relations at Scott Lithgow. *Industrial Relations Journal*, 19(4), Winter, 296–310, and Gennard, J. and Kelly, J. 1991: The role of human resource management in managing change at Royal Rosyth Dockyard 1981–1990. *Human Resource Management Journal*, 1(4), Summer, 77–90.
These examine different management employee relations strategies and styles linked to improved organizational performance.

Kelly, J. 1990: British trade unionism, 1979–1989: change, continuity and contradictions. *Work, Employment and Society*, special issue, May, 29–66.
For somewhat differing and controversial judgements about the impact of HRM on trade unions.

Labour and Society 1987: 12(1).

This journal issue is devoted to aspects of labour market flexibility. Nine well-written articles analyse developments in both Europe and North America, and examine flexibility both within enterprises and more widely in national labour markets.

Legge, K. 1988: Personnel management in recession and recovery. *Personnel Review*, 17, 2–70.

More detailed analysis of changes in the personnel function in the UK.

Marchington, M. et al. 1989: Problems with team briefing in practice. *Employee Relations*, 11(4), 21–31.

This article is especially useful for its specialist treatment of team briefing.

Metcalf, D. 1989: Water notes dry up: the impact of the Donovan proposals, and Thatcherism at work on labour productivity in British manufacturing industry. *British Journal of Industrial Relations*, 28, 1–28.

For a different approach to the impact of HRM on productivity.

Oxford Review of Economic Policy 1988: Education, training and economic performance. 4(3).

This edition provides a very useful overview and analysis of the UK's training problems and an assessment of approaches used towards their resolution. Policies adopted in other countries are also considered.

Pollert, A. 1988: The flexible firm: fixation or fact? *Work, Employment and Society*, 2, 281–316.

This article offers a critique of the flexible firm model, identifying both its conceptual and empirical shortcomings.

Wood S. 1986: Recruitment systems and the recession. *British Journal of Industrial Relations*, 24(1), March, 103–21.

A discussion which raises a number of important questions about the validity of selection procedures.

Other Sources

ACAS 1981: *Recruitment and Selection*, Advisory Booklet no. 6. ACAS.

A helpful short summary of 'best practice' arrangements.

Commission of the European Communities 1991: *The Community Charter of Fundamental Social Rights*. Brussels.

The Charter, adopted in December 1989, sets out the 12 basic principles relating to the social rights of workers within EC countries.

Commission of the European Communities, Director-General for Employment, Industrial Relations and Social Affairs 1990: *Social Europe*, 1/90. Brussels.

This is the Action Programme (AP) relating to the proposals contained in the Social Charter. This publication is helpful when considering the proposals in the Charter, and their relationship to the AP.

Conference Board 1990: *Variable Pay: new performance rewards*. Research Bulletin no. 264. New York: Conference Board.

Describes the variety of recent practice using case studies.

Employment in Europe 1990: European Commission.

Published annually by the Commission, this provides the most up-to-date guide to labour markets and employment policies as well as having specific chapters on HRM issues.

Equal Opportunities Review and *Industrial Relations Review and Report*, both published by IRS Publications.

These are an excellent source of up-to-date information with examples of 'best practice' and recent case law.

Incomes Data Services (who publish two studies each month on employment matters, often focusing on the practical implementation and performance of forms of 'involvement'), or the twice-monthly bulletins of *Industrial Relations Review and Report* (which also report their own surveys and company studies).

These are the best sources for keeping up to date in the 'involvement' field without scouring the academic journals which can be hard work.

Incomes Data Services 1980: *Guide to Incentive Payment Schemes*. London: IDS.

Incomes Data Studies 1979: *Guide to Job Evaluation*. London: IDS.

—— 1985a: *Improving Productivity*. Study no. 331. IDS.

—— 1985b: *Shift Premiums*. Study 336. IDS.

—— 1988: *PRP and Profit Sharing*. Study 397. IDS.

National Board for Prices and Incomes 1967: *Productivity Agreements*. Report no. 36. London: HMSO.

—— 1968: *Payment by Results*. Report no. 65. London: HMSO.

These offer among the best accounts of recent and current practice and offer an adequate coverage of the practical issues and strengths and weaknesses of popular and traditional payment schemes.

Organization for Economic Co-operation and Development 1989: *Labour Market Flexibility: trends in enterprises*. Paris: OECD.

This short collection analyses the components of flexibility and identifies the degree to which different aspects have been emphasized to varying extents in different countries. It offers a useful counter to the picture of overall uniformity given by some writers on flexibility.

Psychological testing 1989: *Personnel Management*, Factsheet no. 24 December.

A short, non-technical discussion of the various considerations involved in the decision to use psychological testing for selection purposes.

Index